Sexual Orientation, Gender Identity and International Human Rights Law

This book identifies, analyses and discusses the nexus of legal issues that have emerged in recent years around sexuality and gender. It audits these against specific human rights requirements and evaluates the outcomes as evidenced in the legislation and caselaw of six leading common law jurisdictions. Beginning with a snapshot of the legal definitions and sanctions associated with the traditional marital family unit, the book examines the subsequently evolving key concepts and constructs before outlining the contemporary international framework of human rights as it relates to matters of sexuality and gender. It proceeds by identifying a set of themes, including the rights to identity, to form a family, to privacy, to equality and to non-discrimination, and undertakes a comparative evaluation of how these and other themes indicate areas of commonality and difference in the approaches adopted in those common law jurisdictions, as illustrated by the associated legislation and caselaw. It then considers why this should be and assesses the implications.

Kerry O'Halloran is a lawyer, social worker and academic who has, for the past 13 years, been Adjunct Professor at Queensland University of Technology, Australia.

Human Rights and International Law
Series Editor: Professor Surya P. Subedi, OBE, QC (Hon), DCL.

This series will explore the place of human rights law within the international legal order, offering much-needed interdisciplinary and global perspectives on the increasingly central role of human rights in the development and implementation of international law and policy.

Human Rights and International Law is committed to providing critical and contextual accounts of the relationship of human rights with international law theory and practice. To achieve this, volumes in the series will take a thematic approach that focuses on major debates in the field, looking at how human rights impacts on areas as diverse and divisive as security, terrorism, climate change, refugee law, migration, bioethics, natural resources and international trade.

Exploring the interaction, inter-relationship and potential conflicts between human rights and other branches of international law, books in the series will address both historical development and contemporary contexts, before outlining the most urgent questions facing scholars and policy makers today.

Available titles:

The Right to Truth in International Law
Victims' Rights in Human Rights and International Criminal Law
Melanie Klinkner and Howard Davis

Sexual Orientation, Gender Identity and International Human Rights Law
Common Law Perspectives
Kerry O'Halloran

About the Series Editor

Professor Surya P. Subedi, OBE, QC (Hon) is Professor of International Law, University of Leeds, member of the Institut de Droit International and former UN Special Rapporteur for human rights in Cambodia.

www.routledge.com/Human-Rights-and-International-Law/book-series/HRIL

Sexual Orientation, Gender Identity and International Human Rights Law

Common Law Perspectives

Kerry O'Halloran

Routledge
Taylor & Francis Group
LONDON AND NEW YORK

First published 2020
by Routledge
2 Park Square, Milton Park, Abingdon, Oxon OX14 4RN

and by Routledge
52 Vanderbilt Avenue, New York, NY 10017

Routledge is an imprint of the Taylor & Francis Group, an informa business

First issued in paperback 2021

British Library Cataloguing-in-Publication Data
A catalogue record for this book is available from the British Library

Library of Congress Cataloging-in-Publication Data
Names: O'Halloran, Kerry, author.
Title: Sexual orientation, gender identity and international human rights law: common law perspectives / by Kerry O'Halloran.
Description: Milton Park, Abingdon, Oxon ; New York, NY : Routledge, 2019. | Series: Human rights and international law | Includes bibliographical references and index. | Identifiers: LCCN 2019031581 (print) | LCCN 2019031582 (ebook) | ISBN 9781138337060 (hardback) | ISBN 9780429442650 (ebook)
Subjects: LCSH: Gender identity—Law and legislation. | Sex and law. | Human rights. | Sex discrimination—Law and legislation.
Classification: LCC K3243 .O37 2019 (print) | LCC K3243 (ebook) | DDC 341.4/83—dc23
LC record available at https://lccn.loc.gov/2019031581
LC ebook record available at https://lccn.loc.gov/2019031582

ISBN: 978-1-138-33706-0 (hbk)
ISBN: 978-1-03-208675-0 (pbk)
ISBN: 978-0-429-44265-0 (ebk)

Typeset in Galliard
Apex CoVantage, LLC

For Elizabeth

Contents

Acknowledgements

This book owes much to the groundwork laid in earlier publications, including *Religious Discrimination and Cultural Context*[1] and my earlier contributions[2] to the series *Human Rights and International Law*, edited by Professor Surya P. Subedi. Given the not dissimilar subject matter and related caselaw, focused on the same jurisdictions, there is inevitably some degree of overlap, and I thank the publishers concerned for their understanding.

There were many who contributed along the way to making this a better book. Particular thanks are due to those who offered comment on draft chapters or related text, particularly: Anthony Langlois[3] and Morgan Carpenter[4] (Australia); Frank Cranmer[5] (England and Wales and international); Judy Walsh[6] (Ireland); Cynthia Burack[7] (USA); Jena McGill[8] (Canada); and Sue Barker[9] (New Zealand). The collegiate support, thoughtful contributions and encouragement have meant a lot, and this book and its author would have suffered without them.

I am very thankful to Routledge, particularly to Alison Kirk, for commissioning the book. Responsibility for any mistakes, inconsistencies or other faults, and for all views expressed, must unfortunately rest wholly with me.

1 Cambridge University Press, 2018.
2 *Human Rights, Religion and International Law*, 2018; *Adoption Law and Human Rights: International Perspectives*, 2018; and *Human Rights & Charity Law: International Perspectives*, 2016.
3 Associate Professor, College of Business, Government and Law, Flinders University, Australia.
4 Co-executive Director of Intersex Human Rights Australia and PhD candidate at the Faculty of Medicine and Health, University of Sydney, Australia.
5 Research Fellow at the Centre for Law and Religion, Cardiff and Director, Central Lobby Consultants.
6 Professor of Law, University College Dublin, Ireland.
7 Professor, Department of Women's, Gender and Sexuality Studies, Ohio State University, USA.
8 Assistant Professor, Faculty of Law, University of Ottawa, Canada.
9 Director of Sue Barker Charities Law, a boutique law firm in Wellington.

Introduction

> We are now called upon to address questions dealing directly with sex, sexual behaviour, and sexual taboos, a discussion fraught with moral, religious, political, psychological, and other highly charged issues. For those reasons (among others), I think it is in the best interests of us all to tread carefully.[1]

The cautionary advice offered by Sack J. seems an appropriate starting point for a book that sets out to explore the law governing contemporary matters of sexuality and gender in six leading common law countries.[2] He is right to urge caution. The subject matter is as it has always been, at the centre of our personal lives, our relationships with family and with society, but the post-binary world promises to be wholly different from that of our predecessors. For millennia, Christianity and other religions structured the role to be played by sexuality and gender. For the past few centuries that role was further conditioned, in the countries profiled in Part II, by the common law and their shared culture. In the course of a few short years, however, it has been deconstructed in ways that could never have been foreseen by previous generations and that, if they had had advance notice, would have caused widespread alarm and disbelief. That we are all now caught up in a process of fundamental but uncertain social change is quite clear. Where that process will end up, and when, is less so. Caution does seem advisable.

As with the "culture wars" more broadly, it is in the US that SOGI issues are acquiring their sharpest edge and proving their capacity to continue the polarisation of society along what appear to be lines drawn by moral imperatives. The current emergence of state-based anti-abortion legislation, for example, is in flat opposition to the Yogyakarta Principles, which require States to

> take all necessary legislative and other measures to ensure access to quality post abortion care, and remove any barriers that may hinder timely access

1 *Zarda v. Altitude Express*, 855 F.3d 76, 79–81 (2d Cir. 2017), per Sack J. at 135.
2 No matter how careful the treading, however, this subject area has become a minefield – not least linguistically – and some readers will inevitably be upset. The author apologises in advance for any offence caused.

to affordable and quality abortion services, without discrimination based on sexual orientation, gender identity, gender expression or sex characteristics.[3]

The proliferation of "religious liberty laws" – providing opt-outs for public health care professionals with non-SOGI compliant beliefs – are now threatening to roll back many of the gains made by the LGBT community over recent decades. It's not that these issues are markedly different from those that other nations are struggling to come to terms with; it's more that, in the US, they feed into already entrenched positions. Current public demonstrations in England, Canada and Australia against the mandatory inclusion of SOGI teaching material in schools are indicative of a wider pushback. This may not be restricted to SOGI-related issues but could be symptomatic of a growing disillusion with the unsparing, relentless levelling effect of the equality imperative. It may even augur the beginnings of a resistance to the spiralling ambit of human rights law.

As this book approaches its subject from a legal perspective, it is perhaps entitled to circle around the more difficult sociological areas where traps, primarily of a cultural and religious nature, proliferate. It also skirts theoretical, philosophical and ideological zones demarcated by the likes of feminism and gender politics. Instead, its objective is simply to identify the relevant law, examine how this is interpreted and applied by judiciary and regulators in relation to human rights themes – such as rights to expression, education, employment and health – and then attempt a comparative assessment of commonality and difference in the jurisdictional treatment of those themes. It is an exercise that hopefully might turn up some indicators as to the direction and extent of the SOGI-driven change process that is currently impacting our society.

Sexual Orientation, Gender Identity and International Human Rights Law: Common Law Perspectives consists of ten chapters. The book takes as its central theme the observation made by Eleanor Roosevelt in 1958 that the ultimate test of human rights rests on how they play out in "the world of the individual person; the neighbourhood he lives in; the school or college he attends; the factory, farm, or office where he works".[4] It therefore proceeds by identifying a specific set of the most relevant human rights and using these to examine six common law jurisdictions; it assesses and compares how those rights intersect with SOGI-related issues to affect such an "individual person" in the fields of health, employment, education and service provision.

Part I begins with a background section of three chapters. The first deals with concepts, social constructs and cultural context. It explores a cultural heritage in which Christian and common law principles provided the framework for a shared understanding of what constituted socially acceptable sexual relationships and

3 See further at: http://yogyakartaprinciples.org/relating-to-the-right-to-the-highest-attainable-standard-of-health-principle-17/.

4 See Eleanor Roosevelt's speech to the UN at the Church Peace Union, *In Your Hands: A Guide for Community Action on the 10th Anniversary of the UDHR*, New York, 1958.

gender conforming roles in those jurisdictions. The second chapter focuses on legal rights and introduces the basic fundamental human rights as initially formulated in the Universal Declaration of Human Rights, identifying and explaining the intersect between human rights and SOGI. It examines SOGI status in law, differentiating between "sex", "sexual orientation", "gender" and "gender identity". The third and longest chapter introduces the main international human rights instruments, such as the ECHR and the ICCPR; the courts, such as the ECtHR and the ECJ; the regulatory mechanisms; and the body of related caselaw. It links specific human rights provisions to key SOGI issues. Drawing from ECtHR caselaw, it outlines a thematic structure for conducting the jurisdictional comparative analysis.

Part II, which constitutes the bulk of the book, deals with contemporary international perspectives and in six chapters focuses in turn on England and Wales, Ireland, the United States of America, Canada, Australia and New Zealand. These jurisdiction-specific chapters closely follow the same format: an overview of the relevant legal framework; a consideration of the SOGI intersect with the core human rights of justice, free speech, association and assembly; a focus on how human rights impact upon SOGI aspects of personal relationships; and then a more detailed study of contemporary SOGI-related caselaw in health, employment, education and service provision. The objective is to identify any governing principles and emerging trends.

Part III, a final section comprising one chapter, concludes the book by drawing from Part II material to examine the nature of the tensions in the present relationship between international human rights law and SOGI-related issues. It does so using the Yogyakarta Principles (YP+10) as a touchstone. It identifies jurisdiction-specific characteristics, weighs them against relevant Principles and considers the more salient aspects of commonality and difference to gauge the way in which this tension now affects "the world of the individual person". It reflects on the significance of cultural context and the relevance of contemporary politics.

Kerry O'Halloran
White Park Bay
Summer, 2019
kerry.ohalloranwpb@gmail.com

Part I

Background

1 Sexuality and gender

Cultural context, concepts and parameters

Introduction

The progenitor common law jurisdiction, and the others profiled in Part II, evolved from the same cultural context. This chapter begins the book by considering that baseline. The roles of these jurisdictions in the former British Empire meant that they grew to share much more than the discipline of the common law: language, Christianity, parliamentary democracy, modes of governance, cultural and social mores and strong family ties were also in the mix. The chapter briefly explores a cultural heritage in which Christian and common law principles provided the orthodox and exclusive framework for sexual relationships in those jurisdictions: gender and sexuality confined in law to familial roles; the criminalisation of sexual relationships outside that framework and the social exclusion and religious rejection of those involved; and the rejection or suppression of any Indigenous culture. It goes on to consider the relevance of "the politics of identity" and the process of social change driven by factors such as single parent welfare benefits, contraceptives and the impact of methods of assisted reproduction on family planning and on female control of that planning etc. It reflects on how much all of this has contributed to shaping the respective jurisdictional responses to contemporary SOGI issues.

The chapter then introduces and explains contemporary concepts, social constructs and emerging issues as they relate to matters of sexuality and gender and their inter-relationship. It identifies theoretical perspectives (e.g. "queer theory") and relates them to social movements (e.g. feminism). It explores our understanding of "sexuality" and "gender", tracing legal milestones in the development of independent rights for males and females. It examines the pivotal importance of reproductive rights, the emergence of which strategically altered the law relating to the family, freeing women and sexuality from roles assigned or constrained by law and opening up the possibility of further diversification from the traditional family law model. It concludes by considering the complex nature, process and consequences of transgendering.

The common law jurisdictions and a common cultural heritage

Prevailing in England since the twelfth century before being exported to its colonies, common law was grounded on the rights and duties of the individual.[1] Often referred to as "judge made law", it was derived not from the prescribed directives of statute but rather from tradition, custom and judicial precedent, as embodied in rules and interpreted and applied by the judiciary adopting an inquisitorial approach on a case-by-case basis. Consequently, it was heavily reliant on established case precedents.

The common law: a shared tradition

The common law made no provision for class or community actions. There was no sense of collective legal interests; it consisted merely of categories of causes actionable by or against individuals, leaving the latter to fit his or her complaint to an established cause. This approach – listing subjects available for legal redress and permitting subsequent empirical extension by analogy – proved to be problematic. Its grindingly logical approach led to the law being constrained by the rigidity of the specified, corralled by established case precedents, where any development to meet emerging needs could only be achieved by painstakingly distinguishing the facts of new cases from the old. The result was a reliance on endless lists and categorisation, producing a consequent patchwork effect rather than a coherent body of law.

The doctrine of precedent

Reliance on this doctrine facilitated the growth of a shared jurisprudence between common law jurisdictions, reinforced, historically, by the role of the Privy Council. The judiciary in one common law jurisdiction would consider it reasonable to apply a principle drawn from a case precedent established in another where there were matching circumstances.[2] This, for example, was standard practice in charity law cases, where the judiciary for centuries were most often drawing from a pooled jurisprudence established in line with principles formulated under the auspices of the English Statute of Charitable Uses 1601. (This, until the mid-twentieth century, was the only formative charity legislation available in the Part II jurisdictions.) Even when not strictly abiding by the doctrine, by "following" the *ratio decidendi* of a judgement, "judicial notice" might well be taken of a ruling issued in another jurisdiction if it was felt to have a bearing on the facts of a particular case. By such means, both law

1 See Blackstone, Sir William, *Commentaries on the Laws of England*, Clarendon Press, Oxford, 1765–1769.

2 Most notably permitting the cross-jurisdiction adoption of principles such as *audi alteram partem*, *nemo judex debet esse in proprio sua causa* and *res judicata*.

and the accompanying moral imperatives were transferred from the progenitor jurisdiction to shape the foundations for justice in all other common law countries.

The common law jurisdictions: a shared cultural heritage

The imperial blueprint that travelled with the forces of the British Empire to all jurisdictions presently being considered is most usually thought of in terms of administrative structure. This comprised a fairly uniform system of parliamentary government, of law and judiciary and of institutional machinery, language and customs that are still recognisable features of the bonds that unify this most developed group within the commonwealth of nations.[3] A conspicuous aspect of that shared cultural infrastructure has been the mosaic of churches, mainly Catholic or Protestant, that have spread much the same web of parishes, ministers/priests and parishioners across many lands. These continue to be highly visible reminders of the shared Christian morality that formed the underpinning foundations of the common law cultural legacy.

Christianity and the common law jurisdictions

Largely unseen but representing the bulk of their shared Christian heritage is the body of values, ethics and principles, strained from the gospels and scriptures, that have been ingrained and passed on from one generation to the next throughout the common law jurisdictions. This shaped a communal sense of right and wrong, of what constitutes morality, immoral conduct and "sin". A matrix of moral imperatives – the violation of which was sinful – was threaded through the justice system of the common law nations.

Sin

The concept of "sin", religion's most basic enforcing mechanism, extended to brand a range of conduct designated by Church and State as "profane" and "heinous", being both criminal and sinful. Conduct regarded as sinful was generally not confined by any religion to transgression of beliefs but included most behaviour that would be construed as breaching secular laws or which in ethical or morality terms could be viewed as "bad". Such prohibited conduct policed the personal life of every individual, mapping out approved relationships, legitimate means of procreation and rules for the properly constituted family. This shared cultural heritage, infused with Christian morality and common law principles, inevitably prepared the ground for the response of the Part II jurisdictions to the emerging challenge of SOGI-related issues.

3 Ireland, in fact, is not among the 52 countries that now constitute the commonwealth.

Sex

The sin of sexual relations – those not conducted between adult heterosexuals, for reasons of procreation and within a marital relationship – was well embedded in Christianity and regulated by statute in the common law nations. One incidental consequence of this was the apparent need to classify types of sexual activity – prostitution, buggery/sodomy, paedophilia etc. – a prequel perhaps to contemporary classifications that now structure our approach to SOGI matters and more generally towards the LGBT community and its constituent parts. Of greater, deeper and more long-lasting significance have been the connotations of immorality that came to be associated with non-marital sex and non-binary gender matters; for some, affirmation of that sinfulness came with the outbreak of AIDS. Fear of being branded sinful, to be tainted with the smear of perversion, has been a very real obstacle that has delayed social and legal acceptance of SOGI issues in the Part II jurisdictions.

Family law

Family law in the Part II jurisdictions evolved within a common law context in accordance with the structures, principles and judicial precedents established in England and Wales. Over the centuries, their shared Christianity and pooling of case precedents gave the common law nations a shared understanding of what constitutes a family and of relationships judged to be sinful or virtuous.[4] As Lord Finlay LC commented in *Bowman v. Secular Society Ltd.*, when reflecting on previous centuries of caselaw:[5]

> It has been repeatedly laid down by the Courts that Christianity is part of the law of the land, and it is the fact that our civil polity is to a large extent based upon the Christian religion. This is notably so with regard to the law of marriage and the law affecting the family.[6]

This developmental framework continued well into the twentieth century, and even now much family law – certainly the basic principles, rules and concepts – can still be read across those jurisdictions fairly seamlessly.

It was a framework that clearly defined the marital family unit, as approved by Church and State, legally and morally demarcating it from all others. It clarified

4 A long catalogue of cases beginning with *De Costa v. De Paz* (1754) 2 Swans 487, Chancery, including *Lawrence v. Smith*, *Murray v. Benbow* (1822) The Times 2 Feb. 1822 and *Briggs v. Hartley* (1850) 19 L. J. (Ch.) 416 and ending with *Pare v. Clegg* (1861) 29 Beav 589, 54 ER 756, established that "the Courts will not help in the promotion of objects contrary to the Christian religion".

5 [1917] AC 406 (H.L.).

6 Ibid., citing: *Briggs v. Hartley* (1850) 19 L. J. (Ch.) 416; *Cowan v. Milbourn* (1867) L. R. 2 Ex. 230; *De Costa v. De Paz* (1754) 2 Swanst, 487; and *In re Bedford Charity* (1819) 2 Swanst. 470, 527.

the respective responsibilities of spouses, conferred legitimacy upon any children born to and of their marriage and established the rules governing inheritance and the rights of dependants on the death of family members. Equally clearly it identified the various forms of relationships that transgressed the approved model. These were not just contrary to law but also morally repugnant. Those involved were to be named, shamed and reviled, denied any form of legitimacy and deprived of many rights and protections enjoyed by their counterparts in a marital family. The stigma, deliberately cultivated to brand as outcasts those who engaged in – or were the product of – sexual conduct outside the ordained framework, served to tarnish all forms of non-conforming relationships.

Changing cultural context: civil rights, welfare benefits and the politics of identity

The separation of Church and State, the fading significance of institutionalised religions and a corresponding increase in secularism, together with the generalised social disruption that followed in the aftermath of WWII – an era dominated by ideologies that competed with religion as much as with each other – were among the contributing factors that led to a weakening of established social mores in the common law nations as elsewhere. As globalisation and consumerism took hold and citizens increasingly moved within and between countries – as never before – in search of security and economic opportunities, so also their ties to extended family and social context, to Christian morality and its institutions and practices, became less binding. Whether as cause or effect of the increased freedom of choice, this was also an era which saw the spread of the civil rights movement and improvements in medicine and welfare benefits. Arguably, the assertion of LGBT rights in the late twentieth century, followed by the ongoing engagement with SOGI-related matters, only fully makes sense when seen against the background of a process of social change that had begun much earlier.

Civil rights

The ongoing elucidation of SOGI-related rights marks the latest in a sequence of stages whereby socially disadvantaged groups emerged to successfully gain recognition for their rights: from the emancipation of black Americans in the 1950s/1960s, through universal suffrage and the rights of the disabled, feminists, children, Indigenous people etc; to the rights of the LGBT community and its various constituencies.

Gay rights as a social movement

The path followed by the LGBT community in all Part II jurisdictions would seem to conform to that taken by other disadvantaged groups, such as those mentioned earlier; indeed, this is substantiated by a considerable body of academic work.[7] An important point of difference is, however, worth noting. Then, the objective and outcome – for black Americans, universal suffrage and women's rights – was assimilation of the disadvantaged into the established mainstream: equal treatment for all. Now, social policy resists assimilation and instead favours multiculturalism: difference and diversity are to be respected and preserved. Recognition of SOGI status should not necessarily lead to assimilation, nor imply uniform treatment for all, but should instead allow for and celebrate distinctive non-binary identities.

Centuries of persecution for deviance by Church and State, reinforced more recently by alarmist reports from medical authorities, media pillorying and social ostracisation, led down the same route – protest marches, riots and legal battles – towards incremental staged recognition, remedial intervention and equality. While the struggle (e.g. Stonewall riots),[8] level of suffering (AIDS crisis)[9] and victimisation (Pulse nightclub shootings)[10] cannot be doubted, the continuing outbursts of homophobia and transphobia, together with the variable legal recognition given to trans and intersex status, are evidence that assimilation and full equality have yet to be achieved.

Health and welfare benefits

By the latter half of the twentieth century, a rising tide of prosperity in the Part II jurisdictions had established improved standards of education, housing and health care and begun to raise quality of life expectations.

Family planning, IVF and surrogacy etc.

Family planning emerged as a respectable public policy in the period between WWI and II, but it was not until the development of more effective contraception in the 1960s and 1970s that birth control gave women freedom of choice in relation to pregnancy and transformed family planning from a public policy strategy into a private lifestyle option. The separation of sex from procreation, a milestone in women's reproduction rights, was followed by a constellation of other significant and related developments in medical science which collectively ended the necessity of a link between sexual mutuality and procreation. Since being pioneered in the 1970s, improvements in the effectiveness and scale of

7 See for example: Stulberg, L.M., *LGBTQ Social Movements*, Polity Press, 2018; Faderman, L., *The Gay Revolution: The Story of the Struggle*, Simon & Schuster, 2015; and Bornstein, K., *Gender Outlaws: On Men, Women, and the Rest of Us*, Routledge, 1994.

8 On 28–29 June 1969, several hundred gay people rioted in Greenwich Village, New York, in protest against a police raid targeting homosexuals.

9 Reaching epidemic levels in the US in the 1980s, the AIDS/HIV crisis caused the deaths of hundreds of thousands.

10 On 12 June 2016, Pulse (a gay nightclub) in Orlando was the site of a mass shooting which left some 50 people dead.

IVF procedures and other reproductive techniques had by 2018 facilitated the birth of some 8 million children worldwide. Increasingly, by the beginning of the twenty-first century, IVF, genetic engineering and surrogacy services were being commercially expanded to cope with the parenting needs of many same-sex couples.

Welfare benefits

It would be hard to overstate the importance of the introduction in the 1970s of welfare benefits and priority social housing for single parents: thereafter, women were no longer financially tied into a traditional patriarchal home ownership system; mothers could leave an emotionally or physically abusing male, take their children and set up home elsewhere. This coincided with a period of reduced stigma and greater social acceptance of marriage breakdown, of single mothers, of non-marital relationships and of serial cohabitation arrangements. Added to which there was easier access to contraception, abortion and divorce, together with increased opportunities for female employment.

The politics of identity

There is a very considerable body of academic work on this subject – largely drawn from psychology,[11] philosophy,[12] anthropology[13] and sociology[14] – but for present purposes a restricted and legal approach is adopted to explore how an entity acquires an identity and the effect of that status.

Identity

An identity is the particular aggregate of constituents, or their configuration, that distinguishes an entity from all others. Once identified, an entity then becomes amenable to classification, which in turn means it can be ascribed a status or be rank-ordered relative to other entities. In effect, identification leads to determining the significance of an entity and its worth; this establishes its value or perhaps power in relation to its context. Not until it acquires or is ascribed an identity can an entity be recognised in law and then deemed to be vested with a "legal personality" with rights and duties that can be the subject of legal proceedings.

11 See Erikson, E., *Identity and the Life Cycle: Selected Papers*, International Universities Press, New York, 1959 and *Identity: Youth and Crisis*, Faber, London, 1968.
12 See Heidegger, M., *Being and Time* (trans. by Macquarrie J. and Robinson, E.), SCM Press, London, 1962.
13 See Brubaker, R. and Cooper, F. Beyond "Identity", *Theory and Society*, 29, pp. 1–47 (2000) and Calhoun, C. (ed.), *Social Theory and Identity Politics*, Blackwell, Oxford, 1994.
14 See Weinreich, P. and Saunderson, W. (eds.), *Analysing Identity: Cross-Cultural, Societal and Clinical Contexts*, Routledge, London, 2003.

Difference

Difference is crucial to identity. To be different is to run the risk of being defined by others: having your identity defined by what you're not. It implies a vulnerability, a fear that the perceived difference may represent a threat to an established identity. It suggests that an "in-group" should distrust others – places it in a position to "name" the other, to "objectify" them – and has been responsible for many forms of discrimination throughout history.

Catering for difference has now become a significant challenge for all institutions in western society. The range of ethnic, racial, religious and other types of groups and communities seeking recognition for separate and distinct identities has multiplied exponentially in recent years, and with this has come legislation requiring that all be respected, accommodated and treated equally. This would seem to have generated a competitive striving to assert a unique identity and is accompanied by international acknowledgement of the human right to do so[15] – which has perhaps licensed an upsurge in identity change as new groups emerge, fragment and reform – to the detriment of the collective. So also for individuals: the freedom to make lifestyle choices, for many in the developed nations, has become emblematic of modern liberal democracy, a means of exercising their right to acquire and shape a unique identity; and for some this is, perhaps, sometimes seen as a sufficient end in itself.

Alienation and exclusion

The Independent Expert on minority issues has referred to the "multiple forms of exclusion" of members of minority communities "based on aspects of their identities and personal realities such as sexual orientation or gender expression that challenge social or cultural norms".[16] While sexual identity usually corresponds to gender as determined at birth (cisgender), for some it does not, and this can lead to profound feelings of alienation: the LGBT community as a whole has long suffered alienation, but because of social rejection rather than a self-perceived disconnect between gender and sexuality. For trans people, the route to realignment of sexuality and gender is likely to involve traumatic self-doubt and possible alienation; may require medical intervention; and may ultimately need social affirmation and acceptance of their acquired identity. Without recognition for their distinct identity, collective or individual, there can be no authentic reciprocal social engagement, no effective representation of an entity's interests in law and a risk of exposure to discrimination for "not belonging".

15 See Mende, J., *The Human Right to Culture and Identity*, Rowman and Littlefield International, 2016.

16 Report of the independent expert on minority issues, Commission on Human Rights, 6 January 2006, E/CN.4/2006/74 at paras 28 and 42.

Types of identity

Prescribed characteristics (imposed genetically or otherwise), experiences, culture and other contextual influences all contribute to the formation and continuity of an individual's identity. In many cultures this is fixed at birth, determined – partly, largely or even entirely – by the family and community into which a person is born, by how they are perceived and treated by others and by the extent to which they conform to a set of stereotypical characteristics. In such circumstances, identity is regarded as immutable, like ethnicity or race, as it has little or nothing to do with personal choice.

On the other hand, identity may be contingent and negotiated, or it may be manufactured for a purpose. It may be elective: the latitude granted to those who "self-identify" – thereby dismissing any need for contextual corroboration or independent validation – has become a particularly complicating factor in modern life with regard to politics and other matters. In such circumstances, identity has an accompanying aura of transience creating uncertainty in the relationships between those affected and others. Some identities are constructed: "asylum seekers", for example, identifies a class of migrants politically designated as deserving of particular assistance.

The "LGBT community"

The above term is used throughout this book in reference to that eclectic group of people who, to a varying degree, have in common some SOGI-related issues. It is admittedly inadequate but has come to be accepted as a form of shorthand to identify those perceived to fall outside rigid binary sex and gender norms.[17] As has been pointed out,

> lesbian, gay, bisexual, trans and intersex people are a diverse population that not only must contend with human rights violations on the basis of their sexual orientation, gender identity and/or sex characteristics, but also face violence and discrimination based on skin colour, ethnic origin, sex, gender, disability, age, migratory status, family status, nationality, religion, health status, income level, and on other grounds.[18]

Cultural identity

"Culture" has been defined as "people's values, languages, religions, ideals, artistic expressions, patterns of social and interpersonal relationships and ways

17 Many different versions of this acronym are in use, and they tend to change in accordance with locally perceived political correctness. One extreme version is LGBTIQCAPGNG-FNBA (lesbian, gay, bisexual, trans, queer, intersex, asexual and gender-non-conforming).

18 U.N., *Living Free and Equal*, New York, 2016, at p. 19. See, further, at: www.ohchr.org/Documents/Publications/LivingFreeAndEqual.pdf.

of perceiving, behaving and thinking".[19] Such characteristics are commonly taken into account when distinguishing the identities of nations, communities or groups. While the Convention on the Rights of the Child (Articles 7 and 8) is the only international convention that explicitly refers to identity as a fundamental human right, others do so at least implicitly.[20] In recent years, rulings of the ECtHR have drawn attention to the need to ensure and respect the right to personal and cultural identity – clearly very SOGI-relevant – which must be considered not only in the context of the developed western nations but also in relation to communities of Indigenous people.

Social homogeneity, conducive to the phased evolution of a nation, has now largely given way to globalised trends determined by changing patterns of consumer demand in conjunction with widespread government reliance upon a policy of multiculturalism. This would seem to typify the Part II jurisdictions. Some, however, see the current spread of populism as evidence of a mass turning away from the dominance of corporate and geo-political concerns and away from international finances, banking and trade, and as indicating instead a retreat to a nation State outlook with revived national cultural characteristics and firmer boundaries that exclude those that don't "belong".

Cultural identity and Indigenous people

For four of the six common law jurisdictions considered in Part II, cultural identity must be seen in relation to their communities of Indigenous people. For several millennia, these communities had their own distinctive religious/cultural mores, the residual vestiges of which they maintained and practised as they co-existed alongside their colonising neighbours. Having avoided, or having neither embraced nor been embraced by, the Christianity and common law of the colonists, the Indigenous people never wholly acceded to the ancillary laws and conventions, including those relating to the marital family and to the stigma and taboo associated with sexual relationships outside that institution. Consequently, they continued to accommodate and respect the same-sex and non-marital relationships that their Christian neighbours rigorously sought to prohibit and punish. This aspect of their cultural identity has remained relatively intact and constant for Indigenous people throughout the long period it has taken for it to be accommodated in the parallel world of their Christian neighbours. It can be seen, for example, in the acceptance traditionally extended to the "sistergirls" and "brotherboys" of the Aboriginal communities in Australia and to the "two-spirit" people in the Native American tribes of the US and Canada. For many Indigenous people everywhere,

19 Manning, M. L. and Baruth, L. G., *Multicultural Education of Children and Adolescents* (5th ed.), Allyn & Bacon Inc., 2009, at p. 24.

20 Including the Universal Declaration of Human Rights, Article 19, and the European Convention of Human Rights, Articles 8, 9 and 10.

the rigid binary distinction imposed on matters of sexuality and gender by Christianity, and the law and social mores of the settlers, was an integral part of a long process of colonisation and, though intended to compromise their cultural identity, largely failed to do so. Moreover, the international human rights framework – also binary-centric – arguably does not fit well with the cultural experience of Indigenous people.

Cultural identity and migrants/refugees/asylum seekers

A theme in the considerable body of academic work on "the politics of identity"[21] concerns striving to acquire recognition and status, not so that an entity may join with others in a community of equals but rather that it may establish its own uniqueness, assert its difference and be free and able to stand its own ground, apart from all others. Since 2015, immigration has been a prominent political issue for many European countries, the US and – though for a longer time – Australia. It is likely to remain prominent for the foreseeable future, as will the accompanying contention about accommodating cultural dissonance.[22]

A large proportion of migrants are Muslims belonging to very different ethnic cultures from those of the countries they seek to enter, and this gives rise to significant tensions for the cultural identity of both parties. The potential loss of cultural identity is a heartfelt issue for the many immigrants forced for various reasons to abandon their country, community and culture of birth. Indeed, as has been pointed out, "many minority populations have attempted to avoid, in various ways, assimilation becoming erasure".[23] It is correspondingly difficult for many in the receiving countries who fear the dilution and gradual erosion of their own cultural identity. In particular, the marked disconnect on SOGI issues constitutes a serious obstacle to efforts to bridge cultural differences. Consequently, government uncertainty regarding the balance to be struck between support of its national culture or in support of multiculturalism would seem to be tipping towards the former and a resurgent "nation State" ethos. A revival of interest in asserting and protecting national cultural identity is now emerging as a legitimate government goal. This will leave many migrants with the forced choice of trading in their cultural identity and accepting the SOGI legal and social norms that conflict with their religious beliefs, in exchange for refuge. It's a choice that carries with it profound questions for how western nations – especially the Part II jurisdictions – are responding to the human rights of migrants.

21 See, for example, Barzilai, G., *Communities and Law: Politics and Cultures of Legal Identities*, University of Michigan Press, 2003, and Campbell, D., *Writing Security: United States Foreign Policy and the Politics of Identity*, University of Minnesota Press, 1998.

22 See Mendelsohn, D., *Waiting for the Barbarians*, NYRB, 2012.

23 See Herman, D., *An Unfortunate Coincidence: Jews, Jewishness and English Law*, Oxford University Press, Oxford, 2011, at p. 51.

Sexuality and gender: binary and post-binary interpretations

The social awareness and eventual legal recognition of sexuality and gender as phenomena in their own right – distinguishable from and now no longer reducible to their traditional familial contextualisation – came about quite suddenly. Within the past few decades, this has impacted most developed western nations more or less uniformly, though it may well take a few more decades before a more balanced approach to SOGI-related matters can be reached.

This is a field of competing theoretical frameworks emanating mostly from the disciplines of psychiatry, psychology and sociology, in which feminism[24] plays a leading role. While a law book cannot hope to do justice to the mountain of academic work that has flowed and is flowing from those and other disciplines, it is necessary to at least note at the outset some primary theories and concepts that may aid an understanding of SOGI issues before relating them to a legal context.

Concepts, social constructs and theoretical frameworks

For centuries, and for all six jurisdictions considered in this book, Christianity and common law provided the framework defining sexuality and gender in terms of the parts they were to play in the family and society. Established by Church and State, the model marital "family" was viewed in private law as an autonomous institution where internal responsibilities were vested in patriarchal hands. "Sexuality" in that context was defined by and confined to purposes of legitimate procreation. Outside that context, it was viewed as a matter for public law and best left to be policed by criminal sanctions. "Gender" was of relevance only insofar as it designated male/female roles in relation to the marital family. As the twentieth century progressed, that framework began to unravel. The effect of various factors, as mentioned earlier, combined to free sexuality from procreation, and in time this freed gender from its prescribed familial role, which in turn began to dissolve the legal rigidity of a private/public distinction.

Feminism

While it is impossible and unnecessary, in the present context, to do justice to this subject, it is important to note its SOGI-related impact.

Advocacy for women's rights, on the grounds of equality of the sexes, proved to be a powerful force for changing the earlier presumptions that for centuries had structured family law in the Part II jurisdictions. In the latter decades of the twentieth century and into the twenty-first, the feminism movement turned away from its earlier preoccupation with affirmative action and protective legislation,

24 See Butler, J., *Gender Trouble: Feminism and the Subversion of Identity*, Routledge, New York, 1999.

with equality in employment, access to divorce and single parent welfare benefits, with the constrictions imposed by family and social roles, and other such issues. This had been a wholly necessary stage, but it was perhaps one in which women were largely perceived, objectively and subjectively, as vulnerable and in need of protection. While that phase had inadvertently contributed to reinforcing stereotypical roles,[25] the new objectives were less to do with equality and more about gender-specific concerns. This was a phase in which the feminist movement developed a strategic focus on women's health, sexual matters and reproductive rights in particular.[26] The struggle to take control of their interests in relation to reproduction – ensuring access to effective contraception, abortion facilities, IVF treatment etc. – generated a new awareness of the social marginalisation endured by those in same-sex relationships, engaged in trans gender processes[27] or otherwise outside the binary dualism that had occupied and confined previous feminists.[28] One product of this has been the emergence of the "Trans-Exclusionary Radical Feminist" (TERF) organisation, representing those feminists who oppose the inclusion of trans (mtf) in female-specific facilities (Women's Refuges, Rape Crisis Centres etc.).[29] Their transphobic tendencies have served both to reinforce the binary gender identity paradigm and to deny trans people their human rights. The protests against such attitudes, from within the feminist movement[30] and from the trans community,[31] have again done much to raise public awareness of ongoing post-binary issues. By 2018, most feminist organisations, including Planned Parenthood, had openly advocated in support of SOGI issues.

Queer theory

Emerging in the 1990s from women's studies and from feminism more generally, queer theory[32] owes a good deal to the academic work associated with the previously-mentioned politics of identity. To that extent, it can be seen as a radical exploration of the power relationships both linking the different constituencies in the LGBT community and linking them to the structures of mainstream

25 Friedan, B., *The Feminine Mystique*, WW Norton, 1963.

26 Greer, G., *The Female Eunuch*, Harper Collins, 1970.

27 Dworkin, A., *Women Hating*, EP Dutton, 1974.

28 Haraway, D., 'A Cyborg Manifesto', in *Simians, Cyborgs and Women: The Reinvention of Nature*, New York, Routledge, 1991, pp. 149–181; Fausto-Sterling, A., *Myths of Gender*, Basic Books, 1992 and *Sexing the Body*, Basic Books, 2000.

29 Raymond, J., *The Transsexual Empire*, Beacon Press, 1979.

30 Butler, J., *Gender Trouble: Feminism and the Subversion of Identity*, Routledge, 1990 and *Bodies That Matter: On the Discursive Limits of Sex*, Routledge, 1993.

31 Stone, S., The Empire Strikes Back: A Post Transsexual Manifesto, *Camera Obscura*, 10(2) (1992).

32 See, for example, Rich, A., *On Lies, Secrets and Silence: Selected Prose*, 1966–1978, WW Norton, 1979.

society. It addresses deviance from the norm and deconstructs the norm to better understand the nature of that relationship. As has been said:

> Queer is by definition whatever is at odds with the normal, the legitimate, the dominant. There is nothing in particular to which it necessarily refers. It is an identity without an essence. "Queer" then, demarcates not a positivity but a positionality vis-à-vis the normative.[33]

This theoretical field of study holds that individual sexuality is a fluid, fragmented and dynamic collectivity of possible sexualities which may vary at different points during one's life.[34] Its post-binary focus on the "mismatches between sex, gender and desire",[35] questioning the differentiation and underlining presumptions, has naturally led it to engage with LGBT issues. This has included a "genderqueer" strand dealing with such topics as cross-dressing, intersex bodies and identities, gender ambiguity and gender-confirmation surgery. The study of misalignment between sex, gender and sexual orientation has been described as "a site of permanent becoming".[36]

SOGI status

SOGI is essentially concerned with what appears to be a non-alignment: of sex and gender; and of gender and sexuality. Although the spectrum of sexualities – heterosexual, gay, lesbian, bisexual, poly-sexual, pansexual, asexual etc. – are now generally viewed as illustrative of the diversity in modern developed societies, they can also indicate insecurity, and in cases of gender dysphoria this may reach levels of acute distress. For many, of course, there is no misalignment and no distress. Social and legal permission to move away from the rigidity of the binary dichotomy to a more nuanced interpretation of sexuality and gender has provided opportunities for finding a better fit among the complexity of possible relationships. Not having to compromise carries a potential for achieving stronger and more enduring relationships.

Sexual orientation and gender identity

These are different entities, and trans people can present with a variety of sexual orientations.[37] Whether someone is lesbian, gay, bisexual or straight is not necessarily

33 Halperin, D., *Saint Foucault: Towards a Gay Hagiography*, Oxford University Press, 1997, at p. 62.

34 Tyson, L., *Critical Theory Today: A User-Friendly Guide*, Routledge, New York, 2006.

35 Jagose, A., *Queer Theory: An Introduction*, New York University Press, 1996.

36 Giffney, N., Denormatizing Queer Theory: More Than (Simply) Lesbian and Gay Studies, *Feminist Theory*, 5(1), pp. 73–78 (April 2004).

37 See International Commission of Jurists, *Sexual Orientation, Gender Identity and International Human Rights Law: Practitioners Guide No.4* (2009), at: www.refworld.org/pdfid/4a783aed2.pdf.

related to whether the individual is trans or cisgender. There is arguably no scientific consensus on how to define sexual orientation: the various definitions proposed by experts produce substantially different groups of people.[38] At the heart of the previously-mentioned nexus of insecurity and apparent non-alignment lies the awkward fact that sexual orientation and gender identity are neither amenable to definition nor are they immutable. These ambiguous, subjective concepts may change over time: for the individuals concerned, it cannot be predicted with any certainty that their SOGI characteristics will in future be as they are now. All relationships, including those built around such characteristics, are open to change and may lead to eventual mismatch. This creates difficulties for the exercise of human rights, which can only function in respect of definable entities (see Chapter 2).

Sexual identity

"Sex" is a matter of biology. It refers to the biological differences between males and females: their reproductive organs and hormones. Sex identity for most people is established in accordance with their physiology at birth and results in their being registered as male or female on their birth certificate. Thereafter, that registered legal status has traditionally determined social role: matters such as schooling, employment, marriage partner etc. Established presumptions have long governed gender and sexuality, the associated values, and their significance for the Christian and relatively homogenous societies which were broadly characteristic of the leading common law jurisdictions until the middle of the last century. Chief among those presumptions was that the family and sexual relationships should necessarily be viewed from a patriarchal and heterosexual perspective.

Sexual orientation

As explained in the Yogyakarta Principles,

> sexual orientation is understood to refer to each person's capacity for profound emotional, affectional and sexual attraction to, and intimate and sexual relations with, individuals of a different gender or the same gender or more than one gender.[39]

Family law, being structured on the perceived mutuality and immutability of gender and sex, for many generations prohibited any non-conforming sexual orientation – specifically, it criminalised homosexuality. Now, sexual orientation is accepted as signifying an inherent and enduring emotional, romantic

38 See further at: www.heritage.org/civil-society/report/sexual-orientation-and-gender-identity-sogi-laws-threaten-freedom.
39 Introduction to the Yogyakarta Principles at: https://yogyakartaprinciples.org/introduction.

or sexual attraction to others and is largely recognised – at least in the Part II jurisdictions – as not necessarily determined by gender; to be "gay" is to have a sexual orientation that is gender non-conforming or non-heterosexual. Many countries, however, continue to categorise sexual orientation discrimination as a subset of sex discrimination rather than designate it as a legal status in its own right (see further below).

Gender identity

As explained in the Yogyakarta Principles:

> Gender identity is understood to refer to each person's deeply felt internal and individual experience of gender, which may or may not correspond with the sex assigned at birth, including the personal sense of the body (which may involve, if freely chosen, modification of bodily appearance or function by medical, surgical or other means) and other expressions of gender, including dress, speech and mannerisms.[40]

Gender, unlike sex, is now understood to be a social construct. Whether a person is female, male, trans or "other" is a matter of gender. For most people, their cisgender – or cis – can be conclusively established at birth on the basis of stereotypical physical characteristics; for most gender and sexuality are in alignment, but for some their development reveals an incongruity between external physiological presentation and self-perceived/experienced gender identity.

The process of determining gender identity has traditionally been a matter for medical aetiology, and in many places continues to be so, where the focus is on stereotypical biological characteristics. Sex at birth may not correspond with an innate gender identity; the latter is not immutable, as subjective interpretation may cause a person to change their gender.

As a social construct, gender may be fluid: it may or may not depend upon biological traits; it is open to being influenced, if not determined, by social norms, attitudes and activities; it may be self-determined. The development of gender identity can be influenced by many factors, including upbringing and life experiences, and it may be a continuing process never to be conclusively resolved.

Gender expression as noted earlier can be through personal choice of dress, hairstyle and behaviour – which may be inconsistent; it can be indicated by mannerisms or through speech. For legal purposes, however, determining gender status may require corroborating evidence, and this is currently a matter of contention in many countries (see further below).

40 Ibid.

Transgender

This term ("trans") refers to the process of "transitioning" from male to female (mtf) or female to male (ftm); it may also include those who intend to do so, though this is contentious.

Gender dysphoria

As has been explained:

> Based on the Greek (*dys-phoria*: hard to bear), this is the medical term for the condition in which a person who has been assigned one gender at birth on the basis of their physical sex self-identifies as belonging to another gender. People who experience gender dysphoria are in no way mentally ill, but they often suffer great stress from hiding their identity.[41]

When birth gender, as assigned, does not correspond with self-perceived gender identity, this can cause significant distress, and as a consequence the person concerned may be clinically diagnosed as suffering from "gender dysphoria". According to the Diagnostic and Statistical Manual of Mental Disorders, this condition causes impairment in social, occupational or other important areas of functioning. The term has replaced "gender identity disorder" in order to "better characterize the experiences of affected children, adolescents and adults" and to avoid continued pathologising of the condition.[42] In a further move to the same effect, the World Health Organisation (WHO) in its 2018 edition of the International Classification of Diseases (ICD-11)[43] moved "gender incongruence" out of mental disorders in the ICD and into sexual health conditions. It now defines gender incongruence as a marked and persistent incongruence between a person's experienced gender and assigned sex. The rationale, as it explains, is that

> while evidence is now clear that it is not a mental disorder, and indeed classifying it in this can cause enormous stigma for people who are transgender, there remain significant health care needs that can best be met if the condition is coded under the ICD.[44]

However, it remains a concern, despite the previous assertion by Jackson J and international re-classification, that a mental health diagnosis is still deemed an

41 *J v. B (Ultra-Orthodox Judaism: Transgender)* [2017] EWFC 4, per Jackson, J. at para. 14.
42 Note the endorsement given by the UN Independent Expert on Protection Against Violence and Discrimination Based on Sexual Orientation and Gender Identity to Moves to Depathologise Trans Identities. Geneva (May 2019), at: www.ohchr.org/EN/NewsEvents/Pages/DisplayNews.aspx?NewsID=24663&LangID=E.
43 WHO, ICD-11, at: www.who.int/health-topics/international-classification-of-diseases.
44 Ibid., Revision of ICD-11: Gender Incongruence.

appropriate pre-condition for gender reassignment therapy; the concern is that it may be used as "a license for the stigmatization or for the deprivation of civil and human rights".[45] Interestingly, as of 2018, some 34 states in Europe still required such a diagnosis in gender recognition procedures[46] and 14 required a trans person to be sterilised for legal gender recognition, though in some, including the UK, gender identity is governed by legislative provisions that do not necessarily require evidence of sterilisation.[47]

Trans

As has been explained:

> This describes people whose gender identity differs from their birth sex, including transsexual people (those who intend to undergo, are undergoing or have undergone a process of gender reassignment to live permanently in their acquired gender).[48]

As the purpose is to achieve conformity with a strongly held self-perception of gender identity, many – but not all – who undergo that process will thereafter be committed to their acquired identity as male or female and will not identify as "trans". They may be among the strongest proponents for the binary gender structuring in family law.

The trans population is heterogeneous: it includes those diagnosed as suffering from "gender dysphoria"; also on the binary spectrum are those who experience, to a varying degree, some gender incongruity but without distress; then there are those who self-perceive as male or female but are cross-dressers or transvestites. Also to be included are a significant number of people who identify as non-binary: some as bisexual, some as androgynous or as other gender variant persons. "Genderqueer" is sometimes used as an umbrella term to refer to all those who are perceived, or self-perceive, as being non-binary.

Intersex

Those known as "intersex" are distinct from the trans population: whereas for the latter their gender identity is open to social conditioning, for the former this is biologically determined; they are "intersex" due to the ambiguity of their sexual characteristics (hormones, chromosomes, genitalia etc.).

45 World Professional Association for Transgender Health, *Standards of Care for the Health of Transgender and Gender Non-Conforming People* (7th Version), 2012, p. 5.
46 See further: *Trans Rights Europe Map & Index 2018*, at: https://tgeu.org/tag/trans-rights-europe-map/.
47 Council of Europe, Commissioner for Human Rights, *Discrimination on Grounds of Sexual Orientation and Gender Identity in Europe*, Council of Europe Publishing, 2011, at pp. 86–87.
48 *J v. B*, op. cit., per Jackson, J., at para. 15.

Although distinctively different, because of social pressure and self-perceived inadequacy many intersex people – usually as children – experience gender dysphoria, or are so diagnosed, and enter the gender reassignment process. For a proportion of those, the surgical realignment of physiological characteristics with perceived gender will fail and compound their identity issues. In short, the trans population will always contain some who are intersex.[49]

The transitioning process/gender reassignment

As Jackson J has explained:

> The complex and protracted process of altering one's birth sex . . . includes some or all of the following cultural, legal, and medical adjustments: telling one's family, friends, and/or co-workers; changing one's name and/or sex on legal documents; hormone therapy to create the physical characteristics of the other gender; and possibly some form of surgery.[50]

More than 30 years ago, the ECtHR noted that those suffering from gender dysphoria "often seek to achieve a more integrated, unambiguous identity by undergoing medical treatment and surgical operations to adapt their physical character to their psychological nature".[51] However, realigning external appearance with subjective perception of gender, so as to achieve social acceptance of an acquired gender identity, is not without its challenges; doing so in order to also achieve legal recognition in law for that identity can be even more problematic.

The courts have recognised three distinct phases of reassignment treatment, all of which occur in the context of "coming out" – expressing to others and gaining affirmation by them of a new gender identity – and accompanying changes in social role. Stage 1 is hormonal-based "puberty blocking treatment", using gonadotropin-releasing hormone drugs (GnRH), which are known not to cause any clinically significant effects on physiological parameters: they do not impact adversely on bone mineral density or affect reproductive function; nor do they cause obesity. The effects of such treatment are reversible when the drugs are used for a limited time, approximately three to four years, ideally commenced in the early stages of puberty (from the ages of 9 to 12). Stage 2 is "gender-affirming hormone treatment", involving the use of either oestrogen or testosterone, which can have irreversible effects and is ideally commenced at an age where the adolescent is sufficiently mature to be able to provide informed consent. Stage 3 involves irreversible surgical intervention (chest reconstruction and genital reconstruction) and, most probably, sterility. For many, the first stage is sufficient

49 See further Carpenter, M., The "Normalisation" of Intersex Bodies and "Othering" of Intersex Identities, in Scherpe, J. M., Dutta, A. and Helms, T. (eds.), *The Legal Status of Intersex Persons*, Intersentia, 2018.

50 *J v. B.*, op. cit., at para. 16.

51 *Rees v. The United Kingdom*, Application No. 9532/81 (1986), at para. 38.

to achieve transition, meaning an alignment between physical presentation and self-perceived gender identity.

Consolidating personal identity is a central part of adolescence. This period, a time of general uncertainty for young teenagers, is when they need space to develop a firm sense of gender identity, but it is also the time when some commit to gender identity treatment. Medical intervention with puberty suppression gonadotropin-releasing hormone analogues often begins during the early stages of puberty, with cross-sex hormonal treatment starting at under 16 years of age and leading to possible surgery in the late teenage years. As increasing numbers of children are being referred to gender identity clinics in all western countries, safeguards are essential to filter out inappropriate referrals and to avoid premature intervention in what may be a normal phase of gender uncertainty. The SOGI intersect with human rights starts with the availability of appropriate counselling facilities for children with gender identity issues.

It might be added that transitioning cannot be seen as an event: it is a process that may take many years and never be completed; it may also happen that sufficient transitioning will be subjectively achieved by merely changing external appearance – name, clothes, hairstyle, speech etc. – to conform with social expectations of desired gender identity. Moreover, gender reassignment is an expensive process, and its availability will often depend on whether national health services or private health insurance policies will pay for it; accessing the gender reassignment process is a human rights issue for all trans people.

Transphobia

Members of the LGBT community, particularly trans persons, are commonly the target of derogatory attitudes, harassment and/or verbal or physical abuse. It may take the form of deliberately "outing" such a person without their permission. This, of course, is discriminatory and prohibited under equality legislation in all Part II jurisdictions, whether or not the abuser is correct in an assumption that their victim belongs to that community.

Trans persons, at any stage in the transitioning process, are particularly vulnerable to unprovoked harassment and verbal or physical abuse, but others who self-identify as non-binary are similarly vulnerable. While transitioning gives many the confidence to thereafter fully live within the genetic identity and the accompanying social boundaries with which they feel most comfortable, others – whether trans or not – can be left fragile and with continuing uncertainty. The latter group, a high proportion of whom are at risk of harm from themselves and/or others, are very much in need of recognition and protection within a human rights framework.

Conclusion

The male/female binary interpretation of sexuality and gender was established in all Part II jurisdictions under the dual rubric of Christianity and the common law. Enforcement mechanisms included being shamed as a sinner and jailed as a criminal by the institutions of Church and court respectively – and sometimes by both as in the case of "heretics" – and were sufficient to maintain a structuring of society around the legal concept of the "marital family" for many centuries. It was sustained by a body of family law, together with ancillary laws relating to property, tax, inheritance etc., all of which applied with a considerable degree of uniformity across all those jurisdictions.

Whether the deconstruction of the central concept of the heterosexual marital family was a cause or an effect of the social changes that have been sweeping through the Part II jurisdictions since the 1960s is uncertain, but the consequences of the retreat of Church and State from the private life of the individual are continuing to emerge. Once the necessity for that unifying structure fell away – no longer reflected in a hierarchy of patriarchal relationships, manifested in ascribed legal status and reinforced by medical science – different interpretations of sexuality and gender seemed possible, accompanied by an array of relationship permutations. How the law has responded to this unravelling, gradually recognising the legitimacy of SOGI status and relationships, is largely what this book about.

2 SOGI, human rights and the common law jurisdictions

Introduction

This chapter begins with an overview of legal rights and international human rights and considers their characteristic differences. It identifies and outlines the main SOGI-related human rights, as they originated in the Universal Declaration of Human Rights (UDHR), before turning to examine the relevance of equality and non-discrimination legislation. It traces the sequential developmental stages in the history of the law as it relates to the SOGI/human rights intersect, from the de-criminalising of homosexuality, through recognition of different LGBT rights, to the current tentative acknowledgement of non-binary status. It then examines the recognition of SOGI status in law: the differentiation of "sex", "sexual orientation", "gender" and "gender identity" and the legal significance of the difference between binary and non-binary. The chapter ends by introducing the book's key underlying narrative: the effect of human rights on the world of the individual person, judged by Eleanor Roosevelt to be the crucial test of its effectiveness; and the importance, 60 years later, of applying the same test to measure how a modern iteration of that law is now affecting the SOGI-related world of such an individual person.

Legal rights and international human rights

Legal rights provide for assertive action in the courts by individuals or legal entities for alleged breaches of duties established in national legislation and/or in international conventions. Certain rights have gained international recognition as being of greater importance than others. These are embodied in various international treaties, conventions, protocols etc., some of which are directly binding upon signatory States; others have been legislatively incorporated into national law (see Chapter 3).

Legal rights

Legal rights and corresponding legal duties, usually underpinned by moral authority and enforced by legal powers, form the basis for national legal systems and are characterised by: acknowledgement of specific rights held by individuals or entities; a "cause of action" or set of facts sufficient to justify legal proceedings; objective adjudication on alleged breach of right and appropriate recompense; and a process for enforcement. While providing specific remedies for specific unlawful acts, legal rights also contribute to generally reinforcing the currency of human rights norms and to the building of human rights compliant practices. On the other hand, it may also be argued that an adversarial pursuit of legal rights as a means of dealing with complex social problems can lead to a strategic failure to "see the wood for the trees" and generate fractious social divisiveness.

Human rights

From the outset – in the American and French revolutions of the late eighteenth century – human rights had a central concern for citizenship and equality. This was forcefully asserted in the US Declaration of Independence on 4 July 1776:

> We hold these truths to be self evident: that all men are created equal; that they are endowed by their Creator with certain inalienable rights; that among these are life, liberty, and the pursuit of happiness.

Although the French Revolution, launched in 1789, drew significantly from the American experience, it went a step further. The French rejection of feudalism – its institutions and its carefully orchestrated social order – together with an ideological insistence on equality and egalitarianism as incidents of citizenship, were instrumental in paving the way for human rights.

From common law to legal rights and social justice

While the foundations for the evolving legal systems of all jurisdictions that formerly constituted the British Empire remained similarly grounded on the bedrock of common law, the changes introduced by the gradual spread of legislation, together with the concepts of legal rights and justice, shifted the dynamic from the personal to the public domain but still left the law anchored on specified causes of action or on "entitlements". This approach – statutorily encoding legal rights and corresponding legal duties, enforced by legal powers – formed the basis for national legal systems, often complemented, in due course, by constitutions enshrining principles of collective justice. It was not until the introduction of international conventions, protocols etc. that such principles acquired a transcending effect.

Following the brutalising experience of two world wars and the harrowing futility of experiments with ideology, sovereign States came together in Paris on 10 December 1948, under the auspices of the United Nations General Assembly, to adopt the Universal Declaration of Human Rights and thereby lay the foundations for contemporary international human rights. Over subsequent decades, an international safety net of provisions has grown which requires standards of equity, equality and non-discrimination to be entrenched in the legislation of signatory nations (see Chapter 3).

Citizenship and human rights

The signature hallmark of human rights lies in the fact that they are vested uniformly in each human being and bring an entitlement: to exercise any such right in the context of relationships either with other human beings or with the State; and to appeal to supra-national authorities to have that entitlement enforced should the State fail in its legal obligation to respect such rights. While the first can be interpreted as an incident of citizenship, derived from nationality, the second introduces a tension with citizenship as it authorises a transcending of the citizen/State relationship when necessary to ensure the protection or enforcement of human rights.

Initially, and for nearly two centuries, the "rights of man" as articulated in both the American and French revolutions were interpreted as the rights of citizens vested in them by virtue of their nationality and assured of protection by the authorities of their sovereign nation State as part of an agreed "social contract". Not until the mid-twentieth century, in the face of irrefutable evidence of the extent of disempowerment inflicted upon citizens – by religion, ideology and nation States – did human rights come to be viewed as being vested in human beings as such rather than by virtue of their being citizens. More recently, the impact of globalisation and mass migration, accelerated by the phenomenon of "Stateless persons" and the volume of cases determined on a supra-national basis, have caused many to see yet further erosion in the relationship between citizenship and human rights. Arguably, the concept of "citizen" is no longer tied to the nation State but has been re-branded to become "citizen of the World", precisely because of the uniform, increasingly comprehensive and supra-national effect of human rights.[1] A new global superstructure of moral verities is perhaps being built and progressively refined, one which holds States to account for safeguarding a designated set of human rights vested equally in everyone.

Refugees, asylum seekers and human rights

The plight of refugees or asylum seekers is of particular significance in the present context of mass migration, which necessarily includes many people with SOGI-related issues. It is a point explicitly addressed in Article 23 of the Yogyakarta Principles, which outlines both the right to seek and enjoy asylum from persecution related to sexual orientation and/or gender and the corresponding duty of a State to ensure that no person seeking asylum on that basis is denied it.

1 See, for example, Benhabib, S., *The Rights of Others: Aliens, Residents and Citizens*, Cambridge University Press, Cambridge, 2004.

Initial formulation of international human rights and freedoms

The Treaty of Westphalia in 1648, ending 30 years of wars in Europe, has been hailed as inaugurating the modern era. It was based upon a multi-national agreement, committing sovereign States to respect each other's independent territory and to respect the responsibility of each ruler for ensuring the protection of those within it. This marked a significant step in establishing the concept of "a comity of nations". Exactly three centuries later, following more wars that devastated Europe and elsewhere, the Universal Declaration of Human Rights (UDHR) sought to revive the 1648 initiative. The 30 fundamental rights entrenched in the UDHR provided the foundations for the development of all subsequent human rights and include those addressed next which have a particular relevance for SOGI-related matters and are therefore the focus of attention throughout this book. Arguably, at least in the view of this author, the ever-expanding platform of human rights can and should be differentiated in accordance with their relative importance. There would appear to be a set of core human rights of truly fundamental importance: access to justice, and the freedoms of speech, association and assembly, and of religion; all are essential to establish and maintain a democratic society. Another set of human rights would seem to govern the legal status of a citizen and their relationships with a significant other, with family and with others more generally; in our introspective western societies, this set is developing exponentially. Then there is an array of operational rights that relate to the functioning of society and to the role of the individual within those functions, including but not limited to standards of health, employment, education and general service provision. This book proceeds on the basis of that differentiation.

Right to justice

Access to justice, as guaranteed under Articles 6–11 of the UDHR, is central to the rule of law and a prerequisite for the recognition and enforcement of all other rights. This composite right is of fundamental importance, encompassing an entitlement to equality before the law and to equality of protection by it. Included within its scope is the right to: access a legal system; to a presumption of innocence and fair trial; to due process. It requires: relevant information to be available that can be readily understood; appropriate processes and proceedings to exist; an opportunity to avail of such resources as may necessary for effective representation; the proceedings to be conducted independently, fairly and with a right of appeal; and that the outcome is fully and fairly enforced.

By extension, this right is applied through Article 14 to asylum seekers in the declaration that "everyone has the right to seek and to enjoy in other countries asylum from persecution". It arises most acutely in respect of the large proportion of those who are Muslims: some fleeing to escape SOGI-related persecution[2]

2 See the Refugee Convention 1951, as amended by the 1967 Protocol.

and others who experience great difficulty in reconciling their SOGI-adverse religious beliefs with the equality laws and social mores that now prevail in Europe.

Rights to freedom of expression, association and religion

These rights are often viewed together as different aspects of the collective right of people to act in concert to achieve a common purpose, though clearly individuals also have the right to choose to act independently in pursuit of the same ends.

Right to freedom of expression

Article 19 of the UDHR establishes the right to articulate opinions and ideas without fear of retaliation, censorship or sanction and directs that it may be exercised through any media and regardless of frontiers. As one of the principal hallmarks of a democratic society, this right is particularly important for those who need to advocate on behalf of a cause, comment on events or challenge an abuse of power. It often functions with other rights such as the freedoms of religion or association. Because it rests on a presumption of permissiveness, it facilitates the growth of a tolerant, diverse and pluralist society, but this is breached by expressions of homophobia, transphobia and/or hate.

Right to freedom of association and assembly

Initially established by Article 20 of the UDHR, this right is crucial for those who wish to join with others to form a legal entity in order to act collectively in pursuit of a common lawful interest. The freedom of association protects the collective pursuit of common goals. It also provides for the right not to be compelled to belong to an association. Essentially it protects the discretion of an individual to form, join or leave an association without interference from the State. This right has proved strategically important for emerging minority groups with a need to lobby for social and legal change.

Right to freedom of religion

Article 18 of the UDHR declared the right to freedom of thought, conscience and religion. It is a right that in recent years has expanded greatly in scope as its definition in law broadened to accommodate a range of new religions, beliefs and subjective interpretations. Enjoyment of this right is necessarily entangled with such other rights and freedoms as those of expression, association and assembly. It includes the right to have, to adopt or to change a religion or belief; to exercise religion or belief publicly or privately, alone or with others; and to exercise religion or belief in worship, teaching, practice and observance. It also provides for the right to have no religion and to have non-religious beliefs protected.

Personal rights

For everyone, those rights which afford recognition and protection for the more intimate aspects of life – that relate to a sense of self and govern our relationships with those dearest to us – are the ones which are most directly relevant. This is particularly true for the application of such rights in a SOGI context and justifies treating them as a distinct set.

Right to an identity

Article 6 of the UDHR states that "everyone has the right to recognition everywhere as a person before the law". For the many and diverse constituents of the LGBT community, there has been no more important human right than that of recognition in law and society for their distinctive SOGI identity.

Right to privacy and family life

State responsibility to ensure that "no one shall be subjected to arbitrary interference with his privacy, family, home or correspondence" was initially stated in Article 12 of the UDHR and has provided the foundations for a considerable body of SOGI-related jurisprudence.

Right to marry and found a family

Article 16 of the UDHR provides for the right of men and women of a marriageable age to marry and to found a family, in accordance with their national law, without hindrance due to race, nationality or religion. It is specifically made conditional upon the free and full consent of the spouses, who are thereafter – for the duration of their marriage and at time of dissolution – entitled to equal rights. While the right does not explicitly refer to heterosexual marriage, it would be disingenuous to suggest that the framers of the Declaration had any other interpretation in mind. Nonetheless, the right as formulated – particularly when read in conjunction with the Article 2 directive that UDHR rights be available to all "without distinction of any kind . . . such as sex" – lends itself to a SOGI-compliant application.

The right to found a family is absolute. The State is required to protect the family unit and cannot interfere with it: there is no legal obligation on the State to provide the services that may be necessary for the right to be exercised, but any State intervention in family affairs is required to be in accordance with the obligation to respect the private and family life of its members. The second part of the right viz. "to found a family" was clearly intended to be construed as dependent upon first exercising "the right to marry": marriage would confer legal status on "family" and vest the spouses with reciprocal duties, parental obligations, inheritance rights etc.

Right to cultural life

An entitlement to realise the "social and cultural rights indispensable for his dignity and the free development of his personality" is established by Article 22 of the UDHR and supplemented by the Article 27 right "to freely to participate in the cultural life of the community". Further, Article 2 of the Vienna Declaration unequivocally states that "all peoples" have the right to "freely determine their . . . cultural development". However, this right has proved contentious in a contemporary SOGI context and was refuted, arguably, by the UN Secretary-General's statement that "where there is tension between cultural attitudes and universal human rights, universal human rights must carry the day".[3] The right of Indigenous people to an authentic cultural life has probably been irretrievably compromised everywhere.

Human rights: equality and non-discrimination

UDHR rights and freedoms are declared by Article 2, as mentioned earlier, to be available to all "without distinction of any kind . . . such as sex . . . or other status". This is reinforced by Article 7, which is unequivocal in its pronouncement that all are equal before the law, all are entitled without any discrimination to equal protection of the law and all are entitled to equal protection against any discrimination or any incitement to discrimination. This fundamental principle of entitlement to equality and non-discrimination is drawn from similar expressions in both the French Declaration of the Rights of Man and the US Fourteenth Amendment. As Eleanor Roosevelt noted, it is how this plays out for the ordinary person living a normal everyday life[4] that ultimately tests the value and effectiveness of human rights. Her warning has a general relevance and is particularly applicable to the individual who belongs to a minority group, and it probably did much to prepare the ground for the civil rights movement in the 1960s.

Equality and non-discrimination

Not until the turn of the century, however, following the widespread introduction of equality and non-discrimination legislation (which drew heavily from the example set by the 1965 US Civil Rights Act), did the provisions of that law really begin to impact upon LGBT issues in the settings she identified some 60 years ago. The traction since gained by the courts and regulatory bodies as they applied and developed this law across the wide sweep of those everyday settings has transformed social relationships, including those that are SOGI-related, in all Part II

3 UN Press Release, Confront Prejudice, Speak Out Against Violence, Secretary-General Says at Event on Ending Sanctions Based on Sexual Orientation, Gender Identity, SG/SM/13311-HR/5043, 10 December 2010.

4 See Eleanor Roosevelt's speech to the UN at the Church Peace Union, *In Your Hands: A Guide for Community Action on the 10th Anniversary of the UDHR*, New York, 1958.

jurisdictions. It justifies the present approach of focusing on the application of equality and non-discrimination provisions – in the fields of health, education, employment and service provision – as identified by Eleanor Roosevelt.

Affirmative action

By the twenty-first century governments had concluded that policies conducive to building a diverse but equitable civil society required intervention and adjustment in some areas more than others: "a one size fits all" strategy for addressing social inequality, in line with the previous UDHR Articles, was insufficient. This led to an acceptance that policies such as "affirmative action" (favouring the more marginalised), "islands of exclusivity" (exempting entities that are liable to be unduly burdened) and "religious exemption" (specifically exempting religious organisations and their emanations) may run alongside equality and non-discrimination provisions to moderate their levelling effect. The application of those provisions, with their accompanying caveats, are examined in some detail throughout this book.

Discrimination

It is salutary to bear in mind that the law relating to discrimination is itself discriminatory: not everyone can claim protection. Specific grounds or "protected characteristics" are identified, and only those that can fit within that category will qualify. Moreover, and paradoxically, a feature of many UN human rights treaties is that they are discriminatory: an international instrument will single out a particular type of person as warranting protection, to the exclusion of others. The selective focus is often clearly indicated in the title: the Convention on the Rights of the Child, the Convention on the Elimination of All Forms of Discrimination Against Women and the Convention on the Rights of Persons With Disabilities. There is an argument that such affirmative intervention is overly concerned with identifying and differentiating, ends up labelling and may be experienced by some as patronising or demeaning and by others as excluding or undervaluing.

Right to health

The right to a standard of living adequate for the health and well-being of an individual and that of their family is guaranteed by Article 25 of the UDHR. This specifies an entitlement to all "medical care and necessary social services" and a "right to security" in relation to "circumstances beyond their control".

Right to education

As stated in Article 26 of the UDHR, this establishes that everyone has a right to education, accessible without cost at least until the secondary stage. It is a vitally important right as it provides a gateway for personal social success and economic security and also the means for facilitating an inter-generational transfer of culture, values and beliefs. Education is understood to mean the provision of factual information, objectively and impartially taught, including health and safety information relating to sexuality, gender and the facts of life.

Right to employment

Article 23 of the UDHR establishes that everyone has a right to employment on reasonable terms. This is a right, not a duty: individuals are free to choose not to work; no-one should be prevented by others from seeking employment; but also the right is exercisable in relation to employment in general, not in relation to any particular type of employment. The right is one which includes an entitlement to a safe and healthy workplace free of intimidation and non-work-related restrictions.

Right to service provision

Public services are to be available to those in need on a non-discriminatory basis. Private service providers are similarly bound by that requirement unless they can claim exemption on grounds of conscientious objection.

Conscientious objection

For religious organisations and for persons with religious belief, the equality and non-discrimination legislative provisions often present SOGI-related difficulties – particularly in the context of employment – requiring them to seek exemption from universal constraints that adversely affect their religious freedom. The ambit of the moral licence to be excused from legislative requirements binding on everyone else is uncertain but steadily widening.

Developmental stages in the law relating to the SOGI/human rights intersect

The western nations, including the Part II common law jurisdictions, passed through much the same stages in changing their laws relating to sexuality and gender, albeit with some differences in timing. It was a process driven essentially by human rights, specifically by the unremitting logic and momentum of equality and non-discrimination laws. How this is now evolving, as illustrated in legislation and caselaw, is examined in detail in Part II. However, to appreciate the pace, sequencing and consequent social impact of that process, it is first necessary to broadly sketch the parameters of the SOGI phenomenon: tracing the stages, noting the key turning points and outlining the timescale.

De-criminalisation of homosexuality

Homosexual relationships, condemned by Church and State for centuries in the Christian west, continue to be so in eastern and mainly Islamic countries, while also presenting challenges for Muslims and others, including many from the more fundamental branches of Christianity and Judaism, now living in the SOGI-accepting cultures of the Part II jurisdictions.

Consensual sex in private

The process of de-criminalising homosexual relationships began in the mid-1960s and rippled across the developed nations in the following decades, with Ireland among the last to take that step, in 1993. In England and Wales, for example, the Sexual Offences Act 1967 largely ended the criminalisation of same-sex relationships,[5] followed in time by a lowering of the age of consent to 16 in 2001 and by repeal of the offence of gross indecency in 2004. This progression was assisted by the forming of gay groups, some notable riots (e.g. the 1969 Stonewall riots in New York) and the effectiveness of public protest marches in all countries.

Enlistment in the armed forces

In many countries there was never an explicit ban on LGBT persons serving in the armed forces – it was largely dealt with on a "don't ask, don't tell" basis – but ambivalence in the top echelons allowed bullying, blackmail and "outing" to prevail in the ranks. By the end of the twentieth century, most of the Part II jurisdictions had introduced laws prohibiting any discrimination on the grounds of sexual orientation in the recruitment of armed forces personnel or in their conditions of service. In England and Wales, such recruitment was permitted from 2000, but not until the Equality Act 2010 did discrimination become legally prohibited.

Gay blood donors

The AIDs pandemic took hold in the USA in the early 1980s before spreading elsewhere, and a lifetime prohibition on blood donations from homosexual men was imposed almost immediately. Not until 30 years later was this ban replaced by a deferral policy: 2011 in the UK (excluding Northern Ireland) and 2015 in the US.

Legal affirmation of same-sex relationships

The shift from prohibition to permission and affirmation was one that came in incremental steps, but once same-sex relationships were de-criminalised, the equality imperative left little doubt about the trajectory; any uncertainty as to outcome was confined to the timing.

5 Repealing the buggery provisions in the Criminal Law Act 1885 and permitting sexual activity in private between consenting males over the age of 21.

Same-sex foster carers, adopters and surrogate parents

The build-up of children in the public care systems in all developed nations, coupled with an acute shortage of the substitute parents necessary to give effect to the national and international legal welfare principles requiring children to be cared for in a family environment, led to the relevant government authorities approving same-sex couples for children in care. At first this was largely restricted to short-term foster parents, and often the approval was in respect of a single carer with a blind eye turned to the probability that he or she was in a same-sex relationship. In time, some such foster parents acquired the right to adopt the child in their care, which brought the issue of the suitability of same-sex parenting before the courts, resulting in judicial notice being taken of the fact that sexual orientation was not of itself a factor in determining parenting capacity. By the beginning of this century, same-sex couples had acquired the same legal right to adopt as their heterosexual counterparts (2005 in England and Wales). Somewhat later the same principle extended to IVF; by the end of that decade, same-sex couples were legally entitled to access IVF treatment, and same-sex surrogate parents could both be registered as their child's parent: 2009 in England and Wales; but still uncertain in Ireland in 2019.

Civil partnerships

Legal recognition conferring positive affirmation on the status of same-sex relationships came some years after de-criminalisation and then in the limited form of an entitlement to civil registration, as opposed to a religious ceremony. In England and Wales, legislation allowing civil partnerships was passed in 2004.

Same-sex marriage

Given the spreading implementation and effects of equality and non-discrimination laws, pushed on by the stream of SOGI-related cases coming before the European courts, the step from civil partnership to same-sex marriage was probably inescapable. The fact that it took some years is testimony to the strength of resistance from religious organisations and from others who feared the erosion of traditional social mores and their related institutions. The second decade of the twenty-first century saw most common law nations successively introducing legislation legalising same-sex marriage: Canada did so as early as 2005, with England and Wales following in 2014, but Australia not until 2017.

The Yogyakarta Principles

The Yogyakarta Principles on the Application of International Human Rights Law in relation to Sexual Orientation and Gender Identity were adopted in 2007 by a group of human rights experts and augmented in 2018 by an additional ten principles.[6] Now recognised internationally as a significant milestone, they state the principles and set out the human rights protection framework applicable in the context of sexual orientation and/or gender identity.

Implications for policy and law

The importance of these principles is evident in the fact that they are constantly cited in SOGI-related court cases around the world. Of particular significance is the recognition they have given to the distinct needs, characteristics and situations of intersex people compared to others in the LGBT community. The weighting attached to them is also apparent in the leverage they wield with policy makers: the removal of transgendering from mental health categorisation is only one example of their influence; the reminder of the importance to be attached to cultural context is another (see Chapter 3).

Legal recognition of SOGI status

Human rights jurisprudence, not unlike the common law itself, is constructed on the basis of categories of people (children, disabled, asylum seekers, women etc.) and of grounds (health, employment, education etc.) judged to be particularly deserving of protection. Human rights proceedings are contingent upon an entity having a legal identity that fits within the specified characteristics of a protected category. This sophisticated classification system functions on the basis of a correlation between a legally recognised entity and a "cause of action". In recent years, first sexual orientation, then gender identity, then non-binary identity – the latter with some equivocation – have acquired such recognition and legal status in the Part II jurisdictions.

Sex

Judiciary and regulators have struggled with the problem of whether such entities could be fitted within the category of "sex" or whether they should be ascribed a distinct legal status in their own right. This proved problematic because neither "sexual orientation" nor "gender identity" has been viewed as definable in terms of having a fixed legal identity: neither is in all cases immutable.

Sexual orientation status

By the end of the second decade of the twenty-first century, a body of law structured around the binary system had grudgingly come to ascribe legal status to

6 ICJ, Yogyakarta Principles – Principles on the Application of International Human Rights Law in Relation to Sexual Orientation and Gender Identity (hereafter "Yogyakarta Principles"), March 2007, at: www.unhcr.org/refworld/docid/48244e602.html.

gay, lesbian and trans causes of action and to accommodate most associated issues alongside corresponding binary system proceedings (marriage, divorce, adoption etc.). Although sexual orientation has now acquired a legal identity and in all Part II jurisdictions has been defined as having the protected characteristics that merit giving it independent recognition, it had taken years of professional legal and health care wrangling before the disaggregation of sex orientation from sex discrimination could be agreed. Human rights law has yet to develop the refinements necessary to recognise and address issues associated with the nuances and greater fluidity of SOGI status.

Gender identity: legal recognition of status

For some time there has been uncertainty in medicine, in law and in society at large as to the necessary steps that must be taken in order to validate a claim of change in gender identity, though such medical evidence as there is has tended to be weighted against the possibility that such a change could result merely from a lifestyle choice. In the event of such a claim being made, further uncertainty then arose as to the form of legal recognition that would be appropriate to identify the status of a trans person. Given that such a claim was most likely to arise in the context of proceedings alleging discrimination – where both human rights law and the equal treatment directives of the European Union operate with closed categories of grounds – it became apparent that the established protected category of "sex" was the only ground available and appropriate to accommodate such proceedings. Indeed, at an early stage the Advocate General had closed off the possibility of providing separate recognition for trans persons by ruling that they did not constitute a third sex and therefore should fall within the scope of equal treatment directives.[7]

The courts, from the outset, focused on verifiable change resulting from Stage 3 (see Chapter 1) medical intervention.[8] For example, the Commission in *D. van Oosterwijck v. Belgium*[9] referred to a post-operative transsexual's "changed physical form, his psychical make-up and his social role". Even now, although the ECtHR has ruled that sex reassignment surgery is not an essential prerequisite for legal recognition of a changed gender identity,[10] in many countries medical affirmation of treatment that has caused irreversible gender change is necessary

7 *P. v S. and Cornwall County Council*, Case C-13/94, Opinion of the Advocate General (14 December 1995), at para. 22.

8 For many years the courts in the Part II jurisdictions applied the test formulated by Ormorod LJ in the English case of *Corbett v. Corbett* [1970] 2 All ER 33, which relied on: (i) chromosomal factors; (ii) gonadal factors (i.e. presence or absence of testes or ovaries); (iii) genital factors (including internal sex organs); (iv) psychological factors. Noting that some would add (v) hormonal factors or secondary sexual characteristics (such as distribution of hair, breast development, physique etc. which are thought to reflect the balance between the male and female sex hormones in the body). See www.pfc.org.uk/caselaw/Corbett%20v%20Corbett.pdf.

9 Application No. 7654/76 (1979), at para. 52.

10 *S.V. v. Italy*, Application No. 55216/O8 (2018).

to obtain an altered birth certificate, though some such countries are prepared to issue other forms of ID, such as a passport or driving licence, on the basis of lesser evidence, and some will accept a self-declaration of gender identity.

Gender identity: self-declared

Although there had long been a widespread acceptance that the trans world accommodated transvestites and cross-dressers etc., the legal and medical professions took a more clinical view of how a trans person should be defined. Essentially, for legal purposes, an acquired gender identity needed to be corroborated by evidence that a person had completed a physiological transition which had erased the physical indicators of one gender and replaced them with those of the other (see Chapter 1). Little short of years of medical treatment, including irreversible genital surgery, would provide sufficient evidence of a change in gender identity to warrant the confirmation available through the issue of an appropriately amended birth certificate, which most usually was the gateway verification needed for such other official ID documentation as a passport, driving licence etc.

Only in very recent years, and then only in very few countries, has it become accepted that gender identity could be a matter for self-declaration. As with other aspects of identity – most notably that of religious belief – the law has come to accept the privacy right of an autonomous individual to believe what they will, subject to the caveats that: the belief is sincerely held; it is cogent and rational rather than fanciful; it is lawful; and that it can be substantiated by the fact that others recognise and respect that individual's belief. Accordingly, by 2018, in countries such as Ireland, a self-declaration of gender identity was determined to be sufficient for all legal purposes, including acquiring an amended birth certificate. This is not without its difficulties. An inescapable corollary to more relaxed legal criteria for verifying biological gender change is that it correspondingly increases the margins of risk of abuse by predatory sex offenders. Some filtering system would seem prudent to protect potential victims by detecting those who may use the opportunity afforded by a less medically driven gender identity change process to access gender-specific services for the wrong reasons.

Non-binary ID

Again, in very recent years and only in one or two countries, an emerging trend has been for legal recognition to be given for the designation of some persons as "non-binary". The social acceptance that not everyone conforms to a binary gender classification[11] has taken many years to translate into recognition for legal

11 By way of contrast, acceptance of non-binary and intersex persons is well established and has a long history in other cultures: the "two-spirit" designation among the First Nations; and the "sistergirls" and "brotherboys" in the communities of the Indigenous people in Australia.

purposes. "Intersex" is only now beginning to be recognised as a legitimate legal status that identifies persons with distinctive characteristics that differentiate them from others on the binary/non-binary spectrum.

Australia, in 2003, first allowed an "X" to be entered on a passport where gender was "indeterminate", but not until 2014 did this become official federal policy for all official documentation, including birth certificates, and on a self-declaration basis. By the second decade of the twenty-first century other countries, including New Zealand and Canada, had moved to placing an "X" instead of "male" or "female" on passports and birth certificates.

SOGI discrimination and "the world of the individual person"

The individual person that Eleanor Roosevelt had in mind was clearly not one whose world was complicated by SOGI considerations. Nevertheless, the binary world as perceived by that person did not differ significantly – in terms of basic social roles and infrastructure – from that occupied by their post-binary counterpart. Now, as then, it remains probably fair to identify health as the area in which human rights most directly impacts the life of such a person. Similarly, its effect on the field of employment continues to be hugely significant due to the expansion in the number of employees, the range of new employment opportunities and the consequent volume and breadth of workforce human rights issues. Since then, however, socio-economic factors together with spread and penetration of equality and non-discrimination legislation have raised the salience of areas such as education and service provision for human rights intervention. It has been the impact of equality and non-discrimination litigation on SOGI-related issues that has challenged and done much to change the world of the individual person over the past 60 years.

SOGI discrimination

As the UN "Living Free and Equal" report[12] indicates, SOGI-related discrimination can take many forms, including:

> criminalization, discriminatory attitudes, harassment by police, stigma, ill treatment in detention and medical settings, lack of protective legislation, absence of complaints mechanisms, lack of trust in law enforcement officials and awareness by judicial operators. . . . Many of them face multiple and intersecting forms of discrimination because of their skin colour, ethnicity, gender, religion, age or migratory status or because they are living with a disability or in poverty.

12 U.N., *Living Free and Equal*, New York, 2016, at p. 11, at: www.ohchr.org/Documents/Publications/LivingFreeAndEqual.pdf.

For present purposes, however, the examination of discrimination will be restricted to the main sources of cases driven by equality legislation and generated within "the world of the individual person".

Definitional matters

In the absence of a specific international human rights instrument dedicated to SOGI protection, any assessment of related anti-discrimination measures must look to relevant provisions contained in a number of different treaties, conventions, protocols etc. (see Chapter 3). It must also be recognised that due to the definitional difficulties referred to earlier, SOGI discrimination caselaw has developed in a patchwork fashion.

Necessarily, the development of discrimination law is built around the parallel closed lists of matching human rights categories. For some time, that meant that SOGI discrimination was tied to the category "sex" in human rights law, and only relatively recently has that category been extended by analogy to include entities with SOGI characteristics. The disaggregation of sex orientation from sex discrimination has, in some jurisdictions, been followed by recognition of gender identity, but fewer jurisdictions provide express protection from discrimination on the grounds of gender identity, because in some this continues to be treated as a form of sex discrimination, which is already a protected category. As of 2019, as will become clear later, it remains the case that there is some way to go before it can be confidently stated that sexual orientation and gender identity have become protected categories in their own right in all Part II jurisdictions.

Religious organisations

Sexual orientation and gender identity, for some religions more than others, are governed by traditional beliefs, and this entitles religious persons and religious organisations to varying degrees of exemption from the SOGI-related requirements of equality and non-discrimination legislation. This is most obviously the case with evangelical Christians, ultra-Orthodox Jews and Muslims, for whom sexuality is held to correspond to gender at birth and will thereafter determine identity, family and social roles, education and employment opportunities etc. The extent to which the "religious exemption" excuses organisations from practices which would otherwise be discriminatory, and the tension between SOGI-related equality issues and religious organisations, are matters explored in each of the Part II chapters.

Dependent groups

The effects of SOGI-related discrimination, harmful in any circumstance, will be particularly so for those already vulnerable. The plight of asylum seekers or migrants/refugees, for example, is compounded if they belong to the LGBT community, and they may well be endangered by a risk of being forcefully returned to their country of origin. Other vulnerable groups in similar dependent situations include Indigenous people, prisoners and school children, who again may be exposed to harm if "outed" for their SOGI status.

Victims

The 2018 report of the Independent Expert on protection against violence and discrimination based on sexual orientation and gender identity refers to daily acts of exclusion and discrimination which, at their root, intend to punish the non-conformity of victims with preconceived and essentially binary notions of what their sexual orientation or gender identity should be.[13] The report draws attention to the corrosive effect of "stigma" – accompanying the role of victim – on the fabric of society, eroding values of fundamental importance, such as empathy, social inclusion and solidarity.[14] This can be exacerbated when the perpetrator has discriminated in a hateful manner.

"The world of the individual person"

The world may have been transformed in many ways since the end of WWII, but the most basic concerns of the individual person – for health, education, employment and services – have remained much the same. These are of particular importance for the LGBT community, as is evidenced by the fact that they have generated by far the greatest proportion of equality and non-discrimination litigation on SOGI-related issues.

Health

The early importance attached to health was due to acute public awareness, sometimes panic, in relation to a contamination risk from HIV and Hepatitis C and the need for those afflicted to access expensive treatment and drugs, together with SOGI status being designated a mental health matter. In fact, the relevance of the health umbrella for SOGI issues can be traced back to at least the mid-1990s when homosexuality was still being treated as an illness, and it continues that relevance nearly three decades later, as gender dysphoria is still largely regarded and treated as an aspect of mental illness with gender reassignment requiring intensive medical involvement. The necessity of this involvement has, arguably, led to the human rights/SOGI intersect functioning with more ambivalence in the field of health than in employment, education or services. Differentiation, if not discrimination, is built into a system that starts from a mental health premise,

13 A/HRC/38/43, report of Victor Madrigal-Borloz, submitted to HRC, pursuant to Council resolution 32/2 (May 2018), at para. 48 (c/f to A/56/156, para. 17, A/HRC/35/23, para. 16 and A/HRC/20/16, para. 71). See www.un.org/en/ga/search/view_doc.asp?symbol=A/HRC/38/43

14 Ibid., at para. 60.

requires medical assessment, prescribes treatment and, until very recently, facilitated "conversion therapy" for those diagnosed as having SOGI status. Accessing treatment can also be compromised: the availability of gender reassignment drugs and possible surgery is expensive and dependent upon national health services and insurance policies which vary in the costs they will subsidise; the availability of surgeons and the willingness of medical personnel to be involved are variable factors that in practice can determine whether or not a right to treatment is realisable. By 2018, however, there were indications that some countries were moving away from the medical model as an appropriate means of determining SOGI status.

Education

Education on matters of sex and gender has probably always to some degree been fitted into school curriculum topics, usually health and hygiene, but not until well into this century did this extend to include an emphasis on LGBT awareness. Usually schools would have regarded such intimate matters as a responsibility that fell to parents rather than teachers, and the parental right to have at least a say in how such matters are taught in schools has been an ongoing point of contention. Only in very recent years have SOGI issues entered the classroom, as more children openly work out their sexual uncertainties, accompanied by an increase in related bullying, and this has resulted in a structured approach to such issues in some national educational curricula. By 2018, the extent to which SOGI-related information should be a taught subject – the level of age-appropriate detail, the degree of necessary religious/cultural contextualising and whether pupil participation was mandatory or not – had generated considerable general controversy and in particular outright resistance from many faith schools.

Employment

Trade unions, always alert to matters with potential to affect working relationships and conditions of employment, responded promptly to EU directives and to principles emerging from ECtHR judgements by introducing training, protocols and guidance for resolving SOGI-related issues in the workplace. From the introduction of legislation that first prohibited sexual orientation discrimination and later gender identity, there has been a steady flow of cases through the courts and regulatory bodies: by far the largest proportion of SOGI cases have been generated from an employment context; this has also been am area in which the religious exemption, privileging religious organisations and those of religious belief, has exercised most leverage. These cases have achieved much not only by making workplaces more SOGI compliant – gender-neutral bathroom facilities etc. – but also by bringing equity to occupational pension schemes and to the rights and welfare benefits of same-sex partners etc. By 2018, it was well established that a trans employee was entitled to access support and health care while undergoing gender reassignment.

Services

While service provision is governed by equality and non-discrimination laws which require non-discriminatory access, a distinction between the respective responsibilities of public and private (or commercial) providers became apparent at an early stage. Public services, paid for by public revenues and provided for the public benefit, are strictly governed by statutes which make the right to service access unequivocal: public service providers must deliver in accordance with that legislation. Private service providers, particularly religious organisations, may have some discretion as regards controlling service access if they can claim exemption from equality and non-discrimination legislation on the grounds of religion or belief. By 2018, a number of countries were beginning to introduce legislation permitting public health care professionals to decline to provide services on the grounds of conscientious objection.

Conclusion

This chapter has laid the groundwork for the one that follows, dealing with the contemporary operation of the international legal framework for addressing SOGI-related issues. In particular, it examined the Universal Declaration of Human Rights as a starting point for recognising and offering protection for those issues. It considered definitional matters, distinguishing sexual orientation from gender identity and binary from non-binary. It traced the long historical route from criminalisation to protection: the process of acquiring SOGI legal status.

Importantly, this chapter made the case for differentiating between international human rights in accordance with their relative bearing on SOGI issues: one block deals with the more fundamental rights of justice and the freedoms of speech, assembly/association and religion, another with rights relating to the identity of the individual and to their intimate relationships, family life and cultural affiliation; the third and largest block addresses rights of equality and non-discrimination in relation to the "world of the individual person" which, in Eleanor Roosevelt's view, comprised areas such as health, employment and education. In short, this chapter has identified a structure and themes around which the rest of this book will be constructed.

3 The international legal framework and themes of intersection

Human rights, sexual orientation and gender identity

Introduction

As the UN Commissioner for Human Rights has explained:

> The case for extending the same rights to lesbian, gay, bisexual and transgender (LGBT)[1] persons as those enjoyed by everyone else is neither radical nor complicated. It rests on two fundamental principles that underpin international human rights law: equality and non-discrimination.[2]

This key chapter examines how and to what extent international human rights law currently gives effect to such principles. It does so by working through different levels of generality in a process which provides an introduction to these and other important principles, to the law and to related issues. In particular, it trawls through the caselaw generated by the ECtHR and other international bodies to identify governing precedents. Drawing from the material in this and the preceding chapters, it assembles a thematic structure for the comparative analysis undertaken in the following jurisdiction-specific chapters.

Beginning with an overview of the regulatory framework, the chapter outlines the international instruments, such as the ECHR and the ICCPR, and the various courts and bodies with a brief for related issues. It then considers the caselaw generated by that framework. Firstly, it examines the relevance of the core internationally established human rights – e.g. the freedoms of expression and association – for matters of sexuality and gender. This is followed by a more focused exploration of rights with a direct bearing on personal relationships, including: the right to identity; to privacy and family life; to found a family; to marriage; and to cultural life. Finally, the chapter considers the impact of the legislation giving

1 Increasingly the reference is to "LGBTI" in order to include those of indeterminate or fluid sexual identity.

2 OHCHR, *Born Free and Equal: Sexual Orientation and Gender Identity in International Human Rights Law*, 2012, per UN Commissioner for Human Rights, at p. 7. Cited in McGoldrick, D., The Development and Status of Sexual Orientation Discrimination Under International Human Rights Law, *Human Rights Law Review*, 16, pp. 613–668 at p. 625 (2016).

effect to the previously-mentioned fundamental principles of equality and non-discrimination. It concludes by examining the specific service provision issues arising at the intersect of the law relating to equality and non-discrimination with that relating to sexuality and gender. For the participation of minority groups in a democratic society, as for everyone else, ease of access, quality of engagement and the relevance of everyday services such as health, education, employment and accommodation are what really matters.

International framework of conventions, protocols etc.

International human rights law is best viewed as a bundle of interdependent strands, a "living instrument",[3] which is constantly evolving and producing new rights and adjusting older ones as the organic body rebalances in response to changes in social context. While none of the growing body of international treaties, conventions and protocols are SOGI specific, many variously impact upon matters of gender and sexuality. Together with a mass of related jurisprudence, and despite much being neither directly applicable to nor enforceable in some nations, this framework has for some decades provided a common set of reference points for judiciary and government in all Part II jurisdictions.

The Universal Declaration of Human Rights (UDHR)

The Universal Declaration of Human Rights (UDHR) 1948 laid the foundation for every subsequent international human rights instrument. The ensuing decades have seen its provisions incorporated into the legal systems of 165 countries, including each of the six nations studied in Part II. Although without a designated enforcement mechanism, it is now accepted that the UDHR imposes an obligation upon the governments of all signatory States to ensure respect for the full body of rights.

Article 2

Proclaiming the right not to be discriminated against, Article 2 requires any difference in treatment to be objectively and reasonably justified.

Articles 6–11

This cluster of Articles provide for a right of access to an equitable justice system, including an entitlement to equality before the law and to equality of protection.

3 It is regarded as such by the UN HR Committee. See, further, HRC General Comment No 31: The Nature of the General Legal Obligation Imposed on States Parties to the Covenant, 29 March 2004, CCPR/C/21/Rev.1/Add.13.

Articles 12, 16 and 17

These Articles concern the legal integrity and autonomy of the marital family unit. Article 12 provides the right for personal privacy and for protection from arbitrary State intervention in the family home. Article 16 protects the right of men and women of a marriageable age to marry and to found a family, according to national law. This right to found a family is absolute and the State cannot interfere with it. Article 17 establishes the right to private property and family life.

Articles 19, 20, 23 and 26

These establish, respectively, the rights to freedom of speech, association, employment and education. Each of these substantive rights is of considerable significance for minority groups.

The European Convention on Human Rights (ECHR)

Established in 1950 under the auspices of the Council of Europe, with effect from 1953, the ECHR has been described by the European Court of Human Rights (ECtHR), which is responsible for enforcing the Convention, as a "constitutional instrument of European public order" in the field of human rights.[4] Its rulings have grown to form a considerable body of ever-evolving principles. As the court noted in *Tyrer v. the United Kingdom*,[5] the Convention "is a living instrument which . . . must be interpreted in the light of present-day conditions".[6]

Article 8

This right to private and family life, initially established by Articles 17 and 23 of the UDHR, has achieved a particularly wide reach, and the principles forged in the related caselaw have proven to be highly applicable to contemporary LGBT issues. The ECtHR has repeatedly stated that "elements such as gender identity or identification, names, sexual orientation and sexual life fall within the personal sphere protected by Article 8".[7]

4 *Bosphorus Hava Yolları Turizm ve Ticaret Anonim* Şirketi v. Ireland, Application No. 45036/98 (2005).

5 Application No. 5856/72 (1978). Wording derived from Article 31 of the Vienna Convention on the Law of Treaties, 23 May 1969, United Nations Treaty Series, vol. 1155, p. 331.

6 This is facilitated by the fact that the ECtHR is not bound to follow precedents, though it normally does (Rule 51 para. 1 of the Rules of Court).

7 *Van Kück v. Germany*, Application No. 35968/97, 2003-VII; *Schlumpf v. Switzerland*, Application No. 29002/06 (2009); *Y.Y. v. Turkey*, Application No. 14793/08 (2015); and *Garçon* and Nicot v. France, Application No. 79885/12 (2017).

Article 9(1)

This replicates Article 18 of the UDHR and together with the conditional Article 14 constitutes the key provisions relating to discrimination.[8] With application throughout Europe, these are therefore directly binding upon the UK and Ireland.[9]

Article 10

This provision, together with Article 19 of the ICCPR, reinforces the right to freedom of expression as established by Article 19 of the UDHR. It protects the right to articulate opinions and ideas without fear of retaliation, censorship or sanction.

Article 11

This guarantee of a right to freedom of peaceful assembly, an essential prerequisite for pluralism and diversity, promotes the growth of a democratic society. The harmonious interaction of persons and groups with varied identities, including all those represented by their sexual orientation, is viewed as essential for achieving social cohesion.[10]

Article 12

This provides the right for men and women of a marriageable age to marry and to found a family, according to national law, and as such is directly relevant to issues of gay marriage, arranged marriages, child marriages, adoption and a host of related matters.

Article 14

This provides that

> the enjoyment of the rights and freedoms set forth in [the] Convention shall be secured without discrimination on any ground such as sex, race, colour, language, religion, political or other opinion, national or social origin, association with a national minority, property, birth or other status.

8 Specifically: Article 9(1); Article 14: and Article 2 of Protocol 1.

9 Though not enforceable: see, for example, *Hirst -v- The United Kingdom (No. 2)*, Application No. 74025/01 (2004), the case of Ms C in *A, B and C v. Ireland*, Application No. 26499/02 (2006), and *Northern Ireland Human Rights Commission, Re Judicial Review* [2015] NIQB 96.

10 See, for example, *Gorzelik and Others v. Poland*, Application No. 44158/98 (2004).

In addition to the listed grounds, the catch-all reference to "any other status" infers that once triggered it may apply to grounds such as sexual orientation, gender transition or marital status.

Protocol 1

This declares that

> in the exercise of any functions which it assumes in relation to education and to teaching, the State shall respect the right of parents to ensure that such education and teaching is in conformity with their own religious and philosophical convictions.

The International Covenant on Civil and Political Rights (ICCPR)

The ICCPR, which came into effect in 1976, has become particularly important because of its wide international application and accompanying monitoring process. The UN HR Committee, the relevant monitoring body, has given extensive attention to issues of sexual orientation, and some of the earliest and leading treaty body jurisprudence was developed by it under the ICCPR.[11]

Article 2

This Article sets out the principle of non-discrimination. Discrimination on the grounds of "sex" is to be interpreted as including "sexual orientation".[12]

Article 17

The right to privacy is protected by this Article.

Article 23

This Article enshrines "the right of men and women of marriageable age to marry".

11 For example: *Toonen v. Australia*, Communication No. 488/1992, U.N. Doc CCPR/C/50/D/488/1992 (1994); *Joslin v. New Zealand*, Communication No. 902/1999, U.N. Doc. A/57/40 at 214 (2002); *Young v. Australia*, Communication No. 941/2000, UN Doc CCPR/C/78/D/941/2000 (2003) 5 IHRR 747, IHRL 1921, UNHRC (2003); and *X v. Colombia*, Communication No. 1361/2005, U.N. Doc. A/62/40.

12 *Toonen v. Australia*, op. cit.

Article 26

This Article, unlike the non-discrimination guarantee in Article 14 of the ECHR, which is merely an accessory right, has been interpreted by the UN HR Committee as a general, free-standing, equality and non-discrimination guarantee which prohibits discrimination in law or in fact in any field regulated and protected by public authorities.[13]

The International Covenant on Economic, Social and Cultural Rights (ICESCR)

Adopted by the UN General Assembly in 1966, the Covenant took effect from 1976. Article 2.2 lists discriminatory categories including "sex" and "other status", which the Committee has determined includes protection for both sexual orientation and gender identity.[14] Article 3, which proclaims equal rights for men and women, provides a basis for the prohibition of sexual orientation-related discrimination. Articles 6 and 7 considerably expand the right to employment as initially established in Article 23 of the UDHR. Article 6 of the Covenant specifically requires State parties to ensure that enumerated rights – e.g. to work,[15] to training, to equal pay, to join trade unions – can be enjoyed without discrimination of any kind. However, in practice the bodies that monitor implementation of United Nations human rights treaties tend to focus on sexual orientation-related discrimination rather than on discrimination on the basis of gender identity. In this context, the monitoring Committee has addressed relevant issues in its General Comments, which include: no. 18 of 2005 (on the right to work)[16] and no. 14 of 2000 (on the right to the highest attainable standard of health).[17] It has indicated that the Covenant proscribes any discrimination on the basis of, inter alia, sex and sexual orientation "that has the intention or effect of nullifying or impairing the equal enjoyment or exercise of [the right at issue]".

The UN Convention on the Elimination of All Forms of Discrimination Against Women (CEDAW)

Agreed in 1979, this Convention comprehensively defines gender discrimination and provides the foundation for achieving gender equality in many areas of life.

13 *Broeks v. The Netherlands* (172/1984) Views, CCPR/C/29/D/172/1984, at para 12.1; HRC General Comment No 18: Non-discrimination (1989), HRI/GEN/1/Rev.1 at 26 (1994), at para 12; and Joseph and Castan, *The International Covenant on Civil and Political Rights: Cases, Materials, and Commentary* (3rd ed.), 2013, at pp. 759–831.

14 Committee on Economic, Social and Cultural Rights, General Comment No. 20: E/C.12/GC/20, 2 July 2009, at para. 32.

15 Committee on Economic, Social and Cultural Rights, General Comment No. 18: The Right to Work, E/C.12/GC/18, 24 November 2005.

16 Committee on Economic, Social and Cultural Rights, General Comment No. 18: The Right to Work, E/C.12/GC/18, 6 February 2006.

17 Committee on Economic, Social and Cultural Rights, General Comment No. 14: The right to the highest attainable standard of health, E/C.12/2000/4, 11 August 2000.

Of central importance is Article 5, which calls for the elimination of "stereotyped roles for men and women". The Committee on the Elimination of Discrimination Against Women has on a number of occasions criticised States for discrimination on the basis of sexual orientation.

The Convention on Preventing and Combating Violence Against Women and Domestic Violence

This 2011 Convention was the first to refer to non-discrimination on grounds of both sexual orientation and gender identity.

The UN Convention on the Rights of the Child (CROC)

Unanimously adopted by the United Nations General Assembly in 1989, the non-discrimination provision enshrined in Article 2 is inclusive of sexual orientation and gender identity, as specifically outlined in General Comment No. 15. Article 34 explicitly provides protection against "all forms of sexual exploitation and sexual abuse", and the Committee has commented on the rights of young people who are "transsexual".

Convention on the Protection of Children Against Sexual Exploitation and Sexual Abuse

This Council of Europe treaty, issued in 2007, was the first to explicitly refer to non-discrimination on grounds of sexual orientation.

The UN Declaration on the Rights of Indigenous People (UNDRIP)

This international Declaration provides recognition for the beliefs of Indigenous people, among other matters, and was adopted by the General Assembly in September 2007 by 144 States, with only four – Canada, Australia, New Zealand and the US (CANZUS) – voting against, though they did sign much later. The Declaration asserts the rights of Indigenous people and individuals to protect their culture (Articles 9–15, 16, 25, and 31), which is important in the present context because a number of cultures recognise intersex or transgender people.

Article 31(2)

This provision requires States, acting in conjunction with Indigenous peoples, to "take effective measures to recognize and protect the exercise of these rights . . . to maintain, control, protect and develop their intellectual property over such cultural heritage, traditional knowledge, and traditional cultural expressions".

Other relevant international instruments

The Yogyakarta Principles (see next), though not part of the legal framework, have come to play a significant role in guiding and informing professional intervention in SOGI-related matters.

The UN Convention Relating to the Status of Refugees

This 1951 Refugee Convention and its 1967 Protocol define "refugee" and "asylum" and establish the protected grounds – which include race, nationality, religion, political opinion, "fear of persecution" and "membership of a particular social group" – while also setting out the responsibilities of signatory States. The UNHCR has issued guidelines for interpreting these grounds. Article 33 expressly prohibits the return or *refoulement* of refugees to a place where they would face persecution.

The UN Declaration on Sexual Orientation and Gender Identity

In 2008, this Declaration affirmed that "all human rights [must] be applied to all human beings, regardless of their sexual orientation or gender identity" and "condemned all human rights violations based on sexual orientation or gender identity, whenever or wherever they might occur".

Treaty on the Functioning of the European Union (TFEU)

This Treaty came into effect in 2009. Article 10 provides that in defining and implementing its policies and activities, the Union shall aim to combat sexual orientation-based discrimination, while Article 19 gives it powers to introduce legislation to eliminate discrimination on grounds that include sex and sexual orientation.

The EU Charter of Fundamental Rights

Promulgated in 2000, the Charter is important because it addresses a broad range of rights and because of its particular focus on equality. Article 20 provides that "everyone is equal before the law", while Article 21(1) reads:

> Any discrimination based on any ground such as sex, race, colour, ethnic or social origin, genetic features, language, religion or belief, political or any other opinion, membership of a national minority, property, birth, disability, age or sexual orientation shall be prohibited.

Treaty on the European Union (TEU)

The various amendments to this Treaty were last consolidated in 2012. Article 6.1 recognises the rights, freedoms and principles set out in the Charter of

Fundamental Rights of December 2000 and declares that they "shall have the same legal value as the Treaties". Article 6.3 recognises "fundamental rights, as guaranteed by the European Convention for the Protection of Human Rights and Fundamental Freedoms and as they result from the constitutional traditions common to the Member States" as general principles of the Union's law.

The Yogyakarta Principles (YP and YP+10)

In 2007, an international group of human rights experts agreed on "a set of international legal principles on the application of international law to human rights violations based on sexual orientation and gender identity".[18] This comprehensive statement on sexual and gender rights ranges across issues such as non-discrimination, legal recognition, security of person, privacy, access to justice, work, social security, housing, education, health, freedom of expression, immigration and refugee issues, founding a family, public participation and effective redress. The Principles have no legal status but are increasingly referenced – at least among western nations and non-Islamic cultures – as international benchmarks with application to issues arising in an LGBT context.

International framework of courts and regulatory bodies

There are a number of forums that exercise important international functions in relation to sexuality and gender issues. Their output, together with the caselaw produced by certain supra-national courts, mainly that of the ECtHR, are steadily building a body of relevant jurisprudence.

The Council of Europe

The Council of Europe, the continent's leading human rights organisation, works to promote, among other things, greater consistency in the domestic laws of its 47 member States, 28 of which are members of the European Union. The Council has a Commissioner for Human Rights – at the time of writing, Dunja Mijatović – elected by the Parliamentary Assembly.

In 2010, its Committee of Ministers adopted a Recommendation to Member States on measures to combat discrimination on grounds of sexual orientation or gender identity. This was followed in 2014 and in 2016 by the appointment of an Independent Expert on Sexual Orientation and Gender Identity tasked with assessing implementation of existing international human rights law, identifying best practices and gaps, raising awareness of violence and discrimination based on sexual orientation and gender identity and facilitating others to address violence and discrimination on those grounds. The first report of that expert, delivered to

18 Yogyakarta Principles 2007, at p. 7. These were augmented in 2018 by an additional ten principles.

UN member States in October 2017, called for the de-criminalisation of same-sex relationships and for effective anti-discrimination measures covering both the public and private spheres.[19]

Parliamentary Assembly

In 2013 this Council body published "Tackling Discrimination on the Grounds of Sexual Orientation and Gender Identity",[20] which was followed in 2015 by the adoption of Resolution 2048, "Discrimination Against Transgender People in Europe".

Commissioner for Human Rights

Established in 1999, this independent and non-judicial official functions in an ambassadorial capacity on behalf of the Council of Europe by engaging with member States to raise awareness about human rights issues and to promote the development of national human rights structures. In 2011, the Commissioner published a report entitled *Discrimination on Grounds of Sexual Orientation and Gender Identity in Europe*.[21]

The European Union

The law of the European Union takes precedence over the domestic law of its 28 member States;[22] one of its aims is to ensure equality of treatment for EU citizens. As regards sexual orientation and gender identity, it does so through a series of Directives such as: the Employment Equality Directive 2000/78/EC, dealing with sexual orientation; Directive 2004/113/EC, Article 4.4 of which provides that instruction to direct or indirect discrimination on the ground of sex shall be considered discrimination; and the Equal Treatment Directive 2006/54/EC,[23] which prohibits direct or indirect discrimination on the grounds of gender in the labour market, including conditions of access to self-employment, and extends protection to anyone suffering from indirect sex discrimination, harassment or sexual harassment. Another is EU Directive 79/7/EEC, on equal treatment in matters of social security, Article 4(1) of which specifically precludes any

> national legislation which requires a person who has changed gender not only to fulfil physical, social and psychological criteria but also to satisfy the

19 See further at: https://news.un.org/en/story/2017/10/569492-action-needed-stop-violations-lgbt-peoples-rights-worldwide-expert-tells-un.

20 Parliamentary Assembly of the Council of Europe ("PACE"), Resolution 1948 (June 2013).

21 Available at: www.coe.int.

22 *Flaminio Costa v. ENEL* (1964) Case 6/64.

23 Replacing the Equal Treatment Directive (76/207/EEC) *and the* Equal Pay Directive (75/117/EEC).

condition of not being married to a person of the gender that he or she has acquired as a result of that change, in order to be able to claim a State retirement pension as from the statutory pensionable age applicable to persons of his or her acquired gender.

The European Institute for Gender Equality (EIGE)

The Institute, based in Vilnius, was established by Council Regulation No. 1922/2006 of 20 December 2006 and inaugurated in 2007. An autonomous body of the European Union, its purpose is to contribute to and strengthen the promotion of gender equality, including gender mainstreaming in all EU policies and the resulting national policies, to combat discrimination based on sex and to raise EU citizens' awareness of gender equality.

The United Nations

Founded in 1945 to promote international co-operation and prevent further wars, the UN is now the world's largest human rights organisation.

The United Nations General Assembly

In 2008, this body, acting on behalf of 66 member countries, issued a Joint Statement on Human Rights, Sexual Orientation and Gender Identity, s.6 of which stated that "we condemn the human rights violations based on sexual orientation or gender identity wherever they occur" and condemned also any associated "deprivation of economic, social and cultural rights, including the right to health".[24]

The United Nations High Commissioner for Refugees

This body issued a Guidance Note *Refugee Claims Relating to Sexual Orientation and Gender Identity* in 2008, stating that a person cannot be expected to conceal their identity nor to act discretely. It also endorsed the Yogyakarta Principles.

The United Nations Human Rights Council

In 2014 the Council adopted Resolution 27/32 on Human Rights, Sexual Orientation and Gender Identity[25] by a vote of 25 in favour and 14 against, the dissenters being mainly Islamic States. Within the Council the debate on sexual orientation discrimination is now being played out by resolutions on "traditional values" and on "protection of the family".

24 See further at: https://arc-international.net/global-advocacy/sogi-statements/2008-joint-statement/.
25 A/HRC/RES/27/32. See further, at: www.right-docs.org/doc/a-hrc-res-27-32/.

In 2016, the Council further extended the mandate of the Working Group on Arbitrary Detention (established by Resolution 1991/42 of the Commission on Human Rights).

Important functions of the Council include its management of the Universal Periodic Review Process and its use of Special Procedures by which special rapporteurs, independent experts or working groups are appointed to undertake discrete projects on behalf of the Council (see next). UN effectiveness is constrained both by the fact that its instruments bind only those States that consent to be so bound and by the absence of any supra-national enforcement mechanism; enforcement is possible only if a State chooses to incorporate provisions within its domestic statute law. Its effectiveness is likely to be further compromised by the 2018 resignation of the US.

Courts, commissions and other regulatory bodies

The judgements handed down by the European courts over many decades not only have grown to constitute an evolving body of jurisprudence for all 47 member States but also serve as benchmarks for courts and regulatory bodies elsewhere when addressing similar issues.

The European Court of Justice (ECJ)

Officially the Court of Justice of the European Union (CJEU), and normally referred to as the ECJ, this body was established in 1952 with a role of ensuring that EU law is interpreted and applied fully and consistently throughout the EU. This court has clearly stated that the principle of non-discrimination on grounds of sex is aimed at attaining substantive and actual equality between persons, and it has played a prominent role in applying that principle.[26]

The European Court of Human Rights (ECtHR)

This court "has played both an essential and a pioneering role at international and European levels by prompting States to make major legislative changes on issues such as sexual orientation and gender identity".[27] Since the ruling in *Dudgeon*,[28] the first ECtHR hearing on an issue of sexual discrimination, its impact can be seen in many decisions on related matters.

In making its determinations, the ECtHR is guided by principles such as "proportionality", "necessary in a democratic society" and "a margin of appreciation". The first requires a fair balance to be struck between the demands of the

26 *P. v. S. and Cornwall County Council*, Case C-13/94, Opinion of the Advocate General, 14 December 1995, at para. 19.

27 See Council of Europe, *Case Law of the European Court of Human Rights Relating to Discrimination on Grounds of Sexual Orientation and Gender Identity* (2015), at: www.coe.int/en/web/sogi.

28 *Dudgeon v. the United Kingdom*, Application No. 7525/76 (1981).

general interests of the community and the requirements of the protection of the individual's fundamental rights.[29] The ECtHR looks at the interference complained of in the light of the case as a whole to determine whether the alleged interference is "prescribed by law" and was: (i) for a legitimate aim which is important enough to justify interfering with a fundamental right; (ii) rationally connected to achieving that aim; and (iii) no more than reasonably necessary to achieve it; and, in light of this, whether it strikes a fair balance between the rights of the individual and the interests of the community.[30] The second imports a liberal measure of balance and tolerance.[31] Frequently the ECtHR can be seen applying the test – is this form of State intervention necessary in a democratic society?[32] The third permits States a degree of latitude in their interpretation of human rights obligations.[33] Each State enjoys a margin of appreciation, meaning that the extent to which there are differences in otherwise similar situations may justify a corresponding difference in treatment.

The UN Human Rights Committee (UN HR Committee)

The Committee is empowered under the First Optional Protocol, now ratified or acceded to by 116 States, to determine alleged violations of ICCPR provisions suffered by individual citizens. However, this is a non-judicial body and its findings are non-binding. Its rulings, "General Comments" and "Views" when concluding such determinations, have acquired a quasi-judicial status, are often important and influential and at times diverge from principles established by other bodies such as the ECtHR. It is in this forum that "the strongest existing explicit protections against discrimination on the basis of sexual orientation" have arisen at the UN.[34]

Regional human rights commissions

It has been customary for human rights issues to be regulated by a designated national or regional Human Rights Commission, with a right of appeal to the

29 See *Olson v. Sweden (No 1)* (1988) 11 EHRR 299; *Sporrong v. Sweden* [1982] 5 EHRR 35 at para. 69; *Tsirlis and Kouloumpas v. Greece* (1997) 25 EHRR 198 at para. 116; *Razgar v. Secretary of State for Home Department* [2004] UKHL 27 at para. 20; and see, *Kozac v. Poland* [2010] ECHR 280 (2010) 51 EHRR 16.

30 See *Huang v. Secretary of State for the Home Department* [2007] 2 AC 167, para. 19; *R (Quila) v. Secretary of State for the Home Department* [2012] 1 AC 621, para. 45; and *Bank Mellat v. HM Treasury (No 2)* [2013] UKSC 39 [2013] 3 WLR 179, 222, para. 20.

31 See *Refah Partisi v. Turkey* (2003) 37 EHRR 1 [2003] ECHR 87.

32 See *Olson v. Sweden (No 1)*, op. cit., where it is explained that to be justifiable such interference must be "relevant and sufficient; it must meet a pressing social need; and it must be proportionate to the need".

33 See, for example, *Lithgow v. United Kingdom* (1986) 8 EHRR 329, *Fredin v. Sweden* (1991) 13 EHRR 784, *Abdulaziz, Cabales and Balkandali v. United Kingdom* (1985) 7 EHRR 471.

34 Kukura, E., Sexual Orientation and Non-Discrimination, *Peace Review*, 17, pp. 181–188 at p. 183 (2005).

appropriate court. Currently, there are eight such regional bodies – including the European Committee of Social Rights, the Inter-American Commission on Human Rights and the African Commission on Human and Peoples Rights – in addition to their national counterparts. In 1991, under the auspices of the UN General Assembly, the "Paris Principles" were agreed which set out a basic template of functions and objectives for every local Commission.

As equality and non-discrimination legislation has grown, it is now not uncommon for all domestic human rights, equality and discrimination issues to be statutorily assigned to and determined by the same local administrative body.

The Venice Commission

This organ of the Council of Europe – more formally known as the "European Commission for Democracy through Law" – was established in 1990 and has a membership of 60 member States (the 47 members of the Council of Europe plus 13 others). Its primary task is to assist and advise individual countries in constitutional matters in order to improve functioning of democratic institutions and the protection of human rights; it does so by appointing a working group of rapporteurs to advise national authorities on relevant issues. It also produces opinions at the request of the Parliamentary Assembly.

Monitoring and review procedures

There are a number of processes that provide for ongoing monitoring and reports, which have a bearing upon matters of sexuality and gender but are without any adjudicative or enforcement functions.

The Universal Periodic Review process

This reporting mechanism was established by the UN Human Rights Council in 2007. It requires each member State to provide a human rights progress report at four-year intervals. This is subject to a peer review by all other States and concludes with agreed, ongoing goals to be monitored and assessed at the next review cycle. So far two cycles have been completed (2008–11 and 2012–16), during which many States have openly rejected recommendations to de-criminalise homosexuality and legalise same-sex marriage or adoption.[35] The overall acceptance rate in the first cycle of the UPR (2008–11) for recommendations related to recognition of sexual orientation and gender identity (SOGI)-related human rights was only 36%.[36]

35 See Cowell, F. and Milon, A., Decriminalisation of Sexual Orientation Through the Universal Periodic Review, *Human Rights Law Review*, 12, p. 341 (2012).

36 Itaborahy, L. P. and Zhu, J. (eds.), *State-Sponsored Homophobia: A World Survey of Laws: Criminalisation, Protection and Recognition of Same-Sex Love*, 2014, at: old.ilga.org/Statehomophobia/ILGA_SSHR_2014_Eng.pdf.

The US country reports on human rights practices

In accordance with the Foreign Assistance Act of 1961 and the Trade Act of 1974, the US Department of State submits annual reports to Congress on all countries receiving assistance and on all United Nations member States. These reports, covering internationally recognised individual, civil, political and worker rights as established by international instruments, also address matters of sexuality and gender.

The reporting process of the UN Convention on the Rights of the Child

Under Article 44 of the Convention, the Committee on the Rights of the Child established and manages a periodic reporting mechanism whereby each State submits a report on Convention implementation for review by the Committee, two years after ratification and at five-year intervals thereafter. As this reporting cycle has matured, so increasingly State parties in their reports are making links between children's human rights and the broader context of civil and political rights and socio-economic rights. Inevitably, this discourse now takes into account rights relating to gender and sexuality.

In a warning regarding the continuing practice of gender reassignment surgery in many countries, including several Part II jurisdictions (e.g. the US, Ireland and Australia), to "normalise" gender ambiguity, the Committee has warned that a State cannot use the "best interests" test to justify violence or "practices that conflict with the right to physical integrity".[37] This was reinforced in 2016 by the Committee on the Rights of Persons with Disabilities, which referred to such practices, conducted without their informed consent of the children concerned, as a form of "cruel or inhuman treatment".[38]

UN special procedures

In 2016 the Human Rights Council adopted Resolution 32/2 entitled "Protection Against Violence and Discrimination Based on Sexual Orientation and Gender Identity" and established the mandate of an Independent Expert on protection against violence and discrimination based on sexual orientation and gender identity. The mandate included (i) assessment of the implementation of existing international human rights instruments with regard to ways to overcome violence and discrimination against persons on the basis of their sexual orientation or gender identity; (ii) raising awareness of such violence; and (iii) identifying and addressing its root causes.

37 Committee on the Rights of the Child, General Comment No. 13 (2011). Report No: CRC/C/GC/13, at p. 23.

38 Committee on the Rights of Persons with Disabilities, General Comment No. 3 (2016). Report No: CRPD/C/GC/3, at p. 9.

Independent human rights organisations

There are a number of important voluntary organisations which maintain a watching brief on human rights issues. Human Rights Watch and Amnesty International are among the more prominent, and they publish reports on international violations of human rights. Increasingly, the work and publications of these and similar NGOs include studies of issues relating to sexuality and gender.

Other

Because of the growing recognition that sexuality and gender issues cannot be confined by discrete categorisation but are often entangled with other human rights, the 1993 Vienna Declaration and Programme of Action urged States to find an appropriate balance between country-specific cultural and religious backgrounds and fulfilling their duty to promote and protect all human rights and fundamental freedoms.[39] As a matter of practice, the Committees of many treaty bodies now also include SOGI issues in their reports.

The European Social Charter

The Charter lays specific emphasis on the protection of vulnerable persons such as elderly people, children, people with disabilities and migrants. It requires that enjoyment of the previously-mentioned rights be guaranteed without discrimination.

The Charter of Fundamental Rights of the European Union

This Charter specifically acknowledges sexual orientation as a prohibited ground of discrimination and, unlike the ICCPR, does not limit the right to marry to heterosexual couples (Articles 21 and 9).

SOGI and related core human rights

The core international human rights with relevance for sexuality and gender matters are those relating to justice, free speech and association.

Right of access to justice

(UDHR, Articles 6–11; ECHR, Articles 6 and 13; ICCPR, Articles 2 and 26; ICESCR, the preamble)

Recognition of this right in ECtHR jurisprudence can be traced back at least to *Airey v. Ireland*,[40] which concerned access to the courts and the availability of

39 A/CONF.157/23, 12 July 1993.
40 Application No. 6289/73 (1979).

legal aid. Most recently, many such applicants have come from within the LGBT community. So, for example, in *Alekseyev v. Russia*,[41] the ECtHR found that the applicant's Article 13 right had been violated by the absence of any State procedure enabling him to obtain authorisation for a "Gay Pride march" before that event took place.

This right broadly requires that relevant information is available and can be readily understood; appropriate processes and proceedings exist and are accessible before an independent and impartial tribunal; free legal aid and advice is available where necessary, with adequate representation and without undue delay; the proceedings are conducted independently and fairly, with a right of appeal; and the outcome is fully and fairly enforced. As regards the latter, in *Van Kück v. Germany*[42] the ECtHR considered the case of a transsexual woman whose health-insurance company had denied her reimbursement for costs associated with sex-reassignment surgery and who had unsuccessfully sought redress in the domestic courts. Citing *Christine Goodwin v. the United Kingdom*[43] and *I. v. the United Kingdom*[44] (see further Chapter 4), the ECtHR found violations of the right to a fair hearing and to private life on the grounds that the approach taken by the domestic courts in examining "whether the applicant had deliberately caused her transsexuality" was wholly inappropriate.[45] Condemning the failure of the State to provide an appropriate legal remedy for the claimant, the ECtHR referred to "the very essence of the ECHR being respect for human dignity and human freedom, protection is given to the right of transsexuals to personal development and to physical and moral security".[46] In *L. v. Lithuania*,[47] the ECtHR took the view that the State was required to legislate for the provision of full gender-reassignment surgery, thereby enabling a person in the "limbo" of partial reassignment to complete the process and be registered with their new gender identity.

Access to relevant information

Access to the information necessary to facilitate the development of an authentic identity is often problematic in a SOGI context.[48] Article 13 of the UNCROC protects the right of children to receive information and the Committee has interpreted this to include information about sexuality and sexual behaviour.[49]

41 Application Nos. 4916/07, 25924/08 and 14599/09 (2010).
42 2003-VII 1; (2003) 37 EHRR 51.
43 (2002) 35 EHRR 18.
44 36 EHRR 53.
45 Ibid., at paras. 62–65.
46 Ibid., at para. 69. See also, K.*B. v. The National Health Service Pensions Agency and the Secretary of State for Health*, Case C-117/01 (2003).
47 Application No. 27527/03 (2007).
48 See, for example, "Concluding Observations of the Committee on the Rights of the Child regarding the United Kingdom", 9 October 2002, CRC/C/15/Add.188 at para. 43.
49 See Committee on the Rights of the Child, General Comment No. 4 (Adolescent Health and Development etc.), 2003, at paras. 26–31.

An effective remedy

Article 13 of the ECHR provides for this right, but the ECtHR and the HR Committee have tended to interpret it somewhat differently.

In *Schalk and Kopf v. Austria*[50] the ECtHR ruled that the Convention did not confer a right to marry on same-sex couples. This decision had the effect of denying the applicant couple, and all others in the same situation, an entitlement to claim the benefits – such as pensions, inheritances, welfare payments and allowances – statutorily available to married couples. While continuing to deny same-sex couples any right to marry, the ECtHR in *Oliari and Others v. Italy*[51] was prepared to acknowledge a right to have the fact of their relationship accorded a legal status in domestic law and to hold that the failure of the State to provide a means to achieve this breached the applicants' Article 8 rights. At much the same time, the court in *Vallianatos and Others v. Greece*,[52] found that Article 13 had been violated by the absence of any domestic process allowing a same-sex couple to challenge the fact that "civil unions" were restricted to heterosexual couples. In contrast, the HR Committee has long demonstrated a willingness to find that State practices which prevent same-sex couples from benefiting from family-related benefits, such as transfer of pension entitlements, violate their human rights.[53]

Asylum seekers/illegal immigrants

As has been said: "Asylum laws and policies should recognize persecution on account of one's sexual orientation, gender identity, gender expression or sex characteristics as a valid basis for an asylum claim and LGBT and intersex refugees should be treated with respect".[54]

Whether SOGI-related status makes any difference to the fate of those deemed by national authorities to be "illegal immigrants" or "asylum seekers" provides a legitimate focus for examining the access routes to justice provided by those authorities and is a question that has exercised the ECtHR and the ECJ from at least the onset of the ongoing migrant crisis in 2015.[55] This brief overview leaves aside the many human rights questions arising from the SOGI-related circumstances that may have precipitated the need to flee, compromised their transit,

50 Application No. 30141/04 (2010).
51 Application Nos. 18766/11 and 36030/11 (2015).
52 Application Nos. 29381/09 and 32684/09 (2015).
53 *Young v. Australia*, Communication No. 941/2000, UN Doc CCPR/C/78/D/941/2000 (2003) 5 IHRR 747, IHRL 1921, UNHRC (2003) and *X v. Colombia*, Communication No. 1361/2005, U.N. Doc. A/62/40.
54 U.N., *Living Free and Equal*, New York, 2016, at p. 35. See further at: www.ohchr.org/Documents/Publications/LivingFreeAndEqual.pdf.
55 The intention to make such a difference was evident in the Recast Qualification Directive (Directive 2011/95/EU), which specifically recognised SOGI characteristics as indicating particular vulnerability.

and could have been an issue at point of disembarkation. It considers only, and then fleetingly, the decisions taken by the authorities processing such immigrants for residence or deportation.[56]

A State duty not to transfer vulnerable migrants to EU countries known to lack appropriate coping capacity was established at an early stage.[57] Moreover, the CJU ruled in 2012[58] that the fact that a gay person could hope to avoid transfer by "exercising greater restraint than a heterosexual in expressing his sexual orientation is not to be taken into account". This became more focused in *O.M. v. Hungary*[59] when the ECtHR determined that where a State detains a person at the border it is obliged to then assess and address any SOGI-related issues in order to avoid placing them in situations "which may reproduce the plight that forced these persons to flee in the first place", especially when they are placed with other people coming from countries "with widespread cultural or religious prejudices against such persons".

In the 2017 case of *X and X*,[60] the ECJ seemed to recognise that positive obligations rested on receiving nations, under international human rights treaties including the EU Charter and Article 3 of the ECHR, to prevent torture, which in turn should prevent them from legally returning migrants with SOGI status to their countries of origin if to do so would expose them to a likelihood of torture because of that status. It implies that to transfer migrants to any other country, without first ensuring their safe treatment there on SOGI grounds, would constitute indirect *refoulement*.[61] This a term was first used in the UN Convention on the Status of Refugees 1954, which in Article 33(1) provides that:

> No Contracting State shall expel or return ("refouler") a refugee in any manner whatsoever to the frontiers of territories where his life or freedom would be threatened on account of his race, religion, nationality, membership of a particular social group or political opinion.

As Danisi puts it "the prohibition of *refoulement* applies to the benefit of people fleeing homophobia and transphobia if 'specific' and 'individualised' assurances to have granted a 'safe place' in the country of destination are not provided".[62]

56 See Danisi, C., *What "Safe Harbours" Are There for People Seeking International Protection on Sexual Orientation and Gender Identity Grounds? A Human Rights Reading of International Law of the Sea and Refugee Law*, 2018 at: http://sro.sussex.ac.uk/id/eprint/79838/3/Danisi%20-%20GenIUS%202-2018%20-%209-24.pdf.
57 *M.S.S. v. Belgium and Greece*, Application No. 30696/09 (2011) and *Tarakhel v. Switzerland*, Application No. 29217/12 (2014).
58 *X, Y, and Z v. Minister voor Immigratie en Asiel* C-201/12, at para. 75.
59 Application No. 9912/15 (2016), at para. 53 (as cited by Dansi, C., op. cit., at p. 21).
60 ECJ, C-638/16 PPU (7th March 2017).
61 See, the UN Convention Against Torture, Article 3, adopted in 1984 and subsequently reformulated.
62 Danisi, C., op. cit., at p. 21.

Right to freedom of expression

(UDHR, Article 19; ECHR, Article 10; and ICCPR, Article 19)

The means of persuasion, of proclaiming identity and explaining differences, can take many forms. It includes transvestism and cross-dressing and, as noted in the Yogyakarta Principles, may encompass "dress, hairstyles, accessories, cosmetics – and mannerisms, speech, behavioural patterns, names and personal references", and significantly, "gender expression may or may not conform to a person's gender identity".[63]

In *Hertzberg et al. v. Finland*,[64] the HR Committee found that the State had not violated the general freedom of expression, as stated in Article 19(2) of the ICCPR, through its implementation of statutory provisions prohibiting "publicly encourag[ing] indecent behavior between persons of the same sex". Thirty years later, however, it came to the contrary decision in *Fedotova v. Russian Federation*,[65] when it considered that the State had not shown that a restriction on the right to freedom of expression in relation to "propaganda of homosexuality" – as opposed to propaganda of heterosexuality or sexuality generally – among minors was based on reasonable and objective criteria. Moreover, no evidence had been advanced which would point to the existence of factors justifying such a distinction.[66] Furthermore, the HR Committee was of the view that, by displaying posters declaring "Homosexuality is normal" and "I am proud of my homosexuality" near a secondary school building, the author had not made any public actions aimed at involving minors in any particular sexual activity or at advocating any particular sexual orientation. Instead, she was giving expression to her sexual identity and seeking understanding for it.[67] Her conviction for distributing "propaganda of homosexuality among minors" amounted to a violation of her rights under Article 19(2), read in conjunction with Article 26 (equality and non-discrimination).

The moral majority

The difference in the earlier two decisions record and reflect a shift in public morality. As the HR Committee stated in General Comment No. 22: "the concept of morals derives from many social, philosophical and religious traditions; consequently, limitations . . . for the purpose of protecting morals must be based on principles not deriving exclusively from a single tradition".[68] Any legitimacy for State action or inaction in relation to the public expression of sexual orientation

63 See Yogyakarta Principles: Preamble.
64 (61/1979) Views, CCPR/C/OP/1 at 124 (1985).
65 (1932/2010) Views, CCPR/C/106/D/1932/2010.
66 Ibid., at para. 10.6, citing *Young v. Australia*, at para. 10.4; and *X v. Colombia*, at para. 7.2.
67 Ibid., at para. 10.8.
68 Human Rights Committee, General Comment No. 22 (the right to freedom of thought, conscience and religion) 1993 at para. 8.

which society as a whole then found offensive seemed to largely disappear as time passed, to be replaced by a broad social acceptance of diversity and equality which set new norms, backed by international human rights, for accommodating difference. For the LGBT community, the in-between phase is the most hazardous, as it was in Northern Ireland prior to the *Dudgeon* decision (see Chapter 4) and as is now the case in Eastern Europe and countries like Turkey.

In *Identoba and Others v. Georgia*,[69] the ECtHR found that the lack of police protection for a peaceful LGBT march, and the resulting violence perpetrated against the marchers by the "moral majority", constituted a breach of the claimants' various rights under the ECHR. It noted that, as in *M.C. and C.A. v. Romania*,[70] the State had a duty to ensure protection for the lawful freedom of expression of the marchers; not to do so indicated prejudice. It had to make sure that in such a context the exercise of free speech did not give rise to violence that breached the Article 3 threshold. The duty of the State includes allowing the publishing and dissemination of information. So, as in *Kaos GL v. Turkey*,[71] when all copies of a magazine published by a cultural research and solidarity association for gays and lesbians were seized by the State, the ECtHR dismissed the Turkish authorities' "protection of public morals" argument and found their actions to be in breach of Article 10. Most recently, in *Bayev and Others v. Russia*,[72] the ECtHR found that legislative provisions, specifically adopted to outlaw the promotion of homosexuality and non-traditional sexual relations among minors, violated the rights to freedom of expression of the applicant representatives of the LGBT community.

Harm to others

Article 19(3) makes the right to freedom of expression subject to "the interests of other persons or to those of the community as a whole". In *Smith and Grady v. UK*,[73] the Court warned that discrimination on the basis of sexual orientation may cause such interests to be harmed if it results in a person feeling degraded:

> treatment may be considered degrading if it is such as to arouse in its victims feelings of fear, anguish and inferiority capable of humiliating and debasing them and possibly breaking their physical or moral resistance. Hate speech directed against the LGBT community or intended to cause harm to those

69 Application No. 73235/12 (2015).

70 Application No. 12060/12 (2016). Also, see: *Sabalić* v. Croatia, Application No. 50231/13 (2014); *Beus v. Croatia*, Application No. 16943/17 (2017); *Women's Initiatives Supporting Group and Others v. Georgia*, Application No. 73204/13 (2015); *Chechetkin v. Russia*, Application No. 42395/15 (2017); and *Romanov v. Russia* and two other applications, Application Nos. 58358/13, 7146/15 and 25887/15 (2017).

71 Application No. 4982/07 (2016).

72 Application Nos. 67667/09, 44092/12 and 56717/12 (2017).

73 (2000) 29 EHRR 493.

> with SOGI related vulnerabilities, for example, would constitute a clear breach of Article 19.[74] Moreover, it is sufficient if the victim is humiliated in his or her own eyes.[75]

So, for example, such interests were found to be violated in *Vejdeland and Others v. Sweden*,[76] where the ECtHR agreed with the domestic courts' finding that the homophobic leaflets were "unwarrantably offensive to others, constituting an assault on their rights".

The ECtHR has warned that the chilling effect of legislative provisions or policies intended to protect such interests may constitute an interference with the freedom of expression.[77] In the past decade there have been a number of ECtHR rulings relating to this freedom, often in conjunction with that of assembly, and most often in Eastern Europe, in the context of organisations demonstrating in support of LGBT rights.[78] Nonetheless, a State may be justified in taking preventative action, involving constraints on the liberty of those intending to engage in a public protest, where it has good reason to believe that such a protest may disturb the public order and cause danger to the public.[79]

Rights to freedom of association and assembly

(UDHR, Article 20; ECHR, Article 11; ICCPR, Articles 18(1) and 22; ICESCR, Articles 8 and 15; UNCROC, Article 15)

The Council of Europe has urged member States to ensure that these rights can be effectively enjoyed without discrimination on grounds of sexual orientation or gender identity.[80] Their exercise is monitored by the Special Rapporteur on the rights to Freedom of Peaceful Assembly and Association and by the Independent Expert on Sexual Orientation and Gender Identity. The former has reported that the LGBT community is particularly vulnerable in terms of the violation of rights to free association and peaceful assembly.[81]

74 See further RefWorld, Policy Brief, *Responding to Hate Speech Against LGBTI People* (2013), at: www.refworld.org/pdfid/525b9eb64.pdf.

75 Ibid., at para. 120. See also *Cyprus v. Turkey* (2002) 35 EHRR 30 at [302] – [311].

76 Application No. 1813/07 (2012).

77 *Smith and Grady v. the United Kingdom*, Application Nos. 33985/96 and 33986/96 (1999).

78 See, for example, *Alekseyev v. Russia*, Application Nos. 4916/07, 25924/08 and 14599/09 (2010); *Bączkowski and Others v. Poland*, Application No. 1543/06 (2007); *Genderdoc-M v. Moldova*, Application No. 9106/06 (2012); *Vejdeland and Others v. Sweden*, Application No. 1813/07 (2012); and *Identoba and Others v. Georgia*, Application No. 73235/12 (2015).

79 *S., V. and A. v. Denmark* [2018] ECHR 856.

80 COE, SOGI unit, at: www.coe.int/en/web/sogi/freedom-of-association.

81 See Maina Kiai, United Nations Human Rights Council, "Report of the Special Rapporteur on the Rights to Freedom of Peaceful Assembly and of Association", A/HRC/26/29 (2013), at para. 43.

Constraints

In *Alekseyev v. Russia*,[82] the ECtHR found that the government ban on the 2006, 2007 and 2008 Moscow Pride gay rights marches in Moscow did not satisfy the requirement of being necessary in a democratic society and therefore violated Articles 11 and 14 of the ECHR and Article 21 of the ICCPR. More recently, in *Lashmankin and Others v. Russia*,[83] the State had imposed such severe limitations on the applicants' plans for public LGBT events – including requirements for the location, time and manner of conduct – that it undermined their purpose. The ECtHR held that the State had violated the applicants' right to freedom of assembly and expression. As the court had advised in the relatively early case of *Bączkowski*:[84]

> A genuine and effective respect for freedom of association and assembly cannot be reduced to a mere duty on the part of the State not to interfere; a purely negative conception would not be compatible with the purpose of Article 11.

The right of an association to take legal action on behalf of the members it represents can be problematic. This was apparent in *Vallianatos and Others v. Greece*,[85] when the court reiterated its established position that it will not necessarily accord victim status to organisations campaigning on behalf of those suffering discrimination, whether or not in the form of sexual orientation, as the individuals should be able to do so of their own accord.

Right to freedom of religion

(UDHR, Article 18; ECHR, Articles 9(1) and 14; ICCPR, Article 18; Charter of Fundamental Rights of the European Union, Article 10)

Article 9(1) of the ECHR provides that everyone has the right to freedom of thought, conscience and religion. This is subject to the Article 9(2) constraint that its exercise may be subject to limitations prescribed by law as necessary in a democratic society or for the protection of the rights and freedoms of others. Article 9, together with Articles 14 of the ECHR and 26 of the ICCPR, provides an international human rights framework for considering issues of discrimination in relation to religion. Clearly, however, "Article 9 does not protect every act motivated or inspired by a religion or belief".[86]

82 Applications Nos. 4916/07, 25924/08 and 14599/09 (2010).
83 Applications Nos. 57818/09 and others (2017).
84 Op. cit., at para. 64.
85 Application Nos. 29381/09 and 32684/09 (2015).
86 *SAS v. France*, Application No. 43835/11 (2014), at para. 126 citing *Arrowsmith v. UK* (1978) 19 DR 5; *Kalac v. Turkey* [1997] ECHR 20704/92 and *Sahin v. Turkey* 19 BHRC 590, IHRL 3279 (ECHR 2005).

SOGI and religion

The doctrines and tenets of the traditional religions – particularly Christianity and Islam – have for centuries been, and most often remain, fundamentally opposed to the changes in law and social mores regarding matters of sexuality and gender that now characterise the developed western nations. The ECtHR and other judicial and regulatory bodies have sought to cope with the resulting clash of rights in the main by utilising exemption privileges; applying the "margin of appreciation" rule and the proportionality principle; and by developing the non-exhaustive list of grounds on which discrimination is prohibited under Article 14 of the ECHR to include matters such as transgender status.[87]

Religious organisations and the religious exemption

The rejection of changes in the law regarding a range of sexuality and gender matters – not least the legitimacy of same-sex marriages and sexual relationships – by traditional religions has presented particular difficulties for the ECtHR. Proceeding cautiously, it has evolved a view that the principles of secularism and neutrality require impartiality towards all religious beliefs on the basis of respect for pluralism and diversity.[88] This approach has led it to reject Shari'a law as incompatible with democracy.[89] So, in *Khan v. the United Kingdom*,[90] it rejected a man's claim that he should be free to marry and have sexual relations with a girl under the legal age of sexual consent as such a marriage was valid under Islamic law. Again, in *Osmanoğlu et Kocabaş v. Switzerland*,[91] it considered that the refusal by Turkish-Swiss parents of Muslim religion to send their daughters to compulsory mixed swimming lessons as part of their schooling did not warrant Article 9 protection. However, in *Molla Sali v. Greece*,[92] the ECtHR seemed to moderate its views and accept in principle the applicability of Shari'a law in Europe unless an "important public interest" opposes it.[93] Not dissimilar difficulties have also emerged – though perhaps not so frequently nor as acute – from within the Christian and Jewish religions.

The UN Declaration on Religious Intolerance provides for the right to "train, appoint, elect, or designate by succession appropriate leaders" and the right to "establish and maintain appropriate charitable and humanitarian institutions".[94]

87 *PV v. Spain*, Application No. 35159/09 (2011).
88 *Ebrahimian v. France*, Application No. 64846/11 (2015).
89 *Refah Partisi v. Turkey* (2003) 37 EHRR 1 [2003] ECHR 87.
90 Application No. 11579/85 (1986).
91 Application No. 29086/12 (2017).
92 Application No. 20452/14 (2018).
93 Frank Cranmer comments that this case "was decided under Art 14 and A1P1, rather than under Art 9. But a more important point is that, under the Treaties of Sèvres and Lausanne, members of the Muslim minority in Thrace have a right, in principle, to choose between Greek civil law and Shari'a" (note to author, 31 May 2019).
94 The UN Declaration on the Elimination of All Forms of Intolerance and of Discrimination Based on Religion or Belief, Article 6(g) and (b) respectively.

The right to appoint clergy and fill other key leadership posts, exempt from the restrictions of anti-discrimination and equality law, has been extended to permit appointments to commercial entities, hospitals, schools etc., and to restrict access to services, schools and social care facilities owned by religious organisations.

SOGI: personal relationships and human rights

As the following tranche of caselaw illustrates, a characteristic hallmark of human rights – their tendency to become entangled – is only too apparent when sexuality and gender issues impact upon the matters of greatest and most immediate concern to members of the LGBT community, those which shape an identity and a sense of belonging: personal relationships, family and community.[95]

Right to an identity

(UDHR, Article 6; ECHR, Articles 6 and 8; and Article 16 of the ICCPR)

Nearly 40 years ago, the UN HR Committee pointed out in the *Mark Rees* case[96] that "in refusing to consider an entry in the birth register reflecting the applicant's change of sex the respondent Government treats the applicant as an ambiguous being"[97] – a criticism it returned to in *Gaskin v. the United Kingdom*[98] and *Sheffield and Horsham v. the United Kingdom*[99] (see further in Chapter 4). Nonetheless, official recognition for the status of those who choose a sexual identity other than that to which they were born was a long time coming.[100]

Trans recognition in law

Not until the ECtHR rulings in *B v. France*[101] and the earlier *Goodwin*[102] and *I*[103] cases was a consensus established as regards the judicial approach to the right to

95 See the Council of Europe, *Sexual Orientation and Gender Identity Caselaw* (2015), at: www.ein.org.uk/news/major-new-council-europe-study-ecthr-sexual-orientation-and-gender-identity-case-law.

96 *Mark Rees against The United Kingdom*, Application No. 9532/81 (1984). Note that two years later the ECtHR took a different view in the same case when it unanimously ruled that the UK failure to provide such a registration procedure was justified as being within its margin of appreciation.

97 Ibid., at para. 48. See, also, *Schlumph v. Switzerland*, Application No. 29002/06 (2009).

98 (1989) 12 EHRR 36.

99 (1999) 27 EHRR 163.

100 According to the *Trans Rights Europe Map & Index*, some 23 European nations still require transsexuals to divorce; 36 systematically demand a mental health diagnosis; and eight have no practical means of recognising transgender people whatsoever. See further at: https://tgeu.org/trans-rights-map-2017/.

101 Application No. 1334/87 (1992).

102 Goodwin v. the United Kingdom, Application No. 28957/95, (1997).

103 *I. v. the United Kingdom,* 36 EHRR 53.

personal privacy under Article 8 of the ECHR and the related duties of the State. The ECtHR in *Goodwin* then declared that

> the very essence of the Convention is respect for human dignity and human freedom. Under Article 8 of the Convention in particular, where the notion of personal autonomy is an important principle underlying the interpretation of its guarantees, protection is given to the personal sphere of each individual, including the right to establish details of their identity as individual human beings . . . the unsatisfactory situation in which post-operative transsexuals live in an intermediate zone as not quite one gender or the other is no longer sustainable.[104]

As a consequence of this ruling, the ECtHR subsequently noted, there was "no longer any justification for failing to recognize the changed gender of post-operative transsexuals"[105] and urged States to provide for the recognition of a gender identity change in official documents. Any room for doubt was removed by the *Van Kück* case[106] when the ECtHR drew attention to the importance of "the applicant's freedom to define herself as a female person", which, the court noted, is "one of the most basic essentials of self-determination".[107] It also referred to the notion of personal autonomy as an important principle underlying the interpretation of Article 8.[108] Not until 2014 did the HR Committee unequivocally state that the word "everyone" in Article 9 of the ICCPR (liberty and security of person)[109] should be interpreted as including, among others, "lesbian, gay, bisexual and transgender persons", an initiative since adopted by the Committees of all UN human rights treaty bodies.

There remains, of course, the very basic issue of what in law should suffice to verify a claim of gender change: self-identification is not always enough,[110] but imposing a condition of sterility is considered a step too far.[111] It is a matter that has attracted the attention of the Council of Europe:

> The Assembly is concerned about the violations of fundamental rights, notably the right to private life and to physical integrity, faced by transgender people when applying for legal gender recognition; relevant procedures

104 *Christine Goodwin v. the United Kingdom* (2002) 35 EHRR 18, at para. 71.

105 *Grant v. United Kingdom*, at para. 41.

106 2003-VII 1; (2003) 37 EHRR 51. But see, also, *Hämäläinen v. Finland*, Application No. 37359/09 (2014).

107 Ibid., at para. 73.

108 Ibid., at para. 69, citing *Pretty v. the United Kingdom*, Application No. 2346/02.

109 HRC General Comment No 35: Article 9 (Liberty and security of person), 28 October 2014, CCPR/C/GC/35, at paras. 6–7.

110 Self-identification provides sufficient legal proof of gender in Ireland, Argentina, Belgium, California, Colombia, Portugal, Denmark, Norway and Malta.

111 *A.P., Garçon, Nicot v. France*, Application Nos. 79885/12, 52471/13 and 52596/13 (2017).

> often require sterilisation, divorce, a diagnosis of mental illness, surgical interventions and other medical treatments as preconditions. In addition, administrative burdens and additional requirements, such as a period of "life experience" in the gender of choice, make recognition procedures generally cumbersome.[112]

This is a very contentious issue in the high proportion of cases where the gender of a trans person is legally but not biologically validated. In *R.L. and P.O. v. Russia*,[113] the applicants challenged the requirement to undergo various medical procedures in order to have their new gender identity officially recognised; neither applicant had complied with the surgery pre-condition. The ECtHR was clear that such a requirement violated Article 8 of the ECHR. A similar breach was established in *S.V. v. Italy*[114] when the court held that the Italian authorities' refusal to authorise a change of name because no judicial ruling had confirmed the successful completion of sex reassignment therapy, even though the applicant had been socially and physically transitioning for several years, was unjustified. Most recently, the ECJ made a forthright and unequivocal statement that "individuals who have lived for a significant period as persons of a gender other than their birth gender and who have undergone a gender reassignment operation *must* be considered transgendered".[115]

Non-binary gender identity

Courts in both Austria and Germany have recently ruled that intersex individuals have a right to register under a gender other than male or female on the grounds that not offering an additional option violated their right to respect for private life as protected by Article 8 of the ECHR.[116]

Right to privacy and family life

(ECHR, Articles 8, 12, 14 and 17; ICCPR, Articles 2 and 26; CROC, Article 3)[117]

"Private life", it has been said, includes the physical and moral integrity of the person; the physical and social identity of the individual, including sexual identity; the right to personal development or fulfilment; and the right to have relationships with other human beings and the outside world.[118] It was largely given effect by Article 8 of the ECHR (reinforced by Article 12) and, until the *Goodwin* case, was subject to a wide "margin of appreciation". It was first

112 See, Resolution 2048, "Discrimination Against Transgender People in Europe", at para 4.
113 Application Nos. 36253/13 and 52516/13 (2017).
114 Application No. 55216/08 (2018).
115 *MB v. Secretary for Work and Pensions*, Case C-451/16 (2018).
116 See *Der Österreichische Verfassungsgerichtshof*, 29 June 2018.
117 See also Yogyakarta Principles: YP 6 and 18.
118 *Van Kück* v. Germany, 2003-VII 1; (2003) 37 EHRR 51, at para. 69.

successfully evoked on an issue of sexual orientation in *Dudgeon v. United Kingdom*[119] (see Chapter 4).

Sexual orientation, identity and private life

The earliest SOGI-related rulings were probably those of the ECtHR in *D. van Oosterwijck v. Belgium*[120] and *Cossey v. the United Kingdom*[121] and of the UN HR Committee in *Hertzberg v. Finland*.[122] The first two concerned post-operative trans persons, both of whom sought appropriate amendments to official registration documents (birth certificates etc.) to reflect their changed gender. The European Commission of Human Rights (as it then was) found no material difference in the facts that would differentiate either or both from its earlier ruling in *Rees*[123] and therefore had no reason to depart from its rationale in that case. Dismissing the applications, the Commission noted that "gender reassignment surgery did not result in the acquisition of all the biological characteristics of the other sex"[124] and that alterations to birth certificates would not be appropriate; and held that there had been no violations of either Article 8 or 12. The third considered the censorship of a radio program on homosexuality when the UN HR Committee found in favour of Finland, arguing that since public morals differ widely, a certain margin of discretion must be accorded to the responsible national authorities, an argument that it was to later wholly reject.

It was the precedent established by the ECtHR in *Dudgeon* that triggered a new vein of jurisprudence. That *ratio decidendi* was subsequently invoked to similar effect in a number of same-sex relationship cases, including in Ireland in 1988[125] and Cyprus in 1993,[126] until it was taken a stage further in the HR Committee's landmark 1994 decision of *Toonen v. Australia*.[127] The Committee found that Tasmania's criminal prohibition on same-sex sexual activity, even if unenforced, constituted an unreasonable interference with the right to privacy and held that there had been a breach of Article 17 of the ECHR: "it is undisputed that adult consensual sexual activity in private is covered by the concept of 'privacy' ", adding that it "cannot accept . . . [that] moral issues are exclusively a matter of domestic concern". It also noted that the reference to "sex", listed among the prohibited grounds for discrimination in Articles 2(1) and 26 of the ICCPR, "is to be taken as including sexual orientation". In *A.D.T. v. United Kingdom* the mere existence of such legislation was held to violate

119 Application No. 7525/76 (1981).
120 Application No. 7654/76 (1980).
121 Application No. 10843/84 (1990).
122 Communication No. 61/1979, UN Doc CCPR/C/15/D/61/1979, IHRL 1713, UNHRC (1982).
123 *Mark Rees Against the United Kingdom*, Application No. 9532/81 (1984).
124 *Cossey*, op. cit., at para. 40.
125 *Norris v. Ireland*, Application No. 10581/83 (1988).
126 *Modinos v. Cyprus*, Application No. 15070/89 (1993).
127 Communication No. 488/1992, U.N. Doc CCPR/C/50/D/488/1992 (1994).

Article 8.[128] This approach was subsequently endorsed by the ECtHR rulings in the previously-mentioned cases of *Christine Goodwin v. the United Kingdom*[129] and *I. v. the United Kingdom*,[130] though not until *E.B. and Others v. Austria*[131] did the ECtHR consider the minimum age at which a party to consensual sexual activity in private could be assured of legal protection.

Family life

As the twentieth century drew to a close, the ECJ in *Grant v. South-West Trains Ltd*[132] was able to assert confidently that "despite the modern evolution of attitudes towards homosexuality, stable homosexual relationships do not fall within the scope of the right to respect for family life under Article 8 of the Convention".[133] However, by the early years of the twenty-first century, ECtHR caselaw had established that the emotional and sexual relationship of same-sex couples constituted "private life". It nonetheless stopped short of finding that this constituted "family life", even where a long-term relationship of cohabiting partners was at stake. It justified its stance by noting that legislative and judicial recognition of same-sex marriages was far from universal and this was a matter best regarded as lying within a State's margin of appreciation. So, for example, in *Mata Estevez v. Spain*,[134] where the claimant complained that the State did not give proper recognition of his relationship with his deceased same-sex partner, the ECtHR stated

> as regards establishing whether the decision in question concerns the sphere of "family life" within the meaning of Article 8 ss. 1 of the Convention, the Court reiterates that, according to the established case-law of the Convention institutions, long-term homosexual relationships between two men do not fall within the scope of the right to respect for family life protected by Article 8 of the Convention.[135]

In *Young v. Australia*,[136] and again two years later in *X v. Colombia*,[137] the HR Committee settled on a wide interpretation of "family". It acknowledged the existence of various forms, such as unmarried couples and their children or single

128 Application No. 35765/97 (2000).
129 Op. cit.
130 36 EHRR 53.
131 Application Nos. 31913/07, 38357/07, 48098/07, 48777/07 and 48779/07) (2013).
132 Case C-249/96 [1998] ECR I-621.
133 Ibid., at para. 33, citing the decisions in Application No. 9369/81, *X. and Y. v. the United Kingdom*, 3 May 1983, Decisions and Reports 32, p. 220; Application No. 11716/85, *S. v. the United Kingdom*, 14 May 1986, D.R. 47, p. 274, at para. 2; and Application No. 15666/89, *Kerkhoven and Hinke v. the Netherlands*, 19 May 1992, unpublished, at para. 1.
134 Application No. 56501/00 (2001).
135 Ibid., at p. 4.
136 Communication No. 941/2000, UN Doc CCPR/C/78/D/941/2000 (2003) 5 IHRR 747, IHRL 1921, UNHRC (2003).
137 Communication No. 1361/2005, U.N. Doc. A/62/40.

parents and their children.[138] If a group of persons is regarded as a family under the legislation and practice of a State, it should be given the protection provided for by Article 23 of the ICCPR – although, as McGoldrick points out, "the Committee has not expressly determined whether same-sex couples can establish a family life".[139] The ECtHR caselaw has evolved similarly, if more cautiously. In *Salgueiro da Silva Mouta v. Portugal*,[140] it found a violation of the right to family life of a man in a homosexual relationship, albeit the family unit under consideration was that of the man and his daughter rather than that of him and his partner, while in *P.B. and J.S. v. Austria*,[141] it extended its recognition of "family life" to include same-sex couples even if, "for professional and social reasons", they do not cohabit.

Not until *Schalk* did the ECtHR take the further step and rule that "a cohabiting same-sex couple living in a stable de facto partnership, falls within the notion of 'family life', just as the relationship of a different-sex couple in the same situation would".[142] This finding, held to derive from Article 8 of the ECHR, was a watershed decision that moved that court away from the position adopted by the HR Committee, which considered the law to be governed by Article 12. Furthermore, the ECtHR gave consideration to the weighting that may be given to cultural context in such matters (see next). In recent years, the ECtHR has extended its recognition of same-sex family relationships to include succession rights[143] and the obtaining of a residence permit for family reunification.[144] Family life was also at issue in *Boeckel and Gessner-Boeckel v. Germany*,[145] when the ECtHR considered the refusal of authorities to register the applicant, a woman in a registered civil partnership, as the parent on the birth certificate of the other partner's child born during their partnership. The application was dismissed as inadmissible, being manifestly ill-founded, as the applicants were not in a relevantly similar situation to a married different-sex couple when it came to the issue of the entries to be made in a child's birth certificate.

Private life, gender reassignment and divorce

The ECtHR has found that a State's refusal to allow a trans person, who had not undergone sterilisation, access to gender reassignment constitutes a breach of their Article 8 right to respect for private life,[146] as does the absence of any law regulating gender reassignment surgery[147] and so too as regards a waiting period

138 HRC, General Comment No 19: Article 23 (The family) (1990) at para. 2.
139 McGoldrick, D., The Development and Status of Sexual Orientation Discrimination Under International Human Rights Law, *Human Rights Law Review*, 16, pp. 613–668 at p. 629 (2016).
140 Application No. 33290/96 (1999).
141 Application No. 18984/02 (2010).
142 Op. cit., at para. 94.
143 *Karner v. Austria* 2003-IX 199; (2003) 38 EHRR 24.
144 *Pajić v. Croatia*, Application No. 68453/13 (2016).
145 Application No. 8017/11 (2013).
146 *Y.Y. v. Turkey*, Application No. 14793/08 (2015).
147 *L. v. Lithuania*, Application No. 27527/03 (2007).

of two years for such surgery.[148] It has also questioned the legitimacy of surgical intervention as a necessary determinant of trans identity.[149]

In *Van Kück v. Germany*,[150] it considered that determining the medical necessity of gender reassignment measures by their curative effects on a trans person is not a matter susceptible to legal definition.[151] The domestic courts' attempts to pursue this matter, coupled with their enquiry as to whether she had *deliberately caused her transsexuality*, had the effect of changing the central issue from one of reimbursement for costs to the more important matter of the applicant's right to respect for her sexual self- determination, this being an aspect of her right to respect for her private life. It noted that the effect of domestic court decisions not only deprived the applicant of a fair hearing as guaranteed under Article 6 but also had repercussions on a fundamental aspect of her right to respect for private life, namely her right to gender identity and personal development. The ECtHR took the view that "the burden placed on a person to prove the medical necessity of treatment, including irreversible surgery, in one of the most intimate areas of private life, appears disproportionate"[152] (see further below).

The traditional requirement that gender reassignment be accompanied by divorce proceedings was considered – in *Parry v. The United Kingdom*[153] as in *Hämäläinen v. Finland*[154] – to be a matter that lay within a State's "margin of appreciation". In the latter case, a significant minority registered their view that this opt-out rationale favoured the moral majority by allowing the "lowest common denominator" among member States to prevail. Instead, they argued that the Court should have asked whether there was "clear and uncontested evidence of a continuing international trend", as it had done in *Goodwin*.[155]

Nonetheless, for same-sex married couples, as for their heterosexual counterparts, there is no human right to divorce.[156]

SOGI, parenting and "the best interests of the child" principle

The record of ECtHR rulings giving recognition to the rights of trans persons probably began with *B. v. France*[157] and *Christine Goodwin v. United Kingdom*[158]

148 *Schlumpf v. Switzerland*, Application No. 29002/06 (2009).

149 For example, in: *B. v. France*, Application No. 13343/87 (1992); *Sheffield and Horsham v. the United Kingdom*, Application Nos. 22985/93, and 23390/94 (1998); *I v. the United Kingdom*, Application No. 25680/94 (2002); and *Christine Goodwin v. the United Kingdom*, Application No. 28957/95 (2002).

150 2003-VII 1; (2003) 37 EHRR 51.

151 Ibid., at para. 54.

152 Ibid., at para. 82.

153 Application No. 42971/05 (2005).

154 Application No. 37359/09 (2014).

155 *Christine Goodwin v. the United Kingdom*, op. cit.

156 *Babiarz v. Poland*, Application No. 1955/10 (2017) and *Piotrowski v. Poland*, Application No. 8923/12 (2016).

157 Application No. 13343/87 (1992).

158 Op. cit.

when, in both cases, the court found there had been a violation of Article 8 of the ECHR. In *Goodwin*, given the "clear and uncontested evidence of a continuing international trend in favour of increased social acceptance" of transgendered persons, the ECtHR established their right to an official record of gender reassignment and determined that a trans should be able to marry a person of the opposite sex. Problems have arisen, however, in squaring that right with Article 3(1) of the Convention on the Rights of the Child, which requires the welfare interests of the child to be the "primary consideration" in all actions concerning children. The ECtHR, when considering domestic court rulings which give greater weighting to welfare interests relative to those of a trans parent, has arguably been inconsistent.

In the previously-mentioned *Salgueiro* case[159] the ECtHR ruled that a decision in which parental responsibility was granted to the mother, because the sexual orientation of the father was considered likely to threaten the best interests of their child, violated Article 8 when taken in conjunction with Article 12 of the ECHR. A decade later, in the not dissimilar case of *P.V. v. Spain*,[160] the ECtHR upheld a decision based upon the same principle. This case concerned an application by a trans (mtf) with regard to restrictions imposed on contact arrangements with her son. The applicant alleged that she had been discriminated against on the ground of her gender modification contrary to Articles 8 and 14. The ECtHR, distinguishing this case from *Salgueiro* on the grounds that the decision was based not on the gender reassignment of the father but on the best interests of the child, found the restrictions to be reasonable. The Spanish authorities had acted in the best interests of the child by progressively accustoming the son to the gender reassignment of his father and found confirmation for this in the gradual extension of the contact arrangements. Accordingly, the ECtHR found no violation of Article 8 in conjunction with Article 12 of the Convention and held that the applicant had not been discriminated against.

Right to marriage and to found a family

(UDHR, Articles 16 and 17; ECHR, Articles 8, 12, 14 and 17; and ICCPR, Article 23)

Article 12 of the ECHR provides that men and women of marriageable age have the right to marry and to found a family. That in so doing they acquire a preferential *locus standi* was confirmed by the ECtHR in its finding that Article 8 did not "impose a positive obligation to establish for unmarried couples a status analogous to that of married couples".[161] For the purposes of the ICCPR, "marriage" has been interpreted as being confined to heterosexual couples due

159 Application No. 33290/96 (1999).

160 Application No. 35159/09 (2010). See, also, *P. v. Portugal*, Application No. 56027/09 (2011).

161 *Johnston v. Ireland*, Application No. 9697/82 (1986).

to the reference in Article 23(2) to the term "men and women", rather than "every human being", "everyone" or "all persons". For the purposes of Directive 2004/38[162] (governing the right to free movement within the EC of citizens and their family members), the concept of "spouse" is considered to be indifferent as to the sex of the persons concerned.[163]

Legal recognition for same-sex relationships and the right to marry

As the court rightly noted in *Schalk*, "same-sex couples are just as capable as different-sex couples of entering into stable committed relationships" and are "in a comparable situation to different-sex couples as regards their need for legal recognition and protection of their relationship".[164] In its General Comment No. 19, the UN HR Committee acknowledged the existence of various forms of "family",[165] and the ECtHR has consistently ruled to the same effect.[166] Neither body, however, has been willing to go so far as to recognise a right for same-sex couples to consolidate their family life within the legal status of "marriage".

The UN HR Committee made its position clear in *Joslin v. New Zealand*[167] when two lesbian couples argued that New Zealand marriage law, which prohibited same-sex marriage, violated their rights under Article 23 of the ICCPR to marriage and under Article 26 to non-discrimination. It found that a "mere refusal to provide for marriage between homosexual couples" did not constitute a human rights violation, nor could it be considered discrimination, and held that States were not required, under the ICCPR, to allow same-sex couples to marry.[168]

In *Schalk and Kopf v. Austria*[169] the ECtHR held that marriage was not essential to provide legal recognition for the status of a same-sex relationship. It found that it could not force States to make marriage available for same-sex couples.[170] However, it noted that the right to marry is granted to "men and women", and this includes the right to found a family, which could be interpreted as granting the right to two men or two women, because, as the court observed, all other Convention rights are granted to "everyone". This ruling was reinforced by the

162 Directive 2004/38/EC of the European Parliament and of the Council (29 April 2004).

163 *Relu Adrian Coman and Others v. Romania*, C-673/16, per Advocate General Melchior Wathelet (11 January 2018).

164 *Schalk and Kopf v. Austria*, Application No. 30141/04 (2010), at para. 99.

165 Human Rights Committee, General Comment No. 19: Protection of the family, the right to marriage and equality of the spouses, HRI/GEN/1/Rev.1, 27 June 1990.

166 See, for example, *Kozak v. Poland*, Application No. 13102/02 (2010) and *X and Others v. Austria* [GC], Application No. 19010/07 (2013).

167 Communication No. 902/1999, U.N. Doc. A/57/40 at 214 (2002).

168 (902/1999) Views, CCPR/C/75/D/902/1999, at para 8.2.

169 Application No. 30141/04 (2010).

170 A matter left to individual States: *Parry v. the United Kingdom*, Application No. 42971/05 (2006).

court's subsequent decisions in *Hämäläinen v. Finland*[171] and *Oliari and Others v. Italy*[172] in which it concluded that States parties were obliged to provide some legal mechanism for the recognition of same-sex partnerships. This approach was strengthened by its finding in *Vallianatos and Others v. Greece*[173] that the blanket exclusion of same-sex couples living in Greece from registering a "civil union" violated Article 14 when taken in conjunction with Article 8 of the ECHR.

In *Oliari*,[174] the ECtHR ruled that State failure to provide same-sex couples with any kind of legally recognised civil union violated their human rights. *Oliari* has been followed by not dissimilar rulings in *Pajić v. Croatia*,[175] *Aldeguer Tomás v. Spain*[176] and *Taddeucci and McCall v. Italy*.[177] However, the right to legal recognition of a same-sex relationship stopped short of an entitlement to marry, as the court made clear in 2018 when it approved a ruling – based on Article 12 of the ECHR – that "there is no right to homosexual marriage".[178]

Trans persons and marriage

Prior to its decisions in *I v. the United Kingdom*[179] and *Christine Goodwin v. the United Kingdom*,[180] the ECtHR had refused to admit that Article 12 was applicable to the union of a trans person and someone of the opposite sex to his/her new sex. Not until *Goodwin* did the ECtHR concede that it would be willing to interpret flexibly the Article 8 right of a man and a woman to marry, taking account of changes in society.[181] It then found that Article 12 had also been breached and that there was "no justification for barring the transsexual person from enjoying the right to marry under any circumstances".[182]

Adoption, surrogacy and child care

In law the creation of a family is not without difficulties: there is neither a right to procreate[183] nor to adopt,[184] but clearly the need to parent and to be parented

171 Application No. 37359/09 (2014).
172 Application Nos. 18766/11 and 36030/11 (2015).
173 Application Nos. 29381/09 and 32684/09 (2013).
174 *Oliari & Ors v. Italy* [2015] ECHR 716.
175 Application No. 68453/13 (2016).
176 Application No. 35214/09 (2016).
177 Application No. 51362/09 (2016).
178 *Relu Adrian Coman and Others v. Romania*, C-673/16, per Advocate General Melchior Wathelet (11.01.2018). See, also, *Chapin and Charpentier v. France*, Application No. 40183/07 (2016).
179 Op. cit.
180 Op. cit.
181 Op. cit., at paras. 98–104.
182 Op. cit., at para. 103.
183 *Sijakova v. The Former Yugoslav Republic of Macedonia*, Application No. 67914/01 (2003).
184 *E.B. v. France*, Application No. 43546/02 (2008) and *Gas and Dubois v. France*, Application No. 25951/07 (2012).

is as strong in the LGBT community as in society more generally. It has been estimated that

> thirty-one percent of LGBT people in the European Union are parents or legal guardians of a child. In countries where same-sex joint adoption is legalised, the number of parents is even higher. In the Netherlands, for instance, sixty-one percent of such persons have children or are legal guardians of a child.[185]

In *Charron and Merle-Montet v. France*,[186] a female married couple complained that their request for medically assisted reproduction had been rejected on the grounds that French law did not authorise such medical provision for same-sex couples. The application was found to be inadmissible on the grounds that the applicants had failed to exhaust domestic remedies.

However, while there is no right to adopt, there is a right to be treated in accordance with equality and non-discrimination provisions when engaged in an adoption process.[187] In *Frette v. France*,[188] a homosexual argued that a refusal to allow him to adopt because of his sexual orientation constituted a violation of the ECHR. In finding against him, the ECtHR referred to the fast evolving and very diverse practice across Europe as well as the conflicting views of experts as to what would be in the best interests of the child.[189] Six years later, in keeping with that fast moving practice, the ECtHR felt justified in coming to the opposite conclusion in *E.B. v. France*,[190] when it held that "in rejecting the applicant's application for authorisation to adopt, the domestic authorities made a distinction based on considerations regarding her sexual orientation, a distinction which is not acceptable under the Convention".[191]

In *Salgueiro da Silva Mouta v. Portugal*,[192] the ECtHR held that a judge's denial of child custody to a homosexual father on the grounds of his sexual orientation constituted a discriminatory infringement of privacy. This was followed by a series of rulings to the same effect on similar matters: the adoption of children,[193] second-parent adoption of children[194] and as regards the rules

185 Alves de Faria, G., Sexual Orientation and the ECtHR: What Relevance Is Given to the Best Interests of the Child? An Analysis of the European Court of Human Rights' Approach to the Best Interests of the Child in LGBT Parenting Cases, *Family and Law* (April 2015), at: www.familyandlaw.eu/tijdschrift/fenr/2015/04/FENR-D-15-00002.

186 Application No. 22612/15 (2018).

187 See, for example, Johnson, Adoption, Homosexuality and the European Convention on Human Rights: *Gas and Dubois v. France*, *Modern Law Review*, 75, p. 1136 (2012).

188 Application No. 36515/97 (2002).

189 *Karner v. Austria* 2003-IX 199; (2003) 38 EHRR 24.

190 *E.B. v France* Application No. 43546/02 (2008).

191 Ibid., at para. 96.

192 Application No. 33290/96 (1999).

193 *E.B. v. France*, Application No. 43546/02 (2008).

194 *X and Others v. Austria*, Application No. 19010/07 (2013). Distinguishing *Gas and Dubois v. France*, Application No. 25951/07 (2012).

on child maintenance.[195] More recently, in *Bonnaud and Lecoq v. France*,[196] the ECtHR rejected an application for joint exercise of parental responsibility made by two women living as a couple, each of whom had a child born as a result of medically assisted reproduction. Upholding the domestic court finding that the criteria for mutual delegation of parental responsibility between the applicants were not satisfied and did not disclose a difference in treatment based on their sexual orientation, the ECtHR dismissed the application.

Surrogacy, which has proven to be a popular route for same-sex couples to achieve family life, can also be problematic. *Menneson v. France*[197] concerned the parents of twins conceived following surrogacy treatment in the US who, following their return to France, were unable to enter the children's birth certificates into the French register of births as French law did not recognise that form of parent–child relationship. Ultimately, the Court found no violation of the applicants' "family life", but it did find that the children's right to an authentic identity and to "family life" were compromised in comparison with their biological counterparts, and for that reason held that France had breached Article 8.

Right to cultural life

(UDHR, Articles 27; ICESCR, Article 15; and UNDRIP, Articles 9–15, 16, 25, and 31)

In the CANZUS nations, the sharp contrast between the cultures of Indigenous people and modern society invariably leads to the latter imposing its norms and laws upon the former; it is also only too apparent in the various culture wars within western nations, some of which centre on SOGI issues. Across the board, the comments of the UN Secretary-General – in his message to the Oslo Conference on Human Rights, Sexual Orientation and Gender Identity – seem equally relevant:

> Some will oppose change. They may invoke culture, tradition or religion to defend the status quo. Such arguments have been used to try to justify slavery, child marriage, rape in marriage and female genital mutilation. I respect culture, tradition and religion – but they can never justify the denial of basic rights.[198]

Also worth bearing in mind is the ECtHR observation that

> far from being opposed to family values – many persons belonging to sexual minorities manifest allegiance to the institutions of marriage,

195 *J.M. v. United Kingdom*, Application No. 37060/06 (2010).
196 Application No. 6190/11 (2018).
197 Application No. 65192/11 (2014).
198 UN Secretary-General, Video Message to the Oslo Conference on Human Rights, Sexual Orientation and Gender Identity, in *International Conference on Human Rights, Sexual Orientation and Gender Identity*, Oslo, 15–16 April 2013: Summary and Toolkit, at 32 ("Oslo Conference Report"), at: geneva.usmission.gov/wp-content/uploads/2013/06/SOGI-conference-summary-and-toolkit.pdf.

> parenthood and adoption, as evidenced by the steady flow of applications to the Court from members of the LGBT community who wish to have access to them.[199]

(See further below.)

Cultural context

Thirty years after its decision in *Dudgeon*,[200] and without any need to take into account the red line issue of criminalisation, the ECtHR in *Schalk and Kopf v. Austria*[201] weighed in on behalf of cultural context. It then held that in relation to the availability of marriage for same-sex couples, the State was best placed to assess and respond to the needs of society, given that marriage had deep-rooted social and cultural connotations differing greatly from one society to another, and could choose not to provide for same-sex marriage.[202] The corollary – that where the law had fallen out of sync with majority cultural values, then the State was remiss in not making available legal remedies appropriate for the needs of contemporary society – seemed to be demonstrated in *Vallianatos and Others v. Greece*[203] and in *Oliari and Others v. Italy*.[204] The former concerned civil partnership procedures available only to heterosexual couples which – as only two of the 19 State parties to the ECHR with such a procedure similarly restricted its use – indicated a cultural weighing in favour of it being available to same-sex couples, such as the claimants, whose rights under Article 14 taken together with Article 8 were held to have been violated.

The significance of cultural context, strongly resonating with that represented by *Dudgeon*, recently surfaced again in *Bayev and Others v. Russia*.[205] The ECtHR then considered the State's argument that "an open manifestation of homosexuality was an affront to the mores prevailing among the religious and even non-religious majority of Russians and was generally seen as an obstacle to instilling traditional family values" and its allegation of an "incompatibility between maintaining family values as the foundation of society and acknowledging the social acceptance of homosexuality".[206] Dismissing this argument, the ECtHR remonstrated that

> negative attitudes, references to traditions or general assumptions in a particular country cannot of themselves be considered by the Court to amount

199 Citing: *Salgueiro da Silva Mouta*, op. cit.; *Oliari and Others*, op. cit.; *X and Others v. Austria*, op. cit.; and *E.B. v. France*, op. cit.
200 *Dudgeon v. the United Kingdom*, Application No. 7525/76 (1981).
201 Application No. 30141/04 (2010).
202 Also stated in *Gas and Dubois v. France*, Application No. 25951/07 (2012).
203 Application Nos. 29381/09 and 32684/09 (2013).
204 Application Nos. 18766/11 and 36030/11 (2015).
205 Application Nos. 67667/09, 44092/12 and 56717/12 (2017).
206 Ibid., at paras. 65 and 67.

> to sufficient justification for the differential treatment, any more than similar negative attitudes towards those of a different race, origin or colour.[207]

In response to the assertion that "the majority of Russians disapprove of homosexuality and resent any display of same-sex relations", the court retorted that

> it would be incompatible with the underlying values of the Convention if the exercise of Convention rights by a minority group were made conditional on its being accepted by the majority. Were this so, a minority group's rights to freedom of religion, expression and assembly would become merely theoretical.[208]

This approach would seem to vindicate the UN Secretary-General's assertion a decade earlier.

SOGI: non-discrimination, affirmative action and equality

The freedom of all citizens to equally access and participate in the full range of everyday facilities and services is the acid test of a healthy, diverse and accommodating democratic society. Clearly, for LGBT citizens, it is crucially important that the human rights framework facilitates such access and is a matter of concern to the Council of Europe.[209] Moreover, as noted in the Introduction, Eleanor Roosevelt stressed in her speech to the UN in 1958, on the tenth anniversary of the UDHR, that these rights are not abstract principles but are rooted in the everyday life of the citizen.[210] In practice, as illustrated in the caselaw next, it is now the equality and non-discrimination provisions together with the affirmative action obligations that are most often called upon by the LGBT community, as by others, for the protection needed to ensure their full participation in society.

Equality before the law: sexuality and gender discrimination

(UDHR, Article 7; ECHR, Articles 1, 8, 12, 14 and Protocol 12; ICCPR, Articles 2, 17 and 26; ICESCR, Articles 2 and 3; CROC, Articles 2 and 34)

207 Ibid., at para. 68, citing: *Smith and Grady*, op. cit.; *Konstantin Markin v. Russia* [GC], Application No. 30078/06 (2012); *Vallianatos and Others v. Greece* [GC], Application Nos. 29381/09 and 32684/09 (2013); and *Hämäläinen v. Finland* [GC], Application No. 37359/09 (2014).

208 Ibid., at para. 70.

209 Council of Europe, *Discrimination on Grounds of Sexual Orientation and Gender Identity in Europe* (2nd ed.), Council of Europe, 2011.

210 As quoted by Ignatieff, M., in *The Ordinary Virtues: Moral Order in a Divided World*, Harvard University Press, Cambridge, MA, 2017, at p. 196, citing the Church Peace Union, *In Your Hands: A Guide for Community Action on the 10th Anniversary of the UDHR*, New York, 1958.

Article 26 of the ICCPR affords general recognition and protection to all suffering from discrimination, while Articles 8 (right to respect for private and family life) and 12 (right to found a family) of the ECHR are also clearly engaged when it comes to recognition of the legal rights of transsexuals. In particular, it is well established that the prohibition of discrimination under Article 14 of the ECHR includes discrimination related to sexual orientation and gender identity. Also of relevance are Article 21 of the EU Charter, the Gender Goods and Services Directive,[211] the Gender Equality Directive (recast)[212] and the Employment Equality Directive.[213] In 2009, the Council of Europe published the report *Discrimination on Grounds of Sexual Orientation and Gender Identity in Europe*, an updated version of which was re-issued in 2011.[214]

Sex discrimination and sexual orientation discrimination

Discrimination on grounds of sexual orientation has been held to violate Article 14 of the ECHR[215] and, in the opinion of UN Secretary-General Ban Ki-moon, is "one of the great, neglected human rights challenges of our time".[216]

The Ban Ki-moon challenge was recognised in Article 21 of the Charter of Fundamental Rights of the European Union and by the UN HR Committee which, in *Joslin v. New Zealand*,[217] expressed the unanimous view that "the prohibition against discrimination on grounds of 'sex' in Article 26 of the ICCPR comprises also discrimination based on sexual orientation". In *Sutherland v. The UK*[218] (see Chapter 4), the then European Commission of Human Rights had noted that it was not clear whether a difference based on sexual orientation was

211 Council Directive 2004/113/EC, implementing the principle of equal treatment between men and women in the access to and supply of goods and services (13 December 2004).

212 Directive 2006/54/EC of the European Parliament and of the Council, on the implementation of the principle of equal opportunities and equal treatment of men and women in matters of employment and occupation (5 July 2006, recast).

213 Council Directive 2000/78/EC, establishing a general framework for equal treatment in employment and occupation (27 November 2000).

214 See Council of Europe Publishing, *Discrimination on Grounds of Sexual Orientation and Gender Identity in Europe* (2nd ed.), Council of Europe Publishing, 2011, at: www.coe.int/t/Commissioner/Source/LGBT/LGBTStudy2011_en.pdf.

Also, see Council of Europe report compiled by Committee on Equality and Non-Discrimination, *Tackling Discrimination on the Grounds of Sexual Orientation and Gender Identity*, 2013, at: http://assembly.coe.int/nw/xml/XRef/Xref-XML2HTML-en.asp?fileid=20010&lang=en.

215 *Salgueiro da Silva Mouta v. Portugal*, Application No. 33290/96 § 28, ECHR 1999-IX and *P.V. v. Spain*, Application No. 35159/09 (2010).

216 UN Secretary-General, Video Message to the Oslo Conference on Human Rights, Sexual Orientation and Gender Identity, in *International Conference on Human Rights, Sexual Orientation and Gender Identity*, Oslo, 15–16 April 2013: Summary and Toolkit, at 32 ("Oslo Conference Report"), at: geneva.usmission.gov/wp-content/uploads/2013/06/SOGI-conference-summary-and-toolkit.pdf.

217 Communication No. 902/1999, U.N. Doc. A/57/40 at 214 (2002).

218 Application No. 25186/94 (1997).

a difference based on "sex" or on "other status" for the purposes of Article 14 of the ECHR. The matter was clarified in 1999 in *Salgueiro da Silva Mouta v. Portugal*,[219] when the ECtHR stated that a difference based on a person's sexual orientation is "a concept which is undoubtedly covered by Article 14 of the Convention", adding that "the list set out in that provision is illustrative and not exhaustive.[220]

This approach had been criticised earlier by the ECJ[221] on the basis that matters of sexual orientation are substantively different from binary men/women issues around which other categories are often constructed. Shortly afterwards, the rulings in the previously-mentioned cases of *Young v. Australia*[222] and *X v. Colombia*[223] indicated that the HR Committee had been converted to the ECJ interpretation: both concerned the denial of a pension transfer to a same-sex partner; and both concluded with a Committee decision that the applicant had been a victim of discrimination on the basis of sexual orientation under Article 26 of the ICCPR. These cases together with *Toonen* showed the Committee relying upon Article 26 as providing a free-standing right to equality and non-discrimination, thereby opening up a line of jurisprudence that would no longer need to consider sexuality issues as subsumed within other rights. This was a period when the Committee repudiated one rule (the "margin of discretion") and consolidated another (that the criminalisation of consensual adult same-sex relations violated the right to privacy protected by Article 17 of the ICCPR). Moreover, as the Committee went on to hold in *Fedotova v. Russian Federation*,[224] strong grounds would need to be established to justify State interference in that right.

This approach was reinforced by a series of ECtHR decisions taken at much the same time. In *Alekseyev v. Russia*,[225] it stressed that particularly weighty reasons needed to be advanced to justify the measure complained of when a distinction based on sexual orientation operated in the "intimate and vulnerable sphere of an individual's private life".[226] In *P.V. v. Spain*,[227] the court stressed that transsexualism was covered by Article 14, which contained a non-exhaustive list of prohibited grounds for discrimination, and in *X and Others v. Austria*[228] it was particularly forthright:

> Sexual orientation is a concept covered by Article 14. The Court has repeatedly held that, just like differences based on sex, differences based on sexual

219 Application No. 33290/96 (1999).
220 Ibid., at para. 28.
221 *Grant v. South West Trains Ltd* C-249/96 [1998] ECR I-621; (1998) 1 CMLR 993.
222 Communication No. 941/2000, CCPR/C/78/D/941/ 2000, (2003).
223 Communication No. 1361/2005, CCPR/C/89/D/1361/2005, (2007).
224 (1932/2010) Views, CCPR/C/106/D/1932/2010.
225 Applications Nos. 4916/07, 25924/08 and 14599/09 (2010).
226 Ibid., at para. 108.
227 Application No. 35159/09 (2010).
228 Application No. 19010/07 (2013).

> orientation require particularly serious reasons by way of justification or, as is sometimes said, particularly convincing and weighty reasons. . . . Where a difference in treatment is based on sex or sexual orientation, the State's margin of appreciation is narrow.[229]

Again, in *E.B. and Others v. Austria*,[230] the ECtHR found that domestic courts had failed, without an objective and reasonable justification, to treat differently persons whose situations were significantly different and that the consequences for the applicants amounted to discrimination on the grounds of sexual orientation. These cases constitute a milestone in judicial recognition of a distinction to be drawn between differences based on sex and on sexual orientation: a distinction of great importance for transsexuals, bisexuals and those of indeterminate orientation. Previously, the ECtHR had in the main been focused on sexual difference as in *L. and V. v. Austria*[231] and *S.L. v. Austria*.[232] The court then considered that Austria's differing ages of consent for heterosexual and homosexual relationships were discriminatory as they "embodied a predisposed bias on the part of a heterosexual majority against a homosexual minority".[233] Not until *Vejdeland and Others v. Sweden*[234] did the ECtHR warn that discrimination based on sexual orientation was as serious as discrimination based on "race, origin or colour".

Gender identity and trans discrimination[235]

The ECHR provides protection for gender identity under the category of "other status", while the HR Committee, in its General Comment of 2014, stressed that for the purposes of Article 9 of the ICCPR the term "everyone" was to be interpreted as including, among others, "lesbian, gay, bisexual and transgender persons".[236] The ECtHR has suggested that "gender identity is one of the most intimate areas of a person's private life"[237] and that the prohibition of discrimination under Article 14 of the Convention undoubtedly

229 Ibid., at para. 99.
230 Application Nos. 1913/07, 38357/07, 48098/07, 48777/07 and 48779/07 (2013).
231 Application Nos. 39392/98 and 39829/98 (2003).
232 Application No. 45330/99 (2003).
233 Ibid., at para. 44. In keeping with the earlier ruling of the European Commission of Human Rights in *Sutherland v. United Kingdom*, Application No. 25186/94 (1997) that the differential in the minimum age for lawful homosexual and heterosexual relationships violated the right to private life under Article 8 of the ECHR.
234 Application No. 1813/07 (2012), at para. 55.
235 See Sivonen, L., Gender Identity Discrimination in European Judicial Discourse, *The Equal Rights Review*, 7, pp. 11–26 (2011).
236 HRC General Comment No 35: Article 9 (Liberty and security of person), 28 October 2014, CCPR/C/GC/35, at para. 3.
237 *Van Kück v. Germany*, Application No. 35968/97 (2003), at para. 56.

covers "transsexualité"[238] and questions related to sexual orientation and *gender identity*,[239] while

> gender and sexual orientation are two distinctive and intimate characteristics . . . any confusion between the two will therefore constitute an attack on one's reputation capable of attaining a sufficient level of seriousness for touching upon such an intimate characteristic of a person.[240]

The ECJ, for its part, has long maintained that discrimination arising from gender reassignment, i.e. the intention of a person to undergo or having undergone gender reassignment, is covered by the principle of gender equality,[241] while the Advocate General has warned that discrimination based on gender reassignment is not to be confused with discrimination relating to sexual orientation.[242]

However, although nearly 40 years have elapsed since the HR Commission recognised that medical science was not determinative of a trans person's legal identity,[243] and despite the earlier evidence of international concern, there is still no UN human rights instrument that explicitly recognises sexual orientation or gender identity as providing rights or grounds for protection under international law. The Convention on the Rights of the Child (CROC) comes closest to doing so in Article 34 with its article on protection against "all forms of sexual exploitation and sexual abuse".

Affirmative action

(UDHR, Articles 7 and 8; ECHR, Articles 8, 11 and 14; CERD, Articles 1(4), 2(2), 4 and 6)

Recognition of a State duty to develop positive measures to offset disadvantages and promote equality of outcomes can be traced back to *Marckx v. Belgium*,[244] when the ECtHR noted that "there may be positive obligations inherent in an effective 'respect' for family life". In *Airey v. Ireland* in 1979 the ECtHR stated

238 *P.V. v. Spain*, op. cit., at para. 30.

239 *Identoba and Others v. Georgia*, Application No. 73235/12 (2015).

240 *Sousa Goucha v. Portugal*, Application No. 70434/12 (2016), at para. 27.

241 See *P. v. S. and Cornwall County Council*, Case C-13/94, Opinion of the Advocate General, 14th December 1995, at paras. 8–13 and 24; *K.B. v. The National Health Service Pensions Agency and the Secretary of State for Health*, Case C-117/01, Opinion of the Advocate General, 10 June 2003, paras. 25, 79 and footnote 15; and *Sarah Margaret Richards v. Secretary of State for Work and Pensions*, Case C-423/04, Opinion of the Advocate General, 15 December 2005, at para. 1.

242 *K.B. v. The National Health Service Pensions Agency and the Secretary of State for Health*, Case C-117/01, Opinion of Advocate General, 10 June 2003, at paras. 25 and 73.

243 *Christine Goodwin v. The United Kingdom*, Application No. 28957/95 (2002), at para. 108.

244 Application No. 6833/74 (1979).

that the "fulfillment of a duty under the Convention on occasion necessitates some positive action on the part of the State; it cannot simply remain passive".[245] The need for positive State intervention was emphasised in the leading case of *Thlimmenos v. Greece*[246] and in a number of ECtHR rulings concerning the social disadvantages suffered by minority groups such as the Roma.[247] The UN Human Rights Committee has also noted that

> the principle of equality sometimes requires States to take affirmative action in order to diminish or eliminate conditions which cause or help to perpetuate discrimination prohibited by the Covenant. For example, in a State where the general conditions of a certain part of the population prevent or impair their enjoyment of human rights, the State should take specific action to correct those conditions.[248]

LGBT issues and affirmative State action

As the ECtHR has frequently reiterated, there is an onus on the State to be proactive in remedying disadvantage. A State must, for example, respect the right of trans persons to sexual self-determination and not make recognition of their right to reimbursement of the medical costs of a sex change operation conditional on proof of the therapeutic necessity of that operation.[249] It should provide differential treatment to trans persons when necessary: additional supports may be needed to offset disadvantages and ensure equality of outcomes, including special facilities for changing name and sex in identity documents and adaptations to the working environment in terms of unisex toilets etc.

In *Rees v. the United Kingdom*,[250] the UN HR Commission then found that the State had failed to protect the interests of trans persons[251] and thereafter the Commission and its successor the UN HR Committee consistently upheld the principle that the State violated its positive obligations under Article 8 when it did not grant official recognition to a trans person's preferred gender. More recently, in *Van Kück v. Germany*,[252] the ECtHR drew attention to the fact that for the State, under Article 8, "there may be positive obligations inherent in an effective respect for private or family life".[253]

245 *Airey v. Ireland*, Application No. 6289/73 (1979), para. 25.
246 Application No. 34369/97 (2000) at paras. 39–49.
247 See, for example, *Horvath and Kiss v. Hungary*, Application No. 11146/11 (2013).
248 See United Nations Human Rights Committee, "General Comment relating to discrimination under the ICCPR", 1989 (No. 18, para. 10).
249 *Thlimmenos v. Greece*, Application No. 34369/97 (2000) at paras. 39–49.
250 Application No. 9532/81 (1987).
251 Ibid., at para. 40.
252 2003-VII 1; (2003) 37 EHRR 51.
253 Ibid., at para. 70.

Right to equality and non-discrimination: health

(ECHR, Articles 2 and 11; ICESCR, Article 2)

The right to the enjoyment of the highest attainable standard of physical and mental health was first articulated on an international basis in the 1946 Constitution of the World Health Organisation (WHO). The preamble defines health as "a state of complete physical, mental and social well-being and not merely the absence of disease or infirmity",[254] and goes on to proclaim that "the enjoyment of the highest attainable standard of health is one of the fundamental rights of every human being without distinction of race, religion, political belief, economic or social condition". The Committee on Economic, Social and Cultural Rights in its General Comment No. 14 of 2000 also asserted this right,[255] as did the European Social Charter,[256] the UN Special Rapporteur in 2004;[257] more recently, specifically in relation to the LGBT community, it can be found in the Yogyakarta Principles.

The health issues raised before the court have tended to allege negative consequences for same-sex relationships. This was the case in *Interights v. Croatia*[258] (see next). In *Van Kück v. Germany*,[259] the ECtHR found that the domestic courts had erred in accepting expert evidence that the applicant was a male-to-female transsexual; her transsexuality constituted a disease, a matter not in dispute between the parties; and that gender reassignment measures could not be expected to cure the applicant's transsexuality, but at best to improve her psychosocial situation. In *Bayev and Others v. Russia*,[260] the ECtHR not only rejected the argument advanced by the State that "the promotion of same-sex relationships had to be banned on the grounds that same-sex relationships posed a risk to public health and the demographic situation" for lack of supporting evidence, but also responded that the dissemination of information and raising awareness of risks would in fact have the opposite effect.[261]

Gender reassignment treatment

Over the last two decades, if not longer, the cases considered by the ECtHR have been focused very largely on variations in the capacity of national law to provide a process, in compliance with Articles 8 and 12, that is sufficient for legally

254 See further at: www.ohchr.org/Documents/Publications/Factsheet31.pdf.
255 Committee on Economic, Social and Cultural Rights, General Comment No. 14: The Right to the Highest Attainable Standard of Health, E/C.12/2000/4 (2000).
256 CoE, European Social Charter, 1996, at: http://conventions.coe.int/Treaty/EN/Treaties/Html/163.htm.
257 Report of the Special Rapporteur on the right of everyone to the enjoyment of the highest attainable standard of physical and mental health, E/CN.4/2004/49/Add.1 (2004), at: https://digitallibrary.un.org/record/517605/files/E_CN-4_2004_49_Add-1-EN.pdf.
258 Complaint No. 45/2007 (European Committee of Social Rights and Article 11(2) of the European Social Charter) (2009), at paras. 60–61.
259 Application No. 35968/97 (2003).
260 Application Nos. 67667/09, 44092/12 and 56717/12 (2017).
261 Ibid., at para. 72.

recognising a gender identity change. In *Van Kück* it took a firm stand and clearly stated that States should provide trans persons with such a process, including surgery, leading to full gender reassignment, and that the cost of any surgery should be covered by insurance plans as "medically necessary" treatment.[262] In 2009, the Commissioner for Human Rights of the Council of Europe warned that:

> medical treatment must always be administered in the best interests of the individual and adjusted to her/his specific needs and situation. It is disproportionate for the State to prescribe treatment in a "one size fits all" manner. . . . States which impose intrusive physical procedures on transgender persons effectively undermine their right to found a family.[263]

This was followed in 2013 by the report of the Special Rapporteur calling on all States "to repeal any law allowing intrusive and irreversible treatments, including forced genital-normalizing surgery, involuntary sterilization".[264] Then, in 2015, the Parliamentary Assembly adopted Resolution 2048 – on discrimination against transgender people in Europe – which called on the member States, among other things, to abolish sterilisation and other compulsory medical treatment, as well as a mental health diagnosis, as a necessary legal requirement to recognise a person's gender identity.

The earlier developments were among those noted by the ECtHR in *Garçon and Nicot v. France*,[265] which concerned complaints from three trans applicants that the authorities had infringed their Article 8 right to respect for their private life by making recognition of sexual identity conditional on undergoing an operation involving a high probability of sterility. The court heard evidence that at that time: in 18 member States (19 in Europe, counting Belarus) legal recognition of the gender identity of trans persons was not subject to a legal requirement to undergo sterilisation; in 22 countries it was required; and that a psychiatric diagnosis was among the prerequisites for legal recognition of trans identity in 36 European countries.[266] The court found that, at the

262 *Van Kück* v. Germany, op. cit., at paras. 47, 73 and 82 and also *L. v. Lithuania*, Application No. 27527/03 (2007) at paras. 59 and 74.

263 The Commissioner for Human Rights of the Council of Europe, *Human Rights and Gender Identity* (2009) at p. 8.

264 The Special Rapporteur on torture and other cruel, inhuman or degrading treatment or punishment paragraph, report to the United Nations Human Rights Council (A/HRC/22/53) (2013), at para. 88.

265 *Garçon* and Nicot v. France, Application No. 79885/12 (2017).

266 Ibid., citing at para. 73, Transgender Europe, *Trans Rights Europe Map 2016* (2016) and the Commissioner for Human Rights of the Council of Europe, *Human Rights and Gender Identity* (2009). Also quoting from: The Committee of Ministers of the Council of Europe, Recommendation CM/Rec(2010)5 (measures to combat discrimination on grounds of sexual orientation or gender identity); the Parliamentary Assembly of the Council of Europe, Resolution 1728 (2010) (discrimination on the basis of sexual orientation and gender identity); and the Parliamentary Assembly, Resolution 1945 (2013), entitled "Putting an end to coerced sterilisations and castrations" and Resolution 2048 (2015) (discrimination against transgender people in Europe).

time, French law made recognition of the gender identity of trans persons conditional on sterilisation surgery or on treatment which, on account of its nature and intensity, entailed a very high probability of sterility; numerous European and international institutional actors, however, had adopted a very clear position in favour of abolishing the sterility criterion, as they regarded this as an infringement of fundamental rights. Accordingly, the court held that French law violated the Article 8 rights of two of the applicants. It referenced in support its earlier findings in *Y.Y. v. Turkey*,[267] that respect for the physical integrity of the applicant (a trans person whose request to undergo gender reassignment surgery was refused on the grounds that he had not demonstrated that he was "permanently unable to procreate" as required by domestic law) precluded any obligation for him to undergo treatment resulting in permanent infertility; and in *Soares de Melo v. Portugal*,[268] that Article 8 had been violated by the requirement for the applicant to undergo sterilisation surgery in order to exercise her parental rights as protected by that same provision. The court also considered the claim that making the legal recognition of trans identity conditional on proof that the person "actually suffered from a gender disorder" labelled them as mentally ill. It noted that a psychiatric diagnosis featured among the prerequisites for legal recognition of transgender persons' gender identity in the vast majority of the EU States. It also noted that "transsexualism" featured in Chapter V of the World Health Organisation's International Classification of Diseases (ICD-10, no. F64.0) entitled "Mental and behavioural disorders", under the category "Disorders of adult personality and behaviour", sub-category "Gender identity disorders". Furthermore, the High Authority for Health had advised that a diagnosis of gender dysphoria is required for the purposes of differential diagnosis, so that doctors can be sure, before administering hormone treatment or performing surgery, that the patient's suffering does not stem from other causes. The court concluded, therefore, that States retained a wide discretion in deciding whether to insist on such a requirement.

The development of the jurisprudence relating to gender reassignment was taken a step further in *S.V. v. Italy*[269] when the ECtHR ruled that the Article 8 rights of a trans person, who had been in sex reassignment therapy for some years, had been violated by the refusal of Italian officials to permit a name change on the basis that no judicial authority had confirmed the completion of that process. In effect, the ECtHR set aside the issue of external proof of gender reassignment (whether by surgical intervention or other treatment) and determined that as she had been self-identifying as having changed gender for some years, and had committed to a process designed to consolidate that transition, she was entitled to official recognition of her civil status as a trans person.

267 Application No. 14793/08 (2015).
268 Application No. 72850/14 (2016).
269 Application No. 55216/O8 (2018).

Trans children

The earlier noted Parliamentary Assembly Resolution 2048 calls upon member States to "amend classifications of diseases used at national level and advocate the modification of international classifications, making sure that transgender people, including children, are not labelled as mentally ill, while ensuring stigma-free access to necessary medical treatment".[270]

Sports and recreational activities

International human rights law does not provide a right to sport nor does it address SOGI issues in relation to sport. Perhaps the most relevant provisions are the UDHR, Articles 24 and 27, with their references, respectively, to rest and leisure and to the cultural life of the community; and CEDAW, Article 12(g), which includes a mention of sport in the context of equality of opportunity for women in education. This omission has not prevented the emergence in recent years of a good deal of contention as to whether trans people have rights – based on equality and non-discrimination – to compete in sports in accordance with their gender identity, most contentious when that gender rests on self-identification.[271] The debate raises allegations of unfair advantage, segregation, discrimination and victimisation, where physiological differences can be compounded by testosterone and hormonal treatment.[272] There is clearly a balance to be struck between personal privacy and the protection of sport: arguably Article 8 of the ECHR may have relevance in a SOGI context in circumstances where privacy rights are in danger of violation by intrusive testing.

Blood donors

A 2011 survey revealed that 12 out of the 15 examined European countries permanently ban homosexuals from donating blood, while the other three countries

270 Parliamentary Assembly Resolution 2048, *Discrimination Against Transgender People in Europe* (2015) at paras. 6.2.2, 6.2.5 and 6.3.3. Note also Resolution 1952, adopted by the Council of Europe (2013), on *Children's Right to Physical Integrity*, which calls on Member States to: "undertake further research to increase knowledge about the specific situation of intersex people, ensure that no-one is subjected to unnecessary medical or surgical treatment that is cosmetic rather than vital for health during infancy or childhood, guarantee bodily integrity, autonomy and self-determination to persons concerned, and provide families with intersex children with adequate counselling and support" at para. 7.5.3. Also see UN Committee on the Rights of the Child, General Comment No. 15 (2013) on the right of the child to the enjoyment of the highest attainable standard of health (Article 24).

271 See the International Olympic Committee (IOC) *Transgender Guidelines*, at: www.olympic.org/search?q=Transgender%20Guidelines&filter=documents.

272 See IAAF, the *Differences in Sex Development* Regulations (2018), at: www.sportsintegrityinitiative.com/iaaf-introduces-new-eligibility-regulations-female-classification/.

provide for a temporary ban,[273] despite the prohibition in Article 21(1) of the EU Charter on Human Rights of any discrimination against homosexuals on grounds of sexual orientation. This serves as a reminder that beneath the rhetoric of inclusiveness towards the LGBT community, many remain cautious.

The ECJ considered this issue in the *Léger* case[274] in 2015 and concluded by recognising that there may be higher health risks from such blood donors but that techniques existed for assessing the level of risk, and it was a matter for the domestic courts to determine whether, in any particular circumstance, proportionate measures had been employed to make that assessment taking into account a donor's ECHR rights.[275] This somewhat ambivalent decision would at least seem to indicate that there is no justification for a permanent deferral of blood donations from homosexuals. The most recent cases to reach the ECtHR on this matter came from Italy in 2002,[276] but by the time the matter reached the court the relevant law had been changed so the proceedings were duly struck out. In 2018, a French application on this matter was lodged at the ECtHR.[277]

Right to equality and non-discrimination: education

(UDHR, Article 26; ECHR, Articles 5 and 13; ICCPR, Article 18; ICESCR, Article 13; CEDAW, Article 10; CROC, Article 28; and Article 2 of Protocol 1)

National public education systems have struggled with varying degrees of success to accommodate international law on LGBT issues, but very little litigation would seem to have reached the international courts or the HR Committee. However, in the *Belgian Linguistics case*[278] the ECtHR considered the right to education under the ECHR, Protocol 1, Article 2 and noted that "measures taken in the field of education may affect the right to respect for private and family life or derogate from it".[279]

Schools

All countries face challenges in creating space at all levels in their education systems for those who wish to express their LGBT identity, as protected under Article 10 of the ECHR, or to represent and advocate collectively on related issues.

273 See UK Advisory Committee SABTO (Safety of Blood, Tissues and Organs), *Donor Selection Criteria Review*, 2011, at pp. 33–34. See, further, at: https://assets.publishing.service.gov.uk/government/uploads/system/uploads/attachment_data/file/216109/dh_129909.pdf.
274 Case C-528/13.
275 Ibid., at para. 69.
276 *Tosto v. Italy*, *Crescimone v. Italie* and *Faranda v. Italy* (2002). See, further, at: www.airecentre.org/data/files/FS_Sexual_orientation_ENG.pdf.
277 See, further, applicant Drelon.
278 *Belgian Linguistic case* (1968) (No. 2), 1 EHRR 252. See further at: https://hudoc.echr.coe.int/eng#{"itemid":["001-57525"]}.
279 Ibid., at para. 7.

In meeting this challenge, the advice of the Commissioner of Human Rights must be borne in mind – children have rights and their views must be taken into account in decisions that concern them.[280] Also of note is the Recommendation issued by the Council of Europe "to take actions to ensure the human rights of LGBTI children in schools, particularly in the areas of school curriculum and of bullying".[281]

Curricula

At primary school level, the debate about how to introduce and disseminate information regarding the issues affecting the LGBT community in a proportionate non-polemic way, without attracting accusations of propagating a "homosexual agenda", is often contentious. The design and use of curriculum material that addresses matters of sexual orientation and gender identity can be problematic for those parents who wish to protect their rights, under Article 13 of ICESCR and Article 2 of Protocol 1 ECHR, to ensure that a child's religious and moral education conforms to their own beliefs.[282] In *Interights v. Croatia*,[283] it was found that certain teaching material used in the national school curriculum was homophobic, as it described and presented people of homosexual orientation in a manifestly biased, discriminatory and demeaning way. This was held to be discriminatory and in violation of the right to health education under Article 11(2) of the European Social Charter.

Colleges/universities

While there would appear to be no ECtHR cases directly involving SOGI issues in a university/college context, the judgements in *Şahin v. Turkey*[284] and *Çam v. Turkey*[285] are of relevance. Both cases concerned the duty of university authorities to promote inclusiveness and ensure that all students had equal access to the education programmes available: in *Şahin*, a physically handicapped engineering student and in *Çam*, a blind music student; but the rulings are applicable to any barrier to access, including an insensitivity to SOGI issues. In *Şahin*, the ECtHR found that the Article 8 right to respect for private and family life required an assessment of the potential impact of the barrier on the student's safety, dignity

280 "LGBTI children have the right to safety and equality", Commissioner's Human Rights Comment (2 October 2014), at: www.coe.int/en/web/commissioner/-/lgbti-children-have-the-right-to-safety-and-equality.

281 Recommendation CM/Rec(2010)5. See, further, Council of Europe, *Equal Opportunities for All Children: Non-Discrimination of LGBTI Children and Young People*, 2016, at: https://edoc.coe.int/en/index.php?controller=get-file&freeid=7051.

282 See, for example, *Folgerø v. Norway* [2007] ECHR 546.

283 Complaint No. 45/2007, 30 March 2009 (European Committee of Social Rights and Article 11(2) of the European Social Charter).

284 Application No. 44774/98 (2005).

285 Application No. 51500/08 (2016).

and independence. In both cases the court found there had been a violation of Article 14 read in conjunction with Article 2 of Protocol No. 1. In *Şahin* it drew particular attention to "the importance of the fundamental principles of universality and non-discrimination in the exercise of the right to education, which have been repeatedly enshrined in international texts".[286]

Right to equality and non-discrimination: employment

(UDHR, Article 23; ICESCR, Articles 6 and 7;[287] Article 141 EC[288] and the Employment Equality Directive 2000/78/EC)

The right not to be discriminated against on grounds of sex is firmly stated in Article 1(1) of Directive 75/117, and as the ECJ has noted, this right "is one of the fundamental human rights the observance of which the Court has a duty to ensure".[289] "Sex" is understood as not being confined to a binary gender distinction but to include those who have undergone or are undergoing gender reassignment. The recast Equal Treatment Directive (2006/54/EC), which gives effect to the principle of equal opportunities and treatment of men and women in employment, prohibits direct and indirect sex discrimination, harassment and sexual harassment in pay, (access to) employment and in occupational social security schemes.

Religious exemption

The Employment Equality Directive largely exempts religious organisations, and those based on a belief ethos, from the prohibition on discrimination in an employment context.

Sexual orientation in the workplace

Homophobia in the workplace is a long-standing social issue and one which came before the ECJ in *Asociaţia ACCEPT v. Consiliul Naţional pentru Combaterea Discriminării*.[290] This concerned a person, perceived as playing a leading role in a football club, who made homophobic comments to the media and rejected any recruitment of homosexual players, but who in fact had no real managerial

286 *Şahin*, at para. 62.
287 Committee on Economic, Social and Cultural Rights, General Comment No. 18: The Right to Work, E/C.12/GC/18, 24 November 2005.
288 Article 141 states that "each Member State shall ensure that the principle of equal pay for male and female workers for equal work or work of equal value is applied". This provision defines "pay" as including "any consideration whether in cash or in kind, which the worker receives directly or indirectly, in respect of his employment, from his employer" such as a pension.
289 *Richards v. UK*, Case C-423/04 (2006) citing: Case 149/77 *Defrenne* [1978] ECR 1365, paras. 26 and 27; and Case C-13/94, *P.* v *S.* [1996] ECR I-2143, para. 19.
290 Case C-81/12 (2013).

responsibility. The ECJ found that the comments were discriminatory and could be imputed to the club employers as they had failed to distance themselves from those comments. It ruled that Directive 2000/78 allows domestic laws to give legal standing to non-governmental organisations, enabling them to challenge homophobic harassment and discrimination even where there is no victim.

In the closing years of the twentieth century, issues concerning sexual orientation in the workplace were the subject of a series of not dissimilar cases. In *Cossey v. the United Kingdom*,[291] the ECtHR took the view that as there had been no noteworthy scientific developments in the area of transsexualism in the period since its judgement in *Rees*, there was no reason for it not to reach the same decision as it had in that case. In *P. v. S. and Cornwall County Council*[292] (see Chapter 4), the ECJ created an important precedent when it ruled that transsexuals "intending to undergo, undergoing or [who] have undergone gender reassignment" are entitled to protection in the workplace and their dismissal for that reason should be construed as unlawful discrimination.

Trans persons and the workplace

Perhaps the earliest relevant international human rights case in this context was *D. van Oosterwijck v. Belgium*,[293] which concerned a trans person who had been refused employment as a police officer by the Belgian authorities on the grounds that such an officer would be unable to fulfil statutory duties that required males to search males and females to search females. The ECtHR declined to rule on the merits of the case, holding that the claimant had failed to exhaust domestic remedies.

Employment in the military

The well-established right to private life, under Article 8 of the ECHR, has repeatedly been challenged in the context of the sex orientation of members of national armed forces. The response of the ECtHR, to expressions of disquiet from State authorities that inclusion of homosexuals would reduce effectiveness in the armed forces, was bluntly stated in *Lustig-Prean*:

> To the extent that they represent a predisposed bias on the part of a heterosexual majority against a homosexual minority, these negative attitudes cannot, of themselves, be considered by the Court to amount to sufficient justification for the interference with the applicants' rights . . . any more than similar negative attitudes towards those of a different race, origin or colour.[294]

291 Application No. 10843/84 (1990).
292 C-13/94 [1996] IRLR 347.
293 Application No. 7654/76 (1980).
294 *Lustig-Prean v. United Kingdom* (2000) 29 EHRR 548, at para. 90.

As in the contemporaneous *Smith and Grady* case,[295] the court emphasised that any such constraint must not simply be "necessary" but must be "necessary in a democratic society", and a democratic society is one characterised by "pluralism, tolerance and broad-mindedness".[296]

In *Perkins and R. v. the United Kingdom*[297] and *Beck, Copp and Bazeley v. the United Kingdom*,[298] the court considered that the measures taken against the applicants had constituted especially grave interferences with their private lives and had not been justified by "convincing and weighty reasons". In *Emel Boyraz v. Turkey*,[299] the applicant was dismissed from her security officer post, three years after her appointment commenced, because she did not fulfil the requirements of "being a man" and "having completed military service". The ECtHR held that the dismissal constituted a breach of her rights under Articles 8 and 14 of the ECHR.

Right to equality and non-discrimination: services

(UDHR, Article 2; ICCPR, Articles 2 and 26; ICESCR, Article 2(2); CEDAW, Article 2; CROC, Article 2; and Directive 79/7/EEC)

The equality principle, in relation to trans persons accessing services and as regards the supply of goods and services, is not specifically addressed in international instruments nor in the EU Directives.

Trans persons and gender-specific services

In general terms, the previously-mentioned *Christine Goodwin v. United Kingdom*[300] was a landmark case in this context as it established the basic human right of a trans person to access services such as social security, pensions and an ability to marry.

Provision of public services

While international instruments have failed to specifically address SOGI issues, the judiciary have done so, if only to a limited extent.

X v. Turkey,[301] for example, concerned the allegation of a homosexual man that his imprisonment in solitary confinement was due to his sexual orientation and constituted a breach of his Article 3 right to freedom from inhuman and degrading treatment or punishment. Finding in his favour, the ECtHR reiterated that

295 *Smith and Grady v. United Kingdom* (2000) 29 EHRR 493.
296 Ibid., at para. 87.
297 Application Nos. 43208/98 and 44875/98 (2003).
298 Application Nos. 48535/99, 48536/99 and 48537/99 (2003).
299 Application No. 30733/08 (2018).
300 Application No. 28957/95 (2002).
301 Application No. 24626/09 (2012).

Article 14 protects people from discrimination on the grounds of sexual orientation and that when a difference in treatment is based on sex or sexual orientation, the margin of appreciation accorded to the state in question is very thin. The principle of proportionality was also relevant. It held that the measures taken were not aimed at protecting the physical integrity of the applicant but were taken because of his sexual orientation and consequently that there had been a violation of Article 14 in conjunction with Article 3. Again, in *OM v. Hungary*,[302] which concerned a homosexual in immigration detention, the ECtHR commented:

> the authorities failed to . . . [consider] the extent to which vulnerable individuals – for instance, LGBT people like the applicant – were safe or unsafe in custody among other detained persons, many of whom had come from countries with widespread cultural or religious prejudice against such persons.[303]

Trans persons and prisons

The treatment of trans people within the criminal justice system is particularly fraught and has long been known to generate human rights issues under Articles 3, 8 and 14 of the ECHR. Towards the end of the last century, the deliberate disclosure of a prisoner's trans status was found to breach Article 8;[304] nearly 20 years ago the Special Rapporteur noted that trans prisoners (particularly trans women) are at "great risk" of physical and sexual abuse.[305] The segregation of prisoners on SOGI criteria has been found to be unlawful;[306] and, more recently, the ECtHR has urged States to take the "necessary preventive measures to preserve the physical safety and well-being" of prisoners,[307] though it has recognised limits of reasonableness in the lengths that prison authorities can be expected to go to protect gay prisoners.[308] Inmate access to adequate health care and appropriate rehabilitation programmes[309] has also been recognised as important.

Private goods and service provision

Accommodation has often provided a context for SOGI disputes. In *Karner v. Austria*,[310] for example, the ECtHR found that the failure of Austria to permit a homosexual man to continue occupying his deceased partner's flat was

302 Application No. 9912/15 (2016).
303 Ibid., at para. 53.
304 *B v. France*, Application No. 13343/87 (1992).
305 Report of the Special Rapporteur on the question of torture and other cruel, inhuman or degrading treatment or punishment, A/56/156, 3 July 2001, at para. 23.
306 *X v. Turkey*, Application No. 24626/09 (2012).
307 *Sizarev v. Ukraine*, Application No. 17116/04 (2013) at para. 112.
308 *Stasi v. France*, Application No. 25001/07 (2011).
309 *James, Wells and Lee v. UK*, Application Nos. 25119/09, 57715/09 and 57877/09 (2012).
310 Application No. 40016/98 (2003).

discriminatory, since this right, enjoyed by other family members under Austrian law, did not apply to same-sex partners. It held that there had been a violation of Article 14 taken in conjunction with Article 8 as the Austrian government had not offered convincing and weighty reasons to justify a law that produced such an outcome. Similar decisions on similar facts followed in *Simpson v. UK*[311] and in *Röösli v. Germany*.[312] Again, in *Kozac v. Poland*,[313] in which the State argued, in part, that a *de facto* marital relationship was a prerequisite for succession to the tenancy of a council flat and this could only exist between persons of the opposite sex, the ECtHR concluded by finding a breach of Articles 14 and 8. Despite the importance of the legitimate aim of protecting traditional families, the State had to take into account developments and changes in society, including the fact that there was not just one way or one choice in the sphere of leading and living one's family and private life. Given the State's narrow margin of appreciation in cases of difference in treatment on the basis of sexual orientation, a blanket exclusion of persons living in a homosexual relationship from succession to a tenancy could not be considered acceptable. More recently, in *Taddeucci and McCall v. Italy*,[314] the ECtHR found a violation of Articles 14 and 8, but this time in circumstances where stable same-sex partners did not enjoy the same rights as different-sex spouses as they had no access to marriage under domestic law. Otherwise, SOGI-related discrimination in the provision of goods and services by public actors (gender neutral toilets etc.) or by private (retail sales etc.) does not appear to have generated much ECtHR caselaw.

Pensions and social security benefits etc.

At the turn of the century, the ECtHR leaned towards respecting the right of States to protect the *locus standi* of the traditional marital family unit from being undermined by claims of parity from those in same-sex relationships. It took the view that States could shelter behind the "margin of appreciation" rule if they chose to avoid recognising any such equivalence. The steps taken by the ECtHR and the ECJ as their rulings moved away from that baseline to accommodate SOGI issues were instrumental in leading a similar process of change in England and Wales and Ireland, as elsewhere in the EU.

In *Grant v. South-West Trains Ltd*[315] (see Chapter 4), the European Court of Justice (ECJ) noted that within the European Community there was considerable contention as to whether any equivalence existed between same-sex partnerships and heterosexual marriages, which explained the different approaches to sexual orientation, and added that it was a matter for domestic legislatures to change

311 Application No. 11716/85 (1986).
312 Application No. 28318/95 (1996).
313 Application No. 13102/02 (2010).
314 Application No. 51362/09 (2016).
315 Case C-249/96 [1998] ECR I-621.

that position. This approach was followed in *Mata Estevez v. Spain*,[316] where the claimant argued that his long-term relationship with the deceased should be construed as "private and family life", analogous to marriage within the terms of Article 8, as under domestic law marriage was restricted to heterosexual couples. On that basis he claimed that a refusal to grant him the pension entitlement for a surviving spouse amounted to discriminatory treatment infringing his right to respect for his private and family life. The ECtHR ruled that the Convention did not guarantee any right to a pension and that even if the refusal did constitute an interference with respect for his private life, that interference was justified under Article 8(2) as the legislation in question had a legitimate aim – the protection of the family based on marriage.[317] Nearly a decade later, the same approach was apparent in *Mannec v. France*,[318] which concerned much the same set of facts: a reversionary pension to the survivor of a same-sex civil partnership was denied on the ground that the requirement of a lawful marriage had not been met; this requirement was alleged to be discriminatory, in general towards persons who had entered into a civil partnership agreement, and particularly towards same-sex couples. The application was found to be inadmissible. The ECtHR held that the French State, like the Spanish State in *Mata Estevez*, had pursued a legitimate aim, namely the protection of the family based on the bonds of marriage; the limiting of the scope of the legislation to married couples, to the exclusion of partners in a civil partnership regardless of their sexual orientation, fell within the broad margin of appreciation. Again, in *Aldeguer Tomás v. Spain*,[319] discrimination on the basis of sexual orientation was allegedly the reason for the refusal of a pension to an applicant following the death of his partner, with whom he had lived in a *de facto* marital relationship, and again the ECtHR found that there had been no discrimination. As the applicant's situation at that time had not been relevantly similar to that of a surviving partner of a heterosexual cohabiting couple, the State was entitled to rely on the margin of appreciation rule.

In the meantime, however, the ECJ's approach to the equality rights of trans persons in relation to pension entitlement in the previously-mentioned *P. v. S. and Cornwall County Council*,[320] as subsequently confirmed in *K.B v. NHS Pensions Agency*[321] and then again in *Richards v. UK*,[322] seemed more straightforward. The latter case, in line with the rationale adopted by the ECtHR in *Grant*, established that national legislation which precluded male to female trans persons from entitlement to the earlier pension age prescribed for females was in breach of EC Directives on employment equality. It then examined sexual orientation

316 Application No. 56501/00 (2001).
317 Ibid. at p. 5, citing *Marckx v. Belgium*, Application No. 6833/74 (1979).
318 Application No. 66686/09 (2010).
319 Application No. 35214/09 (2016).
320 C-13/94, ECR 1–21–43 (1994).
321 Case C-117/01 (2004).
322 Case C-423/04 (2006).

discrimination in an employment context, beginning with a pair of landmark German cases.

In the *Maruko* case,[323] the ECJ considered the legal significance for pensions of a statutory distinction made between registered same-sex partnerships and heterosexual marriage. The claimant argued that the refusal of his employment pension fund to grant him a pension on the death of his partner, equivalent to that normally received by a widower, constituted discrimination because of his sexual orientation. The fund responded that the regulations provided for pensions to be paid only to spouses, not to registered partners. The ECJ found that the issue fell well within the scope of the Directive 2000/78, the purpose of which was to promote equality in employment, and that discrimination based on sexual orientation formed part of the discriminations addressed by the Directive. The court noted that, since 2004, according to German legislation, life partnership was comparable to marriage with regard to the widow or widower's pension. Therefore, in a decision that was to stand as a significant precedent, the ECJ held that, under Articles 1 and 2 of Directive 2000/78, the regulations constituted direct discrimination based on sexual orientation. This was followed shortly afterwards by the not dissimilar *Römer* case,[324] which also concerned the claim of a former employee in a long-term registered same-sex partnership to benefit equally from a pension scheme on the same basis as a married employee. However, the relevant regulations made a clear distinction between the pension entitlements of married and unmarried couples and civil partnerships were intended to be included within the latter category. The ECJ noted that the judgements in *Mangold*[325] and *Kücükdeveci*[326] definitely confirmed that Directive 2000/78 "does not lay down the principle of equal treatment in the field of employment and occupation",[327] that principle was to be found instead in international law. Adopting the same "comparable situation" approach it had applied in *Maruko*, the ECJ found that the situations of couples in registered partnerships and marriage were comparable and, therefore, that the effect of the regulations was to inflict direct discrimination on the claimant on the basis of his sexual orientation. Then came *Frédéric Hay v. Crédit Agricole Mutuel de Charente-Maritime et des Deux-Sévres*,[328] when the ECJ considered provisions in a collective agreement that allowed employees to claim particular benefits on the occasion of a marriage, but not on the occasion of the conclusion of a form of civil partnership. Given the absence, at the relevant time, of any legal possibility of same-sex marriage, the Court found that the provisions constituted direct discrimination based on sexual orientation

323 *Maruko v. Versorgungsanstalt der deutschen Buhnen*, C-267/06 (2007).

324 *Jürgen Römer v. Freie und Hansestadt Hamburg*, C-147/08 (2011).

325 *Mangold v. Helm*, C-144/04 (upholding principle of non-discrimination in respect of age).

326 *Kücükdeveci v. Swedex GmbH & Co KG* C-555/07 (upholding general principle of law in all EU member States, against discrimination and in favour of equal treatment).

327 *Jürgen Römer*, op. cit., at para. 59.

328 Case C-267/12 (2013).

and were therefore prohibited by the 2000 Employment Equality Framework Directive (the Equality Directive). Most recently, in *MB v. Secretary of State for Work and Pensions*,[329] the ECJ in an important ruling held that the UK requirement for transgendered persons to be unmarried in order to qualify for a State pension at the retirement age of their current gender violated EU law (see Chapter 4).

As same-sex relationships gained a level of broad social acceptance, and the persuasive rationale of the ECJ rulings gained traction, the ECtHR took the view that this had a correspondingly narrowing effect on the margin of appreciation available to States as regards their interpretation of "family life" in relation to benefits entitlement. The fact, however, that a same-sex couple living together in partnership satisfied the definition of "family life" and therefore qualified for the protection of Article 8 but did not necessarily confer an entitlement to ancillary statutory family benefits was demonstrated in *M.W. v. UK*[330] and in *Courten v. UK*[331] (see Chapter 4). In *P.B. and J.S. v. Austria*,[332] however, the ECtHR found that the same-sex couple, living together in a partnership, fell within the notion of "family life" protected by Article 8. The issue then was whether the benefits from a specific insurance cover extended to a cohabiting partner during a period when the governing legislation provided that only a close relative of the insured person or a cohabitee of the opposite sex qualified as dependants. As the State had provided no justification for the difference in the treatment of the applicants on the one hand and cohabitees of the opposite sex on the other, it had only a narrow margin of appreciation as regards different treatment based on sex or sexual orientation and was required to demonstrate that such a difference in treatment was necessary in order to realise a legitimate aim. In the absence of justification, the court held that during that period, before a legislative amendment altered the entitlement criteria, there had been a violation of Article 14 in conjunction with Article 8 of the ECHR. In *Hallier and Others v. France*,[333] the ECtHR considered and rejected a claim for paternity leave from the same-sex partner of a woman who had given birth; a claim made on the basis that, being in a *de facto* parenting role comparable to that of a biological father within a heterosexual couple, she should be equally entitled to that benefit. The court took the view that the claimant's position was not comparable: the mother's partner in a heterosexual relationship would not be eligible for paternity leave if he was not the child's father; besides which the mother's partner was now entitled to carer's leave under the same conditions as paternity leave if he or she was not the child's biological parent.

329 Case C-451/16 (2018).
330 Application No. 11313/02 (2009).
331 Application No. 4479/06 (2008).
332 Application No. 18984/02 (2010).
333 Application No. 46386/10 (2017).

Conscientious objection of service providers

(ECHR, Article 9(1))

Public benefit services – e.g. in schools, health and social care facilities – are required to be delivered in a manner wholly compliant with all human rights, equality and non-discrimination legislation, whether delivered by a government agency or by a body funded and contracted to do so on behalf of government. This leaves little room for public officials in such facilities to claim exemption, on grounds of conscientious objection, from any service delivery requirements of their post. However, some protection for matters of personal conscience can be found under Article 9(1) of the ECHR, as has been demonstrated in a refusal to work on registering homosexual civil unions[334] but, as the ECtHR warned in *R.R. v. Poland*,[335] Article 9 does not protect all acts motivated by religion or belief.

SOGI, public service and conscientious objection

The ECtHR ruling in *Eweida*[336] was a milestone judgement for a number of reasons, including its significance for the evolving conscientious objection jurisprudence. The court then found that Article 9(1) of the ECHR provided protection for matters of personal conscience. Nevertheless, in the cases of both *Ladele* and *McFarlane*, the ECtHR upheld the dismissal of UK public officials who had refused to provide public services as required by the terms of their employment. Conscientious objection to the sexual orientation of legitimate service users – however sincere and even if based on religious belief – could not justify such refusal and the resulting dismissal of the service providers could not be construed as religious discrimination. This approach has since been adopted by the European Committee of Social Rights when, in *FAFCE v. Sweden*,[337] it rejected a claim that women could be denied access to legal abortion services by health professionals, on the grounds of the latter's conscientious objection to the provision of such services, stressing that the EU Charter of Fundamental Rights "does not impose on States a positive obligation to provide a right to conscientious objection for health care workers".

Conclusion

This key chapter examined how and to what extent international human rights law currently intersects with SOGI-related issues. It did so by working through different levels of generality in a process which provides an introduction to

334 *Eweida and Others v. the United Kingdom*, Application Nos. 48420/10, 59842/10, 51671/10 and 36516/10 (2013).
335 Application No. 27617/04 (2011).
336 *Eweida and Others v. United Kingdom*, Applications Nos. 48420/10, 59842/10, 51671/10 and 36516/10 (2013).
337 Complaint No. 99/2013 (2015).

governing principles, the law and the related legal issues. In particular, it trawled through the caselaw generated by the ECtHR and other international bodies and identified leading precedents. Drawing from the material in this and the preceding chapters, it assembled a thematic structure for the comparative analysis undertaken in the following jurisdiction-specific chapters.

Part II

Law, policy and practice

4 England and Wales

Introduction

During the early years of this century, estimates of the size of the UK trans community ranged from 65,000[1] to 300,000.[2] While that uncertainty has now extended to the appropriate use of terminology,[3] the number of those self-identifying as non-binary in their sexuality or "likely to be gender incongruent to some degree" has risen to a possible 650,000.[4]

This chapter begins by setting out the current international and domestic legislative framework, noting the ratification of relevant international treaties, conventions or protocols, and considers any relevant observations made in international human rights reports. It then examines the functioning of contemporary domestic law in relation to sexual orientation and gender identity (SOGI). Firstly, it considers the intersect between core human rights and SOGI, giving particular attention to implications arising for the right to freedom of expression. Secondly, and most importantly, it focuses on same-sex relationships and human rights in a SOGI context where issues relating to gender reassignment, sexual identity and establishing family life are often critical for all concerned. Finally, the chapter systematically examines in turn a sequence of distinct themes relating to the interface between SOGI and equality and non-discrimination law (identified in the preceding chapter) as addressed in domestic caselaw, assessing any significant trends and governing principles.

1 Johnson, K., Studying Transexual Identity: A Discursive Approach, in Haynes, F. and McKenna, T. (eds.), *Unseen Genders: Beyond the Binaries* (Eruptions), Peter Lang Press, New York, 2001.

2 Gender Identity Research and Education Society (GIRES), *Gender Dysphoria, Transsexualism and Transgenderism: Incidence, Prevalence and Growth in the UK and the Implications for the Commissioners and Providers of Healthcare*, 2008. See, further, at: www.gires.org.uk/assets/GIRES-Prevalence-Abstract-2.pdf.

3 The Women and Equalities Committee report *Transgender and Equality* (2016) suggests that the terms "gender reassignment" and "transsexual" in the Equality Act 2010 are outdated and misleading and recommends they be replaced by the term "trans". See further at: https://publications.parliament.uk/pa/cm201516/cmselect/cmwomeq/390/39002.htm.

4 Ibid., at p. 6.

While this chapter is entitled "England and Wales", to a very large extent the law outlined in the following pages may be taken as broadly representative of the three jurisdictions that comprise the UK. Where this is clearly not the case, as for example in relation to the law regarding LGBT rights in Northern Ireland, every effort is made to draw attention to that fact as appropriate in the text.

Legislative framework: international and domestic

Since becoming one of the first countries to ratify the UDHR, the UK has been a party to a range of international human rights treaties, conventions and protocols, some of which have been assimilated into domestic legislation to augment the Human Rights Act 1998, the Equality Act 2010 and other ancillary statutes and regulations.

International legislation

For present purposes, the most relevant international instruments binding on the UK are the European Convention on Human Rights (ECHR), ratified in 1951; the International Covenant on Civil and Political Rights (ICCPR), ratified in 1976 with certain reservations and declarations, including the non-adoption of Optional Protocol 1;[5] the International Covenant on Economic, Social and Cultural Rights (ICESCR), ratified in 1976; the International Convention on the Elimination of Race Discrimination (ICERD), ratified in 1969; the International Convention on the Rights of the Child (ICRC), ratified in 1991; the UN Convention on the Elimination of all forms of Discrimination Against Women (CEDAW), ratified in 1986 with its Optional Protocol; and the Convention on the Rights of Persons With Disabilities (CRPD), ratified in 2009. The Yogyakarta Principles, though not part of the legal framework, are nonetheless very influential (see Chapter 3).

Domestic legislation

UK human rights law derives from the governing principles outlined in the United Nations Declaration of Human Rights, as enlarged in the European Convention, the International Covenant and the Charter of Fundamental Rights of the European Union, and now given effect domestically mainly through the Human Rights Act 1998 and the Equality Act 2010.

The Marriage (Same-Sex Couples) Act 2013

The Women and Equalities Committee has drawn attention to the fact that "trans people feel strongly that the provision on spousal consent under the Marriage

5 See Moon, G., Complying With Its International Human Rights Obligations: The United Kingdom and Article 26 of the International Covenant on Civil and Political Rights, *European Human Rights Law Review*, 8(3), pp. 283–307.

(Same-Sex Couples) Act 2013 gives spouses an effective 'veto' on gender recognition".[6]

The Equality Act 2010

Replacing the 2006 Act (which introduced the "gender equality duty"), this prohibits unfair treatment in the UK on any of nine "protected characteristics", which include gender reassignment, sex, sexual orientation, marriage and civil partnership, whether occurring in the workplace, when providing goods, facilities and services, when exercising public functions, in the disposal and management of premises or in education and by associations (such as private clubs); and whether the discrimination is direct, indirect or takes the form of harassment or victimisation. Schedule 9, paragraph 2 (giving effect to Article 4 of the previously-mentioned Framework Equality Directive 2000/78/EC) specifically extends the protection to include "sexual orientation" and "gender identity", among other matters.

The Gender Recognition Act 2004

This crucially important legislation enables trans persons to acquire legal recognition for their changed gender; in particular, it permits the re-issue of a birth certificate to officially register their new gender identity. Under the Act, application may be made to the Gender Recognition Panel and, if successful, the applicant will be issued with a Gender Recognition Certificate permitting the holder to be recognised for all legal purposes (including marriage) as belonging to their acquired gender. While the criteria for obtaining such a certificate does not include evidence of surgical intervention, the first legislation in the world to omit that criterion, it does require the applicant to be at least 18 years of age; psychiatric assessments confirming a diagnosis of gender dysphoria;[7] and proof of living for two years in the gender in which an applicant wishes to be officially recognised.

The Criminal Justice Act 2003

Since 2012, Schedule 21 of this Act has allowed enhanced sentences to be applied to offences that are aggravated by hostility on the grounds of transgender identity. This equates punishment for such offences with offences aggravated by hostility on grounds of disability or sexual orientation.

The Human Rights Act 1998

Section 1 specifically incorporates the rights and fundamental freedoms set out in Articles 2 to 12 and 14 of the ECHR; Articles 1 to 3 of the First Protocol;

6 Ibid.

7 It is noteworthy that the World Health Organisation no longer classifies gender dysphoria as a mental health illness.

and Article 1 of the Thirteenth Protocol; as read with Articles 16 to 18 of the Convention (see Chapter 3). Section 6 declares that it is unlawful for any public authority – including a court or regulatory body – to act in a way incompatible with a Convention right.

The Sex Discrimination Act 1975

Amended by the Sex Discrimination (Amendment of Legislation) Regulations 2008 to expand protection on the grounds of gender reassignment to cover goods, facilities, services and premises.

Other legislation

The Protection From Harassment Act 1997 is important. So also is the Public Order Act 1986, as amended by the Equality Act 2006, which created new offences: s.29B(i) provided that "a person who uses threatening words or behaviour, or displays any written material which is threatening, is guilty of an offence"; subject to the caveat in s.29J that this does not prohibit or restrict discussion, criticism or expressions of antipathy, dislike, ridicule, insult or abuse. The Human Fertilisation and Embryology Act 2008 and the Adoption and Children Act 2002 are of increasing importance for the many same-sex couples who wish to establish families, while the Data Protection Act 1988 offers a degree of protection for confidential information. The Sex Discrimination (Gender Reassignment) Regulations 1999, the Employment Equality (Religion or Belief) Regulations 2003 and the Equality Act (Sexual Orientation) Regulations 2007 are also very relevant. The Gender Identity (Protected Characteristic) Bill 2016–17, now in abeyance, may have a future relevance.

Framework of courts and regulatory bodies

Direct responsibility for giving effect to human rights and SOGI-related legislation lies with the domestic UK framework of courts and regulatory bodies, but in making their determinations, they are required to take into account any relevant rulings of certain European courts.

International courts and regulatory bodies

EU membership brought with it a requirement that the UK accept the superior jurisdiction of the CJEU; it had earlier accepted that of the ECtHR. After UK membership is withdrawn, the direct jurisdiction of the former will be curtailed while that of the latter will continue; the jurisdiction of certain other international committees will also continue.

The European Court of Human Rights (ECtHR)

The ECtHR hears complaints alleging violations of rights enshrined in the Convention and its protocols. In making its determinations, the court is guided by principles such as "proportionality" and "compatibility with democracy".[8] Its decisions are reached in the light of "a margin of appreciation" which permits States a degree of latitude in their interpretation of human rights obligations[9] (see Chapter 3).

The Court of Justice of the European Union (CJEU or ECJ)

Consisting of three distinct courts (Court of Justice, General Court and Civil Service Tribunal), the CJEU functions as the central court for the EU. It has jurisdiction over the actions of EU institutions, the compliance duties of member States in respect of EU laws and the interpretation of those laws at the request of national courts and tribunals (see Chapter 3).

The Human Rights Committee (HRC)

This body, established by the ICCPR, monitors progress made on national implementation of Covenant provisions. This is achieved mainly through analysis of and commentary on reports required to be submitted by each member State usually at four-year intervals (see Chapter 3).

Domestic courts and regulatory bodies

The Equality and Human Rights Commission (EHRC)

Established by the Equality Act 2006, this body acts as the regulator in respect of issues – including those relating to sexual orientation and gender identity – which now arise under the Equality Act 2010. It has issued important reports, such as *Human Rights and Gender Identity* in 2009.[10]

The Employment Appeal Tribunal (EAT)

This body determines allegations of rights abuse in the workplace as referred to it on appeal from the Employment Tribunal.

The Employment Tribunal

This Tribunal, the decisions of which have effect throughout Great Britain – excepting Northern Ireland – hears allegations of discriminatory practices in the workplace.

8 See *Refah Partisi v. Turkey* (2003) 37 EHRR 1 [2003] ECHR 87, when the ECtHR ruled that Shari'a law is not consistent with democracy and therefore the Turkish government was justified in banning a political party seeking to introduce such law.

9 See, for example, *Lithgow v. United Kingdom* (1986) 8 EHRR 329, *Fredin v. Sweden* (1991) 13 EHRR 784, *Abdulaziz, Cabales and Balkandali v. United Kingdom* (1985) 7 EHRR 471.

10 CommDH/IssuePaper(2009)2, at: www.gires.org.uk/wp-content/uploads/2014/09/CommDHIssuePaper20092.pdf.

International reports on human rights in the UK

In September 2017, the HRC issued its third Universal Periodic Review report on UK progress in respect of its human rights record.[11] This contained 227 recommendations for improvements, many of which addressed perceived shortcomings in prosecutions for hate crime and hate speech.

SOGI and related core human rights

For the LGBT community, as for all other socially marginalised groups, it is the core human rights – justice, the freedoms of expression, association and religion – that are fundamentally important.

Right of access to justice

As stated in Articles 6 and 13 of the ECHR and incorporated into Schedule 1 of the 1998 Act, this right has proven to be crucially important for marginalised individuals and groups seeking recognition for their singular needs and redress for injustice.

Access to relevant information

The HR Committee has expressed concern that homosexual and transsexual young people in the UK "do not have access to the appropriate information, support and necessary protection to enable them to live their sexual orientation".[12] Indeed, for that reason, when the Committee considered s.28 of the United Kingdom Local Government Act, it urged the State to repeal it.[13]

In *Rees v. the United Kingdom*,[14] the ECtHR held that the UK had been acting within its margin of appreciation when it failed to provide a means to adjust its birth registration system to record a trans person's change of gender. This was followed by the landmark cases of *Christine Goodwin v. the United Kingdom*[15] and *I. v. the United Kingdom*,[16] which concerned the appeals of two trans women against the refusal of United Kingdom authorities to change their legal identities and papers to match their post-operative genders. The ECtHR then found – contrary to its earlier decision in *Rees v. the United Kingdom*[17] – that the rights of the

11 See, further, at: https://documents-dds-ny.un.org/doc/UNDOC/GEN/G17/192/15/PDF/G1719215.pdf?OpenElement.

12 See *General Comment No. 20 – Non-Discrimination in Economic, Social and Cultural Rights*, UN Doc E/C.12/GC/20 (2009); and Concluding Observations of the Committee on the Rights of the Child regarding the United Kingdom, 9 October 2002, CRC/C/15/Add.188 at para. 43.

13 Ibid., at para. 44(d).

14 Application No. 9532/81, (1987).

15 (2002) 35 EHRR 18.

16 36 EHRR 53.

17 Application No. 9532/81 (1986).

applicants under Articles 8 and 12 of the ECHR had been breached by government failure to offer a means to change its birth registration system to provide an official record of their change of gender. As it noted in *Goodwin*:

> The Court considers that society may be reasonably expected to tolerate a certain inconvenience to enable individuals to live in dignity and worth in accordance with the sexual identity chosen by them at great personal cost.[18]

ECtHR criticism in the later cases focused on the inability of the UK government to afford full legal recognition for the trans person's preferred gender when it had already authorised and financed their gender reassignment treatment. It found that the UK government was obliged to provide a process giving legal recognition to the change of gender of post-operative transgender persons but had failed to do so.

The existence of an in-built information systems failure, as Claire McCann has pointed out,[19] stems in part from s.9 of the Gender Recognition Act 2004: while s.9(1) ensures that, for a person who has been granted a Gender Recognition Certificate, their gender becomes "for all purposes" the acquired gender; s.9(2) provides that this does not affect things done, or events occurring, before the GRC was issued. The difficulties caused by this retrospective caveat were evident in *JK v. Registrar General for England and Wales*,[20] which concluded that a trans woman could not change her child's birth certificate so that she was no longer shown as the "father", and in *C v. Secretary of State for Work and Pensions*,[21] which held that the Department for Work and Pensions was not obliged to change its IT systems so as to mask information which revealed a benefit claimant's trans status.

An effective remedy

The trans process presents a fundamental difficulty. In this jurisdiction, implementing a choice to change gender identity requires satisfying legal criteria that includes a minimum age limit; acquiring supportive endorsement from two doctors; accepting a mental health designation; and submitting to a treatment programme, all of which can take from 3–5 years to complete. This contrasts sharply with the less bureaucratic, and in some instances self-identifying, processes legally available in countries such as Ireland. Effectiveness may also be an issue in relation to the arguably outdated 2004 Act: s.1(i), for example, confines application of the Act to "person[s] of either gender who [are] aged at least 18" thereby, unlike countries such as Ireland, denying access to all children whether "*Gillick*

18 Op. cit., at para. 91.
19 See McCann, C., Gender Recognition and Trans Equality, in *Counsel: Law in Practice* (August 2018), at: www.counselmagazine.co.uk/articles/gender-recognition-and-trans-equality.
20 [2015] EWHC 990 (Admin).
21 [2017] UKSC 72.

competent"[22] or not; moreover, although s.22 offers protection for trans people against "outing", this has yet to lead to any prosecutions.

Asylum seekers/illegal immigrants

In 2017, it was estimated that approximately 6% of persons seeking international protection in the UK were doing so for reasons relating to their sexual orientation; no data was available for those doing so for reasons of gender identity.[23] The history of UK management of its legal obligations to "illegal immigrants" with SOGI-related vulnerabilities is very recent and arguably largely defensive, as may be indicated by the relatively low level of 25% of successful asylum applications based on such vulnerabilities.[24] The Vine Report contributed significantly to an appreciation of the issues in this field.[25]

There is a scarcity of relevant caselaw, but in 2010 the UKSC held that it would violate Article 3 of the ECHR if individuals were to be deported to a State in which they would have to hide their sexual identity and that such individuals cannot be expected to conceal it in order to avoid that outcome.[26] In 2015, it held that non-deportation could be justified where there was, in general, a serious risk of persecution on grounds of sexual orientation without that persecution affecting any particular percentage of the population.[27]

The absence of any official record of the number, variety and outcome of applications based on gender identity or expression would in itself justify the conclusion reached in the 2018 Asylum Policy Briefing paper that "the UK does not yet offer adequate protection to refugees who are at risk of persecution relating to sexual or gender identity or expression".[28]

Right to freedom of expression

This right, declared in Article 10 of the ECHR and incorporated into Schedule 1 of the 1998 Act, has a versatile application in a SOGI context, as illustrated by the "gay cakes" controversy (see further below).

22 See *Gillick v. West Norfolk and Wisbech AHA* [1986] AC 112, which established that a child aged 16 or less would have the legal competence to consent to medical examination and treatment if of sufficient maturity and intelligence to understand its nature and implications.

23 See Home Office, Asylum Claims on the Basis of Sexual Orientation, November 2017, at: https://assets.publishing.service.gov.uk/government/uploads/system/uploads/attachment_data/file/663468/asylum-claims-basis-sexual-orientation.pdf.

24 Ibid.

25 Independent Chief Inspector of Borders and Immigration, *Inspection Report on Asylum Claims on the Grounds of Sexual Orientation* (October 2014), at: www.gov.uk/government/publications/inspection-report-on-asylum-claims-on-the-grounds-of-sexual-orientation-october-2014.

26 *HJ (Iran) and HT (Cameroon) v. Secretary of State for the Home Department* (2010) UKSC 31. See also *M.E. v. Sweden* Application No 71398/12, Merits and Just Satisfaction, 26 June 2014, on whether a short period of discretion can reasonably be expected.

27 *R (Jamar Brown (Jamaica)) v. Secretary of State for the Home Department* (2015) UKSC 8.

28 Asylum Aid, *Policy Briefing* (February 2018), at: www.asylumaid.org.uk/wp-content/uploads/2018/02/Policy-briefing-Sexual-Borders-Feb-2018.pdf.

The moral majority

In giving effect to the s.28 amendment of the Local Government Act 1986, from 1988 to 2003, the government was enforcing a policy to suppress LGBT freedom of expression on behalf of what it then construed to be the moral majority in contemporary society. This initiative specifically prohibited local authorities from "promot[ing] homosexuality or publish[ing] material with the intention of promoting homosexuality" and directly impacted upon the national education system, which was almost exclusively controlled by local authorities.

More recently, the cases of *Dudgeon v. United Kingdom*[29] and *Gareth Lee v. Ashers Baking Company Ltd, McArthur and McArthur*,[30] although both rooted in the singular religious/cultural context of Northern Ireland (see next), are nonetheless broadly representative of the difficulties faced by societies largely integrated around traditional religious values when confronted by SOGI issues. They also illustrate the importance and difficulties of the principle, which states that where a legislative restriction is ostensibly neutral but has a disproportionate effect on a minority, then a particularly heavy onus rests on the State to justify that legislative measure.

It was the ECtHR ruling in *Dudgeon* which first signalled the invalidity of an argument that sought to justify resisting legal change because many viewed it as offensive to their religion and culture: the court found that to do so would be to condone discrimination.[31] This *ratio decidendi* is clearly equally applicable to other religious cultural traditions which can adversely impact upon the LGBT community. Policies for promoting pluralism and diversity in this jurisdiction have yet to find ways of addressing the dark side of minority cultures (fgm etc.) which deny the rights enjoyed by the liberal majority – particularly in areas such as marriage, family life and education.

Harm to others

The caveat to the right of freedom of expression – that its exercise should not breach the rights of others – is one that often brings issues before the courts.

It is impermissible, for example, to cause alarm or distress, as when a Christian preacher displayed signs reading "Stop Immorality", "Stop Homosexuality" and "Stop Lesbianism".[32] So, in *Apelogun-Gabriels v. London Borough of Lambeth*,[33] when an employee complained of religious discrimination because he had been dismissed for distributing "homophobic material" to co-workers during prayer meetings, the tribunal confirmed that the material was offensive and had caused harm to colleagues, and held that any indirect discrimination involved in his dismissal was justified. Similarly, in *Haye v. London Borough of Lewisham*,[34] a

29 Application No. 7525/76 (1981).
30 Neutral Citation No. [2015] NICty 2. Also, see, a US decision to the same effect (Chapter 7).
31 See also *Smith and Grady v. United Kingdom*, 29 E.H.R.R. 493 (1999).
32 *Hammond v. DPP* [2004] EWHC 69 (Admin).
33 (2006), ET Case No. 2301976/05.
34 (2010), ET Case No. 2301852/09.

Christian administrative assistant was held to have been justifiably dismissed after posting derogatory views about LGBT practices on the Lesbian and Gay Christian Movement's website. However, the law does allow for a degree of give and take, as Underhill J explained in *Dhaliwal*,[35] because

> dignity is not necessarily violated by things said or done which are trivial or transitory, particularly if it should have been clear that any offence was unintended . . . it is also important not to encourage a culture of hypersensitivity or the imposition of legal liability in respect of every unfortunate phrase.[36]

Nonetheless, a sensible person does not express negative views towards LGBT people in conversation with colleagues.[37]

Rights to freedom of association and assembly

The right of individuals to meet, form associations or to leave them, is long established and currently greatly valued by the LGBT community. It was declared in Article 11 of the ECHR and subsequently incorporated into Schedule 1 of the 1998 Act.

Constraints

Controversy over SOGI issues has led to considerable concern as to whether equality and non-discrimination provisions will legally permit the continuance of gender-specific organisations and facilities. This has tended to focus on female safety if trans persons are allowed to access organisations such as Girl Guides, Women's Refuges, Rape Crisis Centres, female swimming pools etc.[38]

Right to freedom of religion

Article 9 of the ECHR, as incorporated into Schedule 1 of the 1998 Act, places a duty of neutrality and impartiality on domestic judicial and regulatory bodies when engaged in religious matters,[39] while the Equality Act 2010 provides protection for those exercising their rights in terms of freedom of sexual orientation

35 *Richmond Pharmaceuticals v. Dhaliwal* [2009] ICR 724; though one cannot help wondering if the same view would have been taken had the derisory expletive referred to Muhammad and been directed towards a Muslim employee. See also *Land Registry v. Grant* [2011] ICR 1390.

36 *Dhaliwal*, op. cit., at para. 22.

37 *Mbuyi v. Newpark Childcare* [2015] Case Number: 3300656/2014 and *Wasteney v. East London NHS Foundation Trust* [2015] Case Number 3200658/2014.

38 See further at: https://inews.co.uk/news/hampstead-heath-why-people-are-fighting-over-the-ladies-pond-in-hampstead-heath/.

39 See *Re G (Children)* [2012] EWCA Civ 1233, at paras. 35–38.

and gender reassignment. Where a conflict arises between these two sets of rights on a SOGI issue, it must be resolved on the basis of the outcome – after weighing the respective rights of the parties – most compatible with the requirements of democracy in contemporary UK society.

SOGI and religion

Re M (Children)[40] (see next) is interesting not least because it illustrates the conflicts that can arise at the intersect of traditional religious beliefs – whether Christian, Jewish or Islamic – and matters affecting the contemporary LGBT community. In this instance, the issues concerned standards of parenting and the beliefs of Charedi Jews: a number of expert witnesses testified that traditional doctrines prevented that religious community from accepting the change in social mores represented by the LGBT community. This case is also instructive because the Court of Appeal took a firm view of where the law stood on a conflict between religious beliefs and the protected characteristics – including sexual orientation and gender reassignment – designated as such in the Equality Act. As Sir James Munby P. warned:

> It is well established on authority that discrimination which is motivated by a religious belief (however sincerely held and even if the discrimination is mandated by that religious belief) does not make discrimination under the Equality Act lawful.[41]

Religious organisations and the religious exemption

The Equality Act 2010, para 2 of Schedule 9, permits a body representing an "organised religion" to impose explicitly discriminatory restrictions on employment opportunities in relation to gender, marital status and sexual orientation[42] (see next). Schedule 23, para 2 of the same Act, allows "organisations relating to a religion or belief" – but without a commercial sole or main purpose to discriminate on the grounds of religion or belief or sexual orientation in the way they operate. Their purpose must be to practise, advance or teach, enable adherents to receive a benefit or engage in an activity "within the framework of that religion or belief"; or to foster or maintain good relations between persons of different

40 [2017] EWCA Civ 2164.

41 *Re M (Children)*, op. cit., at para. 95, citing *Regina I v. Governing Body of JFS and another (United Synagogue and others intervening)* [2009] UKSC 15 [2010] 2 AC 728 and *Regina (Williamson and Others) v. Secretary of State for Education and Employment* [2005] UKHL 15 [2005] 2 AC 246.

42 See the Equality Act 2010, Sched. 9. Also see the School Standards Framework Act 1998, s.60, which provides that foundation or voluntary schools with a religious character can give preference in employment, remuneration and promotion to teachers whose beliefs are in accordance with the tenets of that religion.

religions or beliefs. Such organisations may exercise religious discrimination when determining membership of the organisation, participation in its activities, use of its premises or "the provision of goods, facilities or services in the course of activities undertaken by the organisation".

In addition, the sexual orientation provisions of the Equality Act 2010 allow a religious organisation to restrict provision of a service to persons of one sex or to separate services for persons of each sex – but only if this is necessary to comply with the doctrines of the religion, or be for the purpose of avoiding conflict with the strongly held religious convictions of a significant number of the religion's followers.[43] An organisation cannot lawfully discriminate in the provision of goods and services on the grounds of sexual orientation, where such provision is undertaken on behalf of a public body. Further religious exemption is provided by the Marriage (Same-Sex Couples) Act 2013, accompanied by amendments to the Equalities Act 2010, which has relieved the Church of England and the Church of Wales of any duty to conduct gay marriages.

SOGI: personal relationships and human rights

Some 60 years ago the Wolfenden report[44] articulated the central importance of personal relationships in a SOGI context when it referred to such relationships as being part of the "realm of private morality and immorality which is, in brief and crude terms, not the law's business".

Right to an identity

Though not directly expressed as such, this is an implied right within Articles 6 and 8 of the ECHR as incorporated within Schedule 1 of the 1998 Act.

Trans recognition in law

The lack of a means to gain such recognition was the central issue in *Gaskin v. the United Kingdom*,[45] as in the similar case of *Sheffield and Horsham v. the United Kingdom*.[46] In both, the ECtHR found that the UK was remiss for not being more proactive in its response to the need of trans persons to register their change in gender identity. The issue was not that the UK had abstained from acting to the detriment of the applicants but rather that it had failed to take positive steps to modify a system which the applicants had rightly claimed was prejudicial to their interests. Admonishing the UK government, the ECtHR warned that

43 Equality Act 2010, Sched. 23, S. 2(7) and s.2(9).

44 Report of the Departmental Committee on Homosexual Offences and Prostitution, HMSO, 1957.

45 (1989) 12 EHRR 36.

46 (1999) 27 EHRR 163.

State parties had a duty to act to enable individuals to access information about their origins because "everyone should be able to establish details of their identity as individual human beings".[47]

Currently, while acquiring a Gender Recognition Certificate does not require evidence of surgical intervention, it does necessitate submitting to lengthy medical procedures. This process, as outlined earlier, has been described as bureaucratic, expensive and humiliating,[48] and the Act has attracted criticism because "its medicalised approach pathologises trans identities and runs contrary to the dignity and personal autonomy of applicants".[49] In 2017, the government announced its intention to launch a public consultation on possible reforms.

Non-binary gender identity

In January 2016, the Women and Equalities Committee called for non-binary people to be protected from discrimination under the Equality Act, for the X gender marker to be added to passports, and for a wholesale review into the needs of non-binary people.[50] In June 2018, Baker J in the High Court rejected claims that the current requirement to enter "male" or "female" on a passport breached the ECHR, a decision that is being appealed.

Right to respect for private and family life

As stated in Article 8 of the ECHR and incorporated into the Schedule 1 of the 1998 Act, this right protects personal dignity and autonomy, privacy, family life, home and communications. The ECtHR has warned that "serious interference with private life can arise where the state of domestic law conflicts with an important aspect of personal identity".[51] Any legal constraint must be both necessary and proportionate and for the purpose of ensuring public safety or the country's economic well-being; preventing disorder or crime; protecting health or morals; protecting other people's rights and freedoms; or for reasons of national security.

Sexual orientation, identity and private life

In England, the de-criminalisation of consensual private sexual relations between those of the same sex occurred in 1968, although this remained illegal in Scotland until 1980 and in Northern Ireland until 1982. Not until the ECtHR ruling in *Dudgeon* did domestic law begin the switch from prosecuting to protecting same-sex relationships.

47 *Gaskin*, op. cit.
48 2016 report at para. 33.
49 The Women and Equalities Committee report *Transgender and Equality* (2016), op. cit., at p. 3.
50 Ibid.
51 *Goodwin*, op. cit., at para. 77.

As a consequence of the Wolfenden report,[52] legislation was introduced in 1967 to de-criminalise homosexual conduct. The fact that such conduct remained criminal in Northern Ireland, under s.11 of the Criminal Law Amendment Act 1885, led to *Dudgeon v. the United Kingdom*[53] and resulted in the landmark ECtHR ruling which established that sexual conduct, including homosexuality, was "an essentially private manifestation of the human personality" and State interference in it could only be justified by a pressing social need.

Although *Dudgeon* established an important precedent, the ripple effects of which contributed to changes in the corresponding laws of Ireland[54] and Cyprus,[55] it did little to more broadly ameliorate the effect of the State on the lives of other non-traditional sexual relationships. The difficulties and the extent of intrusion into their private lives were illustrated in cases such as *Cossey v. the United Kingdom*,[56] which concerned a post-operative (mtf) trans who alleged violations of Articles 8 and 12 of the ECHR on the grounds that under English law she could not claim full recognition of her changed status and, in particular, was unable to enter into a valid marriage with a man. In fact, she had already undergone a heterosexual marriage ceremony in a synagogue and, following the breakdown in that relationship, then succeeded in obtaining a *decree nisi* on the only grounds available viz. that the marriage was void due to the parties not being respectively male and female. As the court noted, she was then faced with the predicament that "she could not marry at all: as a woman, she could not realistically marry another woman and English law prevented her from marrying a man".[57] Moreover, the courts were satisfied that such circumstances did not constitute a violation of her right to marry and to found a family as guaranteed under Article 12 of the ECHR. Respect for the traditional concept of marriage provided "sufficient reason for the continued adoption of biological criteria for determining a person's sex for the purposes of marriage".[58]

Not until the end of the twentieth century did the ECtHR rule, in *Sutherland v. United Kingdom*,[59] that the fixing of the minimum age for lawful homosexual activities at 18 rather than 16 violated the applicant's right to respect for private life under Article 8 of the ECHR. As a consequence, the Sexual Offences (Amendment) Act 2000 was introduced to lower the age of such consent to 16.

52 The Home Office, 'Report of the Departmental Committee on Homosexual Offences and Prostitution' (the Wolfenden report), 1957 (Parliamentary Archives, HL/PO/JO/10/11/579/1527).
53 Application No. 7525/76 [1981] 4 EHRR 149 [1981] ECHR 5.
54 *Norris v. Ireland*, Application No. 10581/83 (1988).
55 *Modinos v. Cyprus*, 16 EHRR 485 (1993).
56 Application No. 10843/84 (1990).
57 Op. cit., at para. 44.
58 Op. cit., at para. 46.
59 Application No. 25186/94 (1997).

Family life

UK law has, in the main, long since adjusted to accommodate a definition of "family" which includes unmarried couples, non-marital children and more recently lesbian or homosexual relationships.[60]

Private life, gender reassignment and divorce

It took at least three decades of court cases before the right of trans persons to respect for their "private and family life", as guaranteed by Article 8 of the ECHR, was wholly recognised in the domestic law of this jurisdiction.

In *Corbett v. Corbett*,[61] the High Court determined that for the purpose of contracting a valid marriage, "sex" was to be determined by the congruency of chromosomal, gonadal and genital tests, and without regard to any operative intervention. The legal constraints that defended a traditional interpretation of sexuality and marriage also surfaced in the earlier *Cossey* case.[62] Noting that no significant scientific developments had occurred since its decision in *Rees v. the United Kingdom*,[63] in particular "that gender reassignment surgery does not result in the acquisition of all the biological characteristics of the other sex",[64] the court in *Cossey* saw no reason to depart from its ruling in *Rees* and so again found that Article 8 had not been breached. As noted earlier, not until *Christine Goodwin v. the United Kingdom*[65] and in *I. v. the United Kingdom*[66] did that approach change.

The requirement that a married person divorce as a pre-condition for undergoing gender reassignment was considered in *Parry v. The United Kingdom*,[67] when the ECtHR considered that this fell within the State's "margin of appreciation". Noting the invidiousness of legislation that placed a person in the position of having "to sacrifice either her gender or her marriage", the court commented that this constituted "a direct and invasive effect on the applicants' enjoyment of their right to respect for their private and family life",[68] but nonetheless found in favour of the UK. This unsatisfactory legal situation was subsequently reinforced by the Marriage (Same-Sex Couples) Act 2013, which requires both parties to agree to the status of a marriage being changed before one can legally change gender and acquire a Gender Recognition Certificate. If consent of the other spouse is withheld, the marriage must be dissolved by divorce or annulled before

60 See, for example, *Smith and Grady v. United Kingdom* (2000) 29 EHRR 548 and *Goodwin v. United Kingdom* (2002) 35 EHRR 447.
61 [1971] Probate Reports 83.
62 Op. cit.
63 Op. cit.
64 *Cossey*, op. cit., at para. 40.
65 (2002) 35 EHRR 18.
66 36 EHRR 53 (2002).
67 Application No. 42971/05 (2005).
68 Ibid., at para. 10.

a full GRC can be issued; arguably, this is discriminatory relative to heterosexual comparators and in effect this gives the other spouse a power of veto.

SOGI, parenting and "the best interests of the child" principle

The principle that the welfare of the child is of paramount importance in all matters affecting that child's upbringing is entrenched in domestic and international law. It came into play in *Re J (a minor)*[69] when a father alleged that his 7-year-old son was being induced to transgender by the mother. The parents had separated when the boy was a year old and he had since been permanently in his mother's care with visits to his father. The latter complained that the mother was "forcing" the child, who was assigned male gender at birth, to present as a girl. The High Court agreed. It found that the mother had, with professional support, caused the child significant emotional harm by insisting that he dress and behave as a girl; indeed, he was registered as such with the school and with the family doctor. He issued a care order requiring the child to live with his father and a warning that

> it is important that such children are listened to and their views afforded respect but, to my mind, they are ill served by premature labelling. What they require . . . is the opportunity to develop their identity in which ever way it evolves.

Although having already considered two cases concerning trans parents,[70] the Court of Appeal found the issues in *Re M (Children)*[71] particularly challenging due to the fundamentalist religious aspect. This case concerned an appeal against an order dismissing a petition from a father, who had transgendered to a woman, for direct contact with five children who lived with their mother, his former wife, but permitting limited and staged indirect contact.[72] The family were ultra-Orthodox Jews[73] and the petitioner had been shunned by the Jewish community, which led the judge at first instance to conclude that the likelihood of the children and their mother being marginalised or excluded by the ultra-Orthodox community was so real, and the consequences so great, that this one factor, despite its many disadvantages, must prevail over the many advantages of contact. Sir James Munby P, delivering the appeal judgement, disagreed. Noting that the practices of the Charedi Jewish community "involve discrimination and victimisation and where the community's focus is as much on itself and the adults

69 [2016] EWHC 2430 (Fam) [2016] All ER (D) 17.
70 *Re C* [2006] EWCA 1765 and *Re T* [2008] EWCA Civ 85.
71 [2017] EWCA Civ 2164.
72 Cited at first instance as *J v. B (Ultra-Orthodox Judaism: Transgender)* [2017] EWFC 4 [2017] WLR(D) 142.
73 See also *Re X* [2014] EWFC B230; [2015] EWFC B237 and [2016] EWFC B29.

as on concern for the children or child welfare", he regretted that "it is very unfortunate that the judge did not address head on the human rights issues and issues of discrimination which plainly arose".[74] He added, quoting the President in *Re G*, that "in matters of religion, as in all other aspects of a child's upbringing, the interests of the child are the paramount consideration".[75] This carefully considered decision is likely to stand as a benchmark for future judicial deliberations of child welfare in the context of parenting by trans persons.

Right to marriage and to found a family

"The voluntary union for life of one man and one woman to the exclusion of all others" had served as the definition of marriage in English law since at least Lord Penzance's pronouncement some 150 years ago.[76] More recently the Human Rights Act 1998, Article 12, guaranteed the right to marry and to found a family to men and women of marriageable age, while the 2010 and 2013 Acts have further extended this right to accommodate the LGBT community.

Legal recognition for same-sex relationships and the right to marry

Centuries of Church/State solidarity regarding the need to recognise the existence of same-sex relationships, solely for the purposes of the criminal prosecution of the parties involved, ended in England and Wales with the Sexual Offences Act 1967. A similar consensus on the legal definition of "spouse" terminated with the extension of the right to marry, under Article 12 of the 1998 Act, to same-sex couples who contract civil partnerships in accordance with the Gender Recognition Act 2004. Further, the Marriage (Same-Sex Couples) Act 2013, in giving effect to equality principles, ended the statutory monopoly of marriage by heterosexual couples and broadened yet further the legal interpretation of "family".

However, while the law facilitates entering a same-sex marriage, exiting is more problematic. The concept of "adultery", which provides evidence of irretrievable marriage breakdown and thus grounds for divorce in a heterosexual marital relationship,[77] does not transfer across to same-sex marriages.

Trans persons and marriage

According to recent advice issued by the General Register Office, the law and practice as regards this matter is quite straightforward. The Gender Recognition

74 *Re M (Children)*, op. cit., at paras. 77 and 80.

75 *Re G (Children) (Residence: Same Sex Partner)* [2006] UKHL 43, at para. 43.

76 *Hyde v. Hyde*, 1 P. & D. 130 (1868), per Penzance LJ.

77 See *Owens v. Owens* [2018] UKSC 41 (author thanks Frank Cranmer for bringing this case to his attention: note to author, 24 May 2019).

Act 2004 enables a trans person to marry in their acquired gender. A trans person may legally marry/enter into a civil partnership in their acquired gender, provided this has been formally recognised by the Gender Recognition Panel and a Gender Recognition Certificate issued; the latter is a legal requirement.[78]

Adoption, surrogacy and child care

Since 2002, same-sex couples in the UK have had the legal right to adopt, a right fully available to all members of the LGBT community who can otherwise satisfy eligibility and suitability criteria; it has been estimated that by 2018 one in eight of all adoptions were by same-sex couples.[79] The introduction of IVF treatment, now governed by the Human Fertilisation and Embryology Act 1990 (as amended in 2008), inaugurated an era of fertility research and treatment featuring "cloned embryos" and use of stem cells that has greatly assisted the many same-sex couples wishing to establish a "family life". Surrogacy, particularly an overseas surrogacy arrangement, is often legally consolidated by adoption. In that context, legal complications may arise where payments have been made to the birth mother as adoption law prohibits such payments, other than for reasonable expenses.

Right to cultural life

This jurisdiction has a pronounced Christian cultural heritage which may be perceived as overbearing by secularists and possibly as alienating by those of other religions and cultures.

Cultural context

In *Dudgeon v. United Kingdom*,[80] the ECtHR heard submissions that the prevailing religious culture in Northern Ireland was such that removing the criminal sanction on homosexuality "would be seriously damaging to the moral fabric of society". It was suggested that imposing such a change, resisted by the majority as offensive to their religion and culture, would constitute a form of religious discrimination. While pointedly taking into account the particular cultural and religious mores, the court was unable to find a "pressing social need" to make homosexuality a criminal offence and, applying the proportionality principle, considered that any such justification for retaining the law in force was outweighed by its detrimental effects.

The *Dudgeon* decision, representing as it does the basic civil right of a minority to demand equality of treatment and respect by the law and from their fellow citizens, stands as a benchmark for determining contemporary culture clashes on

78 See further at: www.whatdotheyknow.com/request/transgender_people_getting_marri_2.
79 See further at: www.newfamilysocial.org.uk.
80 Application No. 7525/76 (1981).

SOGI issues. In a reversal of roles, such clashes are now most likely to occur when the traditional patriarchal or misogynist practices of minority cultures breach the standards set by modern mainstream equality legislation.

SOGI: non-discrimination, affirmative action and equality

The Human Rights Act 1998 and the Equality Act 2010 provide the basic legislative framework for protecting the interests of the LGBT community. The prohibition on discrimination as stated in Article 14 of the ECHR and incorporated in Schedule 1 of the Human Rights Act 1998 has been extended to provide particular protection for the rights of trans persons by the Sex Discrimination (Gender Reassignment) Regulations 1999; the Gender Recognition Act 2004; and the Sex Discrimination (Amendment of Legislation) Regulation (2008). This protective safety net is supplemented by an affirmative action duty in the 2010 Act, but arguably the interplay between the provisions is too loose to adequately address contemporary SOGI issues.

Equality before the law: sexuality and gender discrimination

The legal recognition and protection broadly available to those in same-sex relationships have only recently and imperfectly been extended to trans persons. Acquiring official recognition for a change in gender identity has, for them, been a protracted issue and one in which the ECtHR initially endorsed the right of domestic authorities to withhold it.[81] As noted previously, this changed with the *Christine Goodwin* case,[82] when the ECtHR ruled that legal recognition of a new gender identity was justified by "the changing conditions within the respondent State and within Contracting States generally" and because of an "evolving convergence as to the standards to be achieved" in the context of official recognition of post-operative transsexual gender identity.[83] More recently, specific protection has resulted from the inclusion of "gender reassignment" as a separate protected characteristic under the Equality Act 2010, which has also brought partial protection in relation to the provision of goods, facilities and services, subject to the caveat that discrimination is permitted where it is a proportionate means to achieve a legitimate aim.

Sex discrimination and sexual orientation discrimination

Since the Employment Equality (Sexual Orientation) Regulations 2003[84] came into effect, sexual orientation discrimination has been a statutorily recognised

81 See *Rees v. United Kingdom* (1987) 9 EHRR 56; *Cossey v. United Kingdom* (1990) 13 EHRR 622; and *Sheffield and Horsham v. United Kingdom* (1999) 27 EHRR 163.

82 *Christine Goodwin v. United Kingdom*, Application No. 28957/95 (2002).

83 Ibid. at para. 74.

84 Giving effect to the Framework Equal Treatment Directive (2000/78/EC).

offence: "sexual orientation" being understood as an orientation towards persons of the same sex, persons of the opposite sex or persons of the same sex *and* persons of the opposite sex.

Under the Equality Act 2010, it became a protected characteristic which prohibits discrimination that is direct, due to a person's sexual orientation; indirect, due to a provision, criterion or practice that places a person of a certain sexual orientation at a disadvantage; amounts to harassment, caused by subjecting a person to harassment related to their sexual orientation; or amounts to victimisation by threatening or causing actual harm to a person because they have or intend to enforce their rights under the 2010 Act.

Gender identity and trans discrimination

In this jurisdiction, trans persons are protected from discrimination: in general by the provisions of the 1998 and 2010 Acts, reinforced by the ECHR; and more particularly by the Sex Discrimination (Gender Reassignment) Regulations 1999, the Gender Recognition Act 2004, the Equal Treatment Directive (2004/113/EC) and the Sex Discrimination (Amendment of Legislation) Regulations 2008. The landmark ECJ case of *P.v. S. and Cornwall County Council*[85] extended the protection of equality and non-discrimination to trans individuals (see Chapter 2). This ruling, requiring UK law to be broadened to comply with the Equal Treatment Directive, prevents discrimination in employment or vocational education in respect of any trans person intending to undergo, undergoing or who has undergone gender reassignment.

Since the Gender Recognition Act 2004 came into effect, trans persons have been able to acquire official documentary evidence – e.g. an amended birth certificate – of their changed gender identity. A notable feature of this Act – unlike comparable legislative provisions in many other countries – is that a record of a gender identity change is not conditional upon proof of completed surgical procedures or other treatment. Protection for those undergoing such a change was provided by the Equality Act 2010 which includes gender reassignment as a protected characteristic in Part 2.

The prohibition against gender reassignment discrimination in the 2010 Act applies in certain specified circumstances: the workplace; the use of public services; the use of businesses and other organisations that provide services and goods; use of transport; when joining a club or association; and when in contact with public bodies. It operates to offer protection at all stages of the transition process. However, it remains a moot point as to whether the existing procedure for accessing most forms of gender reassignment is itself discriminatory, and the failure, to date, to provide any official form of recognition for those who are non-binary in gender is arguably unfair.

85 Case C-13/94 [1996] IRLR 347. See, Opinion of the Advocate General, 14 December 1995, at paras. 8–13 and 24.

The Gender Identity (Protected Characteristic) Bill 2016–17 was intended "to make gender identity a protected characteristic under the Equality Act 2010 in place of gender reassignment and to make associated provision for transgender and other persons; and for connected purposes". This prospect disappeared with the Bill when the latter became a casualty of the election process.

Affirmative action

Introduced by the Equality Act 2010, s.158, affirmative action strengthens the public service equality duties by providing specific opportunities for intervention in circumstances that would otherwise constitute unlawful discrimination.[86] Such action is permitted if it is a proportionate means of addressing the disadvantages of a group sharing one or more of the protected characteristics[87] but is only lawful if the statutory criteria are met: it must be "reasonably thought" that one of the conditions applies, such as disadvantage or disproportionately low participation. Part 2 of the Act makes provision for the "advancement of equality", and s.149 requires public authorities, or private bodies carrying out public functions, when dealing with those the subject of a protected characteristic – including gender reassignment, sex and sexual orientation – to eliminate discrimination, harassment, victimisation and any other conduct that is prohibited by the Act; advance equality of opportunity between persons who share a relevant characteristic and persons who do not share it; and foster good relations between such persons.

LGBT issues and affirmative State action

Rees v. the United Kingdom,[88] which concerned the applicant's unsuccessful claim that government had failed in its obligation to officially recognise his new status following a sex change operation, provided an early opportunity for judicial consideration of the State requirement to be proactive in addressing the impact of a neutral law that adversely affected a minority.

Right to equality and non-discrimination: health

While it is important to note at the outset that this jurisdiction provides access to gender reassignment treatment as a public service, this is subject to the criticism that "trans people encounter significant problems in using general NHS services, due to the attitude of some clinicians and other staff who lack knowledge and understanding – and in some cases are prejudiced".[89]

86 See also the Employment Equality Directive 2000/78/EC, Art 2(2)(b).
87 The "protected characteristics" being age, disability, gender reassignment, marriage and civil partnership, pregnancy and maternity, race, religion or belief, sex and sexual orientation.
88 Application No. 9532/81 (1987).
89 The Women and Equalities Committee report *Transgender and Equality* (2016), op. cit., at p. 3 and para. 374.

Gender reassignment treatment

The criteria for accessing gender reassignment procedures are problematic. In particular, the requirement that two clinicians, one of whom must be medically qualified, have to agree a mental health diagnosis of gender dysphoria, would seem discriminatory and stigmatising when compared with criteria for accessing other health and social services. Concern has been expressed as to the appropriateness of such a "pathologisation of trans identities".[90] The ECtHR rulings in *Y.Y. v. Turkey*[91] and *Garçon and Nicot v. France*[92] would indicate that such concern is well founded.

Trans children

The 2016 *Transgender Equality* states that "there is a clear and strong case that delaying treatment for young people risks more harm than providing it",[93] and yet it is questionable whether this is supported by the evidence.

There are seven Gender Identity Clinics in England which are run by an NHS Mental Health Trust. Referrals to the Tavistock Clinic in London increased from 94 in 2010 to 2,519 in 2018; 70% of those being referred were biologically female. This gateway to gender reassignment treatment is under considerable pressure. An internal review in 2018 (the Bell report), written by the Clinic governor, warned that "the GIDS service as it now functions [is] not fit for purpose and children's ends are being met in a woeful, inadequate manner and some will live on with the damaging consequences".[94]

While a "*Gillick* competent" minor[95] may give consent to embarking on a social and medical programme leading to a change in their gender identity, he or she is prevented from applying for a Gender Recognition Certificate as the 2004 Act restricts applications to "a person of either gender who is aged at least 18".

Sports and recreational activities

The Equality Act 2010, s.195, permits the exclusion of trans persons from competitive gender affected sports where this is deemed necessary to secure fair competition or public safety. Girl Guides now accept biological males who self-identify as women as guide leaders.

Blood donors

On 28 November 2017, new rules came into effect to relax the previous constraints, in force since 2011, which prohibited donations from homosexual men

90 Ibid., at paras. 208–209.
91 Application No. 14793/08 (2015).
92 *Garçon* and Nicot v. France, Application No. 79885/12 (2017).
93 Op. cit., at p. 3.
94 See further at: www.theguardian.com/society/2019/feb/23/child-transgender-service-governor-quits-chaos.
95 *Gillick v. West Norfolk & Wisbeck Area Health Authority* [1986] AC 112.

if they had had sex within the previous year. The changes brought a reduction in the deferral period to three months (though it remains at one year in Northern Ireland), which has made it easier for gay and bisexual men to donate, but many will still be excluded from doing so.

Right to equality and non-discrimination: education

The right to non-discrimination in education is established by Articles 5 and 13 of the ECHR and by Article 2 of the First Protocol, as incorporated in Schedule 1 of the 1998 Act, but in practice is largely governed by Part 6 of the Equality Act 2010.[96] In addition, the ancillary Public Sector Equality Duty provisions require schools to address homophobic and transphobic bullying.

Schools

The Equality Act 2010, s.85, makes it unlawful for a school to discriminate against, harass or victimise a pupil or potential pupil: in admissions; in the way it provides education, or any benefit, facility or service; and by excluding a pupil or subjecting them to any other detriment. Moreover, it makes it unlawful for a school to discriminate against a pupil or prospective pupil by treating them less favourably because of the protected characteristics which include sex, sexual orientation and gender reassignment, or to discriminate because of the pupil's association with someone with those protected characteristics.[97] Attention has been drawn to the risk of trans school children being exposed to transphobic bullying by the charity Mermaids, which has published guidance in the form of a "toolkit" to assist trans children and those working with them.[98]

Curricula

The Department for Education has declared that from September 2020 all children will be taught about SOGI issues as part of compulsory relationship and sex education (RSE) classes and in keeping with the Ofsted policy of promoting fundamental British values, which has generated prototype programmes such as "No Outsiders". The provision of such teaching will be mandatory in all primary and secondary schools, but parents will retain their traditional right to withdraw their children from such classes at secondary level; the fact that they are to lose this right in relation to children in primary school is highly contentious in the light of Protocol 1 of the ECHR. This policy is facing resistance most obviously from Muslims, ultra-Orthodox Jews and evangelical Christians but also more generally

96 See also the Code of Practice on Employment 2011, paras. 2.50–2.61.

97 Reinforced by the Education (Independent School Standards) Regulations 2014, which include a curriculum obligation to encourage respect for other people, paying particular regard to the protected characteristics set out in the 2010 Act.

98 See further at: www.mermaidsuk.org.uk/assets/media/East%20Sussex%20schools%20transgender%20toolkit.pdf.

from those who claim that there can be no "age-appropriate" way to teach primary school age children about homosexual relationships or transgenderism. The protests – particularly from Muslims lobbying under the "Islam RSE" banner – have not yet led to court cases.

Colleges/universities

The proposed changes to the Gender Recognition Act 2004 have triggered considerable vitriol, "no platforming", accusations of transphobia etc. in a number of UK universities. The polarising issue is the suggestion that changes should be introduced that would make it easier for trans people to have their preferred gender legally recognised. On one side are academics opposing trans self-identification as they fear this may endanger females in general. On the other are trans activists, academics supporting trans rights and some vociferous feminists who strongly maintain that it is trans people who are the vulnerable minority group most in need of protection. This threat to free speech has recently been condemned by Parliament's Joint Committee on Human Rights.[99]

Right to equality and non-discrimination: employment

Legal protection for the LGBT community in an employment context is largely provided by the Equality Act 2010 and the Employment Equality (Sexual Orientation) Regulations 2003, subject to the religious exemption; legitimate and proportionate constraints; the "genuine occupational requirement" provision in application to transsexuals and certain other exemptions. Such an exemption, under Sch 9 of the 2010 Act, permits the exclusion of a trans person in circumstances that would otherwise constitute unlawful discrimination.

Religious exemption

The Equality Act 2010, Schedule 9, paragraph 2 (giving effect to Article 4 of the Framework Equality Directive 2000/78/EC) deals with employment "for the purposes of an organised religion",[100] though that term is not defined. The Act permits an employer to discriminate on the grounds of specified protected characteristics, including gender reassignment, same-sex marriage and civil partnership, sex or sexual orientation. The sexual orientation provisions allow a religious organisation, or an employer whose ethos is based on a particular religion or belief, to restrict staff recruitment to applicants who share the same religion or belief. However, there must be evidence that the restriction is linked

99 House of Commons and House of Lords, Joint Committee on Human Rights, *Freedom of Speech in Universities* (2018) at para. 43. See further at: https://publications.parliament.uk/pa/jt201719/jtselect/jtrights/589/589.pdf.

100 See also Equality Act 2010, Sch. 12, para. 5 (Designation of Institutions with a Religious Ethos) (England and Wales) Order 2010, SI 2010/1915.

to the beliefs/religion – e.g. the job can be shown to be governed by prescriptive doctrines or tenets – and that the restriction is an occupational requirement for the job; is genuine and determining; serves a legitimate aim; and is a proportionate means of furthering that aim. Because of the narrowing effect of the "determining" requirement, this exemption was virtually restricted to employing religious organisations.[101] So, for example, in *Muhammed v. The Leprosy Mission International*,[102] a small Christian charity was allowed to refuse applications from non-Christians, because Christianity permeated the organisation. However, where a religious organisation restricts an employment opportunity on SOGI grounds, it must be able to demonstrate that the restriction is a "genuine occupational requirement" for that particular post.[103]

The PSED provisions also apply to any religious organisation undertaking public sector service delivery functions.

Sexual orientation in the workplace

Reaney v. Hereford Diocesan Board of Finance[104] concerned a plaintiff who had acknowledged on his application form for a job as a youth worker with the diocese that he had been in a same-sex relationship until recently. An interview panel decided that he was the best candidate but his appointment was vetoed by the Bishop of Hereford, even though Reaney had undertaken to remain celibate for the time he was employed. The Tribunal noted that requiring Reaney to be celibate could be said to be in compliance with the doctrines of the religion, or it could be justified to avoid conflicting with the strongly held religious convictions of a significant number of the religion's followers. Given, however, that Reaney met the requirement (celibacy), it was unreasonable to refuse to employ him.

Homophobia can be a very real problem in the workplace, as was evident in *Ditton v. CP Publishing Ltd*,[105] when the complainant suffered homophobic comments from work colleagues during his initial training on commencing employment. He was dismissed after only eight days but was successful in his claim of direct discrimination and harassment on the grounds of his sexual orientation. In *English v. Thomas Sanderson Blinds*,[106] the Court of Appeal held that alleged homophobic abuse towards a man who was not gay, and aware that the perpetrators did not believe him to be gay, amounted to harassment on the grounds of sexual orientation. Again, in *Keane v. Dogan and Another*,[107] a docker working for a commercial shipping company was dismissed for his reactions to such abuse,

101 See *R (on the application of Amicus) v. Secretary of State for Trade and Industry* [2004] IRLR 430 QBD [2004] EWHC 860 (Admin).
102 ET 2303459/0989, 16 December 2009.
103 See *Vera Egenberger v. Evangelisches Werk für Diakonie und Entwicklung eV* [2018] EUECJ C-414/16 and *JQ v. IR* [2018] EUECJ C-68/17.
104 ET/1602844/2006.
105 [2007] S/107918/05.
106 [2008] EWCA Civ 1421 CA.
107 ET/2602003/2012, 13 May 2014.

which had been repeated over a period of many weeks. The employment tribunal found that he had been the victim of discrimination and harassment at work on the grounds of sexual orientation and unfairly dismissed because of his reaction to that abuse. On the other hand, not all banter in the workplace constitutes homophobia, as illustrated by the response of Briggs J, in *Smith v. Trafford Housing Trust*,[108] to an employer who had disciplined an employee, a Christian manager, for posting on Facebook his view that holding civil partnership ceremonies in churches was "an equality too far". While accepting that the complainant could have considered this as homophobic and been offended, Briggs J found that "her interpretation was not in my view objectively reasonable".[109] As Underhill J explained in *Dhaliwal*,[110] "it is also important not to encourage a culture of hypersensitivity or the imposition of legal liability in respect of every unfortunate phrase".[111] However, whereas a person could justifiably claim that being outed in the workplace breached their Article 8 right to privacy and constituted sexual orientation discrimination, if they should openly disclose their sexual orientation they cannot – in the absence of any evidence of intent to harass – subsequently hope to succeed in such claims.[112]

The EAT, in *Commissioner of Police of the Metropolis v. Maxwell*,[113] upheld the ET ruling that the respondent was liable in respect of unlawful discrimination by way of direct discrimination, harassment and victimisation on grounds of race and sexual orientation against a gay black police officer. The latter had been present when disparaging comments had been made about discrimination by his superior who, in the knowledge that allegations of discrimination had been lodged by that officer, would have realised that his comments identified and disparaged him in front of his colleagues.

Trans persons and the workplace

Towards the end of the twentieth century there was a reversal in the discriminatory approach towards trans persons in an employment context. In *White v. British Sugar Corporation Ltd*,[114] a trans (ftm), who had not undergone any sex-change treatment but had been employed in a position reserved for men under the Factories Act, was dismissed following disclosure of the biological facts. The Industrial Tribunal treated the claimant as a female for the purposes of the Sex Discrimination Act 1975 and upheld the dismissal. In *P. v. S. and Cornwall County Council*,[115] however, much the same facts produced a different outcome.

108 [2012] EWHC 3221.
109 Ibid. at para. 85.
110 *Richmond Pharmaceuticals v. Dhaliwal* [2009] ICR 724. See, also, *Land Registry v. Grant* [2011] ICR 1390.
111 *Dhaliwal*, op. cit., at para. 22.
112 *Grant v. HM Land Registry* [2011] EWCA Civ 769.
113 UKEAT/0232/12/MC (2013).
114 [1977] Industrial Relations Law Reports 121.
115 C-13/94, ECR 1–21–43 (1994).

This case concerned a trans person who had been dismissed after informing her employers that she was undergoing gender reassignment. The Employment Tribunal accepted that her disclosure had been the cause of her dismissal but because the relevant domestic legislation did not provide for such circumstances, the Tribunal referred the matter to the ECJ for a preliminary ruling under the terms of the Equal Treatment Directive. The resulting landmark ECJ decision[116] effectively extended the scope of legal provisions regarding sex discrimination so that discrimination in employment and vocational training on grounds of "gender reassignment" also became illegal. This was consolidated in 1999 by the introduction of secondary legislation which extended the Sex Discrimination Act 1975 to align domestic law with that ruling.

Employment in the military

In *Smith and Grady v. United Kingdom*,[117] joined with *Lustig-Prean and Beckett v. United Kingdom*,[118] the ECtHR found that the dismissal of personnel from the Royal Navy on the basis of homosexuality breached their Article 8 rights. Shortly afterwards the court reached a similar conclusion in *Perkins and R. v. the United Kingdom*[119] and *Beck, Copp and Bazeley v. the United Kingdom*.[120] Discrimination on the basis of sexual orientation in the British armed forces has been prohibited since the introduction of the Equality Act 2010.

Right to equality and non-discrimination: services

SOGI issues arising in a service provision context have been the subject of guidance issued by the GEO[121] and by the EHRC.[122] The prohibition, in the Equality Act 2010, on direct discrimination in goods and services provision is subject to the caveat that it is only lawful if it is a proportionate means of achieving a legitimate aim. Secondary legislation in 2008, which extended the law on gender discrimination to cover access to and supply of goods and services, also effectively protected people with the characteristic of "gender reassignment".

116 C-13/94 [1996] IRLR 347.

117 (1999) 29 EHRR 493.

118 (2000) 29 ECHR 548.

119 Application Nos. 43208/98 and 44875/98 (2003).

120 Application Nos. 48535/99, 48536/99 and 48537/99 (2003).

121 See *Providing Services for Transgender Customers* and *The Recruitment and Retention of Transgender Staff* (2015), at: https://assets.publishing.service.gov.uk/government/uploads/system/uploads/attachment_data/file/484857/Providing_services_for_transgender_customers-a_guide.pdf and at: https://assets.publishing.service.gov.uk/government/uploads/system/uploads/attachment_data/file/484855/The_recruitment_and_retention_of_transgender_staff-_guidance_for_employers.pdf.

122 See *Provision of Goods, Facilities and Services to Trans People: Guidance for Public Authorities in Meeting Your Equality Duties and Human Rights Obligations* (2010).

Trans persons and gender-specific services

The Equality Act 2010, Sch 3, in keeping with ECtHR principles, provides exemptions from the statutory prohibition on discrimination to permit the exclusion of a trans person from single sex facilities or services where this would be a proportionate means of achieving a legitimate aim. This allows for the provision of separate-sex and single-sex services, or exclusion from such services, in circumstances where criteria of proportionality and legitimacy are satisfied. It gives service providers in settings such as hospitals and prisons a discretionary right to deny trans persons single-sex services as and when this is deemed necessary. In theory, this should provide reassurance for those who fear that the safe space seemingly assured by single-sex schools, swimming pools, women's refuges etc. might be vulnerable to intrusion by biological males who self-identify as females for the purpose of causing harm to the latter. However, there remains considerable uncertainty as to the circumstances that justify the exclusion of someone who is legally but not biologically female from female-only services. There is little clarity regarding when such exclusion satisfies the 'proportionate means of achieving a legitimate aim' test and overcomes the right of a trans person to be treated in accordance with the provisions of equality and non-discrimination.

The sexual orientation provisions allow a religious organisation to restrict service provision to persons of one sex or to provide separately for persons of each sex – but only if this is necessary to comply with the doctrines of the religion, or for the purpose of avoiding conflict with the strongly held religious convictions of a significant number of the religion's followers.[123] Such an organisation cannot lawfully discriminate in the provision of goods and services on the grounds of sexual orientation, where such provision is undertaken on behalf of a public body.

Provision of public services

A key theme in the *Transgender and Equality* report was "the lack of sufficient understanding of trans issues by professionals in the public sector, probably reflecting society's lack of knowledge – and sometimes prejudice".[124] Whether due to ignorance, prejudice or to sincerely held religious beliefs, the cases would seem to bear out the report's misgivings about professional objectivity and sensitive commitment to public service.

In *McClintock v. Department of Constitutional Affairs*,[125] which concerned the request of a JP member of a statutory panel that he be excused from officiating in cases where he might have to decide whether same-sex partners should adopt children, and who resigned when his request was refused, the EAT found that McClintock had not been disadvantaged because of any religious belief he held

123 Equality Act 2010, Sched. 23, S. 2 (7) and s.2(9).

124 The Women and Equalities Committee report *Transgender and Equality*, op. cit., at para. 374.

125 [2008] IRLR 29.

and that, even if he had been, such discrimination would have been justified. This was followed shortly afterwards by *Ladele v. London Borough of Islington*,[126] when the Court of Appeal considered the dismissal of Ms Ladele, a Christian marriage registrar, who refused on religious grounds to be involved in registering same-sex "civil partnerships" in accordance with newly introduced statutory procedures. The court took the view that the registration process was a public service, that it had significant human rights implications for the community and that administering the process formed part of Ms Ladele's contractual duties. Again, in *R (on the application of Johns) v. Derby City Council*,[127] members of the Pentecostal Church with strong religious views against homosexuality were rejected as prospective foster carers by Derbyshire County Council. Their claim that their beliefs would not impede them from offering a foster care service and that their rejection constituted religious discrimination by the Council were dismissed by the court. Munby LJ, following the decisions in *Ladele*[128] and *McClintock*,[129] reasoned that the rejection was due to their stance on sexual orientation, not because of their religious beliefs, and that the Council was entitled, indeed required, to ensure that its public service provision was compliant with equality and non-discrimination legislation – a rationale subsequently endorsed by the ECtHR, which ruled, in relation to both applicants, that their employer pursued a legitimate aim – to provide public services without discrimination.[130] In the same year and on much the same issue, the Catholic Care adoption agency refused to provide its services to same-sex cohabiting couples or civil partners (or to unmarried couples), on the basis that to do so would be contrary to the tenets of the Roman Catholic Church.[131] In the High Court, Briggs J advised that the services could be restricted on the basis of sexual orientation only if the restriction amounted to a proportionate means of achieving a legitimate aim. The regulatory authority concluded that this test was not satisfied because of the public nature of its activities and this decision was subsequently endorsed by the First-tier Tribunal (Charity).[132]

Trans persons and prisons

Public service response to trans issues is of pressing importance for the criminal justice system, particularly following the deaths of Joanne Latham and Vikki Thompson (both trans women in male prisons) in 2015.[133] In *AB, R (on the*

126 [2009] EWCA (Civ) 1357 (15 December 2009).
127 (2011) EWHC 375 (Admin).
128 *Ladele v. London Borough of Islington* [2009] EWCA Civ 1357.
129 *McFarlane v. Relate Avon Ltd* [2010] EWCA Civ B1; [2010] IRLR 872.
130 *Eweida and Others v. United Kingdom* [2013] ECHR 37.
131 See *Catholic Care (Diocese of Leeds) v. The Charity Commission for England and Wales* [2011] EqLR 597.
132 See also *St Margaret's Children and Family Care Society v. OSCR* [2014] SCAP App 02/13, which found in favour of the Society on very similar facts.
133 See further HMSO, *The Care and Management of Transsexual Prisoners* (Prison Service Instruction (PSI) 07/2011).

application of) v. Secretary of State for Justice & Anor,[134] which concerned a 27-year-old *pre-operative* trans (mtf) with a GRC detained in a male prison, the court concluded that there had been a violation of Article 8 of the ECHR due to the extent of the constraint on her personal autonomy. However, the risks to be balanced in such circumstances were later illustrated by the case of Karen White, again a pre-operative (mtf) trans person, found by Batty J in the Leeds Crown Court to be a predator and highly manipulative and convicted in 2018 of sexually assaulting two women while detained in a female prison. The need for a greater awareness of trans-specific services in this context was demonstrated in *R (Green) v. Secretary of State for Justice*,[135] when the court found there was no discrimination in refusing gender-affirming items such as a wig, tights and a prosthetic vagina. A change in government policy can be seen in the 2019 announcement of the opening of the first UK trans prison and of an intention to designate new trans prison wings.[136]

Private goods and service provision

SOGI issues have been generated across a wide range of service provision outlets, but clubs and bars in particular have often provided a context for sexual orientation discrimination. In *Mrs E Hegarty v. The Edge (Soho)*,[137] for example, the ET accepted that a heterosexual woman who had been made redundant, ostensibly in order to allow management to "freshen up" their premises, had in fact been unfairly dismissed and discriminated against on grounds of sexual orientation when it transpired that the premises had reopened with exclusively male homosexual staff. Again, in *Hubble v. Brooks*[138] a pub owner refused to employ Mr Hubble (and his long-term partner) when he learned at interview that Mr Hubble was gay, despite Mr Hubble and his partner having the requisite experience required for the role. The Tribunal accepted evidence that the owner had declared that there was "no way" he would employ a gay couple in his village pub: having invested a lot of money in the pub, he could not afford to lose money through having a gay couple. This was held to constitute direct discrimination on the grounds of sexual orientation. Much the same attitudes were prominent in *Lisboa v. Realpubs Ltd and Others*,[139] when it was found that placing a gay employee under pressure to comply with his employer's policy to make the pub less welcoming to gay customers was discrimination. The employer in this case had taken various steps to re-brand the pub, including erecting a display board which stated, "this is not a gay pub".

134 [2009] EWHC 2220 (Admin).
135 [2013] EWHC 3491 (Admin).
136 See www.bbc.co.uk/news/uk-47434730.
137 Case 2200027/05 (4887/106) (2005).
138 Case no. 1600381/05 (2005).
139 UKEAT/0224/10/RN.

Accommodation is another area prone to disputes concerning LGBT issues, often with a religious component. In *Bull v. Hall and Preddy*,[140] the UKSC confirmed that it was unlawful discrimination for Christian hotel owners to refuse a double-bedded room to a same-sex couple and dismissed their argument that they should not be compelled to run their business in a way which conflicted with their deeply held religious beliefs. Again, among a number of similar cases, the court in *Black and Morgan v. Wilkinson*[141] held that a same-sex couple requesting a double bedroom, who were neither married nor in a civil partnership, had been unlawfully discriminated against on the grounds of their sexual orientation in breach of regulation 4 of the Equality Act (Sexual Orientation) Regulations 2007.

Where the service provider is expected not only to provide a service but, in doing so, to express support for a position with which they disagree, then, it might be argued, the right to freedom of expression comes into play. Some such scenario arose in *Gareth Lee v. Ashers Baking Company Ltd, McArthur and McArthur*,[142] a Northern Ireland case appealed to the UKSC.[143] The court at first instance ruled that it was unlawful direct discrimination on grounds of sexual orientation for a bakery owned by two Christians to refuse to bake a cake which had printed on it a picture of "Bert and Ernie" and the caption "Support Gay Marriage". The ruling was upheld by the Northern Ireland Court of Appeal but subsequently overturned by the UKSC, which found that there had been no discrimination: neither political nor based on sexual orientation. As Lady Hale commented:

> The objection was to being required to promote the message on the cake . . . the bakery would have refused to supply this particular cake to anyone, whatever their personal characteristics. So there was no discrimination on grounds of sexual orientation.[144]

Construed differently, this case might have shed light on the interesting issue of whether, in such circumstances, the Christian baker's right to freedom of religion would trump the gay customer's right to equality and non-discrimination. As it is, this issue remains to be addressed in any one of the number of such cases coming before the courts in this jurisdiction, in the US and elsewhere.

Pensions and social security benefits etc.

The driving force for modernising pensions law in this jurisdiction, as in Ireland, and ensuring it addressed SOGI issues and evolved in incremental steps to

140 [2013] UKSC 73. Also see the similar case *Black v. Wilkinson* [2013] EWCA Civ 820 [2013] 1 WLR 2490.
141 [2013] EWCA Civ 820.
142 Neutral Citation No. [2015] NICty 2.
143 *Lee v. and Ashers Baking Co Ltd and Others* [2018] UKSC 49.
144 Ibid., at para. 62.

become more human rights compliant came from the EU, mainly from rulings of the ECJ (see Chapter 2).

An employer's refusal to grant travel concessions to the same-sex partner of an employee, in *Grant v. South-West Trains Ltd*,[145] raised the question whether this constituted sex discrimination, as such concessions were available to an employee's spouse or to a heterosexual partner.[146] Relying on the earlier *P. v. S.*, the claimant argued that discrimination based on sexual orientation must be interpreted as included in the prohibition on "discrimination based on sex" under Article 14 of the ECHR. The ECJ disagreed.[147] It noted that within the European Union there was considerable contention as to whether any equivalence existed between same-sex partnerships and heterosexual marriages, which explained the different approaches to sexual orientation, and added that it was a matter for domestic legislatures to change that position. It ruled that the law "as it stands at present does not cover discrimination based on sexual orientation, such as that in issue in the main proceedings".[148] Sex discrimination was also the presenting issue in *K.B. v. NHS Pensions Agency*,[149] which concerned a female nurse who had worked for some 20 years for the NHS and was a member of the NHS Pension Scheme. Her trans partner (ftm), had been unable to gain official recognition of his new gender identity, and this prevented the couple from marrying. Having been informed by the NHS Pensions Agency that, as she and her partner were not married, if she were to pre-decease him she would not receive a widower's pension, she then brought the matter to the ET, the EAT, the Court of Appeal and ultimately to the ECJ alleging discrimination based on sex, contrary to the provisions of Article 141 EC and Directive 75/117. The ECJ found that the claimant had suffered inequality of treatment but that "the inequality of treatment does not relate to the award of a widower's pension but to a necessary precondition for the grant of such a pension: namely, the capacity to marry".[150] It held that UK law was in breach of the ECHR because it prevented the claimant and her partner from fulfilling the marriage requirement which was a pre-condition for one of them to access the other's pension entitlement.

Shortly after the previously-mentioned *K.B.* ruling, the ECJ was called upon in *Sarah Margaret Richards v. Secretary of State for Work and Pensions*[151] to consider the refusal to award a trans (mtf), who had undergone surgery, the retirement

145 Case C-249/96 [1998] ECR I-621.

146 Also see *L. v. Lithuania*, Application No. 27527/03 (2007) and *Schumpf v. Switzerland*, Application No. 29002/06 (2009).

147 Ibid., at para. 35 et seq.

148 Ibid., at para. 47. As in *B. v. France*, Application No. 13343/87 (1992), where the court observed that there still remained uncertainty as to the essential nature of transsexualism and as to the effect of surgical intervention. This view changed with the judgements in *I. v. the United Kingdom* and *Christine Goodwin v. the United Kingdom*, op. cit.

149 Case C-117/01 (2004).

150 Ibid., at para. 30.

151 Case C-423/04 (2005).

pension to which a 60-year-old female retiree would be statutorily entitled. She alleged that the refusal constituted a breach of her rights under Article 4 of Directive 79/7 EEC concerning the prohibition of discrimination in statutory social security schemes. The court found that Article 4(1) on the progressive implementation of the principle of equal treatment for men and women in matters of social security was to be interpreted as including the entitlement of a person who has undergone gender reassignment to a retirement pension at the age specified for a female. Accordingly, it held that UK law had unfairly discriminated against the claimant. This decision set an important precedent by establishing that any trans person, living permanently in their new gender and regardless of surgery, can claim personal pay-related benefits – including working family tax credits based on married family status, and other social security benefits – to which they would be entitled had they been born into their acquired gender identity.

Courten v. UK[152] and *M.W. v. UK*[153] both involved a claim for a statutory benefit – available to a widow(er) – made by the survivor of a long-term homosexual couple following the death of their partner; in both the claimant pointed out that for the duration of their relationship, marriage had not been an option legally available to homosexual couples, and in both the claimant alleged discriminatory treatment compared to the analogous situation of married persons or persons in a civil partnership. The first concerned a claim for the equivalent to an exemption from inheritance tax payable under s.18 of the Inheritance Tax Act 1984 and the second a bereavement benefit payable under s.36 of the Social Security Contributions and Benefits Act 1992. Neither was successful. The court noted that under Article 14 not every difference in treatment constitutes discrimination: it must be established that other persons in an analogous or relevantly similar situation enjoy preferential treatment, and that there is no reasonable or objective justification for that distinction. Further, it noted that States enjoy a margin of appreciation in assessing whether and to what extent differences in otherwise similar situations justify a different treatment in law: that margin varies according to the circumstances, the subject matter and its background. It relied on the finding in *Burden*[154] that

> just as there can be no analogy between married and Civil Partnership Act couples, on one hand, and heterosexual or homosexual couples who choose to live together but not to become husband and wife or civil partners, on the other hand, the absence of such a legally binding agreement between the applicants renders their relationship of co-habitation, despite its long duration, fundamentally different to that of a married or civil partnership couple.[155]

152 Application No. 4479/06 (2008).
153 Application No. 11313/02 (2009).
154 *Burden v. United Kingdom* (2008) 47 EHRR 38; [2008] 2 FLR 787.
155 Ibid., at para. 65.

Essentially, the claimants in both cases failed because "in the area of evolving social rights where there is no established consensus, States must also enjoy a margin of appreciation in the timing of the introduction of legislative changes",[156] and "acting as they did and when they did, the United Kingdom authorities remained within their margin of appreciation".[157]

The ECJ again disagreed with UK law in *MB v. Secretary for Work and Pensions*,[158] which concerned a married trans (mtf) person who, on reaching the female age for retirement, found her pension application rejected on the grounds that she had not reached the male retirement age. Although having undergone reassignment surgery, the applicant had not obtained a GRC as to do so would have necessitated a divorce (which neither spouse wanted) and so was unable to provide the officially required form of proof of gender reassignment. Eventually the matter came before the UKSC,[159] which, being divided on the issue, referred it to the ECJ. The latter found that the UK law requiring a trans person to be unmarried in order to qualify for a State retirement pension at the retirement age of their current gender constituted direct discrimination.

In 2017, the UKSC in *Walker v. Innospec Limited & Others*[160] found that an exemption in the UK Equality Act 2010 (allowing pension schemes to exclude same-sex partners from benefits paid into pension funds before December 2005) was discriminatory and in breach of EU equality law. The exemption infringed on EU Directive 2000/78/EC requiring member States to prohibit discrimination in employment on various grounds, including sexual orientation. The Court referred to two CJEU decisions[161] (see Chapter 2) which confirmed that unless evidence establishes that there would be unacceptable economic or social consequences of giving effect to the deceased's entitlement to a survivor's pension for his husband, at the time that this pension would fall due, there was no reason that he should be subjected to unequal treatment as to the payment of that pension. The UKSC concluded that Mr Walker's husband was entitled on Mr Walker's death to a spouse's pension. As a consequence of this ruling, occupational pension schemes will have to provide civil partners and same-sex spouses with the same survivors' benefits as opposite-sex married couples.

Conscientious objection of service providers

The principle of freedom of conscience dates back to 1757,[162] but it was the Human Rights Act 1998 that gave the principle explicit recognition in domestic

156 *Courten*, op. cit.
157 *M.W.*, op. cit.
158 Case C-451/16 (2018).
159 [2016] UKSC 53.
160 [2017] UKSC 47.
161 *Maruko v. Versorgungsanstalt der Deutschen Bühnen* (C-267/06) and *Römer v. Freie und Hansestadt Hamburg* (C-147/08).
162 The Militia Ballot Act 1757 allowed Quakers to be exempt from military service on the grounds of conscientious objection.

legislation with the declaration that "everyone has the right to freedom of thought, conscience and religion".

SOGI, public service and conscientious objection

The previously-mentioned cases of *McClintock*, *Johns*, *McFarlane*, *Ladele* and *Catholic Care* all concerned providers of public service who refused, on grounds of conscientious objection, to perform contractual duties on behalf of representatives of the LGBT community.[163] In all, the outcome indicates that such grounds cannot justify a refusal to perform contractual duties if, as a consequence, the rights of others are disproportionately adversely affected. In the UK as elsewhere, public service staff are with increasing frequency being penalised for refusing to facilitate the delivery of those public services that offend their consciences. In response, the Conscientious Objection (Medical Activities) Bill 2017 was introduced in Parliament as a private Peer's bill to clarify for medical professionals their right to refuse to participate in service delivery, on grounds of conscientious objection, but so far this exemption has failed to become law.[164]

Conclusion

This chapter models the structure to be adopted in each of the following five. The template, constructed from Part I material and applied earlier, is deployed to examine and compare equivalent aspects of the human rights/SOGI intersect throughout Part II.

As the progenitor common law jurisdiction, England and Wales bear responsibility for fostering, and transferring to the Part II jurisdictions, the Church/State partnership that for centuries determined the law relating to SOGI matters. More recently, its influence on the human rights/SOGI intersect has been more positive. From the Wolfenden report some 60 years ago, though a sequence of milestone ECtHR rulings which have set precedents for developing the law in this and other jurisdictions, to the present management of controversy and confrontation on a clash between religious interests and the LGBT community on the inclusion of SOGI-related teaching material in the primary schools of Birmingham, it has often been at the forefront in recognising and addressing key issues.

Currently, however, it is demonstrating a singular lack of leadership in certain important areas. The reluctance to recognise non-binary status in official ID documents such as birth certificates and passports is regrettable. The bureaucratic, lengthy and stigmatising process for granting legal recognition of gender identity is outdated, as is the failure to include it as a specific protected characteristic in the equality legislation. The vitriolic furore, including "no-platforming", in relation to proposed trans inclusive measures has been something of an international

163 See also *Greater Glasgow Health Board v. Doogan and Wood* [2014] UKSC 68.
164 Author acknowledges advice from Frank Cranmer on this matter (note to author, 24 May 2019).

embarrassment. There are also grounds for concern in the practice of deporting migrants with SOGI status to countries known to mistreat such persons. Following two deaths, the recent policy decision to designate prison wings for the exclusive use of trans prisoners is an important step in the recognition and protection of their most basic human rights.

5 Ireland

Introduction

This chapter follows the pattern laid down by its predecessor. Beginning with an overview of the relevant international and domestic legal framework – legislative, judicial and regulatory – it considers the implications of the more fundamental human rights for SOGI issues, specifically rights to justice and to freedom of expression, association and religion. Turning then to matters of direct personal relevance to the LGBT community, it examines the law governing same-sex relationships, family life, parenting and associated matters. This leads into the main section dealing with the impact of equality and non-discrimination law on SOGI issues, as illustrated in the understandably very limited caselaw of this relatively small jurisdiction and in accordance with themes identified in Chapter 2.

Legislative framework: international and domestic

The Republic of Ireland has a domestic legal framework governed by a Constitution – *Bunreacht na hÉireann* – but, as a wholly committed member of the EU, that framework is firmly aligned with European treaties, conventions, protocols and directives. Article 29.4.6 of the Constitution makes express provision for European Union law to prevail over Irish domestic law, where the two are in conflict, but only to the extent that such EU law is "necessitated" by Ireland's membership.

International legislation

The main constituent parts of this framework are as in England and Wales (see Chapters 2 and 3). Essentially they comprise the European Convention on Human Rights, the International Covenant on Civil and Political Rights, other international treaties, conventions and protocols[1] and certain EU

1 In particular: (ICCPR); the UN Convention on the Elimination of all forms of Discrimination Against Women (CEDAW) with its Optional Protocol; and the International Convention on the Elimination of Race Discrimination (ICERD).

Directives.[2] These, together with decisions of the ECtHR, the UN HR Committee and the European Court of Justice, are applied, or referred to, as required to align domestic law with that of the EU.

The European Convention on Human Rights (ECHR)

Articles 8, 9, 12 and 14 of the Convention (right to non-discrimination), as supported by Article 9 (the right to freedom of thought, conscience and religion), now have a direct bearing upon Irish domestic law.

International Covenant on Civil and Political Rights (ICCPR)

The ICCPR is of increasing importance in promoting compliance with human rights in Ireland as elsewhere. While Articles 2 and 19 are significant, of particular relevance for present purposes are the equality and non-discrimination requirements of Article 26. The Covenant also provides authority for the UN Human Rights Committee, which adjudicates on complaints arising under its provisions, and for the Universal Periodic Review Process, under which a review of Ireland's progress in achieving human rights standards is conducted every four years (see Chapter 2).

Domestic legislation

Constitutional authority and principles are augmented by a not untypical range of equality and non-discrimination legislation.

The Constitution

Bunreacht na hÉireann, the Irish Constitution, was enacted by Parliament – the *Oireachtas* – in 1937. It continues to provide the governing authority for domestic law, and its contemporary relevance to developments in Irish society is enhanced through periodic amendments, each preceded by a national referendum. As of 2018, there have been a total of 29 amendments, resulting from 35 referendums, the most recent being on blasphemy and abortion with others pending on matters such "the place of a woman in the home".

Article 40.1. states:

> All citizens shall, as human persons, be held equal before the law. This shall not be held to mean that the State shall not in its enactments have due regard to differences of capacity, physical and moral, and of social function.

2 See, in particular, the Equal Pay Directive (75/117/EEC), the Equal Treatment Directive (76/207/EEC) and the General Framework Directive (2000/78/EC).

This constitutional equality assurance was interpreted by Henchy J, in *Dillane v. Ireland*, as limited – as securing formal, as opposed to substantive equality[3] – in his comment:

> When the State . . . makes a discrimination in favour of, or against, a person or category of persons, on the express or implied grounds of a difference of social function the courts will not condemn such discrimination as being in breach of Article 40.1 if it is not arbitrary, capricious, or otherwise not reasonably capable, when objectively viewed in the light of the social function involved, of supporting the selection or classification complained of.[4]

The Adoption (Amendment) Act 2017

This statute amends the Adoption Act 2010 and the Children and Family Relationships Act 2015 to provide for foster parent adoptions, where the foster parents have cared for the child for at least 18 months, and to allow two people regardless of marital status to adopt children, thus granting married same-sex couples the right to adopt.

The Criminal Justice (Sexual Offences) Act 2017

The legislative intent is to enhance and update laws relating to the sexual exploitation and sexual abuse of children, including new offences relating to child sexual grooming and new and strengthened offences to tackle child pornography. It also criminalises prostitution.

The Gender Recognition Act 2015

This legislation allows gender identity to be given legal recognition, without the requirement of medical intervention or assessment by the State, simply by the self-determination of any person aged 18 or over, who is ordinarily resident in Ireland and registered on Irish registers of birth or adoption or on the foreign birth register. It provides a process whereby an individual can apply to the Minister for Social Protection for a Gender Recognition Certificate. The applicant must make a declaration that he or she: has a settled and solemn intention of living in the "preferred gender" for the rest of their life; understands the consequences; and makes the application of their own free will. Having obtained the certificate, they can then apply to be registered in a register of gender recognition, and a certified copy of that entry will allow the gender marker on their birth certificate to be legally changed. In 2018, the government published the findings

3 Author acknowledges advice from Judy Walsh on this point (note to author, 4 June 2019).
4 [1980] ILRM 167.

of the "Gender Recognition Act Review Group" which, in accordance with s.7 of the Act, had undertaken "a review of the operation" of the statute.[5]

The Marriage Act 2015

Following a referendum amending the Constitution to provide recognition for the status of marriage irrespective of the sex of the partners, this statute placed same-sex and heterosexual marriages on the same legal footing and ended civil partnerships.

The Workplace Relations Act 2015

This legislation establishes the primary mechanisms for determining the rights and responsibilities of employers and employees. It provided a new adjudication process to settle disputes in the workplace by consolidating the various functions of the Labour Relations Commission, the Equality Tribunal, the Employment Appeals Tribunal (EAT), the National Employment Rights Authority and the Labour Court into a single body – the Workplace Relations Commission – which commenced in October 2015. There is a right of appeal to the Labour Court with a further appeal, on a point of law only, to the High Court.

The Employment Equality Acts 1998–2015

This legislation came into effect in 1998 and has since been amended by the Equality Act 2004 (exemption for religious bodies is provided in both this and in the Equal Status Act, s.7), the Civil Partnership Act 2010 and other statutes. It provides protection for workers against discrimination, harassment and sexual harassment in the workplace. It promotes equality in the workplace and prohibits discrimination across nine different grounds, including gender and sexual orientation.

The Equal Status Acts 2000–2018

Taking effect on 25 October 2000, this legislation includes the Equal Status Act 2000, the Equality Act 2004, the Equal Status (Amendment) Act 2012 and the Equality (Miscellaneous Provisions) Act 2015. These provisions prohibit discrimination in the provision of goods and services to which the public generally have access, including education and housing, on any of the nine grounds.

5 See further at: www.welfare.ie/en/pressoffice/Pages/pr180718.aspx.

The European Convention on Human Rights Act 2003[6]

This legislation partially incorporates the ECHR, together with several of its Protocols, into domestic law. Irish courts are consequently instructed in s.2 that

> in interpreting and applying any statutory provision or rule of law, a court shall, in so far as is possible, subject to the rules of law relating to such interpretation and application, do so in a manner compatible with the State's obligations under the Convention provisions.

In s.3, the courts are to ensure that "every organ of the State shall perform its functions in a manner compatible with the State's obligations under the Convention provisions"; in s.4, that "judicial notice" be taken of the Convention provisions and of judgements of the ECtHR or any decision of the Committee of Ministers established under the Statute of the Council of Europe on any question in respect of which it has jurisdiction; and they must also, when interpreting and applying the Convention provisions, take due account of the principles laid down in such judgements or decisions. Under s.5, a court may make a "declaration of incompatibility" where it finds that legislation or a rule of law is incompatible with the State's obligations under the ECHR, in which case the matter must be referred to Parliament.[7]

The Prohibition of Incitement to Hatred Act 1989

Under this statute it is an offence to make, distribute or broadcast "threatening, abusive or insulting" words, images or sounds with intent or likelihood to "stir up hatred", where "hatred" is "against a group of persons in the State or elsewhere on account of their race, colour, nationality, religion, ethnic or national origins, membership of the travelling community or sexual orientation" (see further below).

Other legislation

Other relevant statutes include the Pensions Act 1990–2018 and the Unfair Dismissals Act 1977–2015. Also, and potentially of considerable importance, are a number of currently pending bills (see next).

6 (Commencement) Order 2003 (S.I. No. 483 of 2003).

7 See *Foy v. An t-Ard Chlaraitheoir & Others* [2007] IEHC 470, when a declaration of incompatibility was made concerning the lack of legal recognition for transgender people under Irish law.

Framework of courts and regulatory bodies

As an independent and democratic sovereign State, Ireland has a not untypical structure of domestic courts and regulatory bodies, though their powers are necessarily circumscribed by certain EU supra-national instruments.

International courts and regulatory bodies

Ireland accepted the compulsory jurisdiction of the ECtHR in 1953 and is accountable to international committees for progressing the implementation of various convention provisions. Unlike England and Wales, Ireland is to continue its EU membership for the foreseeable future and will therefore continue to accept the superior jurisdiction of the ECJ.

The European Court of Human Rights (ECtHR)

Under s.4 of the European Convention on Human Rights Act 2003 "judicial notice" is required to be taken of ECtHR judgements. In making its determinations, the ECtHR allows States a wide margin of appreciation[8] when it comes to placing limitations on the manifestation of one's religion and belief. In deciding whether there has been a limitation or interference on the exercise of the applicant's religion, the infringement must be: (i) prescribed by law and (ii) necessary in a democratic society[9] for a permissible purpose, i.e. directed to a legitimate purpose and proportionate in scope and effect (see Chapter 3).

The Court of Justice of the European Union (CJEU or ECJ)

The European Court of Justice and various other committees established by their respective international conventions to monitor implementation have intermittent relevance (see Chapter 3).

The Human Rights Committee (HRC)

This body of independent experts monitors implementation of the ICCPR. Ireland is required to submit a four-yearly progress report to which the HRC responds and makes recommendations as to further goals (see Chapter 3).

Domestic courts and regulatory bodies

As elsewhere, in practice most SOGI-related disputes are addressed by the national regulator for human rights, though the High Court also plays a well-established

8 See, for example, *Lithgow v. United Kingdom* (1986) 8 EHRR 329, *Fredin v. Sweden* (1991) 13 EHRR 784, *Abdulaziz, Cabales and Balkandali v. United Kingdom* (1985) 7 EHRR 471. See also Legg, A., *The Margin of Appreciation in International Human Rights Law*, Oxford University Press, Oxford, 2012.

9 See *Refah Partisi v. Turkey* (2003) 37 EHRR 1 [2003] ECHR 87.

role, as does the new Court of Appeal, and occasionally matters with a constitutional dimension will be determined by the Supreme Court.

The Irish Human Rights and Equality Commission (IHREC)

On 1 November 2014, the Equality Authority (established in 1999) and the Irish Human Rights Commission (established in 2000) merged to become the IHREC, which assumed responsibility for overseeing compliance with the Employment Equality and Equal Status legislation and under the Human Rights Commission Act 2000. Its primary function is to protect and promote human rights and equality and to build a culture of respect for human rights.

The Workplace Relations Commission (WRC)

The Commission was inaugurated under the Workplace Relations Act 2015. It replaces the Employment Appeals Tribunal and consolidates the functions of many other bodies, including the Labour Relations Commission, Rights Commissioner Service, Equality Tribunal and the National Employment Rights Authority. It hears cases of reported discrimination arising in the workplace and under the ESA and Pensions Acts. It operates a discretionary anonymity policy when reporting its rulings.[10]

The Labour Court

Established under the Industrial Relations Act, 1946 the functions of the Labour Court have been altered and extended by subsequent legislation, including the Workplace Relations Act 2015, and it now has sole appellate jurisdiction in all disputes under employment rights enactments. Employment equality claims may be heard by the Labour Court on appeal from the WRC.[11]

International reports on human rights in Ireland

The UN has repeatedly criticised Ireland's record on human rights and government inaction on several fronts.

In 2005, the CEDAW Committee expressed its concern regarding "the persistence of traditional stereotypical views of the social roles and responsibilities of women and men in the family and in society at large which are reflected in Article 41.2 of the Constitution".[12] It reiterated this admonition in 2017 when

10 See further at: www.equalitylaw.eu/downloads/4685-ireland-country-report-non-discrimination-2018-pdf-2-29-mb.

11 See further at: www.workplacerelations.ie/en/WR_Bodies/Labour_Court/Labour_Court.html.

12 CEDAW, *Concluding Observations on Ireland's Combined Fourth and Fifth Reports*, UN Doc. CEDAW/C/IRL/CO/4–5 (2005), at para. 24.

it regretted that "the existing discriminatory provision contained in Article 41.2 of the Constitution, which perpetuates traditional stereotypical views of the social roles and responsibilities of women and men in the family and in society at large, has not been amended".[13]

In July 2014, following its fourth Universal Periodic Review of Ireland's compliance with the ICCPR, the UN HRC advised that both the new abortion legislation and the Constitution must be revised to ensure women who are pregnant as a result of rape, incest or who have a diagnosis of fatal foetal anomaly have access to abortion if they so choose and called for access to abortion where a woman's health is at risk. It reiterated its "previous concern regarding the highly restrictive circumstances under which women can lawfully have an abortion owing to article 40.3.3 of the Constitution and its strict interpretation by the State party". The committee also added to the CEDAW criticism of Article 41.2 and recommended that "the State party should take concrete steps . . . to facilitate the amendment of Article 41.2 of the Constitution to render it gender neutral and further encourage greater participation of women in both public and private sectors". It called for two referendums to be held: on abortion and on the place of women in society.

In 2016, in the course of its consideration of the combined third and fourth periodic reports from Ireland on its progress in implementing UNCROC provisions, questions were asked regarding trans children: what mechanisms were in place to seek acknowledgement of different gender, and at what age was that possible? The committee recommended that Ireland take action in relation to intersex children, including in the area of unnecessary medical and surgical procedures, investigations into these procedures and training for medical staff. More information was sought on the prohibition of non-consensual treatments of intersex children.[14]

More positively, the Transgender Europe (TGEU) organisation has praised the Irish model of gender recognition as among the examples of best international practice and welcomes the fact that the Irish model is "depathologised".[15]

SOGI and related core human rights

For the LGBT community, as for all other socially marginalised groups, it is the core human rights – access to justice, the freedoms of expression, association and religion – that tend to be most important.

13 CEDAW, *Concluding Observations on the Combined Sixth and Seventh Periodic Reports of Ireland*, UN Doc. CEDAW/C/IRL/CO/6–7 (2017), at para. 10.

14 See UN HR Committee on the Rights of the Child (14 January 2016), at: www.ohchr.org/EN/NewsEvents/Pages/DisplayNews.aspx?NewsID=16952&LangID=E.

15 See Transgender Europe, *Human Rights and Gender Identity: Best Practice Catalogue* (2016), at https://tgeu.org/wp-content/uploads/2017/02/2.11-TGEU_BestPractice Catalogue.pdf.

Right of access to justice

There is no express constitutional right of access to justice, and statutory law is restrictive in the terms on which provision is made for legal aid and representation in regulatory and judicial proceedings.[16] In July 2015, the UN Committee on Economic, Social and Cultural Rights expressed concern at the lack of legal aid services in Ireland "which prevents especially disadvantaged and marginalised individuals and groups from claiming their rights and obtaining remedies, particularly in the areas of employment, housing and forced evictions, and social welfare benefits".[17]

Access to relevant information

In 2007, the High Court found the State to be in breach of its positive obligations under Article 8 of the European Convention on Human Rights (ECHR) in failing to provide a trans person with an appropriately amended birth certificate. The lack of such a vital "gateway" document – crucial for purposes such as employment, mortgages, banking etc. – greatly constrains a trans person and leaves them exposed to possible "outing", harassment and continuous interference with their privacy. Not until 2015 did it become possible for a trans person to obtain a new birth certificate through the process outlined earlier.

An effective remedy

The lack of an official procedure for legally recognising gender identity was an issue brought before the High Court in 1997 and again in 2007 by Ms Foy, who had completed a gender confirmation process. Backed by domestic and international human rights bodies – that called on Ireland to institute a gender recognition procedure based on identity and human rights, not surgeries and expert opinions – she sought recognition for her female identity. In 2015, after an overwhelming victory on a same-sex marriage referendum, the government instituted such a procedure in accordance with implementation of EU equality directive requirements regarding effective remedies under the EEA and ESA.[18]

Asylum seekers/illegal immigrants

The legislative and regulatory framework for processing asylum applicants changed in 2015. The Refugee Act 1996 was then repealed and replaced by

16 See, for example, *Michael Lyons v. Longford Westmeath Education and Training Board* [2017] IEHC 272, when the court held that the refusal to allow legal representatives to appear on behalf of the applicant constituted a breach of Article 40(3) (1) and (2) of the Constitution.

17 See further at: www.flac.ie/priorityareas/access-to-justice/.

18 See further at: www.equalitylaw.eu/downloads/4685-ireland-country-report-non-discrimi nation-2018-pdf-2-29-mb.

the International Protection Act 2015, which came into effect in 2017, and the Refugee Appeals Tribunal was replaced by the International Protection Appeals Tribunal, which considers appeals from decisions taken by the International Protection Office, with a further right of appeal lying to the High Court. The 2015 Act, s.8, specifically recognises SOGI as grounds for persecution which warrant asylum.

The asylum appeals system has been busy: the 20-plus High Court cases, dealing with SOGI-related appeals from Tribunal decisions in the period 2006–17, are only the tip of the iceberg, while also attracting considerable public interest.[19] The judiciary have demonstrated a concern to establish guiding principles. For example, *SA (Algeria) v. Minister for Justice*[20] concerned a gay man from Algeria who claimed asylum on the basis of his sexual orientation and whose application had been refused on the grounds that the extent of harassment and discrimination he might face in Algeria would not amount to persecution. This was overturned in the High Court where Hogan J, noting that homosexuality was unlawful in Algeria, admonished the Tribunal with the warning that there was

> no basis in law for saying that just because an applicant did not suffer persecution in the past that he or she cannot qualify as a refugee. What counts is whether there is a well-founded fear that this may occur were the claimant to be returned to their country of origin.[21]

Again, in *ETK v. Refugee Appeals Tribunal*,[22] the refusal of an asylum application from a lesbian woman from Malawi on grounds that focused on her political views as an LGBT activist and was overturned by Flaherty J. This was because undue weight had been given to that ground and insufficient account taken of her sexual orientation and thus of her "membership of a particular social group" which legislatively required specific attention.

Brazil and Arnold[23] have noted that "a significant proportion of judicial decisions in the asylum field concern the assessment of credibility", which some have attributed to a culture of disbelief, and draw attention to four key themes identified with the body of caselaw concerning credibility: the failure to make a clear determination on the core issue of sexual orientation;[24] the correct

19 See, for example: Jansen, S. and Spijkerboer, T., *Fleeing Homophobia: Asylum Claims Related to Sexual Orientation and Gender Identity in Europe*, VU University Amsterdam, 2011; and Noone, C., Keogh, B. and Buggy, C., *Far from Home: Life as an LGBT Migrant in Ireland*, NXF (National LGBT Federation), 2018.

20 [2012] IEHC 78.

21 Ibid., at para. 12.

22 [2016] IEHC 275.

23 Brazil, P. and Arnold, S. LGBTI Asylum Seekers in Ireland, in Guler, A., Shevtsova, M. and Venturi, D. (eds.), *LGBTI Asylum Seekers and Refugees from a Legal and Political Perspective*, Springer, Switzerland, 2019, at pp. 149–150.

24 Citing: *EPA v. Refugee Appeals Tribunal* [2013] IEHC 85; *CC v. Refugee Appeals Tribunal & Ors* [2014] IEHC 491; *ZK v. Refugee Appeals Tribunal anor* [2014] IEHC 543; *MA v. Refugee Appeals Tribunal* [2016] IEHC 16; and *PD v. Minister for Justice & Law Reform & ors* [2015] IEHC 111.

approach to the issue of self-identification;[25] treatment of conflicting country of origin information;[26] and stereotyping, demeanour and cross-cultural expectations".[27]

Right to freedom of expression

Article 40.6.1 of the Constitution protects the right to free speech, in terms similar to those of Article 10(1) and (2) of the ECHR, qualified by the caveat that it may not be used to undermine "public order or morality or the authority of the State". This is supported by the Prohibition of Incitement to Hatred Act 1989, which outlaws hate speech, including incitement to hatred based on sexual orientation. Further reinforcement will be provided by the currently pending Criminal Justice (Aggravation by Prejudice) Bill 2016 with its more punitive provisions for those who commit an "an aggravated offence", including in reference to sexual orientation and transgender identity.[28]

The moral majority

Until at least the late 1960s, Ireland was probably the most religious nation in Europe, with accompanying religion-dictated social mores and familial roles. As noted by O'Higgins CJ in *Norris*,[29] the long established Catholic cultural identity had given the Irish people a "deeply religious conviction and faith and an intention to adopt a Constitution consistent with that conviction and faith and with Christian beliefs". Indeed, the Preamble to, and several Articles of, that Constitution are unequivocal in declaring support for the beliefs and values of the Catholic religion as offering appropriate guiding principles for promoting Irish civic society. While the institutional authority of Catholicism in Ireland has since been eroded by a mix of internal scandals[30] and the external pressures of globalisation and multiculturalism, a legacy of religious protectionism continued to inhibit the modernisation of family law, particularly in relation to matters of sexuality, well into the twenty-first century. Only in very recent years has a moral majority emerged to push for the referendum-mandated reforms needed to address LGBT issues.[31]

25 Citing: *AP v. Refugee Appeals Tribunal* [2013] IEHC 448.

26 Citing: *EPA v. Refugee Appeals Tribunal*, op. cit.

27 Citing: *AF (Nigeria) v. Refugee Appeals Tribunal* [2016] IEHC 430; *PD v. Refugee Appeals Tribunal* [2017] IEHC 56; and *PS v. Refugee Appeals Tribunal* [2016] IEHC 398.

28 See further at: http://enarireland.org/proposed-hate-crime-legislation/. Also see: www.iccl.ie/wp-content/uploads/2018/10/Life-Cycle-of-a-Hate-Crime-Country-Report-for-Ireland.pdf.

29 *Norris v. Attorney General* [1984] IR 36, at p. 64.

30 See Commission of Inquiry into Child Abuse in Orphanages and Schools (the *Ryan report*) at: www.dcya.gov.ie/viewdoc.asp?fn=/documents/Child_Welfare_Protection/RyanImplementation.htm. Also see Inquiry Regarding Sexual Abuse in the Archdiocese of Dublin (the *Murphy report*) at: www.justice.ie/en/JELR/Pages/PB09000504.

31 Ní Mhuirthile, T., Article 8 and the Realisation of the Right to Legal Gender Recognition, in Egan, S., Thornton, L. and Walsh, J. (eds.), *Ireland and the European Convention on Human Rights: 60 Years and Beyond*, Bloomsbury, London, 2014, at pp. 201–218.

Harm to others

In October 2018, the Irish nation voted by referendum to remove Article 40.6.1 – which explicitly criminalised the publication of "blasphemous, seditious, or indecent matter" – from the Constitution. Article 40.3.2, however, continues the constitutional protection of personal civic rights through its assurance that "the State shall, in particular, by its laws, protect as best it may from unjust attack (and, in the case of injustice done, vindicate) the life, person, good name and property rights of every citizen". This is reinforced by the Prohibition of Incitement to Hatred Act 1989 and the Defamation Act 2009 and will in due course be further strengthened when the provisions of the Criminal Justice (Aggravation by Prejudice) Bill 2016 take effect.

Right to freedom of association and assembly

As the International Commission of Jurists point out:

> Freedom of assembly focuses on the process of forming, expressing and implementing political opinions in a democratic society, while freedom of association is about the right to choose, join and form associations relevant to the formation and expression of thoughts and opinions.[32]

The Commission emphasises that these rights are crucial to LGBT activism. The record of peaceful demonstrations, marches and lobbying in Ireland – particularly, since 2015, in the context of the referendums on related matters – testifies to the frequency and responsible manner in which these rights have been exercised. From *Norris v. Ireland*[33] through to the present day, the activism and persuasiveness of associations such as Gay Pride, GLEN and TENI have contributed to significant legislative change and succeeded in bringing the LGBT community into the mainstream of Irish social life.

Constraints

The UDHR, the ICCPR and many other international instruments protect the rights of association and assembly. The Constitution, Article 40.6.1, also does so but makes their exercise subject to legislative requirements protecting public order and morality. Short of inciting hatred; posing a threat to public safety, order or morals; or breaching the rights of others, any exercise of such rights in Ireland is assured of State protection.

32 International Commission of Jurists, *Sexual Orientation, Gender Identity and International Human Rights Law*, Practitioners Guide No. 4 (2018) at p. 124. See further at: www.refworld.org/pdfid/4a783aed2.pdf.

33 Application No. 10581/83 (1988).

Right to freedom of religion

The Constitution acknowledges a duty to "respect and honour religion" (Article 44.1); provides for the freedom of conscience and the free profession and practice of religion, subject to public order and morality (Article 44.2.1); and directs that the State must not impose any disabilities or make any discrimination on the ground of religious profession, belief or status (Article 44.2.3). The European Convention on Human Rights Act 2003 incorporates the ECHR provisions, while further protection is available under the EU Charter of Fundamental Rights and Article 18 of the ICCPR.

SOGI and religion

As Henchy J once rightly pointed out in relation to the previously-mentioned Article 44.2.3, "the primary aim of the constitutional guarantee is to give vitality, independence and freedom to religion".[34] As an inevitable corollary, the constitutional guarantee has had the effect of impeding any developments in the law which might be incompatible with or constrain the exercise of that freedom. Consequently, those advocating on behalf of SOGI issues – homosexuality, gay marriage and gender transitioning – have had to contend with particularly strong resistance from those claiming constitutional support for their opposition.

Religious organisations and the religious exemption

In Ireland, an unusually large proportion of national health, education and social care infrastructure is owned, managed and/or staffed by religious organisations. The religious exemption[35] which had excluded such organisations from many statutory requirements of general application, including equality and non-discrimination provisions,[36] has recently been considerably diluted:[37] the Education (Admission to Schools) Act 2018 amended s.7 of the ESA, so that primary schools can no longer use religion as a selection criterion, in most cases. While there has been some progress in recent years, the continued influence of religious organisations has a correspondingly disproportionate impact on related services, many of which are directly relevant to SOGI issues. Gender reassignment surgery, for example, is not possible in Ireland; those requiring such a service need to travel to England or elsewhere.[38]

34 *McGrath and Ó Ruairc v. Trustees of Maynooth College* [1979] ILRM 166 at p. 187.
35 See, for example, the Equal Status Acts 2000–2012, s.7(3)© and the Employment Equality Acts 1998–2012, s.37(1).
36 *Quinn's Supermarket Ltd v. Attorney General* [1972] IR 1 and *Re Article 26 and the Employment Equality Bill 1996* [1997] 2 IR 321.
37 Author acknowledges advice from Judy Walsh on this point (note to author, 4 June 2019).
38 See Szydlowski, M., The Rights to Health and Health Care of Vulnerable Populations: Reducing the Existing Barriers to Health Equity Experienced by Transgender People in Ireland, *Journal of Human Rights Practice*, 8(2), pp. 239–263 (2016).

SOGI: personal relationships and human rights

In law as in life, sexual orientation and gender identity can give rise to complicated issues. In Ireland, that law has been very largely governed by constitutionally entrenched Catholic precepts with the result that, perhaps for longer than most other developed nations, it eschewed recognition of such complications. Until relatively recently, Irish law perpetuated a symbiotic State/Church approach that punished same-sex relationships, abjured abortion and disallowed same-sex adoption applicants.

Right to recognition as a person before the law

The long saga that constituted the *Foy* legal proceedings[39] – launched in 1997 with repeated unsuccessful hearings in the High Court until 2014 – testifies to the difficulties that faced members of the LGBT community as they sought legal recognition for their status, difficulties that continue to trouble those with an intersex gender identity.

Trans recognition in law

The introduction of the Gender Recognition Act 2015 enabled Ms Foy and other trans persons to obtain legal gender recognition for their gender identity by means of a Gender Recognition Certificate, on the basis of self-declaration, and to have their birth certificates amended accordingly (although, previously, they could be issued with an amended passport). Since then, some 300 trans persons have similarly acquired official recognition. The currently pending Gender Recognition (Amendment) Bill 2017 may well result in a considerable increase in the issue of such Certificates. Those aged 16–18 are treated as normal applicants.

Non-binary gender identity

As yet there is no statutory power or process available whereby legal recognition can be given to those who identify as neither male nor female.[40]

Right to respect for private and family life

The rulings of the ECtHR[41] have been instrumental in injecting a recognition of a right to personal privacy into what, in Irish law, has been traditionally regarded as the public institution of marriage comprised of clearly defined roles and relationships.

39 *Foy v. Registrar General* (No.1) [2002] IEHC 116 and (No.2) [2007] IEHC 470.

40 See further 2018 review group's recommendations at: www.welfare.ie/en/downloads/GRA%20Review%20Report.pdf.

41 In particular, *Goodwin v. United Kingdom* [2002] 35 E.H.R.R. 447 and *I. v. United Kingdom* [2003] 40 E.H.R.R. 967.

Sexual orientation, identity and private life

Following hard on the heels of *Dudgeon*,[42] the ruling in *Norris v. Ireland*[43] was similarly grounded on the right to privacy in Article 8 of the ECHR and had the same effect of establishing that sexual orientation and same-sex relationships should not be matters amenable to State intervention. The litigation began in the Irish courts in 1977 with decisions that a right to privacy was not violated either by the Offences Against the Person Act 1861 nor by the Criminal Law Amendment Act 1885 (criminalising "buggery" and "gross indecency", respectively). The ECtHR, however, found that this legislation failed the tests of being necessary in a democratic society and of being proportionate to a legitimate aim; it imposed harm upon certain people that far outweighed any potential social benefit.

Family life

Article 41.1.1 of the Constitution "recognises the Family as the natural primary and fundamental unit group of Society, and as a moral institution possessing inalienable and imprescriptible rights, antecedent and superior to all positive law", and which guarantees its protection by the State. The conservative conceptualisation of that entity and the constitutional constraints faced by those wishing to modernise Irish family law are nowhere more clearly evident than in Article 41.2, which states:

1 In particular, the State recognises that by her life within the home, woman gives to the State a support without which the common good cannot be achieved.
2 The State shall, therefore, endeavour to ensure that mothers shall not be obliged by economic necessity to engage in labour to the neglect of their duties in the home.

The Irish family unit, as envisaged in the Constitution, is based on marriage (though the spouses need not be heterosexual) and is not dependent upon the presence of children of that marriage.[44] It is also one in which traditional gender stereotyping, if only in relation to the maternal role, continues to take precedence over gender parity considerations. This has attracted a degree of judicial endorsement, as in *Sinott v. Ireland*[45] when Denham J described Article 41.2 as

42 *Dudgeon v. United Kingdom*, Application No. 7525/76 [1981] 4 EHRR 149 [1981] ECHR 5.
43 *Norris v. Ireland*, Application No. 10581/83 (1988).
44 *Murray v. Ireland* [1985] IR 532, 537.
45 [2001] IESC 63.

"a recognition of the work performed by women in the home". However, as the IHREC has noted,

> Article 41.2 is not compatible with Ireland's international human rights obligations, in particular Articles 2, 5, 7 and 11 of the UN Convention on the Elimination of All Forms of Discrimination Against Women (CEDAW) and Articles 3, 25 and 26 of the International Covenant on Civil and Political Rights (ICCPR).[46]

It recommends that "Article 41.2 should be amended to make it gender neutral".[47]

Private life, gender reassignment and divorce

Ireland is one of only four nations to rely on personal self-identification as the route for completing gender reassignment. The Gender Recognition Act 2015 provides a process which minimises State and professional intervention and protects the privacy of the person transitioning (see further below).

Recommendations that married trans persons would have to divorce before they could be recognised in their new gender were included in the report of the Gender Recognition Advisory Group, set up in the wake of the *Foy* ruling[48] (see further below) and published in 2011. At that time there was no provision for same-sex marriage.[49] Despite strong lobbying for its removal, the bar on those in an existing marriage or a civil partnership from qualifying for a Gender Recognition Certificate continued to be included in the Gender Recognition Bill 2014 and in the Gender Recognition Act 2015.[50] Ultimately, due to the successful outcome of the marriage equality referendum,[51] the entire matter ceased to be an issue.

SOGI, parenting and "the best interests of the child" principle

Having signed and ratified the UNCROC, Ireland is bound by Article 3 of that Convention, which requires a child's welfare to be the paramount consideration

46 IHREC, *Article 41.2 of the Constitution of Ireland* (June 2018), at pp. 6–7.

47 Ibid., at p. 15. See further at: https://data.oireachtas.ie/ie/oireachtas/libraryResearch/2018/2018-06-27_l-rs-note-article-41-2-of-the-constitution-women-in-the-home_en.pdf.

48 *Foy v. An t-Ard Chláraitheoir and Others* [2007] IEHC 470.

49 See Department of Social Protection, *Report of the Gender Recognition Advisory Group* (15 June 2011), at: www.welfare.ie/en/pages/Report-of-the-Gender-Recognition-Advisory-Group.aspx.

50 The Gender Recognition Act 2015: s.9(2)(b); s.10(1)(f)(i); s.11(2)(a)(ii); paras. (c) and (d)(ii)(I) of s.15(8); ss.(3) and (8) of s.18.

51 The Gender Recognition Act 2015, as amended by s.24 of the Marriage Act 2015, removed the requirement for an applicant to be unmarried.

in any decision taken regarding his or her upbringing. This principle is also incorporated into domestic law: the Children First Act 2015, s.7; the Children and Family Relationships Act 2015, s. 45; and the Adoption (Amendment) Act 2017, s.9. While as yet there is no caselaw on the subject, it is clear that when issues affecting the upbringing of a child come to court the law will treat a trans parent the same as any other while giving priority to safeguarding and promoting the welfare of a child. Support services are available for trans families.[52]

Right to marriage and to found a family

Article 41.3 of the Constitution declares that "the State pledges itself to guard with special care the institution of marriage, on which the Family is founded, and to protect it against attack", while Article 41.4 provides that "marriage may be contracted in accordance with law by two persons without distinction as to their sex".[53] The High Court, in *Murray v. Ireland*,[54] acknowledged that childless couples were not excluded from the constitutional concepts of marriage and family but, ignoring the possibility of families being reconstituted following divorce, went on to define marriage as "a partnership based on an irrevocable personal consent given by both spouses which establishes a unique and very special lifelong relationship".[55] All of this strongly suggests that family forms not based upon a subsisting marriage are relatively disadvantaged in the eyes of the Constitution.

Legal recognition for same-sex relationships and the right to marry

Homosexuality continued to be a criminal offence in Ireland until 1993, but legitimating same-sex relationships has taken a while longer.[56]

The *Zappone* case[57] in 2006 concerned a lesbian couple who had lived together for 23 years, married in Canada and moved to reside in Ireland where, on being refused tax relief on the basis of their marital status, they claimed discrimination in breach of their constitutional rights under Articles 40, 41 and 43 of the Constitution. Further, they argued that the same refusal amounted to discrimination based on sexual orientation, contrary to Articles 8, 12 and 14 of the ECHR. The court found that as the Constitution's definition of marriage,

52 The Gender Identity Family Support service was launched by TENI in 2018 to provide a helpline for families of trans and gender non-conforming people (01 9073707).

53 Until amended following the decision in *Zappone & Gilligan v. Revenue Commissioners & Ors* [2006] IEHC 404.

54 [1985] I.R. 532.

55 Ibid., per Costello, J., at p. 536.

56 See: Casey, M., Radical Politics and Gay Activism in the Republic of Ireland, 1974–1990, *Irish Studies Review*, 26(2), pp. 217–236 (2018); and Ryan, P., The Pursuit of Gay and Lesbian Sexual Citizenship Rights, 1980–2011, in Leane, M. and Kiely, E. (eds.) *Sexualities and Irish Society: A Reader*, Orpen Press, Dublin, 2013, at pp. 101–126.

57 *Zappone & Gilligan v. Revenue Commissioners & Ors*, op. cit.

as a union between a man and a woman, had repeatedly been reaffirmed by Irish courts; it was therefore impossible to accept the argument that the definition must be reconsidered in the light of contemporary interpretations. If the exclusion of same-sex couples from marriage created a discriminatory distinction based on sexual orientation, the disparate treatment was justified under Article 41 of the Constitution, which pledged the State "to guard with special care the institution of Marriage". This case did, however, generate a momentum for change led by bodies such as Marriage Equality and the Irish Council for Civil Liberties.[58]

The Civil Partnership and Certain Rights and Obligations of Cohabitants Act 2010 gave same-sex couples rights and responsibilities similar, but not equal, to those of married heterosexual couples. Following an overwhelming majority favouring gay marriage in the May 2015 national referendum, the President of Ireland approved legislative provision for same-sex marriage in August 2015, which was duly signed into law as the Thirty-fourth Amendment of the Constitution.[59]

Trans persons and marriage

In *Foy v. An t-Ard Chláraitheoir and Others*,[60] which concerned the legal status of a post-operative trans person, the High Court found that marriage as understood by the Constitution referred to the union of a biological man with a biological woman. McKechnie J ruled that Irish law was deficient and in breach of international human rights, particularly Article 8 of the ECHR, as it failed to provide legal recognition for trans persons. He added that had the issue been presented he would have had no difficulty in finding that her right to marry under Article 12 of the ECHR had also been breached. This ruling resulted in the Gender Recognition Act 2015, which now provides legal recognition for the gender of trans persons. Since 2015, persons of the same gender may now marry under Irish law.

Adoption, surrogacy and child care

Recent legislative developments in child care and adoption[61] (the Children and Family Relationships Act 2015 and the Adoption (Amendment) Act 2017) together with the same-sex relationship statutes (the Civil Partnership Act 2010

58 See the Working Group on Domestic Partnership, *Options Paper on Cohabiting Couples* (the Colley report) (2006), at: www.justice.ie/en/JELR/OptionsPaper.pdf/Files/OptionsPaper.pdf.

59 See Healy, G. (ed.), *Crossing the Threshold: The History of the Marriage Equality Movement*, Merrion, Newbridge, 2017.

60 [2007] IEHC 470.

61 See further: www.lawsociety.ie/News/News/Stories/birth-certificate-fictions-and-assisted-human-reproduction/.

and the Marriage Act 2015) have combined to remove legal impediments to adoption, guardianship or custody arrangements by same-sex or trans parents. For the many same-sex couples unable to "beget" children,[62] the prospect of parenting means taking a route which involves assisted human reproduction services[63] or surrogacy,[64] but as yet there is no specific legislation governing either of these services. Surrogacy agreements, while not illegal, are unenforceable:[65] consequently, it is estimated that there are now several hundred children living in Ireland born to surrogate mothers whose legal status is uncertain and their human rights seriously compromised,[66] a state of affairs which, the Supreme Court pointed out, "makes statutory law reform in this area more than urgent".[67] While this situation was not resolved by the Children and Family Relationships Act 2015, it has been improved somewhat by the Children and Family Relationship (Amendment) Act 2018.

The earlier legislative developments have greatly eased the route to parenting for same-sex and trans parents, but there remains the difficulty that the courts continue to attach considerable weighting to the blood-link factor as a determinant of the welfare test when making decisions regarding arrangements for a child's custody or upbringing. In *N. v. HSE*,[68] as in *J. McD. V. P.L.*,[69] the court stressed the importance of blood or genetic links between a parent and child and intimated, at the very least, that these relationships or links were of paramount importance in deciding parenthood.[70] Subsequently, in *M.R. and D.R. & Others -v- An t-Ard- Chlaraitheoir & Others*,[71] the Supreme Court reaffirmed the principle (*mater semper certa est*) that the birth mother is the legal mother of a child. This judicial approach may well present problems for same-sex or trans persons seeking to secure parenting arrangements through guardianship, custody, surrogacy or adoption.[72]

62 The right to beget children was a matter considered by Costello J. in *Murray v. Ireland* [1985] I.R. 532.
63 Draft legislation now exists: The General Scheme for Assisted Human Reproduction 2017.
64 See further at: www.citizensinformation.ie/en/birth_family_relationships/adoption_and_fostering/surrogacy.html.
65 See the Report of the Commission on Assisted Human Reproduction, Dublin, 2005, which recommended that a child born through surrogacy should be presumed to be that of the commissioning couple. Also, see, *M.R. & Anor v. An tArd Chlaraitheoir* [2013] IEHC 91.
66 See further at: www.aclsolicitors.ie/news-events/current-news/legal-status-of-surrogacy-in-ireland/.
67 *M.R. and D.R. (suing by their father and next friend O.R.) & ors v An t-Ard-Chláraitheoir & ors* [2014] IESC 60 (7 November 2014), per Hardiman, J.
68 [2006] 1 I.R. 374.
69 [2010] 2 I.R. 199.
70 See also *Roche v. Roche* [2010] 2 I.R. 321, when the Supreme Court considered whether a frozen embryo could constitute an "unborn" within the meaning of Article 40.3.3.
71 [2014] IESC 60.
72 See further: https://lgbt.ie/advocacy/campaigns/. Also see LGBT Ireland at: https://lgbt.ie/advocacy/submission/.

Right to cultural life

Conservatism in relation to matters of sexuality has a long history in this country and has been pivotal in shaping the Irish "culture wars" but was successfully challenged in the national referendum to repeal the Eighth Amendment.

Cultural context

In *A, B and C v. Ireland*,[73] the ECtHR considered the rights of a Lithuanian resident in Ireland denied access to abortion and held that a broad margin of appreciation should be accorded to Ireland because of the "acute sensitivity of the moral and ethical issues raised by the question of abortion or as to the importance of the public interest at stake".[74] Interestingly, this was challenged in the dissenting opinion of six judges who considered that such reasoning justified exactly the opposite approach and pointed out that it was "the first time that the court has disregarded the existence of a European consensus on the basis of "profound moral views". They argued that the fact that these "moral views" "can override the European consensus, which tends in a completely different direction, is a real and dangerous new departure in the court's caselaw". It is a line of argument that most obviously resonates with the circumstances surrounding the *Dudgeon*[75] decision but also recalls the moral context prevailing when the court ruled in *Norris*[76] that the "Christian and democratic nature of the Irish State" warranted the criminalisation of homosexuality and when the *Zappone*[77] and *Foy*[78] cases were determined.

SOGI: non-discrimination, affirmative action and equality

Article 40.1 of the Constitution, while recognising that "all citizens shall, as human persons, be held equal before the law", adds that "this shall not be held to mean that the State shall not in its enactments have due regard to differences of capacity, physical and moral, and of social function". As the Chief Justice has noted: "some of these differences, particularly of capacity, are inherent".[79] Hogan J adding that sexual orientation is an "intrinsic and essentially immutable feature of human identity".[80]

73 [2010] ECtHR (GC) (No. 25579/05) (16 December 2010).
74 Ibid.
75 *Dudgeon v. United Kingdom*, Application No. 7525/76 (1981).
76 *Norris v. Attorney General*, IESC 3, I.R. 36.
77 *Zappone & Gilligan v. Revenue Commissioners & Ors* [2006] IEHC 404.
78 *Foy v. An t-Ard Chláraitheoir and Others* [2007] IEHC 470.
79 *MD (a minor) v. Ireland* [2012] 1 I.R. 697, per Denham CJ at para. 43.
80 *SA (Algeria) v. Minister for Justice* [2012] at para. 14.

Equality before the law: sexuality and gender discrimination

The previously-mentioned Article 40.1 declaration and its caveat form the foundations for equality law in Ireland, but, as in England and Wales, domestic legal foundations must also support related EU-initiated developments and adjust accordingly. Although it is true that Irish domestic law in relation to SOGI issues has been transformed over a very short period of time, it must be acknowledged that the impetus for change was to some extent – particularly in relation to employment law – generated by the compliancy requirement in respect of EU law, the trickle of cases through the Irish courts being insufficient to develop the law or apply pressure on the legislature to do so. The initiatives taken by Irish civil society organisations in their push for change have also played a part.[81]

Sex discrimination and sexual orientation discrimination

The Employment Equality Acts 1998–2015 and the Equal Status Acts 2000–2018 provide protection against direct and indirect discrimination on grounds that include gender and sexual orientation, in employment and in the provision of goods, services, facilities, accommodation and education. The Prohibition of Incitement to Hatred Act 1989 provides added protection by prohibiting incitement to hatred based on sexual orientation, as does the Code of Practice on Sexual Harassment introduced by the Department of Justice and Law Reform in 2012.

Gender identity and trans discrimination

The Gender Recognition Act 2015, which came into effect on 8 September 2015, established an Irish gender identity recognition process devoid of any – possibly discriminatory – medical criteria. While gender identity is not explicitly included in the Employment Equality Act 1998–2015 and the Equal Status Acts 2000–2018, it has been interpreted as being covered under the gender ground.[82]

81 See Irish Council for Civil Liberties, *Equality for All Families*, ICCL, Dublin, 2006, at: www.iccl.ie/equality-for-all-families-.html.

82 See *Hannon v. First Direct Logistics Limited*, DEC-E2011-066, www.workplacerelations.ie/en/cases/2011/march/dec-e2011-066-full-caase-report.html, and *Customer Service Advisor v. Financial Services Provider*, ADJ-00012014 (30 October 2018), www.workplacerelations.ie/en/cases/2018/october/adj-00012014.html. In the *Hannon* case, the complainant also successfully invoked the disability ground, arguing that her employer was obliged to afford her reasonable accommodation in the gender transition process.

Affirmative action

That the previously-mentioned Article 40 cannot provide a guarantee of absolute equality was emphasised in *Fleming v. Ireland*,[83] where the court drew attention to the necessity to differentiate in order to take into account the significance of distinct human attributes. The Constitution would seem to acknowledge this in Article 41.2.2, which places a positive – if uncertain – obligation on the State to "endeavour to ensure that mothers shall not be obliged by economic necessity to engage in labour" outside the home. As Walsh points out, "while Article 40.1 permits positive action, it has not to date been interpreted as requiring any such measures".[84]

Statutory law takes this a stage further by recognising a need to differentiate in certain circumstances. The Employment Equality Acts 1998–2015, ss.24(1) and 33, permit affirmative action in certain circumstances by allowing more favourable treatment of employees or prospective employees. This applies not just to accessing jobs but also for more favourable conditions of employment. Similarly, the Equal Status Acts 2000–2018 enable positive action in defined circumstances (s.14(1)(b); 5(2)(h)).

LGBT issues and affirmative State action

The Irish Human Rights and Equality Commission Act 2014, s.42, places a public sector duty on all public bodies, as broadly defined under s.2, to be proactive in taking steps to eliminate discrimination, promote equality of opportunity and protect human rights in respect of employees and service users. Arguably, this duty will have particular implications for the Departments of Education and Health, requiring them to have regard to the need to address LGBT-specific issues in their strategic planning for future service delivery.

Right to equality and non-discrimination: health

Many hospitals and health care facilities have been built, and continue to be managed, by Catholic bodies, and consequently the availability of medical treatment has at times been subject to associated religious beliefs: abortion, contraception and IVF are among the areas where religious sanctions have generated social controversy. The now discredited practice of "conversion therapy", whereby those with a sexual orientation perceived as being at variance with their gender were offered counselling to conform to gender stereotyping, owes a good deal to that once prevailing religious culture.[85]

83 [2013] IEHC 2.
84 Note to author, 4 June 2019.
85 See Prohibition of Conversion Therapies Bill 2018.

Gender reassignment treatment

In Ireland, unlike in the UK, medical treatment or surgical intervention for gender dysphoria is not required in order to legally qualify for a Gender Recognition Certificate. Many, however, do opt for the treatment and/or surgery necessary to realign physical characteristics with their gender identity. In that case, they are required to begin transition by living in the preferred gender identity full time (real life experience) for at least a year before continuing with counselling, hormonal treatment and/or surgery in a process which will probably take two to three years to complete. Gender reassignment procedures are not performed in Irish hospitals but can be arranged in another country and are funded under the Treatment Abroad Scheme. A total of 37 were so funded between 2010 and 2015.

Alternatively, as mentioned earlier, the 2015 Act now provides a process whereby a person may change the gender marker on their birth certificate and be legally recognised by the State in their acquired gender. Prospective trans applicants, aged 16 to 18, require prior approval of the court; this will cease to be the case on the introduction of the Gender Recognition (Amendment) Bill 2017.

Trans children

Children under the age of 16 years fall outside the Gender Recognition Act 2015. Under s.12, however, there is some leeway for adolescents – between 16 and 17 years – to legally undergo transition, as long as they satisfy a series of (strict) access criteria: including having the consent of both parents or guardians (with narrow exceptions); the agreement of the minor's primary treating medical physician and another endocrinologist or psychiatrist; and an order of the Irish Circuit Family Court. Clearly these s.12 conditions create a significant obstacle for 16 and 17-year-old applicants, but adolescence is a confusing time and third-party involvement is perhaps a reasonable safeguard for those at that age contemplating such a life-changing decision with its associated mental health issues.[86] In this context it should be noted that, even in the short lifetime of this scheme, there have already been some applications to revoke Gender Recognition Certificates so as to permit a reversion to original gender.[87]

Sports and recreational activities

The Equal Status Acts in principle provide an assurance that trans persons may participate and compete in sport activities on an equal basis with all others. As of

86 See Higgins, A., et al., *The LGBT Ireland Report: National Study of the Mental Health and Wellbeing of Lesbian, Gay, Bisexual, Transgender and Intersex People in Ireland*, GLEN and BeLonG To Youth Service, Dublin (2016), and at: www.dcya.gov.ie/documents/20180628NatLGBTIYouthStrategy.pdf.

87 See Review of the Gender Recognition Act 2015 (June 2018), op. cit., at p. 43.

2018, there have been no known cases on SOGI issues reported by the courts or regulatory bodies in this context.

Blood donors

The lifetime ban on homosexuals donating blood to the Irish Blood Transfusion Service ended in January 2017. Such a donor, who has not engaged in homosexual relations for 12 months, is now able to donate blood if he meets other blood donor selection criteria. However, many in the Irish LGBT community have called for the deferral period to be reduced in line with other European countries, some of which have eliminated it. The time limit in the UK is now reduced to three months due to improvements in HIV testing, while in Italy and Spain there is no longer any deferral period.

Right to equality and non-discrimination: education

The Equal Status Acts 2000–2018 provide that an educational establishment shall not discriminate in relation to: (i) the admission or the terms of conditions of admission of a person as a student to the establishment and (ii) any other term or condition of participation in the establishment by a student.[88]

Schools

Historically, the national school system has been institutionally discriminatory. It has remained very largely governed by the Catholic Church since the founding of the State: some 97% of primary schools and perhaps 50% of secondary schools are State funded but managed by religious organisations, while 90% of all primary schools are controlled by the Catholic Church.[89] This was reinforced by the Education Act 1998, s.15(2)(b), which conferred authority on school "patrons" to whom Boards of Management are accountable for upholding the ethos of a school. As by far the majority of schools have the Catholic Church, or its representative, as its "patron", the public school system is, in effect, obliged to maintain a Catholic religious ethos which is not always conducive to promoting non-binary gender awareness. However, educational institutions – primary schools, post-primary schools, and third-level educational institutions – may not discriminate against students on a number of grounds, including sexual orientation. Reforms introduced by the Education (Admission to Schools) Act 2018 prohibit Catholic-run primary schools from giving preference to Catholic

88 The Equal Status Acts 2000–2018, s.7(2).

89 Op. cit., which clearly established that the State could support denominationally controlled education in discharging its obligation to provide for free primary education.

children.[90] In addition, the religious exemption in the Employment Equality Act 1998, potentially allowing religious schools to dismiss teachers and staff on SOGI grounds, was removed by the Employment Equality Amendment Act 2015. These reforms will, over time, serve to rebalance the religious bias in the public school system.

Curricula

In Ireland, as noted, State education is faith based, very largely Catholic in nature and perpetuates a Catholic religious ethos; an ethos which has difficulty in addressing SOGI issues and accommodating LGBT perspectives.[91] Moreover, the requirement to provide an "integrated curriculum" in all Catholic schools ensures that religious ethos permeates all teaching, which compromises the rights of staff and pupils to express and address SOGI issues.

International concern has been expressed regarding the constraints which the national education system imposes on facilitating diversity and promoting the delivery of a balanced educational curriculum. In February 2016, the United Nations Committee on the Rights of the Child issued a report[92] which urged Ireland to "expeditiously undertake concrete measures to significantly increase the availability of non-denominational or multidenominational schools and to amend the existing legislative framework to eliminate discrimination in school admissions, including the Equal Status Act".[93] Government initiatives to modify this state of affairs have recently been launched. Most promising is the issue of a draft report by the Oireachtas education committee in December 2018 which recommends that the Education Act 1998 be reviewed and amended so that "ethos can no longer be used as a barrier to the effective teaching of the RSE (Relationships and Sexuality Education) and SPHE (Social Personal and Health Education) curriculum." It suggests that the current 20-year old curriculum should be updated by introducing the Provision of Objective Sex Education Bill 2018 to consider: "the inclusion within curriculums of LGBT specific sexual health issues and the presentation of LGBT relationships without distinction as to their heterosexual counterparts" and the "significant and welcome changes" that have taken place in Ireland in order to produce a gender equality-based, inclusive, holistic, creative, empowering and protective curriculum. Arguably, such legislatively initiated change is necessary to prevail against the religious ethos and permit the integration of SOGI issues into education curricula.

90 Author acknowledges advice from Judy Walsh on this point (note to author, 4 June 2019).
91 See, for example, Neary, A. and Cross, C., *Exploring Gender Identity and Gender Norms in Primary Schools*, at: www.teni.ie/attachments/6d5d22d4-801c-4f2d-b456-299291cc17de.PDF.
92 CRC/C/IRL/CO/3–4, at: http://tbinternet.ohchr.org/_layouts/treatybodyexternal/Download.aspx?symbolno=CRC%2fC%2fIRL%2fCO%2f3-4&Lang=en.
93 Ibid., at para. 64(a).

Colleges/universities

Third-level Irish educational institutions are demonstrating an awareness of SOGI issues by introducing many gender-neutral toilet facilities, using gender-free language in teaching and in internal formal communications and by providing platforms for debate. As of 2018, there has been no equivalent to the vitriolic "no-platforming" confrontations that have troubled some UK universities and no court cases on related matters.

Right to equality and non-discrimination: employment

The law governing equality in an employment context is to be found in the Constitution, the Unfair Dismissals Act, the Workplace Relations Act 2015, the Employment Equality Acts 1998–2015 and various European conventions, protocols and directives.[94] However, while protection can be found under the "gender" and "disability" grounds of this legislation, there are no specific provisions dealing with gender identity discrimination in Irish employment law.

The Department of Justice, Equality and Law Reform introduced the Code of Practice on Sexual Harassment in 2012. This seeks to promote the development and implementation of policies and procedures which establish working environments free of sexual harassment.

Religious exemption

In *Re Article 26 and the Employment Equality Bill 1996*,[95] the Supreme Court held that it was constitutionally permissible to discriminate on grounds of religious profession, belief or status – when hiring or firing staff and other such matters – if this is necessary to "give life and reality" to the constitutional guarantee of freedom of religion.[96] This privilege was promptly given statutory effect in the Employment Equality Act 1998, s.37, which provided an exemption for religious, educational and medical institutions permitting discrimination towards employees and prospective employees where this was deemed necessary to protect the religious ethos of the institution. Subsequently, there have been concerns that the religious exemption was having an adverse effect on the human rights of employees.

The Equality (Miscellaneous Provisions) Act 2015, amending the 1998 Act, retained the religious exemption in s.37.(1)(a), which provides that:

> A religious organisation shall not be taken to discriminate against a person for the purposes of this part or part II by giving favourable treatment on the

94 Mainly, the General Framework (Council Directive 2000/78/EC) but also the Equal Pay Directive (75/117/EEC) and the Equal Treatment Directive (76/207/EEC).

95 [1997] 2 IR 32.

96 The 1996 Bill was declared unconstitutional on other grounds, but s.37(1) of the 1998 Act, its replacement, virtually replicates its predecessor.

religion ground to an employee or a prospective employee where the religion or belief of the employee constitutes a justified occupational requirement.

However, for the exemption to apply, there must be no other discriminatory ground (such as gender or race) on which the differential treatment would constitute discrimination, and this differential treatment must be objectively justified. Organisations are prevented from relying on the exemption unless it is (i) rationally and strictly related to the institution's religious ethos; (ii) in response to conduct of the prospective employee rather than membership of another protected category; and (iii) proportionate to that conduct.

Religious organisations, government funded to deliver public services in areas such as education, health and social care, have traditionally been entitled to rely on their exemption to the statutory prohibition on discriminatory practice to lawfully discriminate in relation to staffing and service access on the basis of religion, belief or sexual orientation. However, this exemption is now restricted by the 2015 Act. Such organisations will only be able to avail of the religious exemption where they can satisfy the three conditions of s.37(1A-1C). In theory, this exemption privilege will therefore continue to potentially affect those employees of such organisations whose SOGI status conflicts with their employers' religious beliefs. However, Judy Walsh comments that "there are no religious ethos exceptions under the Equal Status Acts, save the now limited exception in relation to school admissions".[97]

Sexual orientation in the workplace

There is little caselaw to indicate a significant lack of protection for LGBT persons in the workplace.

The 2013 case of *An Employee v. A Credit Union*[98] concerned the complaint of a gay employee who alleged he had suffered discrimination on the grounds of sexual orientation and associated victimisation. The Equality Officer found that the complainant was constantly referred to as "one of the girls" and that other named colleagues made derogatory comments about his attire and his manner. The Tribunal upheld the allegations both of discrimination on the ground of sexual orientation and of associated victimisation.

In *A Teacher v. A National School*,[99] the Equality Tribunal found in favour of the complainant who alleged she had been discriminated against on grounds which included sexual orientation contrary to s.6(2)(d), (e) and (f) of the Employment Equality Acts 1998 to 2011, in the course of her interview for the post of principal in the national school where she had been employed as a deputy principal for eight years. The Equality Officer found that Sr B., for the interview panel,

97 Note to author, 4 June 2019.
98 DEC-E2012–190. See further at: www.workplacerelations.ie/en/cases/2012/december/dec-e2012-190-full-case-report.html.
99 EE/2012/019 (2014).

had asked the question "What about the homos?" to the complainant, who was not sure whether she was being asked about her own sexual orientation. The Officer was less uncertain: "it is precisely because the interview board did not know Ms A.'s sexual orientation, that I interpret Sr B.'s question as an attempt to ascertain the complainant's sexual orientation without asking the question directly".[100] The Tribunal held that Sr B.'s question was unlawful on the ground of sexual orientation, but its decision was overturned on appeal to the Labour Court.[101]

Trans persons and the workplace

In *Hannon v. First Direct Logistics*,[102] the complaint concerned a business development manager who informed her employer that, having been diagnosed with gender identity disorder, she would begin using a feminine name and living as a woman. The employer responded with a series of measures to limit the employee's exposure to external clients, including: requesting that clients be dealt with over the phone; not changing an email account to the employee's new feminine name; and then asking the employee to only work from home. Management repeatedly asked the employee to continue their male identity to ensure that staff and clients were comfortable. Ultimately the employee resigned and commenced proceedings alleging discrimination, on grounds prohibited under s.85A of the Employment Equality Acts 1998–2008,[103] and constructive dismissal by the employer after the transitioning process commenced. Ruling in favour of the complainant, the Tribunal found that

> the facts of this case clearly reveal how a failure to appreciate the reality of a disability and the exclusion of the person with a disability from the process that aims to integrate her, has resulted in discriminatory treatment on the gender and disability grounds.[104]

This was the first trans discrimination case heard by the Equality Tribunal (now Workplace Relations Commission) in Ireland.

Employment in the military

Homosexuality was de-criminalised in 1993, since which date there has been no evidence of discrimination between homosexuals and heterosexuals in either the

100 Ibid., at para. 4.21.

101 Author thanks Judy Walsh for bringing this to his attention (note to author, 4 June 2019). See further at: www.workplacerelations.ie/en/cases/2015/october/eda1515.html.

102 DEC-E2011-066.

103 *Melbury v. Valpeters* EDA/0917 provides authority for the view that s.85A "places the burden of establishing the primary facts fairly and squarely on the Complainant and the language of this provision admits of no exceptions to that evidential rule".

104 Ibid., at para. 4.8.

recruitment or the conditions of service in the national Defence Forces. A staff LGBT network was set up in 2016 and the Defence Forces take part in Pride.[105]

Right to equality and non-discrimination: services

The Equal Status Acts 2000–2018 prohibit discrimination on nine specific grounds, including gender and sexual orientation. The legislation applies to the provision of goods and services, including housing and education, that are available to the public or a section of the public. It covers both private and public service providers. An exemption applies to any difference in treatment that is required by law.

Trans persons and gender-specific services

There is a concern that the prospective abortion legislation will operate to the exclusion of trans men and non-binary people. This is seen as likely to follow from the fact that under the Gender Recognition Act 2015, s.18, trans men with a Gender Recognition Certificate are legally recognised as men while the proposed abortion legislation "will allow terminations only for women, defined as female persons of any age". The provision of gender-neutral bathroom facilities has been non-contentious, and these have been widely introduced. There has been no equivalent to the level of protest in the UK and the US regarding trans access to female-specific facilities such as Rape Crisis Centres and Women's Aid Shelters.

Provision of public services

Following the publication of the Adoption (Amendment) Act 2016, same-sex couples in Ireland have, for the first time, been able to jointly adopt children and step-children. This is likely to trigger the same problems for Irish Catholic adoption agencies as it has for their counterparts in the UK, the US and elsewhere.

Trans persons and prisons

Prisons, in Ireland as elsewhere, constitute a vulnerable environment for trans inmates, though in terms of scale the problem in this country is less pressing and therefore generates little related caselaw. An exception was *Connolly v. Governor of Wheatfield Prison*,[106] which concerned the intimidation and rape suffered by a gay prisoner in Mountjoy prison who was then transferred to Wheatfield where, at his request, he was kept in protective custody 23 hours a day. After some months he sought to be released on the grounds that the undue duress of

105 See further at: www.irishtimes.com/news/ireland/irish-news/head-of-defence-forces-to-walk-in-dublin-pride-parade-1.3548434.

106 [2013] IEHC 334.

that regime breached his constitutional rights. Hogan J refused, explaining that the circumstances of the detention could not be said to violate the substance of the guarantee of personal integrity under Article 40.3.2. More recently, in 2016 the Irish Prison Reform Trust published its commissioned report "Out on the Inside", which drew attention to the absence of any policies specific to LGBT prisoners and identified trans persons as being most at risk.[107] As of Spring 2019, there had been no government policy change in response to that report.

Private goods and service provision

The Equal Status Acts 2000–2018 prohibit discrimination on the basis of sexual orientation in the provision of goods and services, as well as in other areas, and the Workplace Relations Commission rules on complaints arising in that context with a right of appeal to the Circuit Court. The prohibition extends to cover sexual harassment and harassment, and victimisation. There is a duty on those selling goods or providing services to reasonably accommodate staff with SOGI status unless doing so would impose an undue burden on the employer.

In 2014, the Equality Tribunal found the Allied Irish Bank guilty of discrimination under ss.3(1)(a) and 3(2)(a) of the Equal Status Acts when it refused to recognise the changed name of a trans woman and to alter the name on her bank account after she had legally changed it.[108] In an interesting clash of views, the bank argued that a person who changed their gender also changed their identity, while the claimant countered that she had not changed her identity or gender – rather, she had affirmed her true gender. She argued that because a trans person goes through a transition over various periods of time there is no point at which that person has definitively changed from one gender to another. The Equality Officer, sidestepping that argument, confined his rationale to comparing the claimant's position with that of a woman who changes her name after getting married and concluded that there had been a difference of treatment and this was attributable to the claimant having been discriminated against on gender grounds by the AIB. In the same year, the Equality Tribunal considered a complaint from a trans person (mtf) of discriminatory behaviour by a hospital consultant, who had refused to acknowledge her gender identity (using language such as "his vagina"). Despite a finding that such language had been used, the Tribunal dismissed the charges of discrimination on the grounds of gender and of harassment.[109]

Two cases determined by regulatory bodies, on much the same set of facts but with different outcomes, have concerned alleged discrimination by barbers for men in relation to their treatment of trans persons (ftm). The Workplace

107 See further at: www.iprt.ie/files/IPRT_Out_on_the_Inside_2016_EMBARGO_TO_1030_Feb_02_2016.pdf.

108 *O'Byrne v. AIB*, DEC-S2013–015, at: www.workplacerelations.ie/en/cases/2013/december/dec-s2013-015.html.

109 *A Patient v. A Hospital*, DEC-S2014–020.

Relations Commission in *McLoughlin v. Paula Smith Charlies Barbers*,[110] unlike the Equality Tribunal in the earlier case of *Carroll v. Gruaig Barber*,[111] found that the complainant had suffered discrimination on the grounds of gender when the respondent refused to provide him with a haircut, breaching the Equal Status Acts. In both cases the barber had declared in front of other customers "we do not cut ladies' hair", thereby causing distress to both complainants;[112] but in *Carroll*, because the respondent was constrained by the terms of their lease, the Tribunal found that he was entitled to rely on the exemption provided under s.5(2) of the Equal Status Acts.

Mr. Peter McGuffin and Mr. Enda Harte v. Eyre Square Hotel[113] concerned complainants who, having been told that they could host an LGBT event for their gay friends and others in the Eyre Square hotel, and had advertised that event in posters around the town, were then forced to cancel the event when the hotel proprietor refused to allow it to go ahead because he disapproved of their sexual orientation. The Equality Tribunal ruled that the complainants had been discriminated against on basis of their sexual orientation and directed that that the respondent immediately develop an equal status policy and carry out appropriate training to ensure that all staff are adequately informed of their responsibilities under the Equal Status Acts.

More recently, in *Brennan v. Noel Tuite t/a Beulah Print*,[114] the complainant claimed that he was discriminated against and harassed by the respondent on grounds of sexual orientation and religion when the respondent, a provider of a printing service, refused to print invitations in respect of the complainant's civil partnership. The respondent, a committed Christian, refused the service not because of the complainant's sexual orientation but because he did not believe in or support gay marriage and, in the circumstances, could not provide the personal and bespoke service required for wedding invitations. The Tribunal found that the complainant was discriminated against by the respondent on grounds of sexual orientation but was not discriminated against on the grounds of religion.

Pensions, social security benefits etc.

As has been pointed out: "Section 81E (5) of the Pensions Act 1990 prevents pensioners, who retired more than one year before the Civil Partnership Act, 2010, from challenging the refusal of a survivor's pension for their civil partner".[115] This was due to the continuing effect of the ruling in *Parris v. Trinity College Dublin*,[116] a landmark ECJ decision which found that as Irish law had

110 ADJ-00011948 (2018).
111 DEC-S2015–005.
112 Both cases cited Article 10 of the Framework Directive (Council Directive 2000/78/EEC) and *P v. S and Cornwall County Council* (Case C-13/94) [1996] ICR 795.
113 DEC-S2008–051 (2008).
114 DEC-S2018–020 (2018).
115 See, *Review, the Journal of the Public Service Executive Union* (July–August 2014), at p. 26.
116 Case C-443/15 (2016).

not provided for, nor recognised the status of, same-sex marriage or partnerships prior to 2010, there was no legal requirement to give retrospective effect to the mutual legal obligations arising between the parties in those relationships after the introduction of the 2010 Act. This invidious situation – whereby the law denied a benefit to claimants because the parties were not married or in a civil partnership at a time when the law denied the parties any opportunity to acquire such status – gave rise to the private members Pensions (Equal Pension Treatment in Occupational Benefit Scheme) (Amendment) Bill 2016. Section 1 inserts a new subsection (5) into s.72 of the Pensions Act 1990. This provides that it would be a breach of the principle of equal treatment on the grounds of sexual orientation, for a scheme to fix a requirement that employees would have to have married or entered civil partnership before a certain age, in circumstances where persons were unable to do so because they were not legally entitled to marry because they were in a same-sex relationship. Senator Ivana Bacik, the promoter of the Bill, explained in the *Senead*:[117]

> I see this Bill as a legacy Bill. It deals with a legacy of discrimination against gay couples and gay people. It is an important way of clearing up an anomaly in pension law that exists now despite the fact we passed the referendum in 2015 with such a strong majority. Despite the fact we now have equality for same-sex couples, we still have a legacy of discrimination that is based on archaic age restriction clauses in some occupational pension schemes.

In the meantime, the UKSC determination of the *Walker* case[118] (see Chapter 3), because it was grounded on two EU decisions, in itself required Irish law on this issue to be revised, which it was with the introduction of the Social Welfare, Pensions and Civil Registration Act 2018. This legislation would seem to have finally resolved the Parris anomaly: it provides that if the retired employee was in a committed relationship with a same-sex partner at the time they retired or reached a particular age and then married that partner within three years of the enactment of the Marriage Act 2015, they are deemed to be eligible for a survivor pension; it does not take effect retrospectively.

Conscientious objection of service providers

Article 44.2.1 of the Constitution provides a guarantee that all citizens are entitled to "freedom of conscience . . . subject to public order and morality". Any restriction on this right would have to be rational, intrude as little as possible and be proportionate to the aim it seeks to achieve.[119]

117 See further at: www.kildarestreet.com/sendebates/?id=2017-03-22a.237.
118 *Walker v. Innospec Limited & Others* [2017] UKSC 47.
119 See *Heaney v. Ireland* [1994] 3 IR 531.

SOGI, public service and conscientious objection

Following the referendum in May 2018, which overturned the Eighth Amendment abortion ban, the government prepared a draft Health (Regulation of the Termination of Pregnancy) Bill 2018. This provides, under general head 15, that

> nothing in this Bill shall be construed as obliging any medical practitioner, nurse or midwife to carry out, or to participate in carrying out, a termination of pregnancy . . . to which he or she has a conscientious objection.

Fearing that this clause might jeopardise the government commitment that services for the termination of pregnancy will be provided on a universal basis, the Chief Commissioner of the Irish Human Rights and Equality Commission has warned that:

> The State needs to make sure that, in reality, there are no barriers to safe, timely and equal access to services. This means that, in practice, the right to conscientious objection needs to be effectively balanced with women and girls' right to legal medical care, and that access to a termination of pregnancy should not be determined by what part of the country you live in.[120]

Given that an equivalent exemption already operates in relation to priests, ministers and deacons officiating at same-sex marriages, there is a concern that conscientious objection is becoming more generalised and constitutes a growing constraint on realising the statutorily secured human rights of the LGBT community.

Conclusion

Irish membership of the European Union together with adherence to its conventions, protocols and treaty requirements; to European Council directives and guidance; and to the rulings of the ECtHR and the HR Committee have combined to drive forward an alignment of domestic SOGI law with international human rights. As Walsh rightly points out: "EU law has had a significant impact in relation to employment while ECtHR rulings have been significant as regards gender identity and the most egregious human rights violations relating to sexual orientation (*Norris* etc.)".[121]

The developmental line of progression has been similar to that of other jurisdictions such as the US and the UK: anti-discrimination legislation – covering

120 See further at: www.ihrec.ie/human-rights-and-equality-commission-calls-for-conscientious-objection-and-access-provisions-to-be-clearly-set-out-in-abortion-legislation/.

121 Note to author, 4 June 2019.

sexual orientation, gender identity and transgender status – has followed on from the introduction of such legislation to protect women, racial groups and persons with disabilities. However, while similarly linear, the progressive steps that have brought Ireland to this point in its SOGI-related jurisprudence seem more compressed, most having occurred within the past five years.

6 United States of America

Introduction

In 2017, the LGBT community in the US was noted to be increasing and estimated at some 8.1% of all millennials, or 4.5% of the population at large.[1] These are big numbers and, even if somewhat tentative, and even if numbers are beside the point, this socially marginalised group of vulnerable people does require a human rights response. In fact, the US legal response to SOGI issues has been slow to develop, is reliant on very dated legislation and is currently embroiled in political equivocation and culture wars polarisation.

This chapter tracks the pattern established by its predecessors. Beginning with an outline of the relevant prevailing international and domestic legal framework, it then considers the bearing of core human rights on SOGI issues: the right to justice and the freedoms of association, expression and religion. The heart of the chapter follows with an examination of the SOGI issues that typically arise in a personal relationships context and identifies the resulting implications for human rights. This leads into the main part of the chapter, which starts by assessing the meaning and significance of non-discrimination, affirmative action and equality before surveying the caselaw on SOGI issues relating to such key equality and non-discrimination themes as health, education, employment and service provision.

Legislative framework: international and domestic

The United States was a leading nation in the adoption of the Universal Declaration of Human Rights (UDHR) and in recent decades has become a signatory State to most of the ten core international human rights instruments, some with optional protocols. However, there is no international or federal authority that can ensure a nationwide human rights compliant regime; in that respect, as in others, each state enjoys considerable independence. Indeed, the degree of that independence and the resulting variance between states and between them and

1 Gallop poll at: https://news.gallup.com/poll/234863/estimate-lgbt-population-rises.

federal law and policy is a complicating factor in this as in all studies of contemporary US society.

International legislation

The US has signed and ratified the International Convention on the Elimination of All Forms of Racial Discrimination (ICERD) and has signed but not ratified the Convention on the Elimination of All Forms of Discrimination Against Women (CEDAW); nor has it signed the Optional Protocol; the UN Convention on the Rights of the Child (UNCROC); the International Convention on Economic, Social, and Cultural Rights (ICESCR); and the American Convention on Human Rights (see Chapter 2). The failure to ratify is in part due to a technical issue: a two-thirds Senate majority is required, and in the current political climate this is almost impossible to achieve. In 2010, it declared its support for the United Nations Declaration on the Rights of Indigenous Peoples.

Singularly, among the common law nations, the US protects its sovereignty by denying international conventions any scope for superseding domestic legislation. Since the 1970s it has conducted an annual international human rights audit.

The International Covenant on Civil and Political Rights (ICCPR)

The US has signed and ratified the International Covenant on Civil and Political Rights (ICCPR), thereby undertaking to participate in an international review of its progress on human rights matters through the mandatory Universal Periodic Review process as outlined in Article 40 of the Covenant. However, it has not incorporated the Covenant into domestic law nor has it signed the Second Optional Protocol (see Chapter 3).

Other

Having initially voted against adopting the UN Declaration on the Rights of Indigenous People 2007, the US ultimately removed its objections in 2010.

The Constitution and federal legislation

The Declaration of Rights was proclaimed in Virginia in 1776. The Constitution, originally comprising seven Articles, came into force in 1789 and has since been amended 27 times.

The Constitution

The first ten Amendments, collectively known as the Bill of Rights, offer specific protections for individual liberty and justice and place restrictions on the powers of government. Of particular importance for present purposes are the First and the Fourteenth Amendments: the First guarantees the freedoms of expression, assembly, association and religion; while the Fourteenth asserts federal authority by forbidding states to deny any person their "life, liberty, or property, without due process of law" and guarantees every person within a state's jurisdiction "the equal protection of its laws". The Fourteenth has grounded the development of the Supreme Court's jurisprudence on personal privacy and sex discrimination.

The Hate Crimes Prevention Act 2009

Also known as the Matthew Shepard and James Byrd Jr. Hate Crimes Prevention Act, or the Matthew Shepard Act, it expands the 1969 United States federal hate-crime law to include crimes motivated by a victim's actual or perceived gender, sexual orientation, gender identity or disability. In 2016, it was used for the first time in respect of a gender identity crime when a man was successfully prosecuted for murdering his transgender ex-girlfriend.

The Equal Access Act 1984

This legislation requires federally funded secondary schools to provide equal access to extracurricular student clubs or groups on school grounds. The legislative intent is to counteract perceived discrimination against religious speech in public schools and overturn two appellate court decisions that had held that allowing student religious groups to meet on campus before and after classes would violate the Establishment Clause. As Justice Kennedy pointed out,

> one of the consequences of the statute, as we now interpret it, is that clubs of a most controversial character might have access to the student life of high schools that in the past have given official recognition only to clubs of a more conventional kind.[2]

The Civil Rights Act 1964: Title VII

The Civil Rights Act, an iconic milestone for US and for anti-discrimination laws everywhere, sought to prohibit discrimination in public life on a federal basis, including in commerce and education. Title VII prohibits employers, with 15 or more employees, from discriminating against employees or prospective employees on specified grounds, including "because of . . . sex". Title VII was amended by the Civil Rights Act of 1991, in response to Supreme Court decisions, thereby "expanding the scope of relevant civil rights statutes in order to

2 *Board of Education v. Mergens*, 496 U.S. 226, 110 S.Ct. 2356 (1990) at 259.

provide adequate protection to victims of discrimination"[3] and certainly not to the exclusion of sexual orientation discrimination.[4]

Other legislation

The Civil Service Reform Act 1978 protects federal government employees by prohibiting sexual orientation discrimination.

Currently pending is some proposed federal legislation with potential to significantly impact SOGI issues. Foremost in importance is the Equality Bill[5] which, if passed, would amend the Civil Rights Act of 1964 to prohibit discrimination on the basis of sexual orientation and gender identity in employment, housing, public accommodations, public education, federal funding, credit and the jury system. It defines: "sex" to include a sex stereotype, sexual orientation or gender identity and pregnancy, childbirth or a related medical condition, with "sexual orientation" as homosexuality, heterosexuality or bisexuality; and "gender identity" as gender-related identity, appearance, mannerisms or characteristics, regardless of the individual's designated sex at birth. Also pending, though for longer as it was first introduced in 1994, is the Employment Non-Discrimination Act (ENDA), which would prohibit discrimination in hiring and employment on the basis of sexual orientation or gender identity by employers with at least 15 employees. Its frame of reference has moved well beyond its original bounds of employment to now include "Public Accommodations, Education, Federal Financial Assistance, Employment, Housing, Credit, and Federal Jury Service".

Equality and non-discrimination

The proclamation in the Declaration of Independence that "all men are declared equal" was the starting point for US equality laws, and this principle subsequently found endorsement in the "equal protection of the laws" provision in the Fourteenth Amendment. Currently, in practice, many of the associated SOGI issues are litigated under the provisions of the Civil Rights Act of 1964, particularly under of Title VII of this federal statute, while each state has its own roughly similar framework equality and non-discrimination laws. Litigation is also initiated directly under the Equal Protection Clause, under state law and under other federal statutes.

Framework of courts and regulatory bodies

SOGI issues are adjudicated on an exclusively domestic basis, to be heard and resolved in federal and state courts and administrative proceedings, though there is recourse to review on certiorari by the USSC, at its discretion.

3 Pub. L. No. 102–166, 105 Stat. 1071 (1991) §§ 2(2), 3(2), 105 Stat. at 1071.

4 See *Zarda v. Altitude Express*, 855 F.3d 76, 79–81 (2d Cir. 2017) at 129.

5 H.R.2282 – Equality Act, 115th Congress (2017–2018). See further, at: www.congress.gov/bill/115th-congress/house-bill/2282.

International courts and regulatory bodies

The US continues to refute the jurisdiction of the International Criminal Court in respect of its citizens, on the grounds that it cannot accept any constraints on its sovereignty. A perceived threat to that sovereignty prompted its withdrawal from the United Nations Educational, Scientific and Cultural Organisation (UNESCO) and United Nations Human Rights Council (UNHRC) in October 2017 and July 2018 respectively.

The Human Rights Committee (HRC)

This body of international experts monitors the progress of States parties, including the US, in implementing the provisions of the ICCPR. The US submitted reports, pursuant to the Universal Periodic Review process, in 2010 and 2014 and is due to be reviewed again in 2020.

Domestic courts and regulatory bodies

Each state has its own judicial and regulatory system, including a state Supreme Court. The United States Supreme Court (USSC) is the ultimate court of appeal. Appointments to this court are made on the basis of nomination by the President and confirmation by the Senate. which leaves them open to political bias and has resulted in a very divided bench that makes some seemingly weak decisions.[6]

Federal courts

Article III of the Constitution grants federal courts the authority to hear only "cases" and "controversies".[7] The federal Circuit Court of Appeals hears cases on appeal from rulings issued by state district courts, and when sitting *en banc* the court has authority to review and set aside its earlier precedents. The review jurisdiction of the United States Supreme Court (USSC) is discretionary and is exercisable, in respect of controversies, on a writ of certiorari under Rule 10 of the US Supreme Court's rules of procedure.

The Equal Employment Opportunity Commission (EEOC)

This federal agency administers and enforces civil rights laws and as such is the regulatory body for matters arising under Title VII of the Civil Rights Act 1964. It is responsible for enforcing federal laws that make it illegal to discriminate against a job applicant or an employee because of the person's race, colour, religion, sex (including pregnancy, gender identity and sexual orientation), national origin, age (40 or older), disability or genetic information. Many states have

6 For example, the USSC decision in *Burwell v. Hobby Lobby*, 573 U.S. 134 S Ct 2751 (2014) was on the basis of a 5–4 majority.

7 U.S. Const. art. III, § 2, cl. 1.

equivalent agencies with a right of appeal to the courts, which adjudicate on points of law and may grant leave of appeal to the state Supreme Court.

International reports on human rights in the US

In 2015, at the second Universal Periodic Review, concerns were expressed regarding the increasing restrictions on women's right to abortion in some states,[8] and there were direct challenges regarding the abortion restrictions that the US periodically imposes on the disbursement of its foreign aid. Cynthia Burack[9] notes that under the category "Civil Rights and Discrimination", the report enumerates forms of legal and other progress in resolving "discrimination against lesbian, gay, bisexual, and transgender individuals". These included: the Supreme Court decision in *United States v. Windsor*[10] and policy changes compatible with the partial nullification of the Defense of Marriage Act (struck down in 2016); efforts to resolve discrimination and harassment against LGBT students in public schools; transgender training for law enforcement officers; federal efforts to prohibit SOGI discrimination in federal employment; the extension of the federal ban on sex discrimination in employment to discrimination based on gender identity and transgender status; and final repeal of Don't Ask, Don't Tell.

SOGI and related core human rights

If the law

> is applied and administered by public authority with an evil eye and an unequal hand, so as practically to make unjust and illegal discriminations between persons in similar circumstances, material to their rights, the denial of equal justice is still within the prohibition of the Constitution.[11]

One hundred and thirty years later, it is still the case that the judiciary must often turn to the Constitution to secure equal justice by repairing deficiencies or patching the holes in government protective measures for minority groups; currently, this is necessitated by the many SOGI issues generated by a diverse LGBT community that remain inadequately addressed by legislators.

Right of access to justice

Equality of access to justice is fundamental to the rule of law and is proclaimed in the Fourteenth Amendment, which provides that a State shall not "deny to

8 See further at: www.wired.com/2014/03/united-nations-human-rights-committee-considers-report-united-states/.
9 Burack, C., *Because We Are Human: Contesting US Support for Gender and Sexuality Rights Abroad*, Suny Press, 2018, at p. 57.
10 570 U.S. 744.
11 *Yick Wo v. Hopkins*, 118 U.S. 356, 373–74, 6 S.Ct. 1064, 1073, 30 L.Ed. 220 (1886).

any person within its jurisdiction the equal protection of the laws". This is given effect through provisions for legal aid and representation and by the requirement that government adopt "positive action" measures for facilitating access. Further, a fair trial is a constitutional right, guaranteed to all by the Sixth Amendment. However, Guantánamo,[12] the Detainee Treatment Act 2005 and the 2017 immigration constraints stand as reminders that access to justice is compromised in the US.

Access to relevant information

Accessing the relevant legal document providing information as to the sex with which an individual identifies and which may then be used as proof of sex necessary to obtain further information, other identity documents, and to avail of services, is clearly of fundamental importance to trans persons. The processes for doing so, however, and specifically the ability to change the sex designation on a birth certificate, varies from state to state. If a trans person has had sex reassignment surgery and could provide an affidavit from a doctor confirming it then, as of 2016, 29 states would allow them to change the gender marker on their birth certificates; very few would do so without that corroboration.

Birth certificates, as the USSC noted in *Pavan*,[13] are "more than a mere marker of biological relationships" – they are "a form of legal recognition". It then considered the refusal of authorities in Arkansas to issue birth certificates that included reference to the female spouses of women. It found that "same-sex parents in Arkansas lack the same right as opposite-sex parents to be listed on a child's birth certificate, a document often used for important transactions like making medical decisions for a child or enrolling a child in school" and ruled that the *Obergefell* decision proscribes such disparate treatment.

An effective remedy

In this most litigious of nations, recourse to the courts is often the best means of effecting change. This is evidenced by the record of landmark USSC cases – running, perhaps, from *Lawrence v. Texas*[14] to *Obergefell v. Hodges*[15] – which have altered the legal landscape for the LGBT community. However, as noted earlier, there is a need to have an effective and standardised means of ensuring that in legal ID documentation the gender listed is compatible with an individual's expressed gender identity, thereby allowing that individual to avoid having to disclose their trans status in situations where "being outed" could expose them to

12 Notwithstanding the USSC decision in *Boumediene v. Bush*, 553 US 723 (2008) that detainees at Guantánamo Bay have a constitutional right to habeas corpus.

13 *Marisa N. Pavan et al. v. Nathaniel Smith*, 582 U.S. (2017). Also citing, *DeBoer v. Snyder*, 772 F. 3d, 388, 398–399 (CA6 2014).

14 539 U.S. 558 (2003).

15 576 U.S. (2015).

discrimination or violence. This seemed to be acknowledged in *K.L. v. Alaska*[16] when the court ruled that the state's failure to have a policy permitting an individual to change the gender marker on their driver's license impermissibly interfered with a trans person's right to privacy under the state constitution.

Where there is no law there is no means of legal redress and thus no possibility of securing an effective remedy: there is no federal law prohibiting SOGI discrimination. The enduring judicial gridlock on interpretation of the Title VII term "because . . . of sex" – specifically whether "sex" may be defined as "gender identity" – is obstructing the development of a clear and unequivocal legal remedy for SOGI discrimination. As Cynthia Burack points out, resolving this has become a matter of capricious politics:

> under the Obama administration, the EEOC took the position that "sex" included sexual orientation and gender identity, and many courts followed suit in their rulings. However, in the Trump administration, although the EEOC has continued to take this [Obama-era] position, the Attorney General's office has reversed that interpretation, and the question of "sex" in Title VII is now under litigation.[17]

Asylum seekers/illegal immigrants

The Immigration and Nationality Act 1965, initially enacted in 1952 (and subsequently and frequently amended)[18] authorises the Attorney General to grant asylum where an applicant is unable or unwilling to return to their country of origin because of either past persecution or a well-founded fear of future persecution on the protected grounds of "race, religion, nationality, membership in a particular social group, or political opinion". The SOGI-related caselaw has since largely focused on the Refugee Convention (see Chapter 2) key terms – "particular social group", "well founded fear of persecution" and "*refoulement*".

The term "particular social group" was first defined, in 1985, by the Board of Immigration Appeals (BIA) in *Matter of Accosta*[19] in terms of a membership that shared some innate characteristic (e.g. race, nationality religion), which members should not be required to change. This case, by introducing a new definition of "social group" which was duly extended in 1990 to include sexual orientation[20] and later to trans persons,[21] was of international significance as it provided a model that became widely replicated. In 2008, the BIA introduced the requirement that

16 Case No. 3AN-11–05431 CI.
17 Note to author, 12 May 2019.
18 Based upon the Convention Relating to the Status of Refugees 1951 and its 1967 Protocol and amended by the Refugee Act 1980.
19 19 I&N Dec. 211 (BIA 1985).
20 *Matter of Toboso-Alfonso*, 20 I&N Dec. 819 (B.I.A. 1990).
21 *Hernandez-Montiel v. INS*, 225 F.3d 1084 (9th Cir. 2000).

such a group must be based on an immutable characteristic and be socially visible and particularly defined[22] – a requirement clarified in 2014 to mean merely that the group be recognised as a distinct entity within society.[23] Membership of a particular social group may be a matter of perception: for example, evidence may show that an individual was perceived to be LGBT even if they were not. State courts varied in their response to these BIA rulings, some declining to accept BIA adjustments as to what qualified as a "particular social group" and, for example, finding that same-sex relationships did not so qualify.

The *Matter of A-B*[24] is important for several reasons, including the fact that the Attorney General, in overruling *A-R-C-G-*, then clarified the interpretation of "fear of persecution". This may now be taken as consisting of three strands: the severity of the harm; whether inflicted, or likely to be so, on a protected ground; and whether inflicted by government or by an entity the government is unable or unwilling to control. The presence of all three gives rise to a presumption that a fear of future persecution is reasonable.[25]

Refoulement is a problematic concept in the context of a nation which pioneered "extraordinary rendition" and routinely pre-empts this issue by denying entry to asylum seekers, though by forcing many to remain in dangerous conditions on the Mexico border, or in any other country from which those being persecuted may wish to flee, the US is probably in standing breach of the *refoulement* rules. Indeed, the Trump administration has now become strongly associated with measures intended to curtail the flow of "asylum seekers" and where possible to deport those already in the country without proper documentation. Those measures have so far included: building a wall along the Mexican border; turning back the "migrant caravan" from Honduras; banning Muslim immigrants from six countries (where persecution on SOGI grounds is known to force victims to seek refuge elsewhere) from entering the US; and making the deportation of 11.3 million undocumented immigrants residing in the US a policy priority. These and other restrictive measures have undoubtedly adversely impacted upon those with SOGI vulnerabilities.

Right to freedom of expression

As the USSC has noted, this right is not violated by state penalty-enhancement laws for hate crimes[26] and is one with close links to expressive-association

22 *Matter of S-E-G-*, 24 I&N Dec. 579 (BIA 2008) and *Matter of E-A-G-*, 24 I&N Dec. 591 (BIA 2008).

23 *Matter of M- E-V-G-*, 26 I&N Dec. 227 (BIA 2014) and *Matter of W-G-R-*, 26 I&N Dec. 20 (BIA 2014).

24 *Matter of A-B-*, 27 I&N Dec. 316 (A.G. 2018) which overruled the *Matter of A-R-C-G-*, 26 I&N Dec. 338 (BIA 2014).

25 *Yasinskyy v. Holder*, 724 F.3d 983, 989 (7th Cir. 2013).

26 *Wisconsin v. Mitchell*, 508 U.S. 476.

rights.[27] However, not all views expressed qualify for First Amendment protection: they must touch upon a matter of public concern.[28]

One variant of this right that has found its way into court is the artistic expression of bakers, jewellers, photographers and florists etc. Another is clothing: expressing identity or sense of belonging through choice of apparel is an everyday occurrence; for those undergoing gender transition it can lead to awkwardness, particularly in the workplace where gender-specific clothing may be prescribed by a dress code.[29] Cross-dressing has been a particular issue for the courts.[30]

The moral majority

The USSC, in *Rosenberger v. Rector and Visitors of Univ. of Va.*,[31] held that a university generally cannot withhold benefits from student groups because of their religious outlook: "it may not exclude speech where its distinction is not reasonable in light of the purpose served by the forum, . . . nor may it discriminate against speech on the basis of . . . viewpoint".[32] In the recent *Masterpiece* case,[33] a baker successfully relied upon the protection of the freedom of expression to justify his refusal, as a Christian and culinary "artist", to bake a cake for a gay couple. Justice Kennedy, acknowledging that "religious and philosophical objections to gay marriage are protected views and in some instances protected forms of expression", ruled on behalf of the USSC that the baker's rights under the First Amendment had been violated; though the ruling was based on a finding of religious bias on the part of local officials[34] (see further below).

The legislative intent behind the so-called liberty laws or religious freedom laws, recently introduced in a number of states, has ostensibly been to allow those with religious objections to matters such as same-sex marriage and transgender identity to act in accordance with their beliefs without having to fear prosecution for breaching equality and non-discrimination provisions. Others view such laws as a cynical political exercise: using freedom of expression as a flag of convenience to extend the religious exemption from the moral imperatives of equality laws,

27 *Christian Legal Soc. Chapter of Univ. of Cal., Hastings Coll. Of Law v. Martinez*, 561 U.S. 661, 672, 689, 130 S.Ct. 2971, 177 L.Ed.2d 838 (2010) at 622.

28 *Pickering v. Board of Education*, 391 U.S. 563 (1968).

29 *Carroll v. Talman Fed. Savs. & Loan Association*, 604 F.2d 1028, 1032 (7th Cir. 1979), *Smith v. City of Salem* 378 F.3d 566, 568 (6th Cir. 2004) and *Jespersen v. Harrah's Operating Co.*, No. 03–15045 (9th Cir. 2006).

30 *City of Columbus v. Rogers*, Ohio Supreme Court, 5 March 1975; *City of Chicago v. Wilson*, 44 Ill. App. 3d 620 (1976), 357 N.E.2d 1337; *Doe v. Yunits*, 2000 WL 33162199 (2000); *McMillen v. Itawamba County School District*, 1:10-cv-61, 2010 WL 1172429 (N.D. Miss.).

31 515 U.S. 819, 829. See, also, *Gay Alliance of Students v. Matthews*, U.S. Court of Appeals (4th Circuit), 1976.

32 *Rosenberger*, at pp. 17–19.

33 *Masterpiece Cakeshop v. Colorado Civil Rights Commission*, 584 U.S. (2018).

34 Author acknowledges advice from Cynthia Burack on this matter (note to author, 12 May 2019).

thereby stiffening the resolve of conservative voters and winning some local battles in the nation's culture wars. This may have some resonance with times past when public morality was used as a pretext for animus. To paraphrase Justice O'Connor's observation in the era of Texas sodomy laws: "the law serves more as a statement of dislike and disapproval . . . the inevitable inference that the disadvantage imposed is born of animosity toward the class of persons affected".[35] Following the Trump administration's setting up, in 2018, of the Conscience and Religious Freedom Division of the US Department of Health and Human Services and the White House Faith and Opportunity Initiative, many religious liberty bills were formulated for introduction to legislatures across the country.

Harm to others

As the USSC maintained some 80 years ago: "the democratic response to speech that people disagree with is more speech: by allowing students to express both the popular and unpopular viewpoints society can foster 'enlightened opinion' ".[36]

Although the right to freedom of expression is not vitiated by hate speech, including that which denigrates people on the basis of their gender or sexual orientation,[37] its exercise is subject to the proviso the it causes no actual direct harm[38] – causation and the definition of "harm" being matters open to legal debate. The case of *Brandon v. County of Richardson*[39] – a trans man who was abducted, imprisoned, assaulted, raped and murdered – illustrates the harm to which members of the LGBT community may be exposed and explains the latent accompanying climate of fear. Homophobia would also seem to have been the motivating factor in the horrific Orlando Pulse nightclub shooting in 2016. This is a context in which an inflammatory exercise of free speech has the potential to cause real harm.

Rights to freedom of association and assembly

"Implicit in the right to engage in activities protected by the First Amendment" is "a corresponding right to associate with others in pursuit of a wide variety of political, social, economic, educational, religious, and cultural ends".[40] However, their exercise, in the context of ongoing and socially divisive culture wars, has at times been highly contentious.

An early SOGI school case, set in a context of associational rights, was that of *Colín v. Orange Unified School District*,[41] in which the plaintiff students alleged

35 *Lawrence v. Texas*, 539 U.S. 558.
36 *Cantwell v. Connecticut*, 310 U.S. 296, 310, 60 S.Ct. 900, 84 L.Ed. 1213 (1940).
37 *Snyder v. Phelps*, 562 U.S. 443 (2011).
38 *Schenck v. United States*, 249 U.S. 47 (1919).
39 624 N.W.2d 604, 261 Neb. 636, 2001.
40 *Roberts v. United States Jaycees*, 468 U.S. 609 (1984).
41 83 F. Supp. 2d 1135(C.D. Cal. 2000).

that their rights under the Equal Access Act and their rights of expression and association under the First Amendment were violated when their wish to form a "Gay–Straight Alliance Club" at their high school was denied by the defendant school board. According to the Mission Statement, the goal of the club was to talk about "tolerance", "issues related to sexual orientation and homophobia", the need to "treat everyone with respect" and counterattacking "unfair treatment and prejudice". Reminding the parties that public school students do not "shed their constitutional rights to freedom of speech or expression at the schoolhouse gate",[42] that in a free society we rely on the "marketplace of ideas"[43] and of the danger that public education could transform schools into "enclaves of totalitarianism" and convert students into "closed-circuit recipients of only that which the State chooses to communicate",[44] the court found for the plaintiffs and indicated the strong likelihood that the defendants had violated the Equal Access Act.

Constraints

The equality imperative embedded in the Fourteenth Amendment and in the Civil Rights Act 1964 has at times been called upon to curb the exclusionary tendencies of associations. This has been particularly evident along the often tense interface between religious groups and the LGBT community.

The limits of such curbing were demonstrated in *Boy Scouts of America v. Dale*,[45] which involved the refusal of a youth organisation to admit a particular person on the grounds that his sexual orientation conflicted with its traditional Christian-based values. The court acknowledged that any association was entitled to define its purpose, set its terms of membership and include or exclude accordingly: the freedom of association guaranteed by the First Amendment and the Fourteenth protected the organisation from accepting the forced inclusion of an LGBT activist; his membership would be likely to infringe its freedom of expression by significantly compromising its capacity to give effect to its purpose for associating. Rehnquist CJ cited in support the earlier decision in *Hurley*,[46] when the USSC concluded that a St. Patrick's Day parade organised by a private association should not be compelled to accept an LGBT group which would be likely to represent a message it deemed to be at variance with its associative purpose. Both decisions were limited by the distinctive nature of the organisations involved – expressive associations – whose raison d'être is to represent a particular set of ideas.

42 *Tinker v. Des Moines Independent Community School Dist.*, 393 U.S. at 511, 89 S.Ct. 733, 21 L.Ed. 2d 731 (1969).

43 *Abrams v. United States*, 250 U.S. 616, 630, 40 S.Ct. 17, 63 L.Ed. 1173 (1919).

44 *Tinker*, 393 U.S. at 511, 89 S.Ct. 733.

45 530 U.S. 640, 648.

46 *Hurley v. Irish-AmericanGay, Lesbian and Bisexual Group of Boston*, 515 U.S. 557, 573 (1995).

There have been a number of cases in which university authorities have sought to resolve internal disputes between student religious and LGBT organisations.[47] Recently, in *Christian Legal Soc. Chapter of Univ. of Cal., Hastings Coll. of Law v. Martinez*,[48] the USSC upheld the right of a College of Law to prohibit the Christian Legal Society, a student organisation in the College, from restricting membership to those who signed a "statement of faith" which permitted the exclusion of anyone who engaged in "unrepentant homosexual conduct". As Justice Ginsburg put it:

> Hastings, caught in the crossfire between a group's desire to exclude and students' demand for equal access, may reasonably draw a line in the sand permitting all organisations to express what they wish but no group to discriminate in membership.[49]

Right to freedom of religion

This principle is enshrined in the Constitution and given specific protection by the First Amendment but is also present in a number of supra-national conventions to which the US is a signatory, including the UDHR (Article 18), ICCPR (Article 18), UNCROC (Article 14) and the American Convention on Human Rights (Article 12).

SOGI and religion

The so-called Religious Liberty Accommodations Act – or Protecting Freedom of Conscience From Government Discrimination Act – passed in Mississippi in 2016[50] was a direct response to federal rulings in support of same-sex marriage. This legislation (since replicated in other states), which the USSC declined to review, essentially provides carve-outs for those of religious beliefs – most usually public service providers and typically in relation to LG service users – from the constraints of equality and non-discrimination legislation (see further below).

Religious organisations and the religious exemption

Religious organisations per se are exempt from many regulatory mechanisms imposed upon other entities in the commercial and non-profit sectors. Such exemptions and concessions apply not only to churches but also to the ever extending religiously affiliated non-profit facilities such as universities, hospitals,

47 Including: *Gay Students Organization of University of New Hampshire v. Bonner*, 509 F.2d 652, 660 (1974); *Gay Alliance of Students v. Matthews*, U.S. Court of appeals (4th Cir.), 1976; and *Gay Student Services v. Texas A&M University*, 737 F.2d (1984).

48 Op. cit.

49 *Martinez*, op. cit., at pp. 25–28.

50 Mississippi House Bill 1523 (H.B. 1523).

child care centres and homes for the aged. As these privileges include carve-outs from equality and non-discrimination legislation, they disproportionately impact upon the LGBT community.

The introduction of the RFRA reinforced the protection available to religious organisations from State interference in their affairs.[51] This Act states that the "government shall not substantially burden a person's exercise of religion even if the burden results from a rule of general applicability".[52] It may do so "only if it demonstrates that application of the burden . . . is in furtherance of a compelling governmental interest and . . . is the least restrictive means of furthering that compelling governmental interest".[53]

SOGI: personal relationships and human rights

The need to for the law to intervene and address matters traditionally considered to be both deeply personal and socially shrouded in taboo was recognised by the UN Secretary-General Ban Ki-moon:

> Some say that sexual orientation and gender identity are sensitive issues. I understand. Like many of my generation, I did not grow up talking about these issues. But I learned to speak out because lives are at stake, and because it is our duty under the United Nations Charter and the Universal Declaration of Human Rights to protect the rights of everyone, everywhere.[54]

Right to an identity

"The Constitution promises liberty to all within its reach, a liberty that includes certain specific rights that allow persons, within a lawful realm, to define and express their identity".[55] It is also guaranteed in numerous human rights treaties, including the UDHR, Article 6, to which the US is a signatory nation. Gender recognition in law is important not only in itself but also because it functions as a gateway to the enjoyment of other rights – including privacy, freedom of expression, freedom from arbitrary arrest and rights related to employment, education, health, security, access to justice and the ability to move freely.

51 See, for example: *Navajo Nation v. US Forest Serv.*, 479 F.3d 1024 (9th Cir. 2007); *Gonzales v. O Centro Espirita Beneficente Uniao do Vegetal* 546 U.S. 418 (2006); *Cutter v. Wilkinson*, 544 U.S. 709 (2005); *Tenn. V. Lane*, 541 U.S. 509 (2004); *Kimel v. Fla. Bd. Of Regents*, 528 U.S. 62 (2000); *City of Boerne v. Flores*, 521 U.S. 507 (1997); and *Swanner v. Anchorage Equal Rights Comm'n*, 513 U.S. 979 (1994).

52 42 U.S.C. § 2000bb-1(a).

53 42 U.S.C. § 2000bb-1(b).

54 UN Secretary-General Ban Ki-moon's address to the Human Rights Council, 7 March 2012.

55 *Obergefell v. Hodges*, 576 U.S. (2015), per Justice Kennedy.

Trans recognition in law

In the US as elsewhere, personal identification requires producing evidence of official registration – birth certificate, driving licence, passport etc. – which records biological gender at birth, with a gender change requiring a corresponding change to be officially recorded in such personal ID documentation. There being no federal jurisdiction in respect of such matters, the making of any laws or regulations providing for registration of transgender identities is a responsibility that devolves under the Tenth Amendment to the states, but they vary in the extent to which they recognise acquired gender identities. In practice this, at a minimum, requires official alteration of birth certificates, and much then depends on the steps a person has taken in the transition process, with some states only providing an official record of gender change on completion of surgery, but most permit a change to be made to the gender entry on a birth certificate.

Non-binary gender identity

In 2016, both Oregon and California granted legal recognition to non-binary people: in the latter state, recognition took the form of a birth certificate with "intersex" listed under the category of "sex"; subsequently it passed a bill – SB 179 – implementing a third, non-binary gender marker on California birth certificates, drivers' licenses and identity cards. Other states, including Washington, Maine, Arkansas and Colorado, have allowed a third, non-binary "X" gender marker on amended ID documents such as birth certificates and driving licenses. In *Zzyym v. Pompeo*,[56] the US Court of Appeals (10th Circuit) ruled that the State Department exceeded its authority under the Passport Act of 1926 when it denied a passport to a citizen who is intersex, non-binary and does not identify as male or female: "the authority to issue passports . . . does not include the authority to deny an applicant on grounds pertinent to basic identity".

Right to respect for private and family life

Although an "inalienable right to life, liberty and the pursuit of happiness" was proclaimed in the Declaration of Independence, the Constitution has nothing to say about personal rights to privacy, or the rights of families, parents or children in relation to government interference. However, as a signatory State to the UDHR and the ICCPR, the US is bound by Articles 12 and 17, respectively, which declare in almost identical terms that "no one shall be subjected to arbitrary or unlawful interference with his privacy, family, home or correspondence". It has been left to the USSC to forge, through a series of decisions spread over

56 0:18-cv-01453 (2018).

many decades, a right to individual and family privacy, asserting and protecting a "private realm of family life which the State cannot enter".[57]

Sexual orientation, identity and private life

The Due Process Clause of the Fourteenth Amendment provides a right to personal liberty. The courts established that sexual relations between consenting adults are an aspect of the liberty that falls to be protected by that right.[58] This led to the state-by-state de-criminalising of consensual sexual relations between same-sex couples during the period 1960–90, despite cases such as *Bowers v. Hardwick*[59] in which the USSC upheld state sodomy laws. Ultimately, overruling the *Bowers* decision, the USSC in *Lawrence v. Texas*[60] determined that:

> The petitioners are entitled to respect for their private lives. The State cannot demean their existence or control their identity by making their private sexual conduct a crime. Their right to liberty under the Due Process Clause gives them the full right to engage in their conduct without intervention from the government.[61]

This decision in effect legalised such relations nationwide and established a benchmark – State respect for privacy in sexual relations – which transferred into a contemporary SOGI context (see further below).

Family life

Diversity of family forms and acceptance of different sets of relationships have long been a characteristic feature of US society. This may be partly attributable to factors such as the presence of Native Americans with indigenous tribes and loose extended families; the impact of the varied ethnic and racial immigrant communities; and the sustained cultural/religious pockets of Amish, Mormons, Mennonites, Hutterites etc. More simply, it may be associated with the size of the country and the competitive "free-market" nature of a society that encourages re-locating for employment, starting family life afresh, and discourages State intervention. However, as the culture wars began to bite – probably ever since the 1960s – families, family policy and the related law[62] would seem to have been

57 *Roe v. Wade*, 410 U.S. 113 (1973); *Griswold v. Connecticut*, 381 U.S. 479 (1965); *Prince v. Massachusetts*, 321 U.S. 158, 166 (1944); *Pierce v. Society of Sisters*, 268 U.S. 510 (1925); and *Meyer v. Nebraska*, 262 U.S. 390 (1923).

58 *Eisenstadt v. Baird*, 405 U.S. 438 (1972).

59 478 U.S. 186 (1986).

60 539 U.S. 558 (2003).

61 Ibid., at para. 34.

62 See further Elrod, L.D., Family Law and Human Rights: The United States Perspective, *International Law FORUM Du Droit International*, 7, pp. 167–177 (2005).

drawn into the fray and, increasingly, it would appear, the way families are formed is generating divisive contention.

Private life, gender reassignment and divorce

There is probably no greater privacy safeguard for a trans person than having legal ID, in the same but amended form – a birth certificate, passport, driving licence etc. – as all other citizens. Without it there will be constant intrusions upon their privacy as they respond to enquiries about their gender in all the usual situations where ID may be required, such as employment, banks, health care, public toilets, insurance and myriad other areas of public life.

The history of difficulties in acquiring official documentation that records gender reassignment dates back to a string of unsuccessful cases in various states in the 1960s and 1970s.[63] Changes to passports, licenses, birth certificates, and other official documents remained a theme in court cases from the 1960s through to 2010, when the State Department allowed gender identity on US passports to be altered. The difficulties continue. According to the National Center for Transgender Equality:

> only one-fifth of transgender people who have transitioned in the National Transgender Discrimination Survey have been able to update all of their IDs and records with their new gender and one-third had updated none of their IDs or records. At the time of the survey, only 59% had been able to update their gender on their driver's license or state ID; 49% had updated their Social Security Record; 26% their passport; and just 24% their birth certificate.[64]

By 2018, some states were removing the requirement to have a health care professional affirm a gender change request and some were adding a gender-neutral option of "X" in addition to "M" or "F", which permits allows a greater degree of privacy for trans persons.[65]

The legal reconciliation of marital status and the trans identity of a spouse has historically been at least problematic,[66] but since the USSC ruling in *Obergefell* it has become decidedly less so. Essentially, when the USSC decided that same-sex marriage is a federal right, any legal need for a trans spouse to divorce then evaporated.

63 See, for example, *Mtr. Of Anonymous v. Weiner*, 50 Misc. 2d 380, 270 N.Y.S.2d 319 (1966) and *Anonymous v. Mellon*, 91 Misc. 2d 375, 383, 398 N.Y.S.2d 99 (1977).

64 National Center for Transgender Equality, *ID Documents and Privacy* (2014), at: https://transequality.org/issues/identity-documents-privacy.

65 National Center for Transgender Equality, *The Shifting Landscape of IDs for Trans People* (2018), at: https://medium.com/transequalitynow/the-shifting-landscape-of-ids-for-trans-people-97834478701a.

66 *Littleton v. Prange*, 9 S.W.3d 223.

SOGI, parenting and "the best interests of the child" principle

Article 3 of UNCROC, which the US has signed if not yet ratified, firmly declares that the child's welfare must be the paramount consideration in any decision taken regarding his or her upbringing, a principle often also entrenched in state child care law. In effect this should mean that the transsexual status of a parent should not itself be a determining factor in child custody cases. In *Mayfield v. Mayfield*,[67] for instance, the court upheld a transgender parent's shared parenting plan because there was no evidence in the record that the parent would not be a "fit, loving and capable parent". In practice, however, there is little judicial consistency across the states. This was apparent in *Daly v. Daly*,[68] when the court justified its removal of parental rights with the claim that by transitioning the parent had terminated her rights as a father; in *Cisek v. Cisek*,[69] when the court terminated a transgender parent's visitation rights, holding that there was a risk of both mental and "social harm" to the children; and *In re Marriage of Magnuson*,[70] when it affirmed a ruling against a transgender parent, stating it had "properly considered the children's needs in making residential placement decision, not a parent's transgender status, conforming to the principles in sexual [orientation] cases".

Right to marriage and to found a family

"Marriage is one of the 'basic civil rights of man' fundamental to our very existence and survival".[71] The extension of this social institution – traditionally authorised to bring sexuality and religious belief into legal alignment – to accommodate same-sex relationships was, for religious adherents and for others, a most profound challenge. This seismic shift in social mores, that for centuries had rested on a binary pattern of gender and sexuality, naturally progressed to permeate laws governing relationships, parenting arrangements etc., and in doing so generated ever more challenges in the expanding field of sexual orientation and gender identity.

Legal recognition for same-sex relationships and the right to marry

As the USSC explained in *Obergefell*:

> for much of the 20th century . . . homosexuality was treated as an illness. When the American Psychiatric Association published the first Diagnostic

67 Case No. 96AP030032, 1996 Ohio App. LEXIS 3724 (Ohio Ct. App. 14 August 1996).
68 715 P. 2d 56 (Nev. 1986).
69 WL 6161 (Ohio Ct. App. 1982).
70 170 P. 3d 65, 66 (Wash. Ct. App. 2007). See also *M.B. v. D.W.*, 236 S.W.3d 31 (Ky. Ct. App. 2007).
71 *Loving v. Virginia*, 388 U.S. 12 (1967).

and Statistical Manual of Mental Disorders in 1952, homosexuality was classified as a mental disorder, a position adhered to until 1973.[72]

Not until 2003, with the USSC decision in *Lawrence v. Texas*,[73] was it established on a federal basis that same-sex relations were protected by a right to privacy under the Fourteenth Amendment. This resistance to any undermining of the legal parameters of sexual relationships and marriage, as traditionally understood, reached an apogee of sorts in the federal Defense of Marriage Act (DOMA) 1996 which recognised only unions between a man and a woman and denied federal benefits to any same-sex couple granted the right to marry under state law – a statute replicated by the legislatures of some 40 states.

The landmark *Obergefell* decision, building on the partial reversal achieved by *Windsor*,[74] completed the demolition of DOMA, extended the right to marry to same-sex couples and thereby, in effect, invalidated all state statutes and constitutional amendments that until then had denied them that opportunity. It also finally laid to rest the sustained legal, medical and religious ostracisation of same-sex relationships. Kennedy J on behalf of the USSC, while upholding the right to gay marriage, then warned that the ruling should not be construed as undermining the First Amendment rights of the traditional religions and their adherents. This was an equality ruling: both camps were entitled to equal judicial respect; but both were perhaps left equally unhappy. Laycock, reflecting on the contributors to *Same-Sex Marriage and Religious Liberty: Emerging Conflicts*,[75] comments that "this is a depressing book" from a civil libertarian perspective, because all of the other contributors, whatever their religious or political perspectives, "agree that same-sex marriage is a threat to religious liberty". It is the "whatever" that causes most disquiet.

The recent *Bryant*[76] decision was seen by some as a conservative push back against the *Obergefell* ruling, but in reality it simply left matters as they were. By standing aside, the USSC left the partisan approach adopted by the Mississippi legislature unchallenged. *Obergefell* had set a national bar which this legislature chose to curb (although with effects which would be difficult to confine to religious/cultural groups) in order to affirm the equal rights of those with religious beliefs. If implemented, the consequences of this statute will be far-reaching: permitting an opt out for all state employees whose beliefs align with one or more of the three specified in the statute; licencing

72 *Obergefell v. Hodges*, 576 U.S. (2015) citing Position Statement on Homosexuality and Civil Rights, 1973, *American Journal of Psychiatry*, 131, p. 497 (1974).

73 Op. cit.

74 *United States v. Windsor*, 570 U.S. 744 (2013). Author acknowledges advice from Cynthia Burack on the importance of the *Windsor* ruling (note to author, 12 May 2019).

75 Laycock, D., Picaello Jr.A.R. and Wilson, R.F. (eds.), *Same – Sex Marriage and Religious Liberty: Emerging Conflicts*, Rowman & Littlefield, 2008, at p. 189.

76 *Barber v. Bryant* 17–547, and *Campaign for Southern Equality v. Bryant*, 17–642.

many to withhold service provision, thereby discriminating against and disadvantaging some citizens relative to others; and certain to add to the grief of civil libertarians.

Trans persons and marriage

Although only a state ruling, *M.T. v. J.T.*[77] was important because for the first time in the US a post-operative trans person concluded a valid marriage with someone who, prior to surgery, would have been of the same sex. Subsequently, a series of not dissimilar cases in various states concluded otherwise.[78] Not until the USSC decision in *Obergefell* was the right established on a federal basis.

Adoption, surrogacy and child care

State laws governing adoption by same-sex couples have varied in their progress towards the current consensus that this is an equality right and one supported by evidence of its compatibility with the principle that the welfare interests of a child are of paramount importance in any decision affecting his or her upbringing. Even so, by 2010, according to the US Census, approximately 115,000 children were being raised by same-sex couples, of whom about 16%, or 18,400, were bringing up one or more adopted children. However, not until the USSC ruling in *Obergefell* did such adoptions become legal nationwide. This case concerned two lesbians, raising three children adopted by only one of them, who succeeded in having both a state ban on adoption by same-sex couples overturned and in contesting that state's ban on same-sex marriage.

So-called second-parent adoptions – where one partner has already adopted a child (or has their own birth child) and their new partner wishes to adopt the same child to share parenting responsibilities – are an important legal means for LGBT couples to secure their families. The significance for the second parent was illustrated in *Usitalo v. Landon*[79] when a birth mother sought and failed to void an adoption in order to deprive her long-term former partner of parental rights in respect of the child they had both reared.

In the near future, the introduction in some states of "religious liberty laws" could have the effect of restricting same-sex adoptions by legitimating the right of adoption agencies to refuse, on the grounds of religious belief, to accept applications from or to place children with such couples. Indeed, by 2018, two states – Kansas and Oklahoma – had passed such legislation.

77 140 N.J. 77, 355 A.2d 204, 205 (NJ Super. Ct. 1976).

78 See, for example: *Littleton v. Prange*, 9 S.W.3d 223 (1999) (Texas, seven-year marriage between transsexual woman and deceased "husband" declared invalid); *In re Estate of Gardiner*, 42 P. 3d 120 (Kan. 2002) (Kansas, marriage of a man and a trans woman, voided); and *Kantaras v. Kantaras*, 884 So. 2d 155 (Fla. Ct. App. 2004) (Florida, transgender man seeking to invalidate marriage to "wife", marriage declared void).

79 Case No. 308240, Mich. Ct. App. (2012).

Surrogacy, as a means of forming a family, is as viable an option for same-sex as for heterosexual couples, but its domestic legality varies from state to state, which in practice often prompts recourse to overseas surrogacy arrangements.

Right to cultural life

As a signatory State to the UDHR and the ICESRC, the US is bound to protect the right to participate in cultural life enshrined in Articles 27 of the former and 15 of the latter. Having also endorsed UNDRIP, it is obliged to respect the cultural rights of the Indigenous people.

There can be little doubt that there exists an LGBT culture in the US, perhaps originating in the homosexual communities of New York and San Francisco in the 1960s/1970s. Initially an oppressed and socially marginalised group, with a membership that included many musicians and other artists who needed mutual support, they subsequently formed similar enclaves nationwide. When individuals were not in geographic proximity, they relied on the Internet and social media to cultivate a sense of community. Like many other groups, their culture united around a cause, acquired solidarity (through events such as the Stonewall riots), leadership (from the many prominent individuals who have championed issues in the courts), a flag and are now dispersed and wholly assimilated throughout all sectors of society. A defined cultural group can also become a target. The SOGI-related attack on the Pulse nightclub in Orlando was an extreme example of the homophobic violence that is, from time to time, directed against this group within the singular cultural war context that divides US society.

Cultural context

Decades of confrontation with homophobic groups and police, challenges from religious organisations and endless court cases track the transformation of the LGBT community from social outcasts to their present legally protected and socially accepted status. However, the emergence of a rash of "religious liberty laws" may herald the beginnings of a change in that regard.

The cultural context also needs to take into account Native Americans. Some tribes have a long history of recognising and respecting "two spirits" in the one body: a term acknowledging that a person may belong biologically to one gender but have the sexual orientation of the other. The impact of Christianity has been such that this tradition of acceptance was very largely suppressed and only in recent years, given permission by the mainstream LGBT movement, has it resurfaced. The Native American gay community may well develop to become a culturally different entity from its corresponding mainstream counterpart.

SOGI: non-discrimination, affirmative action and equality

The Equal Protection Clause of the Fourteenth Amendment places a legal obligation on the State, and therefore on all government entities, to ensure that similarly situated individuals are treated equally.[80] This constitutional liberty right has been given added weight by the decision in *Employment Division v. Smith*[81] and is now viewed by many as a beacon for equality rights.[82]

Equality before the law: sexuality and gender discrimination

For many years, courts and regulators struggled to differentiate between gender stereotyping that provided evidence to support an allegation of sex (understood as "gender") discrimination and evidence that pointed instead towards sexual orientation discrimination.[83] The distinction was often found to be unworkable and "illogical"[84] and to produce "untenable results".[85] Ultimately, it was concluded that "the line between sex discrimination and sexual orientation discrimination is 'difficult to draw' because that line does not exist save as a lingering and faulty judicial construct".[86] Instead, it was superseded by the view that sexual orientation discrimination is rooted in gender stereotypes and thus constitutes a subset of sex discrimination. By 2017, a total of 21 states had passed legislation prohibiting discrimination based on sexual orientation and/or gender identity.[87]

Sex discrimination and sexual orientation discrimination

The term "sexual orientation" refers to "[a] person's predisposition or inclination toward sexual activity or behaviour with other males or females" and is commonly categorised as "heterosexuality, homosexuality, or bisexuality".[88] Sexual orientation is a function of sex, and because sex is a protected characteristic under Title VII, it follows that sexual orientation is also protected. Therefore, "allegations of discrimination on the basis of sexual orientation necessarily state a claim of discrimination on the basis of sex".[89] The caselaw history, however, shows that this proposition was not readily accepted by judiciary and regulators and still

80 *Alford v. Consolidated Gov't of Columbus, Ga.*, 438 F.App'x 837, 839 (11th Cir. 2011); citing *Campbell v. Rainbow City, Ala.*, 434 F.3d 1306, 1313 (11th Cir. 2006).
81 48 U.S. 872 (1990).
82 Note that the proposed Employment Non-Discrimination Act (ENDA) would add a prohibition on SOGI discrimination not only to employment law but also to public accommodation, education, federal financial assistance, housing, credit and federal jury service.
83 See, for example, *Hively v. Ivy Tech Cmty. Coll., S. Bend*, 830 F.3d 698, 705–09 (7th Cir. 2016).
84 *Philpott v. New York*, 252 F.Supp.3d 313, 316 (S.D.N.Y. 2017).
85 *Boutillier v. Hartford Pub. Sch.*, 221 F.Supp.3d at 270 (D. Conn. 2016).
86 *Zarda*, op. cit., at 122, citing *Videckis v. Pepperdine Univ.*, 150 F.Supp.3d at 1159, 1160 (C.D. Cal. 2015) (quoting *Prowel v. Wise Business Forms, Inc.*, 579 F.3d at 291 [Court of Appeals, 3rd Circuit, 2009]).
87 See ACLU at: www.aclu.org/other/past-lgbt-nondiscrimination-and-anti-lgbt-bills-across-country.
88 See Sexual Orientation in *Black's Law Dictionary* (10th ed.), 2014.
89 *Baldwin v. Foxx*, 2015 WL 4397641, at 10.

remains to be finally settled (see further below).[90] Many states still have no laws prohibiting discrimination specifically on the basis of sexual orientation; some have no "hate-crime" laws that include sexual orientation among their protected categories, and state protection for transgender identity is even more limited.[91]

Gender identity and trans discrimination

The Equal Protection Clause grants to all Americans "the right to be free from invidious discrimination in statutory classifications and other governmental activity".[92] Yet, gender stereotyping has hindered the development of the law,[93] has been apparent in cases of discrimination against trans persons[94] and is evident in the continued absence of any federal legislation specifically designed to protect them.

Some limited federal initiatives have been taken: in 2009, the Hate Crimes Prevention Act added gender identity to the definition of a hate crime; in 2014, a presidential executive order was issued prohibiting discrimination against transgender people employed by the federal government and its contractors; and in 2016, the Departments of Education and Justice issued informal guidance, since withdrawn by the Trump administration, that publicly funded schools should make the necessary arrangements for students to use bathrooms appropriate to their gender or transgender identities. Currently there is considerable variance in the extent to which states give legislative recognition to gender identity where transgender people are concerned. This will often depend upon whether or not an individual has completed sex reassignment surgery. The judiciary, however, have contributed significantly to changes in the law.

As was noted in *Zarda*,[95] claims of gender discrimination have been "especially difficult for gay plaintiffs to bring",[96] because references to a plaintiff's sexual

90 Including, for example: *Barnes v. Train*, 1974 WL 10628, *1 (D.D.C. 9 August 1974) (discriminated against, not because she was a woman, but because she refused to engage in a sexual affair with her supervisor); *General Elec. Co. v. Gilbert*, 429 U.S. 125, 145–46 (1976) (discrimination based on pregnancy was not discrimination based on sex); *Price Waterhouse v. Hopkins*, 490 U.S. 228, 251 (1989) (sex stereotyping could constitute discrimination based on sex); *Simonton v. Runyon*, 232 F.3d 33, 35 (2d Cir. 2000) (Title VII does not proscribe discrimination because of sexual orientation); and *Prowel v. Wise Bus. Forms, Inc.*, 579 F.3d 285, 287, 289, 291 (3d Cir. 2009) (Title VII protects a gay man for deviating from gender stereotypes but not for his sexual orientation).

91 See Marks, M.S., Global Recognition of Human Rights for Lesbian, Gay, Bisexual, and Transgender People, *Health Hum Rights*, 9(1), pp. 33–42 (2006).

92 *Harris v. McRae*, 448 U.S. 297, 322, 100 S.Ct. 2671, 2691, 65 L.Ed.2d 784 (1980).

93 See, for example: *Price Waterhouse v. Hopkins*, 490 U.S. 228 (1989); *Heller v. Columbia Edgewater Country Club*, 195 F.Supp.2d 1212, 1224 (D. Or. 2002); *Centola v. Potter*, 183 F.Supp.2d 403, 410 (D. Mass. 2002); *Boutillier*, op. cit.; *Terveer v. Billington*, 34 F.Supp.3d 100, 116 (D.D.C. 2014); and *Videckis v. Pepperdine Univ.*, 150 F.Supp.3d 1151, 1160 (C.D. Cal. 2015).

94 See, for example, *Smith v. City of Salem* 378 F.3d 566, 568 (6th Cir. 2004).

95 *Zarda*, op. cit.

96 *Maroney v. Waterbury Hosp.*, No. 3:10-CV-1415, 2011 WL 1085633, at *2 n.2 (D. Conn. 18 March 2011).

orientation were generally excluded from the evidence.[97] This, as mentioned earlier, is because the law for years laboured to hold that the legislative intent in the Civil Rights Act prohibition against discrimination "because . . . of sex" was to direct protection towards women. As contemporary LGBT concerns, such as sexual orientation, could never have formed part of that intent, they should not be allowed to now stray into that frame of reference (see further below). This argument was met by expounding on the parallel development of racial discrimination caselaw and its accommodation of associated discriminatory behaviour (e.g. the discriminatory treatment by a white person of another white person on the basis of the latter's marriage to a black person).[98] Clarification regarding federal law as it relates to gender discrimination and sexual orientation discrimination may be forthcoming as a result of the petition recently filed with the USSC, in *R.G. & G.R. Harris Funeral Homes v. Equal Employment Opportunity Commission*,[99] challenging the approach adopted by the Sixth Circuit and the EEOC which, in effect, replaces "sex" with "gender identity" for the purposes of interpreting discrimination under Title VII.

Affirmative action

While there are no specific federal statutes channelling supplementary funding towards disadvantaged groups, many states have legislated for "affirmative action" provisions. In 1990, Laycock[100] referred to what was then "the great national debate about affirmative action", citing the many academic contributors to that debate, but now, nearly 30 years later, equality caselaw has narrowed State affirmative initiatives to the point where they are so restricted in scope that they do little more than ease the admission of the socially disadvantaged into higher education.

LGBT issues and affirmative State action

Affirmative action underpinned Executive Order 13672. This presidential initiative added "gender identity" to the categories protected against discrimination in hiring in the federal civilian workforce and both "sexual orientation" and "gender identity" to the categories protected against discrimination in hiring and employment on the part of federal government contractors and sub-contractors.[101]

97 *Boutillier*, op. cit., at 269.

98 See Siegel, R. B., She the People: The Nineteenth Amendment, Sex Equality, Federalism, and the Family, *Harvard Law Review*, 115, pp. 947, 949 (2002).

99 6th Cir. No. 16–2424,

100 Laycock, D., Formal, Substantive, and Disaggregated Neutrality Toward Religion, *DePaul Law Review*, 39(4), p. 993 (1990), at p. 997. See further at: http://via.library.depaul.edu/law-review/vol39/iss4/3.

101 For background, see Byrne, J.S., Affirmative Action for Lesbians and Gay Men: A Proposal for True Equality of Opportunity and Workforce Diversity, *Yale Law & Policy Review*, 11(1), Article 3 (1993), at: http://digitalcommons.law.yale.edu/ylpr/vol11/iss1/3.

The obverse of affirmative action was the subject of the USSC ruling in *Romer v. Evans.*[102] The court then held that a state law specifically designed to disadvantage lesbians, gay men and bisexuals violated the Fourteenth Amendment's Equal Protection Clause: the targeted group had the same right to seek government protection against discrimination as any other group. Justice Kennedy noted that a law may prevail under the equal protection clause, even if it seems to disadvantage a specific group, so long as it can be shown to "advance a legitimate government interest".[103] Much the same configuration of arguments currently envelops the dispute regarding transgender military personnel.[104] Also, it might be noted, the USSC has on at least three occasions ruled that public universities have acted unconstitutionally in singling out student groups (largely those whose evangelical Christian beliefs excluded LGBT members) for unfavourable treatment.[105]

Right to equality and non-discrimination: health

The US is a signatory nation to the UDHR, ICESRC, CEDAW and UNCROC, all of which declare a right to health care (Articles 25, 12, 12 and 24 respectively), and yet, in the continued absence of universal coverage, it remains questionable whether health care for US citizens can be considered a right or a privilege. This debate, which acquired heightened salience in light of the reforms introduced by the Affordable Care Act in 2010 (mainly taking effect in 2014), has particular significance for the LGBT community as it is disproportionately affected by health care disparities and costs. It's a debate that has also become more pressing following the USSC decisions in *Windsor* and *Obergefell*, which have resulted in greater openness and willingness to register SOGI status with health care professionals (data collection being a long-standing difficulty), but it is one that has generated very little caselaw.

The Affordable Care Act, particularly s.1557 as amended by the 2016 HHS "Final Rule",[106] in effect prohibits SOGI discrimination by government-funded health care providers and the majority of related insurance companies. It has been an important milestone in establishing equity of health care access for women and the LGBT community. Ease of access, including affordability, is vital for lesbians and for trans people who mostly need or want surgical and/or other forms of treatment, but who also have a particularly high likelihood of being HIV positive,

102 517 U.S. 620 (1996).

103 Justice Kennedy found that an "animus" motivated Amendment 2: "its sheer breadth is so discontinuous with the reasons offered for it that the amendment seems inexplicable by anything but animus toward the class that it affects".

104 See, *Karnoski v. Trump*, 2:17-cv-01297-MJP.

105 *Healy v. James*, 408 U.S. 169; *Widmar v. Vincent*, 454 U.S. 263; and *Rosenberger v. Rector and Visitors of Univ. of Va.*, 515 U.S. 819, 829.

106 See Department of Health and Human Services (HHS), Final Rule, *Nondiscrimination in Health Programs and Activities*, at: www.hhs.gov/sites/default/files/1557-summary-508.pdf.

susceptible to substance abuse and at risk of suicide. For those in prison, the risks and the need for appropriate health care access are greater.[107] The threatened repeal of the ACA by the Trump administration, or the suggested re-defining of "gender" as sex at birth for the purposes of this Act, constitutes a significant danger to trans people and the LGBT community more generally, especially to the many without private health insurance.[108]

Gender reassignment treatment

"Gender identity disorder" (GID) has been replaced in the most recent edition of the American Psychiatric Association manual with the term *gender dysphoria*.[109] While this term might appear more normalising, it retains a pathological resonance as a designated form of mental disorder with all its previous associated stigma. It remains the case that a person wishing to undergo a medically affirmed transition must first be diagnosed as suffering from the condition of GID/gender dysphoria and then submit to medical treatment. Arguably, this positions mental health professionals as gatekeepers to fundamental human rights. The process is also problematic because many health insurance agencies exclude coverage of transgender-specific health care, particularly surgery.

Trans children

As of 2017, according to the Williams Institute at the UCLA School of Law, about 150,000 teenagers aged 13 to 17 identified as trans.[110] It has been estimated that there are currently several hundred de-transitioners in the US.[111] They constitute some of the "growing number of people who believe they were failed by the therapists and physicians they went to for help with their gender dysphoria . . . that well-meaning clinicians left unexplored their overlapping

107 See *O'Donnabhain v. Commissioner*, 134 TC 34 (2010); *Adams v. Federal Bureau of Prisons*, 716 F Supp2d 874 (ED Wisc), 2010; *Fields v. Smith*, 653 F3d 550 (7th Cir.), 2011; and *Kosilek v. Spencer*, CA No. 00–12455 MLW, 2012 WL 3799660 (D Mass), 2012.

108 See Grant, J. M., et al., *Injustice at Every Turn: A Report of the National Transgender Discrimination Survey*, National Center for Transgender Equality and National Gay and Lesbian Task Force, 2011. Also see a 2015 survey in which 55% of transgender participants reported that insurance denied coverage for their gender-affirming surgery, while a quarter were denied coverage for hormone therapy, at: https://eu.usatoday.com/story/news/2018/12/11/transgender-health-care-patients-advocates-call-improvements/1829307002/.

109 American Psychiatric Association. Highlights of changes from DSM-IV-TR to DSM-5, at: www.psychiatry.org/File%20Library/Practice/DSM/DSM-5/Changes-from-DSM-IV-TR-to-DSM-5.pdf.

110 See further at: https://williamsinstitute.law.ucla.edu/research/transgender-issues/new-estimates-show-that-150000-youth-ages-13-to-17-identify-as-transgender-in-the-us/.

111 See further at: www.theatlantic.com/magazine/archive/2018/07/when-a-child-says-shes-trans/561749/.

mental-health troubles or past traumas".[112] According to the testimony given by a trans interviewee,

> she was encouraged to rush into physical transition by clinicians operating within a framework that saw it as the only way someone like her could experience relief. Despite the fact that she was a minor for much of the process, she says, her doctors more or less did as she told them.[113]

Clearly, it is difficult for parents and medical staff to both respect the UNCROC right of a child to make informed decisions while at the same time satisfying themselves that the decision taken is the right one for that child. It is notable that there is little if any US caselaw on this fraught issue.

Sports and recreational activities

The binary gender division in competitive sport is one of the most enduring: as it rests largely on male testosterone, which gives significantly more strength to that gender, this can only continue, or just continue to be contentious, in those sports that are strength dependent. For trans people, this issue is obviously problematic, and more so if they are taking testosterone supplements. The long history of debate, invasive sex verification tests and recourse to the courts dates back to the 1940s, but *Richards v. USTA*[114] was probably the first landmark case, when Justice Ascione found that a rule requiring a trans athlete who had completed reassignment surgery to pass the Barr body test (or thc "women born women" rule) was "grossly unfair, discriminatory and inequitable, and a violation of her rights".[115] Since then the debate, testing and litigation have continued on a matter which so far has defied resolution. In 2015, new guidelines were introduced that require: trans woman athletes to declare their gender, maintain it for four years, and demonstrate a certain testosterone level for at least one year prior to competition and throughout the period of eligibility; while female to male trans athletes are allowed to compete without restriction.

Blood donors

The legacy of the AIDs epidemic, centred on California in the 1980s and 1990s, continues to restrict acceptance of blood donations from non-heterosexuals. Some regard this approach as discriminatory, based on outdated stereotypes and not medically justifiable, as donations from all sources are uniformly tested to filter out viruses such as HIV and hepatitis.

112 Ibid.
113 Ibid.
114 93 Misc.2d 713 (1977).
115 Ibid., at p. 272.

In 2018, in a departure from its 30-year prohibition on blood donations from homosexuals, the US Food and Drug Administration adopted the more positive approach of simply deferring blood donations from them and from their female partners for one year from their last sexual contact. This policy is in keeping with that of countries such as Australia.

Right to equality and non-discrimination: education

While education is a crucial medium for the inter-generational transfer of cultural values, this must be balanced against the opportunity it provides for the promotion of inclusivity and diversity. A particularly heavy onus, therefore, lies on the State to take the necessary steps to ensure that the values and beliefs distinctive and integral to the identity of minority groups are given appropriate representation and are safely accommodated within the education system. The extent of this responsibility extends beyond educational curriculum, methods and material to include in loco parentis obligations such as deployment of SOGI-aware staff, prevention of bullying, provision of appropriate restroom facilities etc.

Schools

> No person in the United States shall, on the basis of sex, be excluded from participation in, be denied the benefits of, or be subjected to discrimination under any education program or activity receiving federal financial assistance.[116]

All schools, other than those that can avail of the religious exemption[117] (see next), must comply with federal legislation, specifically Title VII, Title IX and the Equal Pay and Equal Access Acts. The situation is different, however, as regards state legislation: individual states differ widely in their enactment of laws protecting people from SOGI discrimination in public accommodations.[118] Of particular note is the ongoing equivocation as to whether the reference to "sex" in Titles VII and IX can be defined as including "gender identity" and the fact that the courts have yet to rule that a faith school as a whole is a "public accommodation".

In the early and landmark case of *Nabozny v. Podlesny*,[119] the USSC found that a school pupil who had been harassed and bullied by classmates because of his

116 Title IX of the Education Amendments Act 1972, 20 U.S.C. §§ 1681–1688.

117 Title VII, 42 U.S.C. §§2000e-1(a), 2000e-2(e)(2). See *Doe v. California Lutheran High School Ass'n*, 170 Cal.App.4th 828 (2009), when the court rejected a claim of unlawful discrimination from two former students who had been dismissed from a California Christian school for lesbian conduct.

118 The term "public accommodations" is generally interpreted as referring to property and facilities that are open to the public, such as property that is open to the public e.g. stores, restaurants, hotels, community centres, camps, museums and parks.

119 92 F.3d 446 (1996).

sexual orientation had suffered discrimination based on his gender or sexual orientation. It went on to rule that schools are responsible for any harassment and violence directed against LGBT students. The bearing of the Equal Access Act on the right of pupils to form a gay–straight alliance in schools was examined in *Colín v. Orange Unified School District*[120] (see earlier mention).

The use of school bathrooms has been an ongoing issue of concern for many. In April 2014, the Education Department's Office for Civil Rights released updated guidelines to the 1972 Title IX Education Amendments legislation highlighting that the non-discrimination clause "extends to claims of discrimination based on gender identity or failure to conform to stereotypical notions of masculinity or femininity". This was taken a step further in 2016 in a letter issued by the Obama administration to all educational establishments in receipt of federal funding, expanding on the prohibition on sex-based discrimination in education programs or activities receiving federal funds: "this prohibition encompasses discrimination based on a student's gender identity, including discrimination based on a student's transgender status".[121] The case of *G.G. v. Gloucester School Board*[122] focused attention on this issue. Involving a transgender student using a bathroom in accord with gender identity rather than sex, it led to the Fourth Circuit ruling that "sex" included "gender identity" and that by denying the student access to appropriate facilities the defendants had discriminated against him contrary to the Title IX prohibition. The subsequent USSC hearing, which was to consider whether "sex" in Title IX and ancillary regulations allowing for sex-specific facilities did in fact encompass "gender identity" was overtaken by events, as in February 2017 the Trump administration rescinded the Obama administration's guidance that had allowed the use of bathrooms that corresponded to gender identity.[123] The matter was returned to the 4th Circuit with the definitional issue left judicially undetermined.

Curricula

Title IX of the Education Amendments Act 1972 prohibits discrimination on the basis of sex in any federally funded programme or activity. The USSC ruling in *Grove City College v. Bell*,[124] which restricted the application of Title IX, was effectively overturned by the Civil Rights Restoration Act 1987, which specified that recipients of federal funds, including all schools, must comply with civil rights laws in all areas. The Equal Access Act is also relevant, as was demonstrated

120 83 F. Supp. 2d 1135(C.D. Cal. 2000).

121 See further at: https://www2.ed.gov/about/offices/list/ocr/letters/colleague-201605-title-ix-transgender.pdf.

122 822 F.3d 709 (4th Cir. 2016).

123 News release, *U.S. Departments of Justice and Education Release Joint Guidance to Help Schools Ensure the Civil Rights of Transgender Students*, U.S. Department of Justice, 13 May 2016, at: www.justice.gov/opa/pr/us-departments-justice-and-education-release-joint- guidance-help-schools-ensure-civil-rights.

124 465 U.S. 555 (1984).

in *Board of Education v. Mergens*,[125] which held that the petitioners violated the Equal Access Act by denying official recognition to respondents' proposed "non-curriculum related student group".

As yet, there would appear not to have been any judicial rulings specifically on the relationship between the previously-mentioned legislation and the incorporation of SOGI-related material into school curricula. However, given the controversy generated by California Senate Bill 48 (SB48), the FAIR Education Act, which provides for the inclusion of the LGBT perspectives in K–12 textbooks, it seems probable that such court cases are only a matter of time.

Colleges/universities

The history of court cases addressing the tensions between university authorities and student religious groups[126] has to a large extent prepared the ground for similar difficulties in accommodating contemporary requests from the LGBT community. So, in *Gay Student Services v. Texas A&M University*,[127] the USSC had little difficulty in finding that a university should be allowed to provide official recognition for a gay student organisation. As might be expected, problems have arisen from time to time between LGBT and religious groups, such as in *Christian Legal Society v. Martinez*,[128] when the USSC upheld the right of a College of Law to prohibit the Christian Legal Society, a student organisation in the College, from restricting membership to those who agreed to comply with an explicit set of religious and lifestyle principles. As the court noted, "First Amendment rights must be analysed in light of the special characteristics of the school environment".[129] The same tensions can exist within courses. In *Ward v. Polite*,[130] for example, a final semester student on a counselling course at Eastern Michigan University told her professors that while she had no problem counselling individual gay and lesbian clients, she could not in good conscience assist them with their same-sex relationships; her subsequent expulsion for violating the school's anti-discrimination policy was upheld.

That the religious exemption also applies in this context was demonstrated in *Cabading v. California Baptist University*,[131] which concerned a "male to female pre-operative transgendered person" who sued California Baptist University following her dismissal for purportedly lying about her gender identity on the

125 496 U.S. 226 (1990).
126 See, for example, *Widmar v. Vincent*, 454 U.S. 263, 102 S.Ct. 269, 70 L.Ed. 2d 440 (1981), when the USSC ruled that if state universities make their facilities generally available for use by registered student groups, they could not single out religious groups and prevent them from meeting.
127 737 F.2d 1317.
128 130 S Ct (2010). Also, see, *Ward v. Polite*, 667 F.3d 727 (6th Cir. 2012).
129 Citing *Widmar v. Vincent*, 454 U. S., at 268, n. 5.
130 667 F.3d 727 (6th Cir. 2012).
131 Case No. RIC 1302245 (Cal. Sup. Ct., Co. of Riverside [2014]).

admission application form. The court found that the university was a private religious establishment that was not subject to Title VII constraints and held that it was therefore entitled to restrict admission to its educational programs.

Right to equality and non-discrimination: employment

Title VII[132] provides that:

> It shall be an unlawful employment practice for an employer . . . to fail or refuse to hire or to discharge . . . or otherwise to discriminate against any individual with respect to his [or her] compensation, terms, conditions, or privileges of employment, because of such individual's race, colour, religion, sex, or national origin.

The latter phrase has been of crucial significance for courts and regulators. In deciding whether Title VII prohibits sexual orientation discrimination, they have been guided by the phrase "because of . . . sex", which Congress has defined as making sex "a motivating factor".[133] This has been interpreted as designating a protected characteristic or status rather than an activity.[134] In 2012, the EEOC ruled that the prohibition on discrimination "because of . . . sex" applies to trans people,[135] but this was refuted in October 2018 in a Trump administration directive stating that trans people are not protected from employment discrimination under Title VII.

This contention needs to be viewed in the light of the USSC finding in *Zarda*,[136] that Title VII prohibits not just discrimination based on sex itself but also discrimination based on traits that are a function of sex, such as life expectancy[137] and non-conformity with gender norms,[138] and also the predicating of sexual orientation on a gender stereotype,[139] a finding which would seem to comprehensively embrace SOGI stereotyping. Courts and regulators have also been alert to the capacity for such discrimination to be present in proxy form (e.g. as in *Manhart*),[140] or by association. Again, as noted in *Zarda*,[141] the prohibition on

132 42 U.S.C. § 2000e-2(a)(1).
133 *Rivera v. Rochester Genesee Reg'l Transp. Auth.*, 743 F.3d 11, 23 (2d Cir. 2014).
134 *Holcomb v. Iona College*, 521 F.3d 130, 139 (2d Cir. 2008), at 139; *Univ. of Tex. Sw. Med. Ctr. v. Nassar*, 570 U.S. 338, 133 S.Ct. 2517, 2522, 186 L.Ed.2d 503 (2013).
135 *Macy v. Holder*, No. 0120120821, 2012 WL (2012).
136 *Zarda*, op. cit., at 112.
137 Citing, *L.A. Dep't of Water & Power v. Manhart*, 435 U.S. at 711, 98 S.Ct. 1370, 55 L.Ed.2d 657 (1978).
138 Citing *Price Waterhouse v. Hopkins*, 490 U.S. at 250–251, 109 S.Ct. 1775, 104 L.Ed.2d 268 (1989). See also *Oncale v. Sundowner Offshore Servs., Inc.*, 523 U.S. 75, 79, 118 S.Ct. 998, 140 L.Ed.2d 201 (1998).
139 See *Zarda*, op. cit., and *Simonton v. Runyon*, 232 F.3d 33 (2d Cir. 2000), at 35.
140 *Manhart*, op. cit.
141 *Zarda*, op. cit., at 125.

associational discrimination[142] applies with equal force to all the classes protected by Title VII, including sex. So, if a male employee married to a man is terminated because his employer disapproves of same-sex marriage, the employee has suffered associational discrimination based on his own sex because "the fact that the employee is a man instead of a woman motivated the employer's discrimination against him".[143] In determining whether something is functioning as a proxy for sex, an enquiry is focused on whether a person would have been treated differently "but for" his or her sex (see next).

Employers may not make any employment decisions "because of . . . sex", including hiring, firing, promoting, demoting and determining assignments and workloads.

Religious exemption

Religious organisations, and those with a religious ethos, are permitted to discriminate when hiring and firing, on the basis of religion. The Free Exercise Clause of the First Amendment, together with the Religious Freedom Restoration Act 1993, grants such exemption from equality and non-discrimination legislation, as do both the "ministerial exception"[144] and the bona fide occupational requirement (BFOQ). This is also permitted by the Establishment Clause, as was confirmed in *Corp. of Presiding Bishop of Church of Jesus Christ of Latter-day Saints v. Amos*,[145] when the USSC upheld the constitutionality of a law permitting religious organisations to exercise a religious preference when making employment decisions.

The limits to the religious exemption were recently explored in *R.G. & G.R. Harris Funeral Homes v. Equal Employment Opportunity Commission*,[146] which concerned the complaint of a funeral director who had been fired after informing the owner of his intention to begin dressing as a female at work and refusing to comply with the company dress code for male staff. The owner, a Christian for more than 65 years, said that forcing him to employ the transgender worker would impose a substantial burden on his sincerely held religious beliefs in violation of the Religious Freedom Restoration Act 1993, which states that "government shall not substantially burden a person's exercise of religion even if the burden results from a rule of general applicability". At first instance, the district court had ruled in favour of the owner, noting that under the 1993 Act the government could not force him to act contrary to his religious beliefs unless it demonstrated that doing so is the "least restrictive means" of furthering a "compelling government interest". The 6th Circuit, however, took a different view. In granting the appeal, lodged with the support of the EEOC, it broke new ground

142 *Holcomb v. Iona College*, 521 F.3d 130, 139 (2d Cir. 2008).
143 *Baldwin v. Foxx*, 2015 WL 4397641, at 6.
144 *Hosanna-Tabor Evangelical Lutheran School & School v. EEOC*, 132 S. Ct. 694 (2012).
145 483 U.S. 327, 329, 339 (1987).
146 6th Cir. No. 16–2424.

by becoming the first appeals court to hold that there is no religious exemption to Title VII provisions.

In recent years, opponents of LGBT equality have sought religious exemptions for health care facilities and adoption and foster care agencies funded or licensed by the state. This has resulted in "liberty laws" being enacted in several states, including Missouri, South Dakota, Alabama and Texas.

Sexual orientation in the workplace

The *Blum*[147] backstop continues to shore up discrimination against same-sex relationships in a US employment context. The US Court of Appeals (5th Circuit) then concluded that the plaintiff, a former employee of Gulf Oil who alleged that he had been fired because he was Jewish, male, white and homosexual, had not suffered unlawful discrimination because "discharge for homosexuality is not prohibited by Title VII".[148] This, as was noted nearly 40 years later in *Hively*,[149] results in the paradox that "although federal law now guarantees anyone the right to marry another person of the same gender, Title VII, to the extent it does not reach sexual orientation discrimination, also allows employers to fire that employee for doing so".

The USSC has acknowledged that a "hostile work environment" violates Title VII by affecting the "psychological aspects of the workplace environment".[150] As noted in *Boutillier*:[151]

> In order to determine whether an environment is hostile or abusive, a court must look at all of the circumstances, including: (1) the frequency of the discriminatory conduct; (2) its severity; (3) whether it is physically threatening or humiliating, or a mere offensive utterance; and (4) whether it unreasonably interferes with an employee's work performance.[152] Title VII is violated when the workplace is permeated with discriminatory intimidation, ridicule, and insult that is sufficiently severe or pervasive to alter the conditions of the victim's employment and create an abusive working environment.

The USSC has explicitly rejected the argument that Title VII does not protect male employees from sexual harassment by male co-workers.[153] In *Oncale*, the court held that "Title VII's prohibition on discrimination 'because of . . . sex' protects men as well as women" and extends to instances where the "plaintiff and

147 *Blum v. Gulf Oil Corp.*, 597 F.2d 936, 938 (5th Cir. 1979).
148 Ibid., at 938, citing *Smith v. Liberty Mutual Insurance Co.*, 5 Cir. 1978, 569 F.2d 325, 327.
149 *Hively v. Ivy Tech Community College, South Bend*, 830 F.3d 698, 714 (7th Cir. 2016).
150 *Meritor Sav. Bank, FSB v. Vinson*, 477 U.S. 57, 66–67 at 64, 106 S.Ct. 2399, 91 L.Ed.2d 49 (1986).
151 *Boutillier*, op. cit., at p. 22.
152 Citing, *Harris v. Forklift Systems, Inc.*, 510 U.S. 17, 23 (1993).
153 *Oncale*, op. cit.

the defendant . . . are of the same sex". Nonetheless, for decades, regulators[154] and judiciary[155] more or less held the line and denied that sexual orientation discrimination claims – including claims that being gay or lesbian constitutes nonconformity with a gender stereotype – could be cognisable under Title VII.

The 2015 landmark decision of the EEOC in *Baldwin v. Foxx*,[156] seemed to mark a turning point and an acceptance that the Title VII prohibition "because of . . . sex" could include sexual orientation discrimination.[157] In *Boutillier*,[158] which concerned the alleged discriminatory treatment and sexual stereotyping of a teacher by the school principal, because the teacher was a lesbian – as evidenced solely by the fact of her same-sex marriage – the principal's defence rested largely on the argument that sexual orientation was not a protected category under Title VII. The court adopted the approach earlier established by the 2nd Circuit in *Holcomb*,[159] interpreting "because of . . . sex" to include sexual orientation, and held that the teacher had suffered sex orientation discrimination which had created a hostile work environment resulting in her being "constructively discharged".[160] At much the same time, the 7th Circuit, sitting *en banc* in *Hively v. Ivy Tech Community College of Indiana*,[161] considered the complaint of an instructor who had worked for 14 years but had been denied full-time employment and promotion and was eventually fired because she was a lesbian. The court, following *Baldwin*, then held that Title VII prohibits sexual orientation discrimination because "the

154 See *Kalich v. AT&T Mobility, LLC*, 679 F.3d 464, 471 (6th Cir. 2012); *Prowel v. Wise Bus. Forms, Inc.*, 579 F.3d 285, 289 (3d Cir. 2009); *Medina v. Income Support Div.*, 413 F.3d 1131, 1135 (10th Cir. 2005); *Hamner v. St. Vincent Hosp. & Health Care Ctr., Inc.*, 224 F.3d 701, 704 (7th Cir. 2000); *Higgins v. New Balance Athletic Shoe, Inc.*, 194 F.3d 252, 259 (1st Cir. 1999); *Wrightson v. Pizza Hut of Am., Inc.*, 99 F.3d 138, 143 (4th Cir. 1996); *Williamson v. A.G. Edwards & Sons, Inc.*, 876 F.2d 69, 70 (8th Cir. 1989) (per curiam); *Blum v. Gulf Oil Corp.*, 597 F.2d 936, 938 (5th Cir. 1979) (per curiam); and *Johnson v. Frank*, EEOC Decision No. 01911827, 1991 WL 1189760 (19 December 1991).

155 See *Simonton v. Runyon*, 232 F.3d 33, 35 (2d Cir. 2000) and *Dawson v. Bumble & Bumble*, 398 F.3d 211, 217–23 (2d Cir. 2005).

156 EEOC Decision No. 0120133080, 2015 WL 4397641 (July 15, 2015). Also see: *Winstead v. Lafayette Cty. Bd. of Cty. Comm'rs*, F. Supp. 3d, No. 1:16, CV00054-MW-GRJ, 2016 WL 3440601, at 5–9 (N.D. Fla. June 20, 2016); *Isaacs v. Felder Servs.*, LLC, 143 F. Supp. 3d 1190, 1193–94 (M.D. Ala. 2015); *Videckis v. Pepperdine Univ.*, 150 F. Supp. 3d 1151, 1159–61 (C.D. Cal. 2015); *Deneffe v. SkyWest, Inc.*, No. 14-cv-00348-MEH, 2015 WL 2265373, at 5–6 (D. Colo. May 11, 2015); *Terveer v. Billington*, 34 F. Supp. 3d 100, 116 (D.D.C. 2014); *Boutillier v. Hartford Pub. Schs.*, No. 3:13, CV1303 WWE, 2014 WL 4794527, at 2 (D. Conn. Sept. 25, 2014); *Heller v. Columbia Edgewater Country Club*, 195 F. Supp. 2d 1212, 1224 (D. Or. 2002); see also *Christiansen v. Omnicom Grp., Inc.*, 167 F. Supp. 3d 598, 618–22 (S.D.N.Y. 2016).

157 Also see Dupont, R. and Davis, N., Gender Identity and Sexual Orientation Coverage Under Title VII, *The Digest of Equal Employment Opportunity Law*, XXVI(1) (August 2015), at: www.eeoc.gov/federal/digest/xxvi-1.cfm#article.

158 Op. cit.

159 *Holcomb*, op. cit.

160 *Petrosino v. Bell Atlantic*, 385 F.3d 210, 229 (2d Cir. 2004).

161 853 F.3d at 340–41 (7th Circuit, 2017).

common sense reality [is] that it is actually impossible to discriminate on the basis of sexual orientation without discriminating on the basis of sex". However, the decision of the 7th Circuit in *Hively* was countered almost simultaneously by that of the 11th Circuit in *Evans*:[162] the former affirmed and the latter denied that Title VII prohibited workplace discrimination on the basis of sexual orientation.

Evans v. Georgia Regional Hospital concerned Ms Evans, a gay female security officer in a hospital, who alleged that she had been denied equal pay or work and had been harassed and physically assaulted or battered, in a hostile work environment, because of her sexual orientation and gender non-conformity ("male uniform, low male haircut, shoes, etc."), which ultimately resulted in her resignation. The court at first instance reasoned that – based on caselaw from all circuits that had addressed the issue – Title VII "was not intended to cover discrimination against homosexuals". With regard to Evans's claim of discrimination based on gender non-conformity, the magistrate judge concluded that it was "just another way to claim discrimination based on sexual orientation", no matter how it was otherwise characterised. On appeal to the US Court of Appeals (11th Circuit), Evans with EEOC support pursued in the main a two-pronged argument. Firstly, she argued that the district court erred in dismissing her claim that she was discriminated against for failing to conform to gender stereotypes, because an LGBT person may properly bring a separate discrimination claim for gender non-conformity. Secondly, she argued that sexual orientation discrimination is, in fact, sex discrimination under Title VII.

As regards the first, she contended that her status as a lesbian supported her claim of sex discrimination, because discrimination against someone for her orientation often coincides with discrimination for gender non-conformity. She further asserted that discrimination based on gender stereotypes is a broad claim that encompasses more than just her appearance and also provides for suits based on various other stereotypes, such as family structure. Finding that discrimination based on gender nonconformity was actionable, and allowing the submission of further supportive evidence, it was held that the lower court erred because a gender non-conformity claim is not "just another way to claim discrimination based on sexual orientation", but instead constitutes a separate, distinct avenue for relief under Title VII.

As regards the second argument – that as a consequence of the hostile work environment, due to her sexual orientation, she had suffered discrimination – this the court peremptorily rejected: "She has not. Our binding precedent forecloses such an action".[163] It similarly rejected a suggestion that the decisions in *Price Waterhouse v. Hopkins*[164] and *Oncale v. Sundowner Offshore Servs., Inc.*[165] supported a cause of action for sexual orientation discrimination under Title VII: "*Price Waterhouse* and *Oncale* are neither clearly on point nor contrary to *Blum*".

162 850 F.3d 1248 (11th Cir. 2017).
163 Citing *Blum v. Gulf Oil Corp.*, 597 F.2d 936, 938 (5th Cir. 1979).
164 490 U.S. 228 (1989).
165 523 U.S. 75 (1998).

The court held that its hands were firmly tied by the 1979 decision in *Blum*, pointing to a string of circuit court decisions that had followed the same precedent, and dismissed the sexual orientation claim. Judge William Pryor explained that "just as a woman cannot recover under Title VII when she is fired because of her heterosexuality, neither can a gay woman sue for discrimination based on her sexual orientation".[166]

Then, in 2018, the 2nd Circuit Court of Appeals considered the same issue, in *Zarda v. Altitude Express*,[167] which concerned a claim brought by a former employee that the termination of his job as a sky-diving instructor, following disclosure that he was gay, constituted sex discrimination in violation of Title VII. It ruled that "sexual orientation discrimination, which is based on an employer's opposition to association between particular sexes and thereby discriminates against an employee based on their own sex, constitutes discrimination 'because of . . . sex' ".[168] As Katzmann J on behalf of the court explained:

> Although sexual orientation discrimination is "assuredly not the principal evil that Congress was concerned with when it enacted Title VII," "statutory prohibitions often go beyond the principal evil to cover reasonably comparable evils."[169] In the context of Title VII, the statutory prohibition extends to all discrimination "because of . . . sex" and sexual orientation discrimination is an actionable subset of sex discrimination. We overturn our prior precedents to the contrary to the extent they conflict with this ruling.

However, until the USSC finally determines the matter, it remains the case that the US courts are divided on this crucial issue of interpretation.

Trans persons and the workplace

Modern US jurisprudence on this subject can be safely dated to *Price Waterhouse*,[170] as buttressed by the Civil Rights Act 1991.[171] The USSC then observed that one way to discern the motivation behind an employment decision is to consider whether, "if we asked the employer at the moment of the decision what its reasons were and if we received a truthful response, one of those reasons would be" the applicant or employee's sex. This was a case concerning a female executive who, although eligible in all other respects for a partnership, was denied such promotion because her employer had insisted that she should act in a stereotyped "feminine" manner, and she did not. Finding that the same treatment would not have applied to a male counterpart,

166 Ibid., at 20.2.
167 883 F.3d 100, 132 (2d Cir. 2018) (*en banc*).
168 Ibid., at 128.
169 Citing: *Oncale*, op. cit., at 80.
170 *Price Waterhouse*, op. cit., at 250.
171 Tit. I, § 107(a), 105 Stat. 1075 (codified at 42 U.S.C. § 2000e – 2(m)).

the USSC concluded that being female – while refusing to fit the "feminine" stereotype – was the operative factor in denying her promotion and held that the firm was therefore guilty of committing sex-based discrimination violation of Title VII.[172] This finding, arguably eviscerating *Blum*, broke open the previously tightly confined interpretation of what constituted "because . . . of sex" for the purposes of Title VII.[173] Thereafter, it became possible to consider that a broad range of discriminatory stereotyping lay latent within that formulaic term, including discrimination against transgender persons. The courts, applying the rule that "an individual cannot be punished because of his or her perceived gender-nonconformity",[174] were able to extend the protection available under Title VII.

One such case was *Glenn v. Brumby*,[175] which concerned Glenn, who was fired when the employer learned of his employee's intention to proceed with gender transition. In fact, the employer testified that he terminated Glenn's employment "based on 'the sheer fact of the transition'".[176] Termination was because Glenn "was born a biological male" and the employer believed the choices "to take steps to transition" and to be "dressed as a woman" at work were "unsettling", "unnatural" and "not appropriate".[177] In 2011, the 11th Circuit found that "discrimination against a transgender individual because of her gender-nonconformity is sex discrimination, whether it's described as being on the basis of sex or gender" and upheld the ruling of the district court that Glenn had suffered unlawful discrimination because of the employer's view that his employee had failed to conform to sex stereotypes. It declared that:

> All persons, whether transgender or not, are protected from discrimination on the basis of gender stereotype. For example, courts have held that plaintiffs cannot be discriminated against for wearing jewellery that was considered too effeminate, carrying a serving tray too gracefully, or taking too active a role in child-rearing. An individual cannot be punished because of his or her perceived gender-nonconformity. Because these protections are afforded to everyone, they cannot be denied to a transgender individual.

172 Among many other such cases, see: *Lopez v. River Oaks Imaging & Diagnostic Grp., Inc.*, 542 F. Supp. 2d 653 (S.D. Tex. 2008); *Schroer v. Billington*, 577 F. Supp. 2d 293 (D.D.C. 2008); *Creed v. Family Express Corp.*, 101 Fair Empl. Prac. Cas. (BNA) 609, 2007 WL 2265630 (N.D. Ind. Aug. 3, 2007); and *Tronetti v. TLC HealthNet Lakeshore Hosp.*, No. 03-cv-375E, 2003 WL 22757935, at *4 (W.D.N.Y. 2003).

173 *Manhart*, op. cit.

174 Op. cit., at 1319.

175 663 F.3d 1312 (11th Cir. 2011).

176 Ibid., at 1320–1321.

177 Ibid., at 1314, 1320–1321. Also see *Chavez v. Credit Nation Auto Sales, L.L.C.*, 2016 WL 158820 (11th Cir. 14 January 2016), in which it was noted that, before the plaintiff was fired, the supervisor had remarked that her transgender status made him "nervous" and would negatively impact the business and co-workers.

Again, in *Finkle v. Howard Cty., Md.*,[178] when considering a Title VII claim brought by a volunteer auxiliary police officer, the court ruled that the officer was an "employee" for Title VII purposes, and that her claim that she was discriminated against "because of her obvious transgendered status" raised a cognisable claim of sex discrimination. The court reasoned: "It would seem that any discrimination against transsexuals (as transsexuals) – individuals who, by definition, do not conform to gender stereotypes – is proscribed by Title VII's proscription of discrimination on the basis of sex as interpreted by *Price Waterhouse*". This ruling was followed most recently by that of the US Court of Appeals for the 6th Circuit, in *R.G. & G.R. Harris Funeral Homes v. Equal Employment Opportunity Commission*,[179] which held on similar facts that job discrimination on the basis of transgender status was inherently sex discrimination. Further, as mentioned earlier, the court ruled that the employer could not claim an exemption from the law because of his religious beliefs. This was the sixth time a federal appeals court had found that employees must not be discriminated against because they fail to conform to "stereotypical gender norms", a position flatly contradicted by the Trump administration. In October 2017, Attorney General Jeff Sessions advised that: "Title VII's prohibition on sex discrimination encompasses discrimination between men and women but does not encompass discrimination based on gender identity *per se*, including transgender status".[180]

Employment in the military

The traditional prohibition on LGBT persons serving in the US military was supplanted in 1996 with the introduction of a Congressional "Don't Ask, Don't Tell" (DADT) policy[181] and formally in 2010 following a series of court cases ruling the prohibition unconstitutional.[182] Cynthia Burack adds that:

> DADT was the result of a coerced compromise between Clinton and the military, which refused to consider ending the prohibition as Clinton had promised when he was running for president. DADT actually ended up resulting in more forced separations from the military than the policy it replaced, and women were disproportionately affected.[183]

178 12 F. Supp. 3d 780 (D. Md. 2014).
179 6th Cir. No. 16–2424 (2018).
180 See further at: https://edition.cnn.com/2017/10/05/politics/jeff-sessions-transgender-title-vii/index.html.
181 The Don't Ask, Don't Tell Repeal Act 2010 removed legal obstacles to gay, lesbian and bisexuals serving in the armed forces (author acknowledges advice from Cynthia Burack on this matter: note to author, 12 May 2019).
182 See, for example, *Witt v. Department of the Air Force*, 527 F.3d 806 (9th Cir. 2008) and *Log Cabin Republicans v. United States*, 658 F.3d 1162 (9th Cir. 2011).
183 Note to author, 12 May 2019.

The decades-long prohibition on trans persons serving in the military was due to end in July 2017. The order declaring that "transgender individuals be allowed to serve in the military", and prohibiting the discharge of any service personnel on the basis of gender identity, issued under the Obama administration, was rescinded by the Trump administration the day before it was meant to take effect. Following a good deal of litigation,[184] largely revolving around a district court preliminary injunction[185] granted in December 2017 which prevented implementation of a presidential ban[186] on allowing transgender individuals to openly serve in the armed forces, the USSC ruled that the injunction be lifted. It found that government policy did not violate the respondents' due process or First Amendment rights: there is no fundamental right to serve in the military, much less to do so in a particular manner; and no specific restriction on speech had been identified.

Right to equality and non-discrimination: services

The US Constitution established no obligations on government to provide health, food, education or an adequate standard of living. Nor has there ever been a federal law prohibiting discrimination in respect of LGBT people. Consequently, under the Tenth Amendment, it has fallen to individual states to legislate for such matters, and they have varied greatly in their willingness to do so. According to a 2018 report, at that time only 19 states and the District of Columbia had laws that protected people from discrimination in public accommodations[187] based on sexual orientation and gender identity.[188] Seven of the 19 – Colorado, Delaware, Illinois, Maine, Nevada, New Jersey and New York – had some of the broadest with laws explicitly covering sexual orientation and gender identity for public transportation, hospitals, schools and places like hotels and restaurants.

Trans persons and gender-specific services

Some states have legislation protecting trans individuals from discrimination in public spaces like restaurants and shops. Massachusetts is one such state. However, following the Trump administration's introduction of federal measures that seemingly aim to constrain the rights of trans persons, the citizens of

184 See *Stockman v. Trump*, No. 17-cv-1799 (C.D. Cal. filed Sept. 5, 2017), *Doe v. Trump*, No. 17-cv-1597 (D.D.C. filed Aug. 9, 2017) and *Stone* v. *Trump*, 280 F. Supp. 3d 747 (D. Md. 2017).

185 *Karnoski v. Trump*, 2:17-cv-01297-MJP.

186 Directive-type Memorandum-19–004.

187 The term "public accommodations" is generally interpreted as referring to property and facilities that are open to the public such as property that is open to the public e.g. stores, restaurants, hotels, community centres, camps, museums and parks.

188 See the Movement Advancement Project (MAP), *LGBT Policy Spotlight: Public Accommodations Nondiscrimination Laws* (2018), at: www.lgbtmap.org/policy-spotlight-public-accommodations.

Massachusetts are now to vote on whether or not to repeal a 2016 law that prohibits discrimination against trans persons in public spaces and allows unimpeded access to bathrooms. There is evidence that other states are following suit. The MAP report shows that in 2017 at least 19 "bathroom bills" (excluding trans individuals from restrooms which conform to their acquired gender identity) were filed in 16 state legislatures.[189]

Provision of public services

While Titles III and IV of the Civil Rights Act 1964 provide the main statutory protection from discrimination in accessing public services, Title II prohibits discriminatory practice by any establishment that leases, rents or sells goods or provides services.[190] Specifically, s.2000a(a) of the Civil Rights Act 1964 declares that "all persons shall be entitled to the full and equal enjoyment of the goods, services, facilities, privileges, advantages, and accommodations of any place of public accommodation". The guiding principle, however, as was pithily expressed in *Rosenberger v. Rector and Visitors of Univ. of Va.*,[191] is that "once it has opened a limited [public] forum . . . the State must respect the lawful boundaries it has itself set".

Public services traditionally provided by religious organisations, such as adoption and foster care, have been negatively impacted by equality law. In 2006, Catholic Charities in Boston failed to gain exemption from the state's anti-discrimination statute and terminated its adoption work rather than continue to place children under the "guardianship of homosexuals". Similarly, in Washington DC in 2010 the same body took the same step when faced with a statutory requirement that government-funded religious entities providing public services do so by including same-sex couples. In 2012, the Illinois Department of Children and Family Services revoked its contract with Catholic Charities after its refusal to provide adoption and foster-care services to same-sex couples, causing the transfer of more than 1,000 children to secular agencies. When religious organisations are contracted to provide services on behalf of government – acting as agents of the State – they have been wholly bound by State legislation, but "liberty laws" are now challenging this prescriptive approach, as they are the implicit requirement that public officials will deliver the public services they are contracted to provide regardless of their private beliefs (see further below). In 2018 a new unit – the Conscience and Religious Freedom Division – was established at the Office of Civil Rights in the Department of Health and Human Services. This has the stated purpose of protecting moral and religious convictions, and it has already issued a proposed rule aiming to excuse health care

189 Ibid.

190 See, for example, *Heart of Atlanta Motel Inc v. U.S.*, 379 US 241 (1964) and *Katzenbach v. McClung*, 379 U.S. 294 (1964).

191 515 U.S. 819, at 829.

providers from participating in procedures that conflict with their moral or religious beliefs.[192]

Trans persons and prisons

US prison services vary from state to state in their policies regarding LGBT prisoners; trans inmates are clearly the most vulnerable. The USSC, in the landmark decision of *Farmer v. Brennan*,[193] which concerned a trans prisoner (mtf) who had been repeatedly assaulted and raped by fellow inmates, laid down the general principle that prison officers had a duty of care – when they were aware of a prisoner's particular vulnerability – to take reasonable steps to ensure their safety. This principle may not survive the federal policy announced in May 2018, under the present Trump administration, that prisoners should in future be housed in accordance with their gender as acquired at birth rather than as self-identified or as surgically determined. In practice, however, many state prisons manage the vulnerabilities and health care needs of trans prisoners by segregating them from other inmates, often in solitary confinement.

Private goods and service provision

Private service providers (owners of hotels, boarding houses etc.), claiming exemption from equality and non-discrimination provisions on the protected grounds of personal religious belief, generate a great deal of controversy throughout the US. Cases include the refusal to bake cakes ordered to celebrate gay marriages[194] which led to the USSC decision in *Masterpiece*.[195] Unfortunately the USSC was then unable to make any finding as to whether or not the baker's refusal to provide services was protected by the First Amendment, as it was deflected by process irregularities and had to confine itself to ruling that the Colorado Civil Rights Commission did not act "with the religious neutrality that the Constitution requires"[196] when it considered the bakery's arguments. Had this claim succeeded, the USSC would have thereby licenced similar discretionary religious/ sexual discrimination from a limitless range of "expressive" service providers,

192 Department of Health and Human Services, 83 FR 2802, *Statement of Organization, Functions, and Delegations of Authority* (19 January 2018), at: www.gpo.gov/fdsys/pkg/ FR-2018-01-19/pdf/2018-00820.pdf.

193 511 U.S. 825 (1994).

194 See the decision of the Oregon Bureau of Labour and Industries to fine *Sweet Cakes by Melissa* for such a refusal at: Richardson, V., Oregon Panel Proposes $135k Hit Against Bakers in Gay-Wedding Cake Dispute, *Washington Times*, 24 April 2015.

195 *Masterpiece Cakeshop v. Colorado Civil Rights Commission*, 584 US 138 S. Ct. 1719; 201 L. Ed. 2d 35, (2018)

196 *Church of Lukumi Babalu Aye, Inc. v. City of Hialeah*, 508 U.S. (1993) and *Employment Division v. Smith*, 48 U.S. 872 (1990).

including architects, hairdressers, tailors, designers etc.[197] Arguably, the principle that a religious employer may restrict product availability on the grounds that to do so would violate sincerely held religious beliefs has already been conceded in *Burwell v. Hobby Lobby*.[198] So, this matter is sure to return to the USSC.

State pensions and social security benefits etc.

The USSC decision in *Manhart*[199] did more than establish that gender inequality in pension contributions violated Title VII; it also introduced the "simple test of whether the evidence shows treatment of a person in a manner which *but for* that person's sex would be different".[200] Its conclusion, after applying the test to the correlation between life expectancy, sex or gender of employee and amount of contribution, was that life expectancy functioned as a proxy for "sex" and therefore the pension policy constituted discrimination "because of . . . sex". This test proved transferable and useful for identifying other proxies that served for "sex" in cases of alleged discrimination against LGBT persons, with "religion" often being one such proxy.

In *United States v. Windsor*,[201] which concerned federal tax benefits and tax liabilities, the USSC held that s.3 of the federal Defense of Marriage Act 1996 violated the Fifth Amendment's guarantee of equal protection of the laws insofar as certain tax laws discriminated against persons of the same sex who were legally married under the laws of their State. Consequently, the Employee Retirement Income Security Act of 1974 (ERISA), the federal law that sets minimum standards for most voluntarily established pension and health plans, has been re-interpreted – taking into account also the ruling in *Obergefell v. Hodges*[202] – to extend certain entitlements to married same-sex couples. The extent to which a survivor's legal claim to a share in their deceased's partner's pension, or accommodation, or to their health or social service benefits, will be geographically determined – in accordance with whether or not the state in which they are resident legalised same-sex marriage following the *Windsor* ruling – remains to be explored.

The USSC rulings in *Windsor* and *Obergefell*, together with subsequent changes in agency policy and guidance, resulted in expanded access for many LGBT family members to a range of benefits, including dependent health coverage and family and medical leave and also to Medicare for same-sex couples.

197 See further Laycock, D. and Berg, T., *Symposium: Masterpiece Cakeshop – Not as Narrow as May First Appear*, at: www.scotusblog.com/2018/06/symposium-masterpiece-cakeshop-not-as-narrow-as-may-first-appear/.
198 573 U.S. 134 S Ct 2751 (2014).
199 *L.A. Dep't of Water & Power v. Manhart*, 435 U.S. 702, 707 n.13, 98 S.Ct. 1370, 55 L.Ed.2d 657 (1978).
200 Ibid., at 711.
201 570 U.S. 744 (2013).
202 576 U.S. (2015).

However, federal recognition of same-sex legal status did not translate into nationwide legislation; consequently, legal entitlement to some benefits differs from state to state.

Conscientious objection of service providers

The USSC confirmation of the constitutionality of the Obama administration's Patient Protection and Affordable Care Act (ACA) brought with it considerable controversy regarding public health measures which restrict personal choice: in particular, there were arguments that some requirements violated the right to freedom of conscience by mandating access to contraception as a form of public service provision which breached the beliefs of many religious organisations and individuals. Some states responded by introducing so-called religious liberty laws that provide opt-outs for service delivery staff, permitting them to decline involvement in services on the grounds of personal conscience.[203] This trend was consolidated by the Trump administration when it repealed crucial aspects of the ACA contraceptive provisions and established the Conscience and Religious Freedom Division, as part of the Office of Civil Rights, within the Department of Health and Human Services.

The remit of this new Division, tasked with enforcing federal laws protecting civil rights and conscience in health and human services, has been reinforced by the aforementioned "liberty laws". One such was the Religious Liberty Accommodations Act in Mississippi, in respect of which the USSC declined to hear a challenge due to the plaintiff's lack of standing.[204] The Mississippi legislation is not untypical in that it permits state employees to refuse to participate in service provision to LGBT persons if doing so would contravene their religious beliefs (see further below). It specifies three beliefs that qualify the holder for exemption: that marriage happens only between a man and a woman; that sex should only take place in that kind of marriage; and that a person's gender is decided at birth and cannot be changed. The ramifications of this USSC decision not to grant a hearing are currently difficult to predict, but the law remains on the statute books, even if not yet implemented.

SOGI, public service and conscientious objection

The number of doctors, nurses and other health care workers who decline to take part in aspects of health care service provision – because to do so would violate their religion, beliefs or morals – has increased in recent years. The previously-mentioned Division of Conscience and Religious Freedom is intended to protect

203 See further Laycock, D. (ed.), *Same-Sex Marriage and Religious Liberty*, Rowman & Littlefield, 2008.

204 Also known as the Patient Protection and Affordable Care Act 2016, or HB 1523. See, *Barber v. Bryant* 17–547, and *Campaign for Southern Equality v. Bryant*, 17–642.

such professionals. Building upon recent USSC decisions[205] and state "religious liberty law" initiatives, it marks an important point of departure from the law which generally does not permit public service providers to choose those aspects of legally mandated provision with which they will comply. There is an argument that such freedom of choice is prohibited under the Fourteenth Amendment.

While clearly aimed at offering protection to staff engaged in abortion and contraception services, the potential remit of this Division is uncertain. It seems likely that it extends to matters addressed in the Mississippi legislation – such as protection for those refusing to deal with LGBT and transgender issues – and may accommodate issues such as assisted suicide or capital punishment and could possibly reach beyond direct service providers to those in ancillary positions such as radiographers or even receptionists. Differentiating between a justifiable right to protect beliefs and any unjustifiable resulting conduct that discriminates against others has become a dangerous fault-line that runs throughout the "culture wars". This is rapidly becoming more complex. Establishing a rationale for limiting the potential scope of an opt-out for those who protest that service provision obligations compromise their consciences could prove difficult.

Conclusion

The absence of any federal legislation specifically prohibiting discrimination based on sexual orientation and gender identity, together with the fact that less than half of all states do so, is a curious anomaly in a nation that pioneered State protection of civil rights in general and discrimination against trans persons[206] in particular. That anomaly has forced courts and regulators to rely instead on creative interpretations of the "because of . . . sex" clause in Title VII, as amended by the Civil Rights Act of 1991 (in response to Supreme Court decisions). This clause has become a key part of the foundations supporting the weight of SOGI-related jurisprudence in the US. However, although that form of words is now accepted as encompassing "sexual orientation", there is continuing judicial deadlock at federal appeals court level as regards whether "sex" may be interpreted as including "gender identity".

Judicial ambivalence on SOGI matters is now in danger of being bypassed and made redundant by the clarity of political purpose demonstrated by the Trump administration. The 2017 advice given by the Attorney General (arguably acting as a spokesperson for the administration) that the earlier-mentioned clause did not "encompass discrimination based on gender identity *per se*, including transgender status"[207] indicated a certain sense of direction. This was confirmed in 2018 with the setting up of the Conscience and Religious Freedom Division of

205 *Burwell v. Hobby Lobby*, 573 US 134 S. Ct. 2751 (2014) and *Zubik v. Burwell*, 136 S. Ct. 1557–2016.

206 See, for example, *Smith v. City of Salem* 378 F.3d 566, 568 (6th Cir. 2004).

207 See further at: https://edition.cnn.com/2017/10/05/politics/jeff-sessions-transgender-title-vii/index.html.

the US Department of Health and Human Services and the White House Faith and Opportunity Initiative. Subsequent initiatives have strengthened the realisation that the Trump administration is not interested in upholding the doctrine of State neutrality towards religion but instead is intent on demonstrating State support for traditional, conservative and essentially religious values, by curtailing the gains made in recent years by the LGBT community and more specifically by imposing constraints on the trans sector of that community. These initiatives have included: the directive that prisoners should in future be housed in accordance with their gender as acquired at birth rather than as self-identified or as surgically determined; that trans persons should not be enlisted or permitted to serve in the national armed forces; encouragement for state repeal of bathroom laws that allow trans persons to use facilities that correspond with their declared gender identity; and encouragement also for the introduction of state "religious liberty laws" which excuse public health officials from service provision where involvement might compromise their religious beliefs, including not approving same-sex couples as adopters. Such developments do not augur well – at least for the immediate future – as regards the response to SOGI-related issues in the US.

7 Canada

Introduction

In 2018, Statistics Canada introduced two new standards – "sex" and "gender" – to be used from 2021 as indicators in national population data surveys.[1] These closely defined and carefully differentiated terms should in future prove invaluable for measuring, profiling and tracing trends in Canada's developing LGBT community, though further refinement that includes non-binary indicators would help give a fuller picture. In the meantime, the meagre and undoubtedly under-reported statistics for 2014 reveal Canadians in the age group 18 to 59 disclosing that 1.7% considered themselves to be homosexual (gay or lesbian) while 1.3% were bisexual.

This chapter sketches a broad overview of the SOGI landscape, noting the features that are most characteristic of this jurisdiction. It begins by explaining the relevant international and domestic legal context and identifying the main laws, courts and governing principles. It considers the relationship between the more fundamental human rights and contemporary SOGI issues before examining those rights which have a direct relevance for the LGBT community: same-sex relationships, family life, parenting and associated matters. The main part of the chapter then focuses on the caselaw generated by equality legislation which has driven much of the legal development achieved in those areas. This identifies the principal cases arising within the thematic structure outlined in Chapter 3: equality and non-discrimination in relation to SOGI issues, arising in the context of health, education, employment and service provision.

Legislative framework: international and domestic

Canada has a well-earned international reputation of being at the forefront in building a domestic framework of SOGI-related legislation and in developing the law and practice on SOGI issues.

1 See Statistics Canada at: www.statcan.gc.ca/eng/concepts/definitions/gender-sex-variables.

International legislation

Canada has played a leading role in endorsing international treaties, conventions, protocols etc. relevant to ensuring SOGI rights (see Chapter 3).

The Universal Declaration of Human Rights (UDHR)

Canada signed and ratified the Universal Declaration of Human Rights in 1948.

The International Covenant on Civil and Political Rights (ICCPR)

Having ratified the ICCPR in 1976, Canada subsequently ratified Optional Protocol 1.[2]

Other

Also of relevance for present purposes are the ratifications of the International Convention on the Elimination of All Forms of Racial Discrimination (1970); the International Covenant on Economic, Social and Cultural Rights (1976); the Convention on the Elimination of All Forms of Discrimination Against Women (CEDAW) (1981); and the UN Declarations on the Rights of Indigenous Peoples (UNDRIP) (2007) and on human rights, sexual orientation and gender identity. In addition, certain protocols and directives have a bearing upon SOGI issues (see further Chapter 3).

Domestic legislation

The Constitution Act 1982, containing the Canadian Charter of Rights and Freedom, is of central importance.[3] In total, Canada has 14 different human rights statutes, one for each province and territory and for the federal jurisdiction, all of which include sexual orientation and gender identity as prohibited grounds of discrimination.

The Constitution

This consists of the Constitution Act 1982, together with its predecessor the Constitution Act 1867 (formerly the British North America Act 1867), and all other statutes and orders referred to in the schedule and any amendments.

The Canadian Charter of Rights and Freedoms, which constitutes the first part of the Constitution, takes priority over all other federal and provincial legislation. Section 2 declares that everyone has the following "fundamental freedoms: (a)

2 See *Waldman v. Canada*, Communication No. 694/1996.

3 Canadian Charter of Rights and Freedoms, s.8, Part 1 of the Constitution Act, 1982, being Schedule B to the Canada Act 1982 (UK), 1982, c 11.

freedom of conscience and religion; and (b) freedom of thought, belief, opinion and expression".[4] Under s.1, this is subject "only to such reasonable limits prescribed by law as can be demonstrably justified in a free and democratic society" and to a requirement that "freedom" be interpreted in accordance with the "preservation and enhancement of the multicultural heritage of Canada" (s.27).[5] The freedoms specified in s.2 and ss.7–15 are all subject to Clause 33, the "notwithstanding" caveat, which allows the federal or any provincial government to pass laws that breach Charter rights in relation to such matters. Section 15(1) provides a specific guarantee of equality and has been held to import a requirement that all provincial human rights legislation include the ground of sexual orientation.[6]

Bill C-16

Passed in June 2017, this federal legislation amends the Canadian Human Rights Act to include "gender identity" and "gender expression" among the grounds protected from discrimination. It also adds "gender identity" and "gender expression" to two sections of the Criminal Code: first, to the definition of "identifiable group" in s.318, which makes it a criminal offence to advocate or promote genocide against members of an identifiable group; and second, to the sentencing provisions in s.718.2, leading to increased sentences for those who commit crimes motivated by hatred or prejudice based on gender identity or expression.[7]

The Civil Marriage Act 2005

This federal legislation legalised same-sex marriage across all of Canada.

Bill C-23 2000

Introduced in the 36th Parliament, 2nd Session, which ended in October 2000, this statute gave same-sex couples the same social and tax benefits as heterosexuals in common law relationships.

The Employment Equity Act 1996

This legislation promotes equity in the workplace for the four designated groups: women, Aboriginal peoples, persons with disabilities and members of visible minorities. In addition, the Canadian government has passed into law a set of regulations, the Federal Contractors Program 1986 and the Employment Equity Act 1996, to address employment opportunities and benefits.

4 Charter, s.2.
5 See, for example, *R. v. S. (R.D.)* (1997), 118 CCC (3d) 353 (SCC), per Cory, J., at 385.
6 *Vriend v. Alberta*,[1998] 1 S.C.R. 493.
7 Code, RSC 1985, c. C – 46 at ss. 318 and 718.2.

The Canadian Human Rights Act 1985

This statute improved and extended the largely ineffective Canadian Bill of Rights 1960. It was amended in 1996 by the addition of s.3(1), which broadened the law to ensure equal opportunity for individuals, to expressly prohibit discrimination on a federal basis (replicated at province and territory levels) and to prohibit discrimination – on grounds which include sex and sexual orientation – in relation to employment and the provision of goods, services, facilities or accommodation within a federal regulated industry.

The Criminal Law Amendment Act 1969

Among the many matters addressed in this omnibus federal legislation – Bill C-150 – an exception clause was added to the provisions of the Criminal Code criminalising "buggery" and "gross indecency", permitting same-sex relations between consenting adults over the age of 21 in private.

Framework of courts and regulatory bodies

In Canada, as in the US, SOGI issues are adjudicated on an exclusively domestic basis and very largely by the courts and regulatory bodies at provincial and territorial levels, though naturally some of the most important decisions have come from the SCC.

International courts and regulatory bodies

The Universal Periodic Review process, admittedly neither judicial nor regulatory in nature, does provide an international peer monitoring forum for the ongoing review of Canadian progress in addressing human rights concerns, including SOGI issues.

Domestic courts and regulatory bodies

The jurisdictional division between federal and provincial government naturally affects the courts and regulatory machinery for law relating to religion: the system of Human Rights Tribunals with a right of appeal to a court and possibly to a local Supreme Court is replicated in each province and territory.

The Supreme Court of Canada (SCC)

This final court of appeal has a federal jurisdiction enabling it to adjudicate on, and to formulate governing principles in relation to, cases drawn from all areas of law, including those relating to human rights.

Appellate courts, provincial and federal

There is a right of appeal to this tier of courts from decisions of judicial and regulatory bodies taken at provincial and territorial levels.

The Canadian Human Rights Commission (CHRC)

This independent body, established at federal level, was created to administer the Canadian Human Rights Act 1977 and subsequently undertook regulatory responsibility for the Employment Equity Act 1996.

The Canadian Human Rights Tribunal

Established under the Canadian Human Rights Act 1977, the jurisdiction of this Tribunal is restricted to federally regulated activities and thus most human rights claims come before the provincial tribunals. It is independent of the Canadian Human Rights Commission, which refers cases to it for adjudication under the Act.

International reports on human rights in Canada

In the 2015 sixth periodic report,[8] the UN Human Rights Committee expressed its concern regarding several issues, including the human rights of Indigenous people, and urged Canada to "renew its traditional commitment to the promotion and protection of the exercise of freedom of assembly, association and expression".[9] In the 2018 UPR, the recommendations of the Committee included that Canada ratify those international human rights instruments to which it is not yet a party; strengthen measures to combat structural discrimination against African Canadians, Indigenous peoples, lesbian, gay, bisexual, transgender, queer and intersex persons and religious minorities, in particular by establishing effective mechanisms of investigation and punishment of perpetrators of acts of discrimination and violence against them; and that it take further measures to address hate crimes.

SOGI and related core human rights

The core human rights are largely as articulated within the Canadian Charter of Rights and Freedoms 1982. These are supplemented by the Canadian Human Rights Act 1985 and provincial human rights legislation as reinforced by various international treaties, together with the seven ratified UN human rights conventions and covenants. Some elements of this framework, such as the voluntary Yogyakarta Principles,[10] have a specific relevance for SOGI matters.

8 See UN International Covenant on Civil and Political Rights, *Concluding Observations on the Sixth Periodic Report of Canada*, at: http://tbinternet.ohchr.org/_layouts/treatybodyexternal/SessionDetails1.aspx?SessionID=899&Lang=en#sthash.XzzyC1Bz.dpuf.

9 Ibid., at para. 15.

10 Yogyakarta Principles 2007, as augmented in 2018 by an additional ten principles. See further at: https://yogyakartaprinciples.org.

Right of access to justice

Although there is no explicit constitutional or statutory right of access to justice, s.7 of the Charter proclaims that "everyone has the right to life, liberty and security of the person and the right not to be deprived thereof except in accordance with the principles of fundamental justice".

Access to relevant information

As regards gender identity, the federal processes for acquiring official identity documentation such as birth certificates and passports for use in normal social transactions (banking, employment, mortgages, health coverage, insurance, marriage, drivers' licence, travel visas etc.) are notably straightforward and transparent.[11]

An effective remedy

The Canadian approach to issues relating to a person's SOGI status, which essentially rests on respecting individual self-determination and relies more on a legal than a medical frame of reference, has been widely acclaimed. It would seem comprehensive and coherent and has gained a higher degree of acceptance among the LGBT community than is the case with most other national responses to such issues. However, the constitutional anomaly – embodied on the Constitution Act 1867, s.93 – that skews the significance of religion and extends the effects of the religious exemption, does constrain the legislative intent to embed equality principles and practice throughout Canadian society (see further below).

Asylum seekers/illegal immigrants

The definitional terms that structure the 1951 UN Convention on Refugees (see Chapter 3), to which Canada is a signatory State, have determined the resulting pattern of Canadian caselaw, which has largely revolved around the key concepts of "fear of persecution" and "particular social group".

Persecution (meaning a degree of serious harm),[12] or a well-founded fear of it, on SOGI-related grounds in their country of origin will qualify a displaced person for refugee status in Canada:[13] the mere inability of the State of origin to provide protection is sufficient to establish a claim for persecution;[14] and there is

11 See, for example, *XY v. Ontario (Government and Consumer Services)*, 2012 HRTO 72, where the HR tribunal struck down the surgery requirement to change legal sex on birth certificate in Ontario.

12 *Cuesta v. Canada (Minister of Citizenship and Immigration)* VA3–00908 (RPD), 2003.

13 See Immigration and Refugee Board of Canada, *Guideline 9: Proceedings before the IRB Involving Sexual Orientation and Gender Identity and Expression* (May 2017), at: www.irb-cisr.gc.ca/en/legal-policy/policies/Pages/GuideDir09.aspx.

14 *Canada (Attorney General) v. Ward* [1993] 2 S.C.R. 689.

no requirement that such a person should be discreet or take certain steps so as to avoid persecution.[15]

That SOGI characteristics could constitute the basis of "a particular social group", for Convention purposes, was established some 20 years ago: both sexual orientation[16] and trans[17] were recognised as valid grounds for refugee status, together with an acceptance that such group membership was a matter of perception (if the "persecutor" believed that the victim belonged to a particular group, it was of no legal consequence that in fact they did not);[18] this in turn could provide the basis for a "well-founded fear of persecution".[19]

The *Ogunrinde* case[20] concerned a refusal of refugee status by the Refugee Protection Division of the Immigration and Refugee Board because the petitioner's claim of being a homosexual was found not credible; this was not the first time the authorities had taken a somewhat dismissive attitude.[21] The grounds for appeal were that the immigration officer had given inadequate consideration to the evidence on the sexual orientation of the petitioner before rejecting the Pre-Removal Risk Assessment (PRRA) application. Corroborating evidence is necessary in such cases,[22] but must be reasonable,[23] and the Federal Court of Appeal heard that both the RPD and the PRRA officers had accepted that homosexuals were at risk in Nigeria and agreed that the applicant would possibly face risk or persecution in Nigeria if his homosexuality had been proven.[24] Although he failed to establish his homosexuality to the satisfaction of the PRRA Officer, he was regarded as a homosexual by his male companion and was wanted by the authorities in Nigeria for his homosexual activities. The court found that the risk of *perceived* homosexuality in Nigeria had not been appropriately analysed: the question was not whether or not the applicant was gay but rather the belief of Nigerian authorities about his sexual orientation. In overturning the earlier decision, the court stated an important principle:[25]

> The (PRRA) Officer's reasoning on this point also suggests that she had in mind a set of actions or behaviours which would convince her that the Applicant is homosexual. It is inappropriate for officers to rely on stereotypes

15 *Fosu v. Canada (Citizenship and Immigration)*, 2008 FC 1135, 335 FTR 223 and *Sadeghi-Pari v. Canada (Minister of Citizenship and Immigration)*, 2004 FC 282.
16 *Ward v. Canada*, op. cit., at p. 739.
17 *J(HA) (Re)* (1994) Vancouver V93–01711 (CRDD).
18 *Dykon v. Canada* (1994), 87 FTR 98, 25 Imm L.R. (2d) 193.
19 See, for example, *Kadah v. Canada (Citizenship and Immigration)*, 2010 FC 1223 and *Vasallo v. Canada (Citizenship and Immigration)*, 2012 FC 673.
20 *Francis Ojo Ogunrinde v. Canada* 2012 FC 760.
21 *Muckette v. Minister of Citizenship and Immigration*, 2008 FC 1388.
22 *Zakka v. Canada (Minister of Citizenship and Immigration)*, 2005 FC 1434 and *Birsan v. Canada (Minister of Citizenship and Immigration)* (1998), 86 ACWS (3d) 400.
23 *Essa v. Canada (Minister of Citizenship and Immigration)*, 2011 FC 1493.
24 *Mohacsi v. Canada (M.C.I.)*, 2003 FCT 429 and *Okoli v. Canada (Minister of Citizenship and Immigration)*, 2009 FC 332.
25 *Francis Ojo Ogunrinde v. Canada*, op. cit., per Russell, J., at para 46. See also: *Trembliuk v. Canada (Citizenship and Immigration)*, 2003 FC 1264; *Herrera v. Canada (Citizenship and Immigration), 2005 FC 464; and Ponniah v. Canada (Citizenship and Immigration)*, 2013 FC 386 (CanLII).

when evaluating whether or not a person has established any ground of risk, including sexual orientation.

Right to freedom of expression

The Canadian Charter of Rights and Freedoms proclaims the fundamental freedom of thought, belief, opinion and expression, including freedom of the press and other media of communication.

In Canada as elsewhere, the conflict between religious belief and sexual orientation has generated considerable litigation. The complainant in *Schnell v. Machiavelli and Associates Emprize Inc. and John Micka*[26] was a gay man who alleged that he had suffered sexual orientation discrimination by the respondents, who had posted messages on a website likely to expose homosexuals to hatred and contempt, in contravention of s.13 of the Canadian Human Rights Act. The Commission found that messages had been transmitted by means of a telecommunications facility; that they equated homosexuality with paedophilia, bestiality and had depicted homosexuals having an agenda to lure and abuse children; that they were likely to expose a person or persons to hate or contempt; and that such person or persons were identifiable on the basis of a prohibitive ground of discrimination, contrary to s.13(1) of the Canadian Human Rights Act.

A more explicit prohibition on hate propaganda, or the incitement of hatred, directed against persons on the grounds of their perceived sexual orientation, gender identity or gender expression can be found in the Criminal Code 1985, s.318(4) and s.319(1), which criminalises speech that wilfully promotes hatred based on such grounds, but this is subject to constraints. *Boisson*,[27] for example, concerned a letter written by the appellant to a newspaper, expressing disparaging comments about homosexuals. In overturning the HRC finding of incitement to hatred and upholding the relative importance of freedom of speech, Wilson J ruled that the language used must disclose a real intention to discriminate or incite others to discriminate. The same approach was taken in *Saskatchewan (Human Rights Commission) v. Whatcott*[28] regarding flyers that denounced gays and lesbians, when the SCC emphasised the need to pursue true hate speech, not just offensive language. In an important ruling, the SCC then denounced hate speech with the warning that it "lays the groundwork for later, broad attacks on vulnerable groups that can range from discrimination, to ostracism, segregation, deportation, violence and, in the most extreme cases, to genocide".[29]

The moral majority

The freedom to express SOGI issues would seem particularly prone to being inhibited by the actions of, or the chilling effects of initiatives taken by, the

26 HRT, 2002-08-20, T.D. 11/2, T594/5200 and T595/5300.
27 *Boisson v. Lund* 2009 ABQB 592.
28 [2013] 1 SCR 467.
29 Ibid., at para. 74.

moral majority. The existence and nature of the "covenant" in the *Trinity Western* cases,[30] for example, must function, as it is surely intended to, as such a restraint throughout the TWU community and as a model for conduct in the wider society. In one of that series of cases the court found no concrete evidence that covenant beliefs about homosexuality would result in actions by its graduates that would be discriminatory, despite any contrary covenant intention (see further below).

Harm to others

There have been a number of provincial cases involving individuals placing advertisements in newspapers protesting about LGBT issues. One such was *Owens*,[31] where the court ruled that although an advertisement, connecting Bible verses related to homosexuality with gay marriage, was "offensive and jarring to many", it did not constitute an offence, but warned that statements designed to provoke "extreme emotions and strong feelings of detestation, calumny and vilification" may be deemed hate speech.[32] It should also be borne in mind that it is the effect of the conduct, or action, not the intent, that is relevant in determining whether discrimination has occurred.[33]

Right to freedom of association and assembly

Freedom of association is guaranteed under s.2(d) of the Charter, this right entitles individuals to establish, belong to, maintain or leave any legal organisation. It's a right that has in the past been, and continues to be, invaluable to those representing LGBT concerns.

The first exercise of this right on behalf of such concerns took the form of public marches and protests in Vancouver and Ottawa in August 1971, and these have spread and continued across Canada ever since.

Constraints

Through the 1980s and into the early years of this century, the LGBT right of assembly was generally treated by the Canadian police as a threat to public order and often ended with mass arrests. The series of "bath house raids" by the police in Toronto in the 1980s being an example, which prompted an official apology from the Chief of Police in 2016.

30 *Trinity Western University v. British Columbia College of Teachers* (2001), 39 C.H.R.R. D/357. 2001 SCC 31; *Law Society of BC v. Trinity Western University*, 2018 SCC 32; and *Trinity Western University (TWU) v. Law Society of Upper Canada*, 2018 SCC 33.

31 *Owens v. Saskatchewan (Human Rights Commission)* 2006.

32 See, also, *Ross v. New Brunswick School District No. 15* [1996] 1 SCR 825.

33 *Ontario Human Rights Commission v. Simpson-Sears Ltd.* [1985] 2 S.C.R. 536.

Right to freedom of religion

Freedom of conscience and religion, as guaranteed under s.2(a) of the Charter, includes

> the right to entertain such religious beliefs as a person chooses, the right to declare religious beliefs openly and without fear of hindrance or reprisal, and the right to manifest religious belief by worship and practice or by teaching and dissemination.[34]

The right to freedom of religion is infringed, as the SCC stated in *Ktunaxa Nation*, when a claimant demonstrates:

> (1) that he or she sincerely believes in a practice or belief that has a nexus with religion, and
> (2) that the impugned State conduct interferes, in a manner that is non-trivial or not insubstantial, with his or her ability to act in accordance with that practice or belief.[35]

The State adopts a policy of neutrality towards religion which places it in a position to claim that it thereby offers equal recognition to all those who profess adherence to religion or belief or to secularism.

SOGI and religion

The Charter, s.15, provides a right to equality. This, following the decision in *Egan*,[36] is construed as extending by analogy to include sexual orientation. The SCC has consistently held that there is no hierarchy of Charter rights and "that clashes between rights should be approached by reconciling the rights through accommodation if possible, and in the end, if a conflict cannot be avoided, by case-by-case balancing" under s.1 of the Charter".[37]

The ambit of this restraint was examined most recently and thoroughly by the SCC in the last of the *Trinity Western* cases,[38] which concerned the university's mandatory covenant requiring the conduct of students, staff and professors to be in compliance with anti-SOGI principles. It then noted previous rulings where it had held that religious freedom can be limited where an individual's religious beliefs or practices have the effect of "injuring his or her neighbours

34 *R. v. Big M. Drug Mart* [1985] 1 SCR 295, per Dickson CJ.
35 *Ktunaxa Nation v. British Columbia* [2017] SCC 54, at para. 68, citing *Syndicat Northcrest v. Amselem* [2004] 2 S.C.R. 551.
36 *Egan v. Canada* [1995] 2 SCR 513.
37 *R v. NS*, 2012 SCC 72 [2012] 3 SCR 726, at para 52.
38 *Law Society of British Columbia v. Trinity Western University*, 2018 SCC 32.

or their parallel rights to hold and manifest beliefs and opinions of their own"[39] and that State interference with religious freedom can be justified "when a person's freedom to act in accordance with his or her beliefs may cause harm to or interfere with the rights of others".[40] Asserting that "being required by someone else's religious beliefs to behave contrary to one's sexual identity is degrading and disrespectful", the SCC found the Law Society to have been reasonable in its decision to deny accreditation because freedom of religion was subject to the limitation of upholding the fundamental rights and freedoms of others.[41]

Religious organisations and the religious exemption

Freedom of religion most obviously privileges churches and permits priests, ministers and clergy in general to abstain from officiating at same-sex marriages.[42] It also exempts a wide range of organisations that constitute the outworkings of religion. This includes many hospitals, residential care facilities, schools, and universities such as Trinity Western University which, as Cambell J pointed out, "like churches and other private institutions, does not have to comply with the equality provisions of the Charter".[43] This "religious exemption" permits such facilities to ensure that service provision, staff recruitment and staff conduct complies with religious belief rather than with the constraints of equality legislation (see further below). The exemption is strengthened by the *Wall* decision,[44] in which Justice Rowe was at pains to stress that religious groups are free to manage their own affairs and that the "courts will not intervene in such matters save where it is necessary to resolve an underlying legal dispute".[45] Inevitably, given the extensive spectrum of service facilities with their roots in religious organisations and the continuing effects of the Constitution Act 1867, s.93 – as preserved by s.29 of the Charter (explicitly guaranteeing the rights of denominational schools) – the potential impact of the religious exemption on SOGI matters is considerable, though it remains to be seen whether the previously-mentioned SCC 2018 TWU ruling, together with Bill C-16 and the Canada Summer Jobs programme, will have a curbing effect (see further below).

39 Ibid., citing *Big M*, at p. 346.

40 Ibid., citing *Multani*, at para. 26.

41 Ibid., at para. 101.

42 *Nichols v. M.J.* 2009 SKQB 299. Also, see *Marriage Commissioners Appointed Under the Marriage Act (Re)*, 2011 SKCA 3 (CanLII).

43 *Trinity Western University v. Nova Scotia Barristers' Society* 2015 NSSC 25 at para. 10 and endorsed in *Law Society of British Columbia v. Trinity Western University* 2018 SCC 32 at para. 335.

44 *Wall v. Judicial Committee of the Highwood Congregation of Jehovah's Witnesses*, 2018 SCC 26.

45 Ibid., at para. 39.

SOGI: personal relationships and human rights

Any consideration of the SOGI/human rights intersect must start with that set of human rights with potential to recognise and protect our most significant personal and family relationships.

Right to recognition as a person before the law

Legislative provisions in provincial Vital Statistics Acts, requiring a person to have "transsexual surgery" before he or she could acquire legal recognition for their gender identity by means such as changing the sex designation on their birth certificate, were found to be discriminatory and to violate the human rights of those concerned.[46] Now the right to an authentic, SOGI-compliant identity is well established throughout Canada, as is the right of a trans person to have their gender identity recognised in official documents such as birth certificates, drivers' licenses and passports.[47]

Trans recognition in law

All provinces and territories have introduced legislation to ensure that a process for changing gender identity is available, which allows official citizenship documents to be amended accordingly, and this is not dependent upon evidence of surgical intervention.

Non-binary gender identity

As of 31 August 2018, Canadians can indicate that they do not identify as male or female by choosing to state their sex as "X" on their passport and other government-issued identification.[48]

Right to respect for private and family life

In Canada as elsewhere, it was essentially a developing awareness and respect for the more personal aspects of life that gradually removed matters from the arena of public law and designated them as private.

46 *A.B. v. Minister of Transportation and Minister of Government Services* (Settlement, HRTO 2006), *XY v. Ontario (Government and Consumer Services)*, 2012 HRTO 726 (CanLII) and *C.F. v. Alberta*, 2014 Alberta Queen's Bench 237.

47 Bill C-16 added "gender identity and expression" to Canada's Human Rights Code and its Criminal Code.

48 Government of Canada, at: www.canada.ca/en/immigration-refugees-citizenship/services/canadian-passports/change-sex.html.

Sexual orientation, identity and private life

The Criminal Law Amendment Act 1968–69[49] de-criminalised certain same-sex sexual activity between consenting adults in private. This relaxing of long-standing punitive legislation relating to homosexuals continued with initiatives such as amending the Canadian Immigration Act in 1977 to allow them to freely immigrate. More recently, the Civil Marriage Act 2005 and Bill C-16 in 2017 have done much to extend the normalisation of same-sex relationships. While Canada is now recognised internationally as providing a particularly welcoming legal and social environment for the LGBT community, it is possible that the contention surrounding Trinity Western,[50] SOGI 123 and the Summer Jobs programme etc. may herald a broad-based push-back favouring the more conservative and religious elements in Canadian society.

Family life

"Society is continuously changing and family structures are changing along with it. This must be recognized as a reality and not as a detriment to the best interests of the child". So Fowler J stated in *C.C. (Re)*,[51] when judicial notice was taken of the fact that a family could comprise three legal parents (two fathers and one mother), based on the throuple's sexual relationship; both men were declared fathers. The judge commented that "I can find nothing to disparage that relationship from the best interests of the child's point of view".[52]

The federal Civil Marriage Act 2005 allows same-sex couples to marry, while the federal Divorce Act 1985, as amended, permits their divorce.

Private life, gender reassignment and divorce

For many years, to be a trans person meant abandoning any prospect of private life. This is still largely the case.

Not until the late 1960s did Gender Identity Clinics (GICs) began to emerge and become distributed at a variable rate across Canada. These brought specialist professionals who assessed patients for what in 1994 became generally known as "gender identity disorder" and which, if confirmed, would lead to referrals for hormone therapy and gender reassignment surgery. When this invasive process was completed, this still left a trans person having to produce evidence of completed surgical procedures from two doctors in order to have an official change made to the gender recorded on their birth certificate. Most trans persons,

49 Bill C-150, passed by Parliament in May 1969.

50 This has perhaps gone into abeyance given the last SCC ruling together with the TWU decision to make the covenant voluntary – at least for its students.

51 2018 NLSC 71. Following on from *A v. B*, 2007 ONCA 2, 83 OR (3d) 56 I when Ontario recognised a three-parent family.

52 Ibid., at para. 34.

however, do not have such surgery, and for them it remained necessary to repeatedly explain and provide proof of acquired gender on each and every occasion that proof of identity was required (bank accounts, mortgages, passports etc.).

Only comparatively recently has the law governing gender identity become simplified and more respectful of the privacy of trans persons. In *C.F. v. Alberta (Vital Statistics)*,[53] the court found that "the VSA birth registration system, and in particular the parts of it which relate to the issuing of birth certificates contribute to the disadvantage experienced by transgendered persons by perpetuating the prejudice and stereotyping to which they are subject".[54] Justice Burrows held that because this system did not permit the issuance of a birth certificate which recorded the claimant's sex as female, it therefore violated her rights under s.15(1) of the Charter. This led to the introduction of regulations, first in Alberta and then spreading to other provinces, with some degree of variation, which eliminated the surgical requirement and substituted a declaration of acquired gender identity from the applicant, supported by a letter from a physician or psychologist attesting that the requested birth certificate amendment was appropriate.

A combination of same-sex legislation and the pervasive effect of equality law has meant that in Canada, unlike in many other countries, divorce is no longer a legal pre-condition for a married person to undergo the transitioning process.

SOGI, parenting and "the best interests of the child" principle

Canadian courts have a well-established record of not allowing SOGI considerations to deflect from the legal requirement to apply this principle in determining the future care or custody arrangements for a child.

Forrester v. Saliba,[55] for example, concerned a mother's application to vary a custody order, issued in respect of her now 5-year-old daughter, following the revelation that the child's father had commenced a transitioning process. The court took the view that "the applicant's transexuality, in itself, without further evidence, would not constitute a material change in circumstances, nor would it be considered a negative factor in a custody determination".[56] The onerous burden of proof, specifically focused on the welfare of the child, to show a material change such that the joint custody order could not continue, had not been discharged. Being satisfied that there were sufficient safeguards in place to ensure the child's future health and safety, Justice Walder dismissed the application. The welfare of three children was at issue in *Anger v. Anger*,[57] following the breakdown of their parents' marriage

53 2014 ABQB 237.
54 Ibid., at para. 59.
55 2000 CanLII 28722 (ON CJ). See, also, *Ghidoni v. Ghidoni*, 1995 CanLII 1018 (BCSC).
56 Ibid., at para. 19.
57 1998 CanLII 4490 (BCSC).

due to the mother embarking on a same-sex relationship and the father filing custody proceedings as he found mother's sexual orientation "repugnant on religious and moral grounds". Finding that there was no reason to be concerned about the quality of parenting as "there does not appear to be anything abnormal or particularly disturbing about the behaviour of these particular children",[58] Master Nitikman ordered that the existing shared custody arrangements be continued. Again, in *Bubis v. Jones*[59] as in *Murphy v. Laurence*,[60] the fact that in both cases the birth mothers were in same-sex relationships was not a factor in determining applications for custody orders: the court noted, respectively, "there is no evidence that families with heterosexual parents are better able to meet the physical, psychological, emotional or intellectual needs of children than are families with homosexual parents"[61] and "the best interests of [the child] are, of course, what will govern any decision relating to custody in this matter . . . same sex parents seeking custody are no different than opposite-sex parents seeking custody".[62] In *Boyce v. Boyce*,[63] the court was clear that "gender dysphoria is not relevant to the issue of custody". More recently, in *K. (N.) v H. (A.)*,[64] which concerned a parental dispute regarding their child's transitioning process, Skolrood J noted that "the overriding consideration in making that determination is the best interests of the child".[65]

Right to marriage and to found a family

The family model as traditionally known to Canadian law, and as long supported by the well-established religious institutions, has been Christian. Consequently, the issues arising in recent years have tended to be in relation to homosexuality; same-sex marriages; abortion services; and as regards a range of gay,[66] lesbian and transgender[67] matters or the consequences thereof.[68]

Legal recognition for same-sex relationships and the right to marry

"Anyone stumbling through life even half-awake is aware that the myths and stereotypes which have followed same-sex partners for centuries are disappearing", as Quinn J succinctly put it in *Bubis v. Jones.*[69]

58 Ibid., at para. 23.
59 2000 CanLII 22571 (ONSC).
60 [2002] O.J. No. 1368 (ONSC).
61 *Bubis v. Jones*, op. cit., at para. 21.
62 *Murphy v. Lawrence*, op. cit., at para. 12.
63 2004 CanLII1602 (Ont Ct J.) at para. 26.
64 2016 BCSC 744.
65 Ibid., at para. 44.
66 See *Egan v. Canada* (1995) 2 SCR 513, where a statutory definition of "spouse" which excluded homosexual partners was deemed to discriminate against a homosexual couple.
67 See, for example, *Vancouver Rape Relief Society v. Nixon*, 2005 BCCA 601.
68 See *P. (S.E.) v. P. (D.D.)*, 2005 BCSC 1290, where the British Columbia Supreme Court ruled that the definition of adultery should include affairs between two people of the same gender.
69 Op. cit., at para. 21.

The Criminal Law Amendment Act 1969 (Bill C-150) de-criminalised aspects of same-sex relationships, and by the turn of the century many provinces such as Québec were beginning to follow suit. This was a period when several cases concluded with judicial rulings to the effect that restricting marriage to heterosexual couples was discriminatory. For example, in 1995 the SCC ruled that s.15 of the Charter, guaranteeing the "right to the equal protection and equal benefit of the law without discrimination", should include sexual orientation, and in *M. v. H.*[70] it found that the exclusion of same-sex partners from the definition of common law spouse under s.29 of the Ontario Family Law Act similarly violated that provision. These decisions paved the way for recognition of the rights of same-sex couples to equal treatment under the Constitution and led to the introduction of Bill C-23, which gave such couples the same social and tax benefits as their heterosexual counterparts. Not until *Halpern*,[71] however, did the judiciary conclude that the common law definition of marriage as "the voluntary union for life of one man and one woman to the exclusion of all others" infringed the equality rights of same-sex couples under s.15 of the Charter. This was followed immediately by *Reference Re Same Sex Marriage*,[72] where the SCC found that the meaning of marriage is not frozen in time, in accordance with its definition under s.91(26) of the Constitution Act 1867, but must be allowed to evolve with Canadian society, which currently represents a plurality of groups – a principle with a capacity for limitless transferred application. Promptly afterwards, the federal government introduced the Civil Marriage Act 2005 which legalised same-sex marriage, making Canada the first nation outside Europe to do so.

Trans persons and marriage

When same-sex marriage was federally mandated in 2005, the legal issues that had previously faced a spouse intending to undergo gender transitioning fell away. The legal status of "marriage" no longer required such a spouse to first divorce in order to avoid violating traditional marriage law.

Adoption, surrogacy and child care

Altruistic surrogacy, without payment to the surrogate mother (other than for "expenses"), the creation of embryos for assisted reproduction procedures and access to those procedures by same-sex couples have been legally possible since the Assisted Human Reproduction Act came into effect in 2004. Same-sex adoption has also become legal in all provinces and territories under varying rules, though in some there remain human rights issues around birth registration and the legal anomalies that necessitate birth parents adopting their own children.

70 [1999] 2 SCR 3.
71 *Halpern v. Canada (Attorney General)* [2003] O.J. No. 2268.
72 [2004] 3 SCR 698.

Right to cultural life

Canada, as a signatory State to the UDHR, ICESRC and UNDRIP, is bound to respect the provisions relating to cultural life enshrined in those international instruments, including the obligation to protect the cultural rights of its Indigenous people (see Chapter 3).

Cultural context

Currently, the relevant cultural context is one in which tensions in the law between religious freedom and equality are having a considerable influence.

In *Mouvement laïque québécois*,[73] the SCC closely followed the sentiment expressed in *R. v. Big M Drug Mart Ltd*[74] that "what may appear good and true to the majoritarian religious group, or to the State acting at their behest, may not for religious reasons, be imposed upon citizens who take the contrary view". Warning against a benign stance favouring Christianity (or any other religion/culture), the SCC advised that "if the State adheres to a form of religious expression under the guise of cultural or historical reality or heritage, it breaches its duty of neutrality".[75] At much the same time in *Loyola*,[76] followed later by *Wall*,[77] the judiciary reinforced an approach which respected but firmly contained the religious sphere of influence. This position has hardened with the most recent of the SCC *Trinity Western*[78] decisions. Taken in conjunction with such federal government initiatives as Bill C-16 and Canada Summer Jobs programme, it would seem that equality – and with it SOGI-compliant principles and practice – is being steadily entrenched, despite resistance from religious organisations.

The Indigenous people – the First Nations, Inuit and Métis – originally spread across all of Canada, each tribe with its own distinctive culture and set of beliefs, customs, ceremonies and rituals, usually with strong spiritual references to specific animals and to nature in general, and all equally susceptible to the effects of a Christian culture imposed by Church and State. Under the Indian residential schools programme, consolidated by the Indian Act 1876, some 150,000 Aboriginal children were removed from their homes, communities and culture to residential educational institutions: the first such residential school opened in 1620 and the last closed in 1986; the net effect was, as intended, to substitute an enforced compliance with a veneer of Christianity for centuries of Indigenous cultural beliefs and practices. Nonetheless, the acceptance of "two spirit" identities – a blending of male and female "spirits" in the same person – among

73 *Mouvement laïque québécois v. Saguenay (City)* [2015] 2 SCR 3.

74 *Big M*, op. cit., at para. 337.

75 Ibid., at para. 78.

76 *Loyola High School v. Québec (Attorney General)* 2015 SCC 12.

77 *Wall v. Judicial Committee of the Highwood Congregation of Jehovah's Witnesses*, 2018 SCC 26.

78 *Trinity Western University (TWU) v. Law Society of Upper Canada*, 2018 SCC 33.

the First Nations was never wholly suppressed. The accommodation of a range of sexual orientation and of gender identity within the community life of the tribes and bands preceded contemporary SOGI awareness and, arguably, the First Nations were always much more attuned to recognising and protecting non-binary gender distinctions than is currently provided for in human rights law.

The Canadian Human Rights Act, s.35 of the Constitution Act, s.25 of the Charter of Rights and Freedoms and the United Nations Declaration of the Rights of Indigenous Peoples all now include legal protections for the fundamental right of Indigenous peoples to freely practice their religious and spiritual traditions, and to be treated equally and with dignity.[79]

SOGI: non-discrimination, affirmative action and equality

The Charter, s.15(1), provides the federal umbrella governing non-discrimination and equality in the actions of government bodies and officials – federal and provincial – in a broad and general sense throughout Canada. As the SCC explained in *Andrews v. Law Society of British Columbia*:

> discrimination may be described as a distinction, whether intentional or not but based on grounds relating to personal characteristics of the individual or group, which has the effect of imposing burdens, obligations, or disadvantages on such individual or group not imposed upon others, or which withholds or limits access to opportunities, benefits, and advantages available to other members of society. Distinctions based on personal characteristics attributed to an individual solely on the basis of association with a group will rarely escape the charge of discrimination, while those based on an individual's merits and capacities will rarely be so classed.[80]

In addition, each and every province and territory in Canada has enacted human rights statutes that prohibit discrimination and harassment on several grounds – including gender identity and sexual orientation – in private and public sector employment, housing, public services and publicity. Consequently, discrimination, including harassment, based on real or perceived sexual orientation, gender identity or HIV/AIDS status is prohibited throughout Canada in comprehensive coverage which includes many aspects of employment (e.g. benefits for spouses and long-term partners) and of service provision (e.g. credit, insurance, government programs, hotels and public schools).

79 *Kelly v. British Columbia (Public Safety and Solicitor General) (No.3)*, 2011 BCHRT 183 (CanLII).
80 (1989) 1 SCR 143 at para. 37.

Equality before the law: sexuality and gender discrimination

The grounds of "sex" and "physical disability", as listed in s.15(1) of the Charter, have been interpreted as including transsexuality.[81] Prohibited discrimination occurs not only when someone is treated less favourably or is harassed on a prohibited ground, but also, as in the US, when a uniform policy or practice has a disproportionately adverse effect on a particular disadvantaged minority group (e.g. *Alberta v. Hutterian Brethren of Wilson Colony*[82] or *Syndicat Northcrest v. Amselem*).[83] Moreover, as noted in the previously-mentioned *Jurban* case, it is the effect of the conduct, or action, not the intent of the perpetrators, that is relevant in determining whether discrimination has occurred.[84]

Sex discrimination and sexual orientation discrimination

The SCC has stated that sexual orientation "is a precise legal concept that deals specifically with an individual's preference in terms of gender" in sexual relationships, and is not vague or overly broad.[85] In the landmark case of *Egan v. Canada*,[86] the SCC recognised that sexual orientation was implicitly included in s.15 as an "analogous ground" and was therefore a prohibited ground of discrimination. Since then, sexual orientation has been recognised as an immutable personal characteristic that forms part of an individual's core identity, and discrimination on that basis is prohibited throughout Canada.

The *Trinity Western* cases can be seen as representing a conflict between the right to equality and to non-discrimination on the basis of sexual orientation on the one hand and, on the other, the right to freedom of conscience and religion.[87] This conflict – at the heart of the cultural wars here as in the US – is currently playing out in a number of different arenas, including the Summer Jobs programme and in the schools of British Columbia in relation to SOGI 123.

Gender identity and trans discrimination

Bill C-16, prohibiting discrimination based on gender identity and gender expression throughout Canada, became law in June 2017 and makes it illegal

81 See: *Sheridan v. Sanctuary Investments Ltd. (No.3)* (1999), 33 C.H.R.R. D/467, at paras. 80–94; *Mamela v. Vancouver Lesbian Connection* [1999] B.C.H.R.T.D. No. 51 (Q.L.); and *Ferris v. O.T.E.U., Local 15* [1999] B.C.H.R.T.D. No. 55 (Q.L.).
82 2009 SCC 37 [2009] 2 SCR 567.
83 (2004) 2 SCR 576.
84 *O'Malley, supra, Ontario Human Rights Commission v. Simpson-Sears Ltd.* [1985] 2 S.C.R. 536), *Bhinder v. Canadian National Railway Co.* [1985] 2 S.C.R. 561, and *British Columbia (Public Service Relations Commission) v. BCGSEU* [1999] 3 S.C.R. 3.
85 *McAleer v. Canada (Human Rights Commission)* (1996), 132 D.L.R. (4th) 672.
86 [1995] 2 SCR 513.
87 *Trinity Western University, et al. v. Law Society of Upper Canada* (2017); *Law Society of British Columbia v. Trinity Western University, et al.* (2017).

to deny services, employment, accommodation and similar benefits to individuals based on their gender identity or gender expression. In the same year, New Brunswick became the last province to enact explicit legislative protections against discrimination on the basis of either gender identity, gender expression or both. These initiatives followed on from cases such as *C.F. v. Alberta*,[88] in which trans persons were prevented by state law from having their new gender officially recognised because they had not undergone sex change surgery. The legislation is significant as it gives gender identity the status of a separate and distinct human right. It also marks a clear line of departure from the US "liberty laws".

Affirmative action

The equality provision in the Canadian Charter of Rights and Freedoms, s.15(1), is subject to the s.15(2) exception that it

> does not preclude any law, program or activity that has as its object the amelioration of conditions of disadvantaged individuals or groups including those that are disadvantaged because of race, national or ethnic origin, colour, religion, sex, age or mental or physical disability.

However, the view that affirmative action does less to facilitate diversity and more to reinforce stereotypes, build-in new layers of inequality and fuel resentment is less persuasive in Canada than in the US because the equality provision in s.15 has been interpreted as guaranteeing substantive equality (as opposed to formal equality in the US).

LGBT issues and affirmative state action

Recent federal government initiatives, such as introducing the "X" option for gender identity on passports, Bill C-16 and the attestation requirement inserted into the Summer Jobs programme, can be realistically seen in terms of affirmative action on behalf of the LGBT community (see further below).

Right to equality and non-discrimination: health

As has been said, health care providers must keep from imposing their own values on a chronically marginalised group of people.[89] It must always be borne in mind, as the SCC ruled in *Ciarlariello v. Schacter*,[90] that patients have a "clear legal right" to autonomy and self-determination in health care.

88 [2014] ABQB 237.
89 *Kavanagh v. Canada (Attorney General)*, 2001–08–31, D.T. 11/01.
90 [1993] 2 SCR 119.

Gender reassignment treatment

Gender Identity Clinics (GICs), for those with gender identity disorder (GID) problems – providing services of assessment, diagnosis and referrals for hormone therapy and sex reassignment surgery – have been operational to a varying extent across the provinces and territories since the late 1960s. However, as mentioned earlier, evidence of having undergone gender reassignment treatment is no longer a prerequisite for amending official citizenship documents.

In *Waters v. BC Medical Services Plan*,[91] the respondents – the Ministry of Health Services (BC Medical Services Plan) and the Medical Services Commission (the "Ministry") – were held to have discriminated against the trans complainant (ftm), as they had denied him a service or facility customarily available to the public. The issue was one of costs: the Ministry had refused to pay the full amount for the first and second stages of surgery, performed outside BC, and refused to pay for the third. As the Tribunal found that equivalent costs would have been paid in respect of a male to female trans it was able to conclude the case on the basis of discrimination based on sex rather without having to consider the further issue of sexual orientation discrimination. Three years later, in the similar case of *Hogan v. Ontario (Minister of Health and Long-Term Care)*,[92] the issue was again one of costs when the Tribunal found that the complainants, who had reached the surgery stage in the trans reassignment process, had been unfairly treated by the Minister, who had terminated the related insurance cover programme which it would not have been unduly burdensome for him to have maintained.

Trans children

There is no specific federal law prohibiting conversion therapy, but a minority of provinces and territories now have such statutes. In very recent years, the practice has been banned in Vancouver, Manitoba and Ontario.[93]

The right of children to be heard in decisions taken on their accessing transitioning therapy was upheld in the previously-mentioned case of *K. (N.) v. H. (A.)*,[94] which concerned a parental dispute as to whether or not J.K., their 11-year-old child, should engage in such therapy. Justice Skolrood was firmly of the view that "these issues cannot be properly considered without J.K.'s direct participation, nor would it be fair to J.K. for the court to attempt to do so".[95]

Sports and recreational activities

U Sports, the organisation that governs university intercollegiate and varsity athletics in Canada, now has an inclusive policy for trans student-athletes which

91 2003 BCHRT 13 (CanLII).
92 2006 HRTO 32 (CanLII).
93 In Ontario by the Affirming Sexual Orientation and Gender Identity Act 2015.
94 2016 BCSC 744.
95 Ibid., at para. 40.

allows them to compete on teams that correspond with their acquired gender identity. There does not appear to be any reported Canadian caselaw on SOGI issues arising in this context.

Blood donors

From the mid-1980s until 2013 a homosexual relationship, however brief, disqualified a prospective blood donor. From then until 2016, the rule was amended to permit a donation if the donor had abstained from such a sexual relationship for five years. Since 2016, the time ban on gay and bisexual men donating blood has been reduced to one year, when similar eligibility criteria for trans persons also came into effect. In 2019, the deferral period was further reduced to three months. This differentiation in treatment between homosexual and heterosexual donors, even if reduced, continues to cause feelings of stigma and generate allegations of discrimination.

Right to equality and non-discrimination: education

The rights of LGBT students and staff in an educational institution vary considerably depending on whether the institution is religious and/or open to the public.

Schools

The Constitution Act 1867, s.93 – as preserved by s.29 of the Charter – explicitly guarantees the rights of denominational schools, thereby preferencing Catholic and Protestant schools above all others. These "denominational privileges" continue in the constitutional obligation to fund Catholic schools in the provinces of Ontario, Alberta and Saskatchewan.[96] In practice, this may restrict the right to equality based on sexual orientation under s.15 of the Charter, as such schools may exercise a discretion, aligning religious beliefs with *bona fide* service provision requirements, not to accommodate staff and pupils with SOGI issues. This archaic anomaly has often given rise to cases alleging religiously biased preferential treatment,[97] but the recent SCC ruling in the latest of the *Trinity Western* cases[98] may have foreclosed future options in that regard.

Exemption from the constraints of equality and non-discrimination legislation applies to religious organisations that provide, staff and determine pupil access to schools across Canada. The limitations on this exemption – in relation to the

96 Note also that many Canadian universities, including St. Francis Xavier University, Queen's University, McGill University and Concordia University College of Alberta, have long been religiously affiliated.

97 See, for example: *Tiny Township Catholic Separate Schools Trustees v. The Queen* (1928) A. C. 363; *Attorney General of Quebec v. Greater Hull School Board* [1984] 2 SCR 575; *Reference Re Bill 30* [1987] 1 SCR 1148; *Adler v. Ontario* [1996] SCR 609; and *Waldman v. Canada*, Comm No 694/1996.

98 *Law Society of BC v. Trinity Western University*, 2018 SCC 32 and *Trinity Western University (TWU) v. Law Society of Upper Canada*, 2018 SCC 33

rights of pupils not to be discriminated on SOGI grounds – have been examined in a number of cases. In *Ross*,[99] the SCC stressed that the freedom of religion is "subject to such limitations as are necessary to protect public safety, order, health or morals, or the fundamental rights and freedoms of others" and stated that "the School Board has the duty to provide students with an educational environment that does not expose them to discriminatory harassment".[100] In *Hall*,[101] which concerned a Roman Catholic school board which had refused permission for a same-sex couple to attend a school graduation dance, MacKinnon J noted that "there is an obvious tension between the individual's free expression and equality rights when contrasted against the equality rights and the religious freedom of Catholic schools",[102] and ordered the school to admit the couple. In *Jubran*,[103] where the plaintiff had endured years of persistent, homophobic harassment despite not being homosexual, the court endorsed the Tribunal's finding that the School Board was liable for the discriminatory conduct of the students because of its duty to maintain a non-discriminatory environment.[104] It noted that it was the effect of the conduct, or action, not the intent of the harassers, that was relevant in determining whether discrimination had occurred.[105] Quoting McIntyre J in *O'Malley*:[106] "we are dealing with consequences, not intent or perception". The SCC declined to hear an appeal from this decision, thus adding to its authoritativeness. Anti-bullying legislation, intended to identity and prevent bullying in school, including in respect of SOGI issues, has recently been introduced in most provinces and territories.

Curricula

The tension between the rights to freedom of religion and freedom of expression has become steadily more fraught in the context of school curricula. Given that parents undoubtedly have the right, established in international[107] and domestic law,[108] to raise their children in accordance with their religious beliefs,[109] the

99 *Ross v. New Brunswick School Dist. No. 15* [1996] 1 S.C.R. 825.
100 Ibid., at para. 116.
101 *Hall v. Durham Catholic School Board* [2002] OJ No. 1803.
102 Ibid. at para. 57.
103 *School District No. 44 (North Vancouver) v. Jubran*, 2005 BCCA 201 (B.C. C.A.).
104 Ibid., at paras. 115–116, citing *Kafé et Commission des droits de la personne du Québec* c. *Commission scolaire Deux-Montagnes* (1993), 19 C.H.R.R. D/1 (at para. 84) (Que. Trib.), for the proposition that schools have a duty to educate students regarding human rights and implement principles to prevent harassment and discrimination.
105 Ibid., citing *Ontario Human Rights Commission v. Simpson-Sears Ltd.* [1985] 2 S.C.R. 536. See also *British Columbia (Public Service Relations Commission) v. BCGSEU* [1999] 3 S.C.R. 3 per McLachlin C.J.C. at para. 49.
106 *O'Malley*, op. cit.
107 See, for example, the ECHR, Protocol 1.
108 See, for example the Charter of Rights and Freedoms, s.2(a).
109 *B(R) v. Children's Aid Society of Metropolitan Toronto* [1995] 1 SCR 315.

question then arises as to how that right can be protected in a State education system which treats all religions with impartial neutrality. Specifically, is there any discretion available to schools – faith schools and State schools – to choose whether or not to incorporate SOGI issues in classroom teaching? This question is very much to the fore in Ontario, where there has been a recent rash of cases challenging the government's roll-back of sex education curricula to exclude conversations about same-sex families and trans identities.[110] Similar contention is currently evident in British Columbia.

In *Chamberlain*,[111] the SCC considered the refusal of the Surrey School Board to approve three controversial books depicting same-sex parented families, which had been promoted as supplementary learning resources, as teaching aids in the family life education curriculum. The court found that "children cannot learn unless they are exposed to views that differ from those they are taught at home" and held that Board members, by refusing to permit the use of such books, were imposing their own religious values and seeking to deny children an important learning opportunity. This decision was followed by the ruling in *SL v. Commission scolaire des Chênes*,[112] when the SCC dismissed the appeal of Catholic parents who requested exemption for their children from the mandatory "Ethics and Religious Culture" (ERC) course because the curriculum (treating all religions with equal impartiality) was considered incompatible with their family beliefs, and added that "the early exposure of children to realities that differ from those in their immediate family environment is a fact of life in society". This sentiment which seemed to be reinforced in *Loyola*,[113] when the SCC noted that "in a multicultural society, it is not a breach of anyone's freedom of religion to be required to learn (or teach) about the doctrines and ethics of other world religions in a neutral and respectful way".[114]

However, the SCC ruling in *Loyola*[115] proved to be something of a watershed in this debate. The court was then concerned with the Québec government's mandatory core curriculum for high schools, the ERC programme, in respect of which Loyola, a Catholic high school founded by Jesuits, sought permission to teach beliefs, ethics and religious culture from a Catholic rather than a neutral perspective, which would clearly have implications for the recognition, acceptance and appraisal of SOGI issues. Ultimately, the SCC unanimously found that to direct a faith school to teach matters of faith from a neutral perspective would be to violate its right to freedom of religion under s.3 of the Charter. The *Loyola*

110 See, for example, *LM and the Corp. of Canadian Civil Liberties Assoc. v. Minister of Education (Ontario)* 2019 ONSC 1308 (Divisional Court File Nos. 526/18 and 554/18).

111 *Chamberlain v. Surrey School Board District 36* (2002), 221 D.L.R. (4th) 156 (SCC) at para. 19. Also see *Hall v. Powers* (2002), 213 D.L.R. (4th) 308 (Ont. S.C.).

112 [2012] 1 SCR 235.

113 *Loyola High School v. Québec (Attorney General)* 2015 SCC 12.

114 Ibid., per Deschamps, J., citing *SL v. Commission scolaire des Chênes* [2012] 1 SCR 235, at para. 40.

115 *Loyola High School v. Québec (Attorney General)* 2015 SCC 12.

decision would seem to represent a rejection of the *SL* rationale and a give a green light to all other faith schools that may wish to frame their curriculum so as to deal with SOGI issues – if at all – from their specific religious perspective. The same tensions generated by the ERC programme in Québec are now likely to be triggered in Western Canada, leading to similar courtroom confrontations, following the introduction of the SOGI 123 programme.[116]

Colleges/universities

Over the best part of the last couple of decades and over a large proportion of Canadian provinces and territories, the previously-mentioned tensions have been starkly polarised in the slew of Trinity Western University (TWU) cases. These concerned a teacher training college (TWU), an emanation of the Evangelical Free Church of Canada, which chose to manifest its beliefs in a Community Standards Contract that all students were required to sign. The contract stated its evangelical Christian values, including abstinence from sex outside marriage and rejection of homosexual relationships, most of which were clearly antithetical to SOGI. In its first consideration of these tensions, the SCC in a majority ruling held in favour of TWU.[117] It found that the refusal of the British Columbia College of Teachers (BCCT) to accredit the TWU school of education degree, on the basis that graduates would be inadequately prepared to provide educational services without discrimination in BC's diverse public school classrooms, was unjustified. However, in its last and quite recent hearing, the SCC ruled that the Law Societies were justified in refusing accreditation to graduates of a proposed TWU law school because that decision represented a proportionate balance between the limitation on freedom of religion guaranteed by s.2(a) of the Charter and the statutory objectives pursued by the Law Societies as a regulating authority and was therefore reasonable; any interference with religious freedom was minor and the Law societies were entitled to take the view that the contract imposed "harm" on LGBTQ law students.[118]

These two cases were admittedly framed differently: the teachers case was about whether graduates would discriminate in the classroom and there was no evidence that this was the case; the law societies case was about whether the law societies of Ontario and BC had acted in accordance with their statutory mandates in refusing accreditation – there was no argument that TWU-educated lawyers would discriminate against clients. Both, however, rested on the TWU covenant with its set of non-SOGI compliant values, and it remains a puzzle to

116 See further at: www.sogieducation.org. Also see Daly, P. and Cameron, A., Furthering Substantive Equality Through Administrative Law: Charter Values in Education, *Supreme Court Law Review*, 63, p. 169 (2013).

117 *Trinity Western University v. British Columbia College of Teachers* (2001), 39 C.H.R.R. D/357. 2001 SCC 31.

118 *Law Society of BC v. Trinity Western University*, 2018 SCC 32 and *Trinity Western University (TWU) v. Law Society of Upper Canada*, 2018 SCC 33.

some why this did not present a block to the accreditation of TWU teachers but did for prospective TWU lawyers. The subjective standard of "reasonableness" may be about to become a new benchmark for balancing SOGI and freedom of religion issues, but it has proven to be a slippery indicator when judicially deployed in other contexts such as matrimonial and child care law.

Right to equality and non-discrimination: employment

The legislative intent underpinning the Employment Equity Act 1995 was to achieve equality in the workplace by measures that would, where necessary, effect remedial intervention and accommodate differences. This, along with the Charter, the Canadian Human Rights Act, the Privacy Act and Bill C-16 are the main components of the federal legislative framework relating to SOGI issues in the workplace.

Religious exemption

Canadian religious organisations have long enjoyed special privileges: they may organise as they see fit, largely free from government regulatory requirements; this includes hiring staff on the basis of religious affiliation. They also enjoy other exemptions in relation to matters such as sexual orientation and gender parity. Indeed, religious communities such as the Hutterian Brethren have always been largely left to regulate their own affairs.

In addition to the right to discriminate when employing staff in accordance with the "bona fide occupational requirements" (BFOR)[119] rule, the Constitution Act 1867, s.93(1), protects denominational school privileges from the anti-discrimination strictures of modern human rights law and the Canadian Charter of Rights and Freedoms.

When the Civil Marriage Act[120] was introduced, which extended the meaning of marriage to include same-sex relationships under Canadian federal law and inserted ss.149.1 into the Income Tax Act,[121] it provided that religious organisations would not have their charitable registration revoked solely because they or any of their members exercised freedom of conscience and religion in relation to the meaning of marriage. The SCC had also ruled to similar effect in *Reference Re Same Sex Marriage*.[122] All of this was in keeping with an established acceptance, clearly evident in testamentary dispositions, that religious beliefs conferred a degree of immunity from the otherwise non-differentiating application of the law. Much the same rationale was evident in *Heintz v. Christian Horizons*,[123]

119 See, for example, *Canada Trust Co. v. Ontario Human Rights Commission* (1990) 69 DLR (4th) 321, per Tarnopolsky, J., at para. 98.
120 SC 2005, c. 33.
121 RSC 1985 (5th Supp.), c. 1, as amended.
122 [2004] 3 SCR 698.
123 2008 HRTO 22, 2010 ONSC 2105 (Div. Ct.).

which concerned a complaint of discrimination by a support worker employed by Christian Horizons who resigned after commencing a same-sex relationship as she felt she could no longer honour her employer's beliefs, but subsequently commenced proceedings alleging discrimination. Ultimately the court found for the employers and, in an important ruling for all religious organisations in Canada, declared that there is an entitlement to exemption from the law barring discriminatory hiring "if they are primarily engaged in serving the interests of their religious community, where the restriction is reasonable and *bona fide* because of the nature of the employment".

Sexual orientation in the workplace

Federal and provincial human rights legislation grants general protection to trans employees and job candidates. In particular, the "duty to accommodate" governs employer responsibilities regarding such SOGI issues as may arise in the workplace and is outlined in sections 2–15 of the Canadian Human Rights Act: s.15 lists the 13 grounds, including sexual orientation and gender identity, on which discrimination is prohibited; while s.7 declares that it discriminatory practice, directly or indirectly, to refuse to employ or continue to employ any individual or, in the course of employment, to differentiate adversely in relation to an employee. The duty generally requires an employer to adjust, modify or adapt an employment standard or task to accommodate the particular needs of an employee unless to do so would impose an undue burden on the business.[124] This might include facilitating a name change, medical treatment, access to gender appropriate washrooms etc.

In *O'Malley v. Simpson Sears*,[125] an early SCC human rights case, it was determined that a neutral rule of universal application could have inadvertent discriminatory consequences for an employee. In finding the employers liable, because they could have readily made adjustments to the work environment, the SCC thereby introduced a two-step test to determine whether adverse discrimination is really a *bona fide* occupational requirement and therefore permitted: is the rule/standard rationally connected to the necessities of the job, and have employers accommodated the individual to the point of undue hardship? Shortly afterwards, in *Robichaud v. Canada (Treasury Board)*,[126] a leading case on sexual harassment, the SCC held that a corporation can be liable for the discriminatory conduct of its employees who are acting "in the course of their employment", as the employer is the only one in a position to remedy the discriminatory conduct and able to provide "the most important remedy – a healthy work environment".[127] Again, in another significant ruling on sexual harassment and one clearly

124 *Corbière v. Canada* [1999] 2 S.C.R. 203.
125 [1985] 2 SCR 536.
126 [1987] 2 S.C.R. 84.
127 Ibid., at para. 94.

applicable in a SOGI context, Dickson CJ in *Janzen v. Platy Enterprises Ltd.*[128] held that discrimination on the basis of sex occurs where there is a "practice or attitude which had the effect of limiting the conditions of employment of, or the employment opportunities available to, employees on the basis of a characteristic related to gender".

Trans persons and the workplace

The previously-mentioned "duty to accommodate" also governs the employer relationship with a trans employee. As in other jurisdictions, there have been a number of cases concerning the use of washrooms,[129] the outcome of which has been to emphasise both the significance of access to appropriate washroom facilities in confirming the identity of a trans person and that the denial of access to a washroom that conforms to the employee's declared gender identity will be regarded as discriminatory. Also typical have been the cases illustrating employer discrimination in refusing to hire a trans person,[130] and inappropriate and discriminatory employer response to an employee undergoing a transitioning process.[131]

Employment in the military

The Canadian military operated an exclusionary policy towards homosexuals until the early 1990s. Since the landmark ruling in *Douglas v. Canada*,[132] however, there has been no legal obstacle to members of the LGBT community enrolling or serving in the Canadian armed forces.

Right to equality and non-discrimination: services

The Canadian Human Rights Act 1985, s.5, prohibits discriminatory practice in the provision of goods, services, facilities or accommodation customarily available to the general public (i) to deny, or to deny access to, any such good, services, facility or accommodation to any individual, or (ii) to differentiate adversely in relation to any individual, on a prohibited ground of discrimination. Under s.3(1), for all purposes of the 1985 Act, the prohibited grounds of discrimination include sex, sexual orientation and gender identity or expression. Bill C-16, which took effect in June 2017, amends that Act to specifically prohibit discrimination

128 [1989] 1 S.C.R. 1252.

129 *Ferris v. Office and Technical Employees Union, Local 15* [1999] BCHRTD No 55 and *Sheridan v. Sanctuary Investments Ltd* [1999] BCHRTD No 43.

130 *Sheridan*, ibid., *Kavanagh v. Attorney-General of Canada* (2001), C.H.R.R. D/119 and *Montreuil v. National Bank of Canada*, 2004 CHRT 7.

131 *M.L. and Commission des droits de la personne et des droits de la jeunesse du Québec contre Maison des jeunes* (1998) 33 CHRR D/623 (Tribunaux du Québec); *Montreuil v. Canadian Forces*, 2009 CHRT 28.

132 [1993] 1 F.C. 264 (Fed. Ct).

based on gender identity and gender expression in relation to the previously-mentioned goods, services, facilities or accommodation within a federal regulated industry.

Trans persons and gender-specific services

Canada's long, drawn-out litigation in relation to a trans woman's access to a gender-specific service – a Rape Crisis Centre – finally concluded with the SCC rejecting her appeal application. The 12-year-long saga, which began when the plaintiff was refused training for peer counselling services provided by the Vancouver Rape Relief Society and came to constitute *Kimberly Nixon v. Vancouver Rape Relief Society*,[133] ended with the court affirming that although the Society had discriminated against her, it was entitled to do so as it was it was exempted from equality and non-discrimination legislation by s.41 of the Human Rights Code, which allows charitable or social organisations to exercise positive discrimination in respect of certain groups of people.

Provision of public services

The Summer Jobs programme, which provides summer job opportunities for students and young persons aged 15–30 throughout Canada, has focused attention on SOGI issues in a public service context. The controversy, divisive in itself, raises the wider question as to whether this is to serve as a test case for SOGI compliance as a standard requirement to be adhered to by all government bodies and all organisations in receipt of government funding.

Employers in 2018, if they wished to receive government funding, were required to attest that "both the job and the organization's core mandate respect individual human rights in Canada, including the values underlying the Canadian Charter of Rights and Freedoms as well as other rights". The accompanying Applicant Guide added that "rights" and "values" included "sexual and reproductive rights" and the "right to access safe and legal abortions". For 2019, the reference to "values" is removed and employers are now required to "attest" that "any funding under the Canada Summer Jobs program will not be used to undermine or restrict the exercise of rights legally protected in Canada". The reference in the Guide to "to sexual and reproductive health services" has been retained, and these are defined as "including comprehensive sexuality education, family planning, prevention and response to sexual and gender-based violence, safe and legal abortion, and post-abortion care". The Guide also indicates that projects or job activities are ineligible for funding if, among other things, they "advocate intolerance, discrimination and/or prejudice".[134]

133 2007 CanLII 2772 (SCC).

134 See further at: www.canada.ca/content/dam/canada/employment-social-development/services/funding/CSJ2019_applicant_guide.pdf.

Neither the 2018 or 2019 attestation explicitly addresses SOGI issues, but they can be taken as incorporated within such terms as "rights legally protected", "sexual and gender-based violence" and "discrimination". Much will depend on how these terms are interpreted. At the very least, it may be assumed that the many thousands of churches and religious organisations with their outreach community development projects will have difficulty in reconciling their traditional beliefs in marriage, heterosexual relationships, binary gender etc. with an attestation for funding that requires a stated adherence to rights that include sexual orientation and gender identity or expression.

Trans persons and prisons

Since 2017, Canadian prisons – unlike their US counterparts – have been placing trans inmates in institutions of their preference, "regardless of their anatomy (sex) or gender on their identification documents, unless there are overriding health or safety concerns which cannot be resolved".[135] This policy change has been a long time coming: it was in 2001 that the CHRT established the human rights of trans prisoners by ruling that sex-reassignment surgery cannot be prohibited while an individual is incarcerated.[136]

Clearly, if multiculturalism, social diversity and religious pluralism are to be more than empty slogans, then government public services must be as inclusive as possible. The tensions between traditional religious/cultural values and the contemporary social mores epitomised in SOGI rights are becoming difficult to balance in public service provision. This is perhaps particularly the case in education, as illustrated in the controversy around SOGI 123, but the earlier noted policy developments in the Canadian Correctional Services seem propitious.

Private goods and service provision

In Canada, as elsewhere, the provision of commercial services can provide a context for discrimination which is often rooted in a conflation of religious belief and sexual orientation. In *Brillinger v. Brockie*,[137] this involved the competing claims of sexual orientation discrimination and violation of freedom of religion. The Ontario Board of Inquiry found that Brockie, a born-again Christian, had discriminated against Brillinger (and the Canadian Lesbian and Gay Archives) on the prohibited ground of sexual orientation by refusing to provide printing services to homosexuals and homosexual organisations and ordered Brockie and

135 For further information on this and other policy changes, see: Correctional Service Canada (CSC) news release at: www.chrc-ccdp.gc.ca/eng/content/joint-news-release-changes-way-transgender-offenders-are-accommodated-canadas-federal prison?utm_source=Email_marketing&utm_campaign=Monday_November_27_2017&cmp=1&utm_medium=HTMLEmail.

136 *Kavanagh v. Canada (Attorney General)* [2001] CHRD No 21, QL.

137 (No. 3) (2000), 37 C.H.R.R. D/15).

his company to provide the same printing services to them as they provided to others. However, on appeal, the Ontario Superior Court of Justice held that the Board's order went further than was necessary and added a condition to the effect that the order should not require Brockie to print material of a nature that could reasonably be considered to be in direct conflict with the core elements of his religious beliefs.

In *Knights of Columbus*,[138] a same-sex couple alleged religious discrimination when their rental application for a facility they wished to use to celebrate their marriage was rejected by the Catholic organisation that owned it. The tribunal concluded that renting out the hall for the purpose for which it was required would have forced the organisation to act against its religious beliefs and would breach its rights under s.2(a) of the Charter. Nevertheless, the organisation was fined as it had failed in its duty of reasonable accommodation, as no consideration had been given to the consequences for the couple, and no attempt had been made to meet with them and explain the reasons for rejection. Again, in *Eadie and Thomas v. Riverbend Bed and Breakfast and Others*,[139] a gay couple had reserved a room in bed and breakfast accommodation offered by a Christian couple in their own home, but when the husband learned that the couple were gay, the booking was cancelled. The Tribunal ruled in favour of the gay couple, who had been denied a service because the provider had unlawfully discriminated against them.

Pensions, social security benefits etc.

In *Mossop*,[140] the HRT found that the Treasury Board had discriminated against its employee, contrary to the Canadian Human Rights Act, when it refused him a day of bereavement leave to attend the funeral of the father of his same-sex partner. Such disputes led to the introduction of the federal Modernization of Benefits and Obligations Act 2000, which extended recognition to same-sex common law partners, affording them the same rights and obligations as their heterosexual counterparts, as regards entitlement to federal income tax, pensions etc. As mentioned earlier, from the turn of the century, Bill C-23 (36-2) has given same-sex couples the same social and tax benefits as their heterosexual counterparts.

Conscientious objection of service providers

Section 2(a) of the Charter – which extends protection to "freedom of conscience and religion" – applies, self-evidently, to those whose actions or inactions are grounded on either religious objections or on matters of conscience or morality.

138 *Smith and Chymyshyn v. Knights of Columbus and Others* 2005 BCHRT 544 (CanLII). See also *Whiteley v. Osprey Media Publishing*, 2010 HRTO 2152 (CanLII).

139 *(No 2)* 2012 BCHRT 247.

140 *Mossop v. Secretary of State*, Canadian Human Rights Tribunal, 1989–04–13, D. T. 6/89.

The previously-mentioned cases of *Brockie*, *Eadie* and *Moore*[141] are among the many instances where service refusal by individual providers, on the grounds of their conscientious objection to the values represented by prospective service users, have resulted in the former being found to have violated the human rights of the latter: generic laws of universal application disallowing exceptions that negate legislative intent.[142] However, the SCC in *Loyola* and the *TWU* cases can be seen wrestling with the issue of whether accommodation can be made for pockets of institutional beliefs that run counter to legislative intent. The "conscientious objection" jurisprudence building up in other countries is becoming increasingly credible as a rationale for challenging what some see as the prescriptive dictates of equality provisions, and it is gaining traction as an argument for facilitating diversity in a democratic society. The cautionary counsel of McLachlin CJ may yet prove persuasive in encouraging support for the *locus standi* of a conscientious objector:

> The demand for tolerance cannot be interpreted as the demand to approve of another person's beliefs or practices. When we ask people to be tolerant of others, we do not ask them to abandon their personal convictions.[143]

SOGI, public service and conscientious objection

As SOGI issues become more salient, a corresponding growth can be seen in conscientious objection as a legitimate ground for refusal to co-operate in related service provision. In *Moore*,[144] for example, a Catholic public service employee who, having objected to abortion and on refusing to work with a client who sought a termination, was disciplined and eventually fired; the HR Tribunal, however, found that because the employer knew of her religiously based objection, an onus rested on the employer to accommodate the employee by transferring the client to other employees. More recently, in *C. v. A.*[145] the HR Tribunal acknowledged that a family medical clinic had appropriately accommodated a Christian employee's pro-life beliefs by not requiring her to refer patients for abortions. Abortion referrals were processed by other individuals without compromising patient care. It remains to be seen whether the pointed constitutional reference to freedom "of conscience" in s.2(a) of the Charter will provide a platform for a more broad-based legitimisation of conscientious objection as grounds for resisting what is perceived by some to be a creeping SOGI agenda.

141 *Moore v. British Columbia (Ministry of Social Services* (1992), 17 C.H.R.R. D/426 (B.C.C.H.R).

142 See further at: www.ohrc.on.ca/en/learning/part-3-examples-competing-rights-situations/example-3-code-right-v-code-right-muslim-barber-and-woman-denied-service.

143 *Chamberlain v. Surrey School District No. 36* [2002] 4 S.C.R. 710, 2002 SCC 86, at para. 66.

144 *Moore v. British Columbia (Ministry of Social Services* (1992), 17 C.H.R.R. D/426 (B.C.C.H.R).

145 (2002), 43 C.H.R.R. D/395, 2992 BCHRT 23.

Conclusion

The challenges of geography, together with the duality of its colonial experience and the patchwork of First Nations, Inuit and Metis communities, have perhaps proven particularly conducive to growing the plurality of cultures that are now to be found in Canada. The vibrant, authentic cultural lives of Jews, Hutterites, Sikhs, Muslims and others, the openness towards asylum seekers and the growing assertiveness of secularism are all evident in the earlier caselaw. Evident also is the sense of proud independence of individual provinces and territories, most clearly apparent in the judicial and legislative initiatives of Ontario. This would seem to have fostered an environment where mutual respect and accommodation of differences have prepared the ground for a more positive response to SOGI-related issues than has been experienced elsewhere.

So often defined by characteristics that merely demonstrate how unlike the US it is, Canada in fact – at least in relation to the SOGI/human rights intersect – is different, not just from its neighbour but also from the other Part II jurisdictions. It has led the way in permitting self-identification of gender identity without the necessity for medical or surgical corroboration; legislating to prohibit a refusal of services, employment, accommodation and similar benefits to individuals based on their gender identity or gender expression; and providing official recognition for non-binary status. As the US retreats further down the road of traditional conservatism, rolling back LGBT rights and access to abortion, so the differences with Canada become increasingly more apparent. Judicial firmness in containing the potential of religion to undermine equality principles has been demonstrated in *Loyola*,[146] *Wall*[147] and in the most recent of the SCC *Trinity Western*[148] decisions, while legislators and policy makers have demonstrated equal resolve in the Bill C-16 and the Summer Jobs programme initiatives. At this point it seems unlikely that the conscientious objection jurisprudence developing in the US and the UK, extending opt-outs to public health professionals and perhaps to others on grounds of religion or belief and thereby inevitably imposing constraints on professional responses to SOGI-related issues, will also take hold in Canada.

146 *Loyola High School v. Québec (Attorney General)*, 2015 SCC 12.
147 *Wall v. Judicial Committee of the Highwood Congregation of Jehovah's Witnesses*, 2018 SCC 26.
148 *Trinity Western University (TWU) v. Law Society of Upper Canada*, 2018 SCC 33.

8 Australia

Introduction

The data gathered in the 2016 national Census, the first to collate information on sex/gender diversity, is acknowledged by ABS to have been affected by considerable margins of error. Nonetheless, it recorded around 46,800 same-sex couples and some 1,260 sex and/or gender diverse people. It noted that Aboriginal and Torres Strait Islander people are more likely to live with a same-sex partner than non-Indigenous people. About 1.2% of Aboriginal and Torres Strait Islander people lived with a same-sex partner, while only 0.9% of non-Indigenous people did so.[1]

This chapter, in keeping with the format adopted for its predecessors, begins with an outline of the legal framework relating to SOGI matters: the governing legislation, courts and regulatory bodies, both domestic and international. Turning from structure to content, it opens a consideration of human rights by examining the interface between SOGI and the more fundamental rights of justice, expression, association and religion. It then switches to SOGI and the law in a more personal context, exploring matters such as identity, privacy, same-sex relationships, family life and parenting; and, reflecting on the broader cultural dimension, with particular reference to the Indigenous people. This leads into the central section dealing with the patterns of SOGI-related caselaw, resulting from contemporary equality and non-discrimination legislation, focusing on themes of health, education, employment and service provision. The chapter concludes by reflecting on the growing significance of conscientious objection and its potential to exempt professionals – particularly in health care – from statutory public benefit service delivery duties.

Legal framework: international and domestic

Australia, alone among the common law nations currently being considered, retains the singular distinction of not having any designated human rights legislation.

1 See further at: www.abs.gov.au/ausstats/abs@.nsf/Lookup/by%20Subject/2071.0~2016~Main%20Features~Sex%20and%20Gender%20Diversity%20in%20the%202016%20Census~100.

International legislation

Human rights are statutorily defined at federal level[2] to mean the rights and freedoms recognised or declared by the International Convention on the Elimination of All Forms of Racial Discrimination 1965; the International Covenant on Economic, Social and Cultural Rights 1966; the International Covenant on Civil and Political Rights 1966; the Convention on the Elimination of All Forms of Discrimination Against Women 1979; the Convention Against Torture and Other Cruel, Inhuman or Degrading Treatment or Punishment 1984; the Convention on the Rights of the Child 1989; and the Convention on the Rights of Persons With Disabilities 2006. Although Australia is a party to all the above, it should be noted that these international instruments cannot be used to "override clear and valid provisions of Australian national law".[3]

The International Covenant on Civil and Political Rights (ICCPR)

Ratified in 1980, although not assimilated into its domestic law, ICCPR provisions and the UPR process are fully binding upon Australia, and it has acceded to Optional Protocol 1.[4] Articles 2(1) and 26 deal with principles of non-discrimination and equality respectively, while Articles 17 and 23 set out the rights to privacy and the right to marry and found a family. The ICCPR is supplemented by General Comment 22 (see also Chapter 3).

Other

Australia initially voted against adopting the UN Declaration on the Rights of Indigenous People 2007 but ultimately removed its objections in 2009 (see Chapter 3). Also, because of the tendency for Australian litigation to conflate matters of racial and religious discrimination, ICERD has considerable relevance (see further Chapter 3).

Domestic legislation

Having neither a national human rights statute nor a constitutional bill of rights, Australia's weak commitment to such protection for its citizens regularly attracts protests, most recently from the AHRC.[5]

2 See the Human Rights (Parliamentary Scrutiny) Act 2011, s.3(1).
3 *Minister for Immigration v. B* (2004) 219 CLR 365, per Kirby, J., at 425.
4 See *Toonen v. Australia*, Communication No. 488/1992, U.N. Doc CCPR/C/50/D/488/1992 (1994).
5 Australian Human Rights Commission, *Religious Freedom Review* (2018), at para. 90.

The Commonwealth of Australia Constitution Act 1900 (the Constitution)

Human rights are not among the "heads of power" available to Parliament for legislative purposes. While this does not prevent Parliament legislating on some aspects of such matters, it can only do so incidentally. Although the Constitution does not contain a "bill of rights", it does provide, directly or implicitly, for certain rights and freedoms.

The Marriage Amendment (Definition and Religious Freedoms) Act 2017 (Cth)

This statute amended the Marriage Act 1961, changing the federal definition of marriage to one that simply referred to two persons of marriageable age, regardless of their gender.

Sex Discrimination Amendment (Sexual Orientation, Gender Identity and Intersex Status) Act 2013 (Cth)

Amending the Sex Discrimination Act 1984, this statute makes it unlawful to discriminate against a person on the basis of sexual orientation, gender identity and intersex status under federal law, supplemented, in due course, by the Australian Government Guidelines on the Recognition of Sex and Gender.[6]

The Human Rights (Parliamentary Scrutiny) Act 2011

Taking effect on 4 January 2012, the 2011 Act requires all new legislation introduced to the Federal Parliament to be assessed for compatibility with human rights, but it stopped short of creating a Charter of Rights. This legislation is illustrative of Australia's very weak orientation towards human rights in domestic law which, as Langlois points out, "is a very clear marker of Australia's preferred mode of dealing with human rights".[7]

The Fair Work Act 2009 (Cth)

This protects freedom of association and extends the specific legal protection previously given to religious non-discrimination in the workplace.[8]

6 See further at: www.ag.gov.au/RightsAndProtections/HumanRights/Pages/Australian-Government-Guidelines-on-the-Recognition-of-Sex-and-Gender.aspx.

7 Note to author, 11 June 2019.

8 Neil Foster points out that employment protections in relation to discrimination on the grounds of religion only apply where the relevant state or territory provides such protection, citing s.351(2)(a) (note to author, 20 February 2017).

The Human Rights (Sexual Conduct) Act 1994

This ended the criminalisation of sexual conduct involving consenting adults (18 years or over), in private, on a federal basis.

The Human Rights and Equal Opportunity Commission Act 1986 (Cth)

This statute established the Human Rights and Equal Opportunity Commission which, in 2008, was renamed the Australian Human Rights Commission (AHRC). It implements Australia's human rights obligations under the International Labour Organization Convention (No. 111) concerning discrimination in respect of employment and occupation. The Commission has the function of inquiring into and attempting to reach a settlement of complaints through conciliation.

The Sex Discrimination Act 1984 (Cth)

Initially providing protection from discrimination in relation to the protected characteristics of sex, marital or relationship status, pregnancy and breastfeeding, in 2013 this legislation was amended to also prohibit discrimination on the grounds of sexual orientation, gender identity and intersex status in a range of areas of public life.

The Racial Discrimination Act 1975 (Cth)

For clarification as to what constitutes "discrimination", s.9 refers to the rights established in Article 5 of ICERD, while s.10 establishes a general right to equality before the law. Section 18(c) prohibits speech that insults, offends or humiliates people based on their race.

Other legislation

At federal level, equality and anti-discrimination provisions are to be found in a range of legislation such as the Fair Work Act 2009 (Cth). In November 2012, the government released a draft of its Human Rights and Anti-Discrimination Bill 2012, but this was suspended and the government settled for amending some aspects of the Sex Discrimination Act.

All states and territories provide various laws prohibiting the vilification of persons, singularly or as a group.

Framework of courts and regulatory bodies

Law in the Commonwealth of Australia is promulgated, adjudicated and administered at various levels – federal, state and territory – and is built on foundations laid down by English common law. Jurisdictional complexity is further complicated by the fact that Australia has not achieved the status of a republic, although in 1986 the Australia Act established domestic legislative sovereignty and ended the appeal jurisdiction of the Privy Council in England.

International courts and regulatory bodies

Although the SOGI-related decisions of Australian courts and regulatory bodies are not amenable to any international judicial oversight, domestic law and practice remains subject to the UN HR Committee monitoring role conducted through the Universal Periodic Review process.

Domestic courts and regulatory bodies

The states and territories of Australia each have their own hierarchy of courts and tribunals with a right of appeal to a supreme court and thereafter to a federal court.

The High Court of Australia (HCA)

This is Australia's supreme court and final court of appeal. Its federal jurisdiction is derived from authority vested in it by the Constitution, s.75 and s.76, and its appellate jurisdiction is defined by s.73. Appeals lie to it from the Federal Court of Australia (FCA).

The Federal Court of Australia (FCA)

This superior court has jurisdiction to deal with most civil disputes governed by federal law. It includes an appeal division, the Full Court, comprised of three judges.

The Australian Human Rights Commission

A national independent statutory body with responsibility for investigating matters protected by Australia's anti-discrimination legislation. It has published some significant SOGI-related reports.[9]

9 See: the *Resilient Individuals: Sexual Orientation Gender Identity & Intersex Rights Report* (2015); the *Sexual Orientation, Gender Identity and Intersex Human Rights: Snapshot Report* (2012); *Addressing Sexual Orientation and Sex and/or Gender Identity Discrimination Consultation Report* (2011); the *Sex Files Report* (2009); the *Same Sex Same Entitlements Inquiry Report* (2007); and *Human Rights for Australia's Gays and Lesbians Report* (1997).

The Human Rights and Equal Opportunity Commission

The Commission is the regulatory body for such law and practice as is governed by the Racial Discrimination Act 1975; the Sex Discrimination Act 1984; the Disability Discrimination Act 1992; and the Human Rights and Equal Opportunity Commission Act 1986. Since February 2014, the Human Rights Commissioner has performed the role of Commission spokesperson for SOGI issues.

The Human Rights Law Centre

This independent, not-for-profit organisation advocates for the protection and promotion of human rights in Australia. It works across a range of areas, including advocating for reform to anti-discrimination laws and stronger protection for human rights.

International reports on human rights in Australia

In 2009, the UN HR Committee reported its concern that "the rights to equality and non-discrimination are not comprehensively protected in Australia in federal law".[10] Concern was also expressed about specific matters – such as the high level of violence against women and the need for greater promotion and protection of the rights of people who are lesbian, gay, bisexual, trans, gender diverse and intersex. In 2017, the Committee reiterated its previous recommendations that Australia should "adopt comprehensive federal legislation giving full legal effect to all Covenant provisions across all state and territory jurisdictions".[11] This should include a Commonwealth Human Rights Act, a Commonwealth Religious Freedom Act and a consolidation of Commonwealth anti-discrimination laws.

Human Rights Watch, in its 2017 World Report, notes that Australia continues its policy of intercepting asylum seekers and forcibly transferring them to Nauru and, until 2016, to Manus Island in Papua New Guinea. This is of concern because asylum seekers or refugees perceived to have SOGI issues face harassment and abuse in Nauru, where same-sex conduct has only recently been de-criminalised, and also in Papua New Guinea, where it remains criminalised. In 2018, the UN working group on arbitrary detention, which reports to the Human Rights Council, was also critical of this policy, as was the Commissioner for Refugees.[12]

10 See UNHR Committee, *Concluding Observations: Australia* (2009), at para. 12.5.

11 See UNHR Committee, *Concluding Observations: Australia* (2017), at para. 6.

12 UN High Commissioner for Refugees, *Fact Sheet on Situation of Refugees and Asylum-Seekers on Manus Island, Papua New Guinea* (21 January 2018), at: www.unhcr.org/5a6512507.html.

SOGI and related core human rights

These most basic and interlocking rights have essentially been imported into the legal system by way of common law. In the absence of a national bill of rights and with little if any related federal legislation, human rights litigation is dependent upon the varying statutes of states and territories together with reference to the influential but unenforceable provisions of international treaties, conventions and protocols.

Right of access to justice

The failure to ensure that Indigenous people and detained asylum seekers have adequate access to justice has been repeatedly criticised by the HRC.[13]

Access to relevant information

For trans persons, the process of providing the evidence necessary to be issued with appropriately amended ID documentation – medical card, bank account, drivers' licence etc. – has traditionally been torturous and invasive. This has recently been greatly simplified by the introduction of a less intrusive federal process that provides legal recognition for a change in gender identity. The Australian Government Guidelines on the Recognition of Sex and Gender Identity instituted a consistent, standardised procedure for all trans persons in Australia to change or establish sex and/or gender on general personal records – excepting birth certificates – without any need to produce evidence of having undergone hormone treatment or surgery. In 2014 and 2016, the Australian Capital Territory and South Australia, respectively, passed legislation removing the surgery requirement as a condition for altering the gender identity on a birth certificate. Instead, an adult trans person simply applies to the Registrar for Births, Deaths and Marriages, self-identifying their gender, accompanied by a medical statement to the effect that they have received appropriate clinical treatment. Nonetheless, it remains the case that in most states and territories trans people must still produce evidence of surgery when applying for an amended birth certificate. The fact that unconditional access to a birth certificate specifying appropriate gender identity is denied to trans persons, but not to others, raises questions of discrimination.

An effective remedy

Court authorisation, as a prerequisite for the surgical intervention deemed necessary to align children's physiology with preferred gender identity, has had a long

13 See, for example, the 2015 UPR, at: https://documents-dds-ny.un.org/doc/UNDOC/GEN/G16/004/89/PDF/G1600489.pdf?OpenElement.

and controversial history in Australia, attracting criticism that such a procedure was not human rights compliant. The recent FCA decision in *Re Matthew*[14] would seem to have brought closure to this episode. The court then confirmed that – where there is no disagreement between parents and medical professionals – a *Gillick* competent[15] adolescent may consent to all stages of their proposed gender reassignment treatment without any need for court involvement (see further below). Similarly, the ruling of the UN HR Committee in *G v. Australia*[16] was decisive in ending the effect of s.45 of the federal Sex Discrimination Act 1984, which required a trans person to divorce if they were to be eligible for an amended birth certificate that reflected their new gender identity (see further below). In terms of contributing towards a change in domestic law that delivered a more effective remedy, this decision can be seen alongside the Committee's earlier landmark rulings in *Toonen v. Australia*[17] and *Young v. Australia*[18] (see further below).

Asylum seekers/illegal immigrants

Australia is a signatory nation to the Refugee Convention 1951, and as with other such nations, the caselaw of judicial and regulatory bodies tends to be structured in accordance with key Convention definitional terms. For example, as regards whether an applicant falls within the protection afforded by the Convention to a "particular social group", the following principles were identified in *Applicant S*:

> First, the group must be identifiable by a characteristic or attribute common to all members of the group. Secondly, the characteristic or attribute common to all members of the group cannot be the shared fear of persecution. Thirdly, the possession of that characteristic or attribute must distinguish the group from society at large. Borrowing the language of Dawson J in *Applicant A*, a group that fulfils the first two propositions, but not the third, is merely a "social group" and not a "particular social group.[19]

The Convention requirement that an applicant have a "well-founded fear of persecution or serious harm" formed a ground of appeal in *SZQRM v. Minister for Immigration and Citizenship*,[20] which concerned the claim of a married Lithuanian homosexual/bisexual couple that as their conduct and views had led to them being attacked in the past – causing the man to suffer severe depression and

14 [2018] FamCA 161.
15 *Gillick v. West Norfolk and Wisbech* AHA AC 112 ((HL)) 1986.
16 CCPR/C/119/D/2172/2012 (2017).
17 Communication No. 488/1992, UN Doc CCPR/C/50/D/488/ (1992).
18 CCPR/C/78/D/941/2000; 11 IHRR 146 (2004).
19 *Applicant S v. Minister for Immigration and Multicultural Affairs* (2004) 217 CLR 387, at para. 36.
20 [2013] FCCA 772.

to attempt suicide – this would happen again if they were forced to return. The court considered the finding made by the Administrative Appeals Tribunal that this ground could not substantiated because the couple had in fact not engaged in non-marital sexual activity for the past two years and they could take steps to avoid recognition, such as residing in a different part of Lithuania. Noting that "intolerance against homosexuals and bisexuals is widespread throughout Lithuania" but taking the view that "this was not a relevant consideration", the court upheld the Tribunal's finding and dismissed the appeal.

The distinction between these two key Convention terms – persecution and social group – was emphasised in *RRT Case No. 1207970*,[21] when the Tribunal held that homosexuals in Sudan were a particular social group – identified not by their fear of persecution, but by their sexuality.

Since 2013, Australian policy towards those seeking refuge, on SOGI or other grounds, has been overshadowed by the government decision to establish offshore detention centres on Papua New Guinea and on Manus and Nauru islands, where a fluctuating population of up to 2,000 refugees, including children, have been forcibly detained, some for several years.[22]

Right to freedom of expression

This right, although not explicitly stated in the Constitution nor in any federal statute, is one to communicate and receive opinions, information and ideas without interference. Judicial notice has been taken that the right to free speech, which is declared in several international conventions – such as Article 19 of the ICCPR – to which Australia is a signatory, exists in domestic law at least in the form of an implied right of political speech.[23]

In practice, the right to freedom of speech often conflicts with the right to religious freedom.[24] In *Gaynor*,[25] for example, an officer in the armed forces had his commission terminated when he refused to stop publicly expressing offensive views, which he claimed were related to his Catholic religion, on matters such as LGBTI rights. While the court found that the plaintiff was entitled to exercise his right to freedom of speech, and duly set aside the decision terminating his commission, Buchanan J made the point that he was "satisfied that the applicant acted by choice to make the statements which he did" and did not accept "that even

21 [2012] RRTA 757.

22 See further Amnesty International report, *Punishment Not Protection* (2017), at: www.amnesty.org/download/Documents/ASA3477812018ENGLISH.pdf.

23 *Nationwide News Pty Ltd v. Wills* (1992) 177 CLR 1, *Australian Capital Television Pty Ltd v. the Commonwealth* (1992) 177 CLR 106 and *Unions NSW v. New South Wales* [2013] HCA 58.

24 See, for example: *Fletcher v. Salvation Army Australia (Anti Discrimination)* [2005] VCAT 1523 (1 August 2005); *Bropho v. Human Rights and Equal Opportunity Commission* [2004] FCAFC 16; *Judeh v. Jewish National Fund of Australia Inc* [2003] VCAT 1254; and *John Fairfax Publications Pty Ltd v. Kazak* [2002] NSWADTAP 35.

25 *Gaynor v. Chief of Defence Force (No 3)* [2015] FCA 1370.

as a matter of conscience, he felt he had no choice but to defy the instructions and orders given to him".[26] Moreover, the courts have been clear that the exercise of this right cannot be constrained in order to prevent "hurt feelings" or to secure "the civility of discourse",[27] and it "does not provide a licence to breach a contract of employment";[28] it only confers "a freedom to communicate ideas to those who are willing to listen, not a right to force an unwanted message on those who do not wish to hear it".[29]

The moral majority

The morality of a significant sector of contemporary society can compromise the right to free speech. Recently this would seem to have occurred in the 2018 "no platforming" by the University of Western Australia of an American paediatrician, known for denying much of the science concerning trans people. His invitation to give a talk at an Australian Family Association event was abruptly cancelled – on health and safety grounds – due to the high level of student protest. It has also been represented by the protests against the erection of "safe access zones" to protect abortion clinics in Victoria and Tasmania. While far from being exclusively a matter of concern to the LGBT community, the focus on reproductive rights does clearly have implications for many of its members, as does any constraint on the right to freedom of assembly and the entitlement to safe passage. This has been the subject of prolonged litigation and is currently before the HCA in *Clubb v. Edwards and the Attorney-General*,[30] where the court is considering whether such zoning impermissibly burdens the implied freedom of political communication insofar as it prohibits communicating in relation to abortions.

Harm to others

As was noted in *Iliafi*,[31] the right to freedom of expression does not guarantee "linguistic freedom as such", nor does it "guarantee a right to use the language of one's choice" in all circumstances. Expressions that stray beyond being offensive to become "errors of fact, distortions of the truth and inflammatory and provocative language" violate the rights of others and are unlawful.[32]

In *Menzies & Ors v. Owen*,[33] the court upheld a charge of publicly vilifying homosexuals and incitement to hatred despite an assertion that this was sourced in "ancient religious text such as the Bible, the Torah or the Koran".[34] The *Three-*

26 Ibid. at p. 215.
27 See, respectively, *Coleman v. Power* (2004) 220 CLR 1 at 78–79 and *Monis v. The Queen* (2013) 249 CLR 92 at 168–169.
28 *Banerji v. Bowles* [2013] FCCA 1052.
29 *Brown v. Tasmania* (2017) 91 ALJR 1089 at 1141.
30 No M46 of 2018.
31 *Iliafi v. The Church of Jesus Christ of Latter-Day Saints Australia* [2014] FCAFC 2 at p. 92.
32 *Eatock v. Bolt* [2011] FCA 1103.
33 [2008] QADT 20, at para. 129.
34 *Youssef v. Khani* [2006] TASADT 8.

wisemonkeys[35] decision is of relevance as it again illustrates a legal conflation of sexual orientation with religious belief. The case concerned a pamphlet, published by a representative of an organisation known as the "Threewisemonkeys" and distributed in the Sandy Bay area of Hobart in 2013. It stated that "homosexuality should not be tolerated" and that "Scripture rejects homosexuality as utterly abominable" and set out alleged statistics on lifespan expectations and causes of death for gay men and lesbians compared to heterosexual men and women. The complainant claimed that publishing and distributing this pamphlet constituted incitement to hatred on the grounds of sexual orientation under the Tasmanian Anti-Discrimination Act 1998, s.19, while the respondent claimed that such conduct was protected by the right to freedom of religion under s.116 of the Constitution. The court found in favour of the complainant, noting that "any 'freedom' must be balanced against the rights of others, as is the case with the rights to freedom of speech and freedom of association".[36]

Right to freedom of association and assembly

There is no express constitutional right to freedom of association. It is recognised only in an employment context by the Fair Work Act 2009 (Cth), which protects the right of persons to join or not join an industrial association. Its importance has, however, been confirmed by the HCA[37] and by inclusion in several international conventions (e.g. Article 22 of the ICCPR and Article 8 of the ICESR) to which Australia is a signatory nation. As was noted in *Barclay v. The Board of Bendigo Regional Institute of Technical and Further Education*, the right is "not simply a freedom to join an association without adverse consequences, but is a freedom to be represented by the association and to participate in its activities".[38]

The right to associate provides opportunities to build group solidarity and to create a platform for representation from which to lobby for change. As such, it has proven invaluable to socially marginalised groups such as the LGBT community. In 1979, Australia's first transgender rights and advocacy organisations were established, the Melbourne-based Victorian Transsexual Coalition and the Victorian Transsexual Association, followed in 1981 by the Sydney-based Australian Transsexual Association.

Constraints

As in other countries, the right to associate is exercisable subject to laws governing public order, safety and criminal activity.[39] It is also affected by anti-discrimination legislation which reinforces the collective identity of those who share

35 *Williams v. "Threewisemonkeys" and Durston* [2015] TASADT.
36 Ibid. at para. 50.
37 *Unions NSW v. New South Wales* [2013] HCA 58.
38 (2011) 191 FCR 212.
39 *South Australia v. Totani* (2010) 242 CLR 1, 54.

protected characteristics and may, thereby, attract affirmative action from government bodies.

Right to freedom of religion

The "freedom of religious belief and expression" has been judicially declared to be an "important freedom generally accepted in Australian society".[40]

However, in *Grace Bible Church v. Reedman*,[41] the court gave short shrift to the appellant's claim that "there was an inalienable right to religious freedom". Parliament, as White J commented, had "an absolute right to interfere with religious worship and the expression of religious beliefs at any time that it liked"[42] and indeed had done so when the nation was at war, as illustrated in the Jehovah's Witnesses cases. More recently, the same dismissiveness was evident in the *Iliafi* case,[43] which concerned an internal dispute regarding language, when the full Federal Court confirmed that in such circumstances an individual's freedom of religion was protected only by the right to leave the Church. The tension between rights in relation to religion and to sexuality is well established in Australia.

SOGI and religion

The Sex Discrimination Amendment (Sexual Orientation, Gender Identity and Intersex Status) Act 2013, while revising certain exemption privileges traditionally enjoyed by religious organisations, specifically exempted private schools and hospitals owned by such organisations from SOGI-specific legal requirements. Given the number, spread and status of such facilities, this privilege has a significant human rights impact. It also inserted a new exemption stating that "conduct is not unlawful when . . . it constitutes a request for information and keeping of records in relation to sex and/or gender" which may permit the "outing" or at least the compromising of trans persons. In addition, the Marriage Amendment (Definition and Religious Freedoms) Act 2017 (Cth) exempts ministers of religion from any obligation to officiate at same-sex marriage ceremonies, as in other Part II jurisdictions, but goes a step further by extending the exemption to civil registrars where to do so would compromise their beliefs (e.g. same-sex marriages, a trans marriage or a marriage involving previously divorced or interfaith couples); and to religious organisations, enabling them to refuse to provide facilities, goods or services if to do so would compromise either their beliefs or those of their religious communities.

40 *Evans v. New South Wales* (2008) 168 FCR 576, per French, Branson and Stone, J. J., at p. 596.
41 (1984) 54 ALR 571.
42 Ibid. at p. 385.
43 Op. cit., at pp. 85–86.

Religious organisations and the religious exemption

Federal religious exemptions are addressed primarily in the Sex Discrimination Act 1984 (Cth) and the Fair Work Act 2009 (Cth) but also in all state and territory anti-discrimination statutes.[44] These provide that religious organisations and religious educational institutions[45] (see further below) are exempted from legislative provisions where a discriminatory act or conduct is required to ensure conformity with doctrines, tenets or beliefs of a religion, or is necessary to avoid injury to the religious sensitivities of adherents of that religion. It allows such bodies to discriminate in the provision of accommodation; in the ordination or appointment of priests, ministers of religion or in the training or education of such persons or in the appointment of persons to perform religious duties or functions and any other act or practice of a body established for religious purposes; and by educational institutions established for religious purposes in relation to the employment of staff and the provision of education and training, provided that the discrimination is in "good faith". However, an organisation will only qualify for exemption if it satisfies the definition of "religious", which the St Vincent de Paul Society, surprisingly, failed to do. In *Walsh v. St Vincent de Paul Society Queensland (No. 2)*,[46] the respondent was found to be a society of lay faithful closely associated with the Catholic Church, rather than a "religious body", and therefore were not entitled to avail of the religious exemption.

This exemption was clearly central to the lengthy proceedings that constituted the *OV and OW* case[47] and *Cobaw Community Health Services Limited v. Christian Youth Camps Limited & Anor.*[48] In the latter, Hampel J referred to the need to balance two key principles: that the exemption should be applied narrowly so as to advance the statutory purposes or objects to prohibit discrimination while the right to equality and freedom from discrimination was to be interpreted broadly; and the protection of religious freedom must be interpreted as far as possible in a manner which is compatible with the rights to equality and freedom from discrimination. Having heard expert evidence from theologians on the meaning of "doctrines of religion", Hampel J found that the beliefs of the Christian Brethren about marriage, sexual relationships and homosexuality could not be construed as "doctrines of the religion". Not everything in the Scriptures

44 Tasmania is the only exception. The absence of a religious exemption in its anti-discrimination legislation means that it is illegal to discriminate there on the grounds of sexuality or gender identity.

45 Note that the Sex Discrimination Amendment (Removing Discrimination Against Students) Bill 2018 proposes to amend s.37 of the Sex Discrimination Act 1984 in order to prevent educational institutions relying on the exemption in that section to engage in discriminatory practices against students on SOGI-related grounds.

46 [2008] QADT 32.

47 *Member of the Board of the Wesley Mission Council v. OV and OW* (No 2) [2009] NSWADTAP 57; *OV & OW v. Members of the Board of the Wesley Mission Council* [2010] NSWCA 155.

48 [2010] VCAT 1613 (8 October 2010).

amounts to "doctrine"; the prevailing cultural beliefs at the time must also be taken into account.[49]

The exemption was also central to *Mornington Baptist Church Community Caring Inc.*,[50] when a Baptist Church unsuccessfully sought to avail of it to restrict staff selection to those who had "publicly confessed Jesus Christ" and were "walking in daily fellowship with Jesus". Their claim failed because the organisation was unable to show why its religious beliefs required it to so restrict employment in order to fulfil the functional tasks of its community care projects.

SOGI: personal relationships and human rights

Cultural context sets the parameters for SOGI issues in Australia as it does in other nations. Given the long-established presence of Indigenous people, it might be expected that the law relating to such matters would be more complicated here than elsewhere. In fact, there is little indication of Indigenous culture being taken into account in SOGI-related legislation – at federal, state or territory level – nor of it impacting upon the resulting caselaw.

Right to an identity

While the de-criminalisation of same-sex relationships, followed by the introduction of their legislative rights to marry and adopt etc., removed traditional obstacles to legal recognition of sexual orientation status, equivalent recognition for a trans person's acquired gender identity required, for many years, evidence of sexual reassignment surgery.

In this context it must also be noted that identity itself, let alone any additional SOGI-related nuances, has long complicated the legal status of Indigenous people. From the time when Australia was designated "terra nullius",[51] through the decades of the "White Australia" policy, until 1967 when they were first included in the national Census, the Indigenous People were not even recognised as citizens.[52] Since then, while in theory the legislation – federal, state and territory – applied as much to them as to the non-Indigenous, in practice a non-inclusive ethos has prevailed: equality legislation in general, including the law relating to SOGI issues, was not seen as particularly relevant to their circumstances. In fact, their history reveals that gender and sexual diversity has always been important components in the life of Indigenous communities.[53]

49 Also see *Ananda Marga Pracaraka Samgha Ltd v. Tomar* (No 6) [2013] FCA 284.
50 (2006) EOC 93-422 (VCAT).
51 So designated by Cook in 1770 – when there were some 750,000 Indigenous inhabitants – and meaning empty or no one's land.
52 See, for example, Horne, D., *The Lucky Country*, Penguin Modern Classics, 1964.
53 See, for example, Hodge, D., *Colouring the Rainbow: Blak Queer and Trans Perspectives*, Wakefield Press, 2015.

Trans recognition in law

Requirements for ID documentation, including gender identity recognition, are subject to jurisdiction: birth certificates and drivers' licences, for example, are regulated by the states and territories, while Medicare and passports are matters for the Commonwealth. Acquiring an amended birth certificate from the Births, Deaths and Marriages Registry has generally required fulfilling the usual criteria and providing evidence of surgery. This approach, established across most states and territories, was challenged in a sequence of seminal cases.

In contrast to prior decisions that had looked to gender reassignment surgery as a threshold requirement for legal recognition of a change in gender identity, Justice Chisholm in *Kevin and Jennifer*[54] recognised Kevin's claim to be a man and to be in a lawful heterosexual marriage despite his not having fully completed the requisite surgical procedures. In reaching this decision, a persuasive factor for the judge had been the fact that Kevin was perceived to be, and was accepted as, a man by his family, friends and work colleagues: such social contextualising seems a precursor to the rationale later deployed to define "marriage" in accordance with contemporary social mores rather than as traditionally understood.[55] This approach was endorsed by the HCA decision in *AB v. Western Australia*[56] when the ruling of the Supreme Court of Western Australia – which focused on the sufficiency of the limited surgery to satisfy "gender characteristics" – was overturned. Instead, the HCA took the view that what was determinative of gender identity was not the extent of surgery but the extent of the resulting social acceptance of the trans person's appearance and behaviour. Then came the 2017 ruling of the UN HR Committee in *G v. Australia*,[57] which reverberated internationally. It concerned a trans person – biologically male but self-identifying as female – who, on that basis, had been issued with a passport, driver's licence, Medicare card, bank and credit cards reflecting the chosen gender identity. Following a same-sex marriage and completion of sex affirmation surgery, she requested an appropriately amended birth certificate, but this was refused. The Committee noted that the federal Sex Discrimination Act 1984 prohibits discrimination on the basis of marital status but not discrimination against persons who are sex and gender diverse and indeed that s.40(5) specifically permits State and Territory Governments to "refuse to make, issue or alter an official record of a person's sex if a law of a State or Territory requires the refusal because the person is married" – which, in this case, it did. Consequently, she was placed in a position whereby she could not acquire an amended birth certificate unless she divorced, which

54 *Re: Kevin and Jennifer v. Attorney-General for the Commonwealth* [2001] FamCA 1074.

55 See *Cobaw Community Health Services Limited v. Christian Youth Camps Limited & Anor* [2010] VCAT 1613.

56 [2011] HCA 42.

57 CCPR/C/119/D/2172/2012 (2017).

constituted a direct arbitrary interference with her right to privacy under Article 17 of the ICCPR. As the Committee pointed out,

> marital status should not be a relevant consideration as to whether or not a person can request a change in legal sex . . . a person should not be forced to end their marriage in order to have a change in sex legally recognised.[58]

It held that

> by failing to implement legislation which prohibits discrimination on the basis of marital and transgender status and guarantees to all persons equal and effective protection against such discrimination, the State party violated the author's rights under Articles 2(1) and 26 of the Covenant.[59]

Specifically, Australia had breached its human rights obligations under Article 26 of the ICCPR by not providing a means for a transgender person to have their birth certificate amended in accordance with their new gender identity. As mentioned earlier, this was followed in 2013 by amendments to the Sex Discrimination Act 1984, which introduced new protections from discrimination on the grounds of sexual orientation, gender identity and intersex status, and by the federal introduction of the Australian Government Guidelines on the Recognition of Sex and Gender Identity in 2013, which dispensed with the need for evidence of hormonal or surgical treatment as a requirement for a Gender Recognition Certificate.[60]

Non-binary gender identity

"Not all human beings can be classified by sex as either male or female", as the HCA noted in *Norrie*,[61] and indeed Australia is now at the forefront of those nations prepared to recognise that gender identity need not be legally confined to a binary definition. This is reflected in the fact that the LGBT community in Australia self-identifies as the LGBTI community and related discourse is pointedly inclusive of those who are "intersex".[62]

In 2003, after some equivocation, the Department of Foreign Affairs and Trade Australian issued a passport to an Alex MacFarlane marked with an "X" to signify unspecified sex or intersex, in acknowledgement that the holder's chromosome mix (47 XXY) fell outside the binary definition. In 2011, the

58 Ibid., at para. 2.13(a).
59 Ibid., at para. 3.4.
60 See further at: www.ag.gov.au/Publications/Pages/AustralianGovernmentGuidelinesontheRecognitionofSexandGender.aspx.
61 *NSW Registrar of Births, Deaths and Marriages v. Norrie* [2014] HCA 11, per French, C.J. and Justices Hayne, Kiefel, Bell and Keane.
62 See further Carpenter, M., op. cit.

Department revised its policy to include non-binary trans and non-binary intersex persons within the "X" category on the basis of a supporting letter from a doctor. This approach was extended to birth certificates following *NSW Registrar of Births, Deaths and Marriages v. Norrie*,[63] when the HCA ruled that the respondent, having undergone sex affirmation surgery, was now androgynous and should be registered as neither male nor female in the NSW Registry of Births, Deaths and Marriages. These developments would seem to lend weight to Carpenter's argument:

> assumptions that to be intersex is to be nonbinary, or to be nonbinary is to be intersex . . . are harmful. They fail to recognise the diversity of the intersex population, and in this case even the existence of intersex girls and boys, and intersex women and men. These misconceptions can be experienced as stigmatising. . . . They harmfully reduce intersex human rights issues to a matter of legal gender recognition. They do not reflect intersex diversity, and nor do they reflect the diversity of the nonbinary population. . . . Intersex as identity is polymorphic; that is, there are many different ideas about what this means . . . intersex as identity is best described as an affirmative label to describe people born with variations of sex characteristics.[64]

Right to respect for private and family life

It was the series of landmark rulings by the UN HR Committee that drove home the need for change in Australian law relating to SOGI issues and provided the impetus for similar changes in other countries. In *Toonen v. Australia*,[65] the Committee held that the ICCPR references to "sex" (Article 2) and the right to privacy (Article 17) included sexual orientation. This led directly to the Humans Rights (Sexual Conduct) Act 1994 (Cth), in which the federal government asserted the right of individuals not to suffer "any arbitrary interference with privacy" from state or territory officials. In *Young v. Australia*,[66] it held that distinctions made between same-sex couples and opposite-sex couples in relation to veterans entitlements were discriminatory and in breach of Article 26. In *G v. Australia*,[67] it reiterated its view that "the interference with the author's privacy and family is not necessary and proportionate to a legitimate interest, and is therefore arbitrary within the meaning of Article 17 of the Covenant".[68]

63 [2014] HCA 11.
64 Carpenter, M., *Intersex Human Rights Australia: Identification Documents*, at: https://ihra.org.au/identities/.
65 Communication No. 488/1992, UN Doc CCPR/C/50/D/488/ (1992).
66 Communication No. 941/2000, UN Doc CCPR/C/78/D/941/ (2003).
67 CCPR/C/119/D/2172/2012 (2017).
68 Ibid., at para. 7.10.

Sexual orientation, identity and private life

In *Simpson v. Brockmann*,[69] the Family Court ruled that that a lesbian couple, living together as partners with their children for more than nine years, met the definition of "parents". Since then, the legal definition of what constitutes a family unit has been broadened by legislation such as the Sex Discrimination Amendment (Sexual Orientation, Gender Identity and Intersex Status) Act 2013, which amended the 1984 Act to provide new protections from discrimination on the basis of sexual orientation, gender identity and intersex status.[70]

Family life

"The Australian family law system remains mired in a two-parent model of legal parentage, a paradigm that does not always reflect the reality and diversity of same-sex families".[71] However, as Sifris also points out, Australian society and its associated family laws have changed greatly in recent years.

Private life, gender reassignment and divorce

Until 2018, in most states and territories, divorce was a legal prerequisite for any married person intending to complete a trans process and have their birth certificate amended accordingly.[72] This had been reinforced in 2011 by the inclusion of the s.40(5) exemption clause in the Sex Discrimination Act, which allowed a state or territory "to refuse to make, issue or alter an official record of a person's sex if a law of a State or Territory requires the refusal because the person is married". As mentioned earlier, the UN HR Committee ruling in *G. v. Australia*[73] set in train a process of legal change culminating in the introduction of federal same-sex marriage legislation in 2018 which in effect negated the divorce requirement. Since then, states and territories have legislated to remove it: Queensland, Victoria, New South Wales and Western Australia did so in the latter part of 2018/19.

SOGI, parenting and "the best interests of the child" principle

As long ago as 1994, Australian judiciary were rightly asserting that "the nature of a party's sexual relationships is relevant to the Court's proceedings only to

69 [2012] FamCAFC 37.

70 See further the Australian Human Rights Commission, *Same-Sex: Same Entitlements* (2007), at: www.humanrights.gov.au/our-work/sexual-orientation-sex-gender-identity/publications/same-sex-same-entitlements.

71 Sifris, A., Gay and Lesbian Parenting: The Legislative Response, in Hayes, A. and Higgins, D., *Families, Policy and the Law: Selected Essays on Contemporary Issues for Australia*, Australian Institute of Family Studies, 2014, at pp. 89–101.

72 See *AB v. Registrar of Births, Deaths and Marriages* [2007] FCAFC 140.

73 CCPR/C/119/D/2172/2012.

the extent that it affects the parenting abilities or the welfare of a child in a particular case".[74]

The recent upsurge in recourse to overseas surrogacy arrangements has created some unique legal concerns with respect to citizenship and parenting rights. In 2008, as a consequence of a number of cases of disputed parental rights resulting from IVF and surrogacy arrangements,[75] s.60H of the Family Law Act 1975 (Cth) was amended to provide legal parentage status for non-biological parents in same-sex relationships. As illustrated in *Re Michael*,[76] the amendment promptly gave rise to issues regarding the legal rights of non-genetic parents. The surrogacy arrangement in this case was not recognised by Watts J, who dismissed the adoption application lodged by the commissioning couple as, in his view, they had no *locus standi* under the amended s.60H. Much the same approach was evident in *Wilson and Anor & Roberts and Anor (No.2)*.[77] This concerned two same-sex couples – one female and one male – who collectively concluded a co-parenting agreement whereby the latter donated sperm to the former resulting in the birth of a girl. Initially the child was co-parented to a varying degree by all four adults until their relationship broke down and brought the couples to court in competing claims for parental rights. Dessau J found that the child's primary attachment was to the mothers and she could not be equally parented by all four adults due to the conflict between the parties – particularly to the threat the mothers believed the fathers presented to their family unit. Referring to the amended s.60H, the judge accordingly awarded parental responsibility to the mothers.

Right to marriage and to found a family

Marriage is "the union of a man and a woman to the exclusion of all others, voluntarily entered into for life" declared the Marriage Act 1961 (Cth), s.5(1). This binary paradigm, for centuries entrenched by Church and State, enabled Justice Bell in 1979 to annul the marriage of an intersex man "since the respondent was a combination of both, a marriage in the true sense could not have taken place and did not exist".[78] However, following a series of judicial rulings to the effect that the meaning of "marriage" in the Constitution could not be regarded as

74 *Re K* (1994) *FLC 92–461*, at p. 9, citing: *N and N* (1977) FLC ¶90–266; *Spry and Spry* (1977) FLC ¶90–271; *Cartwright and Cartwright* (1977) FLC ¶90–302; *L and L* (1983) FLC ¶91–353; and *Doyle and Doyle* (1992) FLC ¶92–286.

75 For example, *Re Patrick* (2002) 28 Fam LR 579; FLC 93–096 and *Re Mark* (2003) 31 Fam LR 162; [2003] FamCA 822.

76 *(Surrogacy Arrangements)* (2009) 41 Fam LR 694.

77 [2010] FamCA 734.

78 *In the marriage of C and D (falsely called C)* (1979) FLC 90–636. Cited in *Tien-Lao & Tien-Lao* [2018] FamCA 953 when the court held that the "wife mistakenly believed she was marrying a man, so the marriage was void" at para. 55.

frozen in time,[79] that the meaning of "man" includes a post-operative female to male trans[80] and that a post-operative trans person could lawfully marry,[81] the federal government introduced same-sex marriage and throughout Australia the traditional definition thereafter ceased to be good law.

Legal recognition for same-sex relationships and the right to marry

Not until the introduction of legislation enacted after *Toonen v. Australia*[82] were same-sex relationships finally de-criminalised nationwide. The extent of discriminatory treatment was such that in 2007 the Australian Human Rights Commission issued a report documenting the many areas in which same-sex couples continued to be unfairly treated in domestic law.[83] The Marriage Amendment (Definition and Religious Freedoms) Act 2017 finally amended the Marriage Act 1961 to make marriage between two persons of marriageable age legally valid, regardless of their gender. It took a further 12 months, until December 2018, for the s.40(5) exemption in the Sex Discrimination Act to be repealed in all states and territories.

Trans persons and marriage

In the earlier-mentioned 2001 case of *Kevin and Jennifer*,[84] the FCA recognised the reassigned gender status of a trans person, and their consequent right to marry someone of the now opposite sex, but did so only after taking into account evidence of hormonal therapy and irreversible surgery. The court gave considerable weight to the social context affirmation of Kevin's gender identity: at the time of marriage, he was perceived as a man by his family, friends and fellow employees due to his appearance, characteristics and behaviour; he was accepted as a man for a number of social and legal purposes; and his marriage as a man was accepted in full knowledge of the circumstances by family, friends and work colleagues.[85]

79 See, for example: *Cormick & Cormick v. Salmon* [1984] HCA 79; *Re: F ex parte F* [1986] HCA 41; *The Queen v. L* [1991] HCA 48; and *Re: Wakim; ex parte McNally* (1999) 198 CLR 511.
80 See, for example: *R v. Harris and McGuiness* (1988) 17 NSW LR 158; *Secretary, Department of Social Security v. SRA* [1993] FCA 573; and *Corbett v. Corbett (otherwise Ashley)* [1971] P83.
81 *Attorney-General for the Commonwealth & "Kevin and Jennifer" & Human Rights and Equality Commission* [2003] FamCA 94. Also see *Re: Wakim ex parte McNally* (1999) 198 CLR 511.
82 Communication No. 488/1992, UN Doc CCPR/C/50/D/488/1992.
83 Noting: the absence of equal recognition of same-sex relationships; discriminatory treatment in relation to the recognition of children of same-sex couples; employment; workers' compensation; tax; social security; veterans' entitlements; health care costs; family law; superannuation; aged care; and migration.
84 *Re: Kevin and Jennifer v. Attorney-General for the Commonwealth* [2001] FamCA 1074.
85 Ibid., at paras. 76 and 170.

Adoption, surrogacy and child care

Although commercial surrogacy is banned nationwide, surrogacy is legal on an altruistic basis within all Australian jurisdictions – except Western Australia (where it is illegal for singles and same-sex couples). Surrogacy arrangements very often involve adoption proceedings, and with the passing of the Adoption of Children Legislation Amendment (Equality) Bill 2017 in the Northern Territories, same-sex and unmarried couples are now legally able to adopt children anywhere in Australia.

Right to cultural life

Historically, there have been two main cultural groupings in Australia: the "Westernised" cosmopolitan and pluralist mainstream society; running alongside are the communities of Indigenous people, the members of which are disproportionately disadvantaged in terms of poverty and health. While the former has transformed in recent years from a markedly conservative society anchored mainly on a twin Protestant and Catholic cultural orientation to becoming more eclectic, and typically "modern", with much the same tensions as in other developed nations, the latter has largely struggled to keep alive remnants of its traditional culture while maintaining a "third world" existence in parallel with its "first world" neighbours. While in recent years major waves of immigration have produced different cultural groupings, greatly diversifying Australian society and adding a plurality of cultural strands, nonetheless these two parallel basic groupings remain firmly in place.

Cultural context

Judicial notice has been taken of the distinctive ethnicity and culture of the Indigenous people. For example, it has been noted that "the Nyungah elders are an ethnic group in that they have a shared history, separate cultural tradition, common geographical origin, descent from common ancestors, a common language and a religion different to the general community surrounding them".[86] Although the policies of Christian proselytising and assimilation, which continued up until the mid-twentieth century and included the tragically misguided "Stolen Generation" episode, eroded and depleted their traditional beliefs and practices, it would seem to have left intact a cultural acceptance of SOGI differences. This is perhaps evidenced in the contemporary references to "sistergirls" and to "brotherboys" which indicate a long-standing accommodation of gender diversity that predates equality and non-discrimination legislation.

86 *Wanjurri v. Southern Cross Broadcasting (Aus) Ltd* (2001) EOC 93–147, per Commissioner Innes. See also *ALRM v. State of South Australia* (1995) 64 SASR 551 and *Macabenta v. Minister for Immigration & Multicultural Affairs* (1998) 90 FCR 202.

SOGI: non-discrimination, affirmative action and equality

Federal anti-discrimination legislation is dated and limited. It is targeted at the characteristics of race,[87] sex[88] and disability,[89] offering protection only where federal acts and legislation are engaged, such as in relation to federal government matters involving immigration or federal government employment. However, the anti-discrimination legislation of every state and territory provides protection from discrimination on SOGI grounds (albeit defined differently), and there is some express protection from discrimination on the ground of intersex status. These limitations bring to mind the warning of Brennan J in *Marion's* case: "if equality under the law, human rights and the protection of minorities are more than the incantations of legal rhetoric, it is in this area of the law that they have real work to do".[90]

Equality before the law: sexuality and gender discrimination

The Australian legislature has pioneered some developments in human rights law. It did so when it became the first nation to officially recognise non-binary gender identity. The Sex Discrimination Amendment (Sexual Orientation, Gender Identity and Intersex Status) Act 2013 amended the Sex Discrimination Act 1984 (Cth), to make it unlawful on a federal basis to discriminate against a person on grounds that include intersex status as well as sex, sexual orientation and gender identity, in areas of public life such as employment, education and the provision of goods, services and facilities. However, the impact of equality legislation has been constrained by the religious exemption. It must also be borne in mind that while SOGI discrimination is unlawful, there is a dearth of related caselaw because, as noted by Chapman and Mason, "the vast majority of discrimination and vilification complaints lodged in Australia under all prescribed grounds are brought to a conclusion through investigation and conciliation".[91]

Sex discrimination and sexual orientation discrimination

The Sex Discrimination Act 1984 (Cth) permits a voluntary body to discriminate against a person on certain grounds and in connection with membership and the provision of members' benefits, facilities or services.

87 The Racial Discrimination Act 1975.
88 The Sex Discrimination Act 1984 (as amended).
89 The Disability Discrimination Act 1992.
90 *Secretary, Department of Health and Community Services v. JWB and SMB (Marion's Case)* [1992] HCA 15; 1992 175 CLR 218, at para. 25.
91 Chapman, A. and Mason, G., Women, Sexual Preference and Discrimination Law: A Case Study of the NSW Jurisdiction, *Sydney Law Review*, 21(4), p. 1 (1999).

Gender identity and trans discrimination

The 1984 Act makes it unlawful to treat one person less favourably than another in a similar situation because of the gender-related identity, appearance, mannerisms or other gender-related characteristics of that person.[92] Trans vilification also breaches anti-discrimination law: vilification is defined as any public act that could encourage hatred, serious contempt or severe ridicule towards those who are trans, or who are thought to be so.

Affirmative action

This term refers to action taken that aims to foster equality by providing targeted support to offset the particular disadvantages suffered by certain specific groups.

LGBT issues and affirmative state action

The 2014 *Going Upstream* initiative,[93] launched to address SOGI issues, can be seen as an illustration of affirmative action. Recognising that the incidence of mental health problems, including suicide, disproportionately affects the LGBT community, this programme aims to specifically target the development and implementation of strategies for the promotion of mental health and well-being and the prevention of associated mental health problems towards members of that community.

Right to equality and non-discrimination: health

As a signatory nation to the UDHR, ICESRC, CEDAW and UNCROC, Australia is bound to respect and deliver on the right to health care proclaimed in these international instruments. However, there have been occasions when its SOGI-related health policies have instead attracted international criticism.

Gender reassignment treatment

In the absence of federal legislation for self-identification of a change in gender identity, procedures for legal recognition vary across the states and territories: most require evidence of having completed gender reassignment treatment, usually entailing evidence of surgical intervention. However, following the HR Committee ruling in *G v. Australia*,[94] the Australian Government Guidelines

92 See AHRC at: www.humanrights.gov.au/quick-guide/12104.

93 National LGBTI Health Alliance, *Going Upstream: A Framework for Promoting the Mental Health of Lesbian, Gay, Bisexual, Transgender and Intersex (LGBTI) People* (2014), at: www.beyondblue.org.au/docs/default-source/default-document-library/bw0257-going-upstream-online-o-lgbti-mental-health-promotion-framework.pdf.

94 CCPR/C/119/D/2172/2012 (2017).

on the Recognition of Sex and Gender Identity has now instituted a procedure for trans persons to change or establish sex and/or gender on personal records, excluding birth certificates, without having to produce evidence of hormone treatment or surgery.

Trans children

Under the Family Law Act 1975, s.67ZC, the court for many years exercised its *parens patriae* power to make orders relating to the welfare of children, most controversially in order to authorise sterilisation procedures.[95] In 2013, the Australian Senate published a report which condemned the practice of "normalising" surgeries and made 15 recommendations, including ending cosmetic genital surgery on infants and children and providing for legal oversight of individual cases.[96] Between 2004 and 2017, the federal courts considered a number of cases[97] in which its authority was sought to permit medical treatment to "normalise" genital irregularities in infants and young children.[98]

In 2004, the FCA in the *Alex* case[99] authorised stages 1 and 2 of transgender treatment for a 13-year-old. The court then ruled that only the FCA, and not parents or legal guardians, had the legal authority to authorise such treatment. Moreover, because of the nature of the treatment, no adolescent, whether or not "*Gillick* competent",[100] could give the required legal consent. For some years thereafter, this "special medical procedure" required all adolescents to seek court authorisation before they could access pubertal suppression and hormone treatment. Nine years after *Alex*, the FCA in *Lucy*[101] found that the 13-year-old subject was not "*Gillick* competent" to give a valid consent to stage 1 of the treatment process, but neither was court authorisation required; instead, it could be determined by the agencies and professionals concerned (in the absence of parents). In that same year the FCA examined the case of *Jamie*,[102] aged 11 at the initial hearing, in which the focus was squarely on whether treatment of

95 *Department of Health & Community Services v. JWB & SNB* ("Marion's Case") [1992] HCA 15 and *Re Sean and Russell (Special Medical Procedures)* [2010] FamCA 948. See further Jones, M., Intersex Genital Mutilation – A Western Version of FGM, *The International Journal of Children's Rights*, 25(2), pp. 396–411 (2017).

96 See The Senate: Community Affairs Reference Committee, *Involuntary or Coerced Sterilisation of Intersex People in Australia* (October 2013), at: http://www.aph.gov.au/~/media/Committees/Senate/committee/clac_ctte/involuntary_sterilisation/second_report/report.ashx.

97 For example, *Re Lesley (Special Medical Procedure)* [2008] FamCA 1226; *Re: Sally (Special Medical Procedure)* [2010] FamCA 237; *Re: Carla (Medical procedure)* [2016] FamCA 7; and *Re: Kaitlin* [2017] FamCA 83.

98 See further Carpenter, M., The Human Rights of Intersex People: Addressing Harmful Practices and Rhetoric of Change, *Reproductive Health Matters*, 24(47), pp. 74–84 (2016).

99 *Re Alex: Hormonal Treatment for Gender Identity Dysphoria* [2004] FamCA 297.

100 *Gillick v. West Norfolk Area Health Authority* [1985] UKHL 7; [1986] AC 112.

101 *Re: Lucy (Gender Dysphoria)* [2013] FamCA 518.

102 *Re: Jamie* [2013] FamCAFC 110.

childhood gender identity disorder constituted a medical procedure for which court authorisation was required. It concluded that such authorisation was not needed for stage 1 treatment – if the child, the parents and medical practitioners agree – but it was for stage 2, which the court found to be irreversible, even without surgical intervention. Significantly, it also ruled that, if *Gillick* competent, the child can consent to both stages 1 and 2 and no court authorisation is required. Then, again in 2013, the separate cases of *Sam and Terry*,[103] both aged 16 but neither judged to be *Gillick* competent, were jointly considered by the FCA, which concluded that parental consent was sufficient to authorise stage 1 treatment; notwithstanding the availability of parental consent, court authorisation was required for stage 2. However, in 2017, the FCA in *Kelvin*[104] reversed the *Jamie* ruling and held that its authorisation – where the consent of parents, the 16-year-old child and the medical professionals had been given – was not required for either stage 1 or 2. Moreover, the court ruled that determination of *Gillick* competence should not be its concern. Most recently, in *Matthew*,[105] the court determined that its authorisation would no longer be required for stage 3 treatment where the child is *Gillick* competent, it is agreed that the treatment is therapeutic and there is no controversy as between the parents and medical professionals. At much the same time, the AHRC launched its inquiry into the human rights of those born with variations in sex characteristics and subject to non-consensual medical intervention.[106]

The ruling in *Matthew* brought to an end Australia's reputation of being the only nation in the world that required trans teenagers to get court authorisation before they could start taking transitioning drugs. Nonetheless, as has been pointed out, the broader issue of forced and coercive medical procedures on infants, children and adolescents with intersex variations will continue until legislative reform is introduced.[107]

Sports and recreational activities

It is not unlawful to discriminate against a trans person in some circumstances relating to single-sex sport, but the law does not require sports clubs to apply the exception, and there is an absence of any related caselaw. However, the limit on the amount of testosterone transgender athletes can have before they gain an unfair advantage in competitive sports is as contentious in Australia as elsewhere.

103 *Re: Sam and Terry (Gender Dysphoria)* [2013] FamCA 563.

104 *Re: Kelvin* [2017] FamCAFC 258.

105 *Re: Matthew* [2018] FamCA 161.

106 Australian Human Rights Commission, *Protecting the Human Rights of People Born with Variations in Sex Characteristics in the Context of Medical Interventions*, 2018. See further at: www.humanrights.gov.au/our-work/lgbti/projects/protecting-human-rights-people-born-variations-sex-characteristics-context.

107 See Carpenter, M., The "Normalization" of Intersex Bodies and "Othering" of Intersex Identities in Australia, *Journal of Bioethical Inquiry*, 15 (4), pp. 487–495 (1–9 May 2018).

Blood donors

The 2012 Therapeutic Goods Administration review of blood donor rules left unchanged the 12-month deferral, from date of last sexual relationship, for donations from gay men. This unusually long deferral period is being challenged as discriminatory, given the sophisticated techniques now available to screen samples and the reliability rate of detection for HIV antibodies whether or not the donor is of LGBT status.

Right to equality and non-discrimination: education

The education sector contains a high proportion of religious-based institutions. These are permitted, under s.37 and s.38(3) of the Sex Discrimination Act 1984, to discriminate against staff and students on SOGI-related grounds provided this is done "in good faith in order to avoid injury to the religious susceptibilities of adherents of that religion". The extent to which they can do so varies across the states and territories according to the governing legislation; some, notably Tasmania, do not permit exemptions, while in others like Western Australia they are narrowly defined. This right to religious exemption has been the subject of a recent review.[108]

Currently, the government is proposing to introduce the Sex Discrimination Amendment (Removing Discrimination Against Students) Bill 2018, which will amend the 1984 Act and remove the capacity of bodies, established for religious purposes and providing education, to directly discriminate against students on the basis of their sexual orientation, gender identity or intersex status. The AHRC has formally welcomed this proposed legislation and stated that "the Bill protects the right of students to be free from discrimination on the basis of sexual orientation or gender identity by removing the ability of schools to discriminate against them on this basis".[109] For added clarity, so as to ensure that religion-based educational institutions cannot continue to rely on the general exemption in s.37(1)(d), the AHRC supports a proposed amendment specifying that the Bill is directed towards the education and training activities of educational institutions.[110] It also supports a proposal to extend the operation of the Bill to include staff and contract workers of such institutions, and suggests that this be considered as part of a broader reform of the 1984 Act.[111]

108 Ruddock P. (Chair), *Religious Freedom Review* (2018); see further at: www.ag.gov.au/RightsAndProtections/HumanRights/Documents/religious-freedom-review-expert-panel-report-2018.pdf.

109 Australian Human Rights Commission, *Sex Discrimination Amendment (Removing Discrimination Against Students) Bill 2018: Submission to the Senate Legal and Constitutional Affairs Legislation Committee* (January 2019), at para. 15.

110 Ibid., at para. 38.

111 Ibid., at para. 57.

Schools

As the AHRC has noted, educational institutions established for religious purposes are currently permitted to discriminate against students on SOGI-related grounds by measures which include[112] refusing or failing to accept the person's application for admission as a student; discriminating in relation to the terms or conditions on which the institution is prepared to admit the person as a student; denying the student access, or limiting the student's access, to any benefit provided by the institution; expelling the student; and subjecting the student to other forms of detriment.[113] Such religion-based constraints on SOGI matters[114] are reinforced by the federally funded school chaplains programme, which provides an exclusively Christian counselling service to schools across Australia.

Needless to say, trans pupils in single-sex schools face particular difficulties. While equality and non-discrimination legislation ensures their entitlement to be educated in the school for the gender with which they identify, this can cause practical problems in terms of shared washrooms, gym facilities etc.

Curricula

Christian organisations have lobbied, sometimes successfully, for the use of conceptual material relating to gender and sexuality to be prohibited in State primary schools. Faith-based schools have generally gone a step further and relied upon the exemption in s.38(3) of the Sex Discrimination Act 1984 to tailor teaching activities in accordance with the doctrines, tenets, beliefs or teachings of their particular religion or creed. The government has indicated it is prepared to protect that exemption in the proposed Sex Discrimination Amendment (Removing Discrimination Against Students) Bill 2018. This is a matter of concern for the AHRC, as it fears that to do so "could make certain forms of direct discrimination lawful, which would undermine the agreed objective of the Bill".[115]

In 2010, the Safe Schools programme was launched in Victoria, expanding nationally in 2014, to provide an education framework to help schools and teachers respond to SOGI issues and deal with homophobic and transphobic bullying and discrimination. Managed by the Safe Schools Coalition,[116] it received annual federal government funding of $8 million but has proved highly controversial. Following a government review in 2016, federal funding was withdrawn the following year. The review was largely positive; it recommended no major changes to the program and found that it was consistent with the national curriculum.

112 Citing: the Sex Discrimination Act 1984 (Cth), ss.21 and 38(3).
113 Australian Human Rights Commission, op. cit., at para. 27.
114 Also see Human Rights Law Centre, *Freedom from Discrimination in Religious Schools* (2018), at: www.hrlc.org.au.
115 Australian Human Rights Commission, op. cit., at para. 48.
116 See further at: www.safeschoolscoalition.org.au.

However, it suggested greater parental involvement and confinement to secondary schools, and it found that some aspects of the programme were inappropriate. The Safe Schools Coalition continues to deliver the programme in Western Australia and in the Northern Territories.

Colleges/universities

The tensions, evident in schools, between religious freedom and the rights of the LGBT community to equality and non-discrimination transfer into a college environment, probably in particular to the more religious institutions such as the Australian Catholic University and St Leo's Catholic College in Brisbane. For example, in November 2017, the South Coast Baptist College is reported to have removed a relief teacher from the roster after it emerged he was in a same-sex relationship.[117]

Right to equality and non-discrimination: employment

SOGI-related protection in an employment context is provided through a number of international and domestic provisions. For example, the International Labour Organisation's Discrimination (Employment and Occupation) Convention, ratified by Australia in 1973, requires the removal of employment-related discrimination on grounds which include sex. The Fair Work Act 2009 (Cth), s.351(1), prohibits any adverse action against an employee or prospective employee on grounds which include sex and sexual preference, while, from 2010, the National Employment Standards – specifically including same-sex couples – regulate employment conditions on a federal basis. Further, the Sex Discrimination Act 1984 (Cth) makes it unlawful to treat a job applicant or employee less favourably because of sexual orientation, gender identity, intersex status, appearance, mannerisms or any other gender-related characteristics. Other relevant federal legislation includes the Racial Discrimination Act 1975, the Disability Discrimination Act 1992 and the Age Discrimination Act 2004. In addition, each state and territory has its own employment-related legislation providing variable protection for SOGI-related matters.

Religious exemption

In the workplace, religious beliefs (or non-belief) have long found protection under the Human Rights and Equal Opportunity Commission Act 1986. More recently, the Sex Discrimination Amendment (Sexual Orientation, Gender

117 See further at: https://thewest.com.au/news/wa/gay-teacher-fired-by-south-coast-baptist-college-in-waikiki-sparking-debate-about-discrimination-rights-of-religious-schools-ng-b88665819z.

Identity and Intersex Status) Act 2013 very largely reaffirmed the traditional religious exemption privilege, subject to some narrowing of its scope (see next), but it specifically exempted private schools and hospitals owned by such organisations from SOGI-specific legal requirements. For those who regard this privilege with some scepticism, the comment "religious conviction is not a solvent of legal obligation",[118] made by Mason ACJ and Brennan J some 40 years ago, continues to resonate.

In *Cobaw Community Health Services Limited v. Christian Youth Camps Limited & Anor*,[119] the Court of Appeal, endorsing Hampel J's ruling, held that CYC was not "a body established for religious purposes" and therefore could not rely on the religious exemption. It found that staff selection on the basis of criteria that included an applicant's religious belief did not constitute religious discrimination for the purposes of the 1986 Act if: this is necessitated under Part (d) of the definition of "discrimination" in s.3 to ensure compliance with the doctrines, tenets, beliefs or teachings of a particular religion, and is made in good faith and in order to avoid injury to the religious susceptibilities of adherents of that religion; or is necessary to fulfil the inherent requirements of the post.[120] This narrow definition of what constitutes a religious organisation was in keeping with an earlier ruling, mentioned previously, which excluded the St Vincent de Paul Society.[121] In that case, the tribunal rejected the respondent's claim that being a Catholic was a "genuine occupational requirement" for the post of president of that society. This assertion was viewed as particularly weak given that the respondent knew that the claimant was not a Catholic, welcomed her as a member, saw her elected as president of three of its conferences, saw her inducted as a president of a conference by a priest of the church and allowed her to work without challenge for years as a conference president.

Sexual orientation in the workplace

Discrimination against lesbian, gay, bisexual, transgender and intersex people has been illegal throughout Australia since the amendment of the Sex Discrimination Act 1984 by the introduction of the Sex Discrimination Amendment (Sexual Orientation, Gender Identity and Intersex Status) Bill 2013. In *Griffin v. Catholic Education Office*,[122] for example, the complaint of a LGBTI activist teacher who had been refused employment in Catholic schools was upheld.

118 *Church of the New Faith v. Commissioner of Pay-Roll Tax (Victoria)* (1983) 154 CLR 120 at para. 136.
119 [2010] VCAT 1613 (8 October 2010).
120 See also *X v. The Commonwealth* (1999) 167 ALR 529, per Justices Gummow and Hayne; where the discrimination concerned disability rather than religion.
121 *Walsh v. St Vincent de Paul Society Queensland (No. 2)* [2008] QADT 32.
122 (1998) EOC 92–928 (HREOC).

Sexual harassment has been found to constitute sex discrimination,[123] a single act being sufficient,[124] but a claim of sexual harassment against a fellow employee must be substantiated by evidence if action subsequently taken by the employer is to be attributed to that claim.[125]

Trans persons and the workplace

The Sex Discrimination Act 1984 (Cth), s.5B, provides that a person discriminates against another person on the ground of gender identity if the discrimination occurs by reason of: the gender identity of the aggrieved person; a characteristic that applies generally to persons who have the same gender identity as the aggrieved person; or a characteristic that is generally imputed to persons who have the same gender identity as the aggrieved person. This includes trans persons and those with an intersex status. An employer is required to ensure that a trans person is able to access their preferred bathroom facility. As in other countries, not all discriminatory acts against trans persons will necessarily breach equality and non-discrimination provisions (see further below).

Employment in the military

SOGI factors have ceased to present a legal obstacle to enlistment or to conditions of service in Australia's armed forces. The prohibition on enlisting lesbian, gay or bisexual personnel was lifted in 1992, though restrictions on trans persons continued until 2010, and not until 2015 did the Australian Defence Force provide protective guidance regulations for those undergoing a trans process.

Right to equality and non-discrimination: services

A significant proportion of Australian social service provision is delivered by religious organisations, but the Marriage Amendment (Definition and Religious Freedoms) Act 2017, in keeping with the Sex Discrimination Act 1984 (as amended by the 2013 Act), exempts religious organisations from providing facilities, goods or services if to do so would compromise either their beliefs or those of their religious communities. However, s.38 of the 1984 Act ties that exemption to the "doctrines, tenets, beliefs or teachings of a particular religion or creed", thereby narrowing its potential application. Moreover, private schools and hospitals owned by religious organisations are specifically exempted under the 2013 Act from SOGI constraints.

123 *Birch v. Wesco Electrics* (1966) *Pty Ltd* (2012) 218 IR 67 [81]; citing *Aldridge v. Booth* (1988) ALR 1 [16]–[17]; *Hall v. A & A Sheiban Pty Ltd* (1989) 20 FCR 217, 274–276; *Elliott v. Nanda & Commonwealth* (2001) 111 FCR 240, 278–282.

124 *Hall v. A & A Sheiban Pty Ltd*, ibid.

125 *Evangeline v. Department of Human Services* [2013] FCCA 807.

Trans persons and gender-specific services

It is a generally accepted rule that in addition to the religious exemption, organisations have some limited scope to avoid the constraints of equality and non-discrimination legislation if they can show that to do so is absolutely necessary to the organisation's raison d'être. For example, in *Hanover Welfare Services Ltd (Anti-Discrimination Exemption)*,[126] a women's refuge residential facility applied to the relevant regulatory body seeking exemption from equality and non-discrimination legislation so as to allow that facility to be staffed and occupied exclusively by females. It also sought permission

> to refuse to provide accommodation (in the nominated facilities) to a person who identifies as a male-to-female transsexual or transgender person unless and until that person provides to the Applicant a medical certificate certifying that the person had gender reassignment surgery.

The Tribunal, which adjudicated on the matter, ruled that Hanover was so exempt, thereby allowing it to reject male-to-female transgender persons as "women" for the purposes of providing shelter.

Provision of public services

From the early years of this century, public services across Australia have undergone a systemic re-adjustment to ensure greater SOGI compliance.

From 2003, all states and territories began granting domestic partnership benefits and relationship recognition to same-sex couples, culminating in federal legal recognition for same-sex couples in 2009 and for same-sex marriage in 2017. Since April 2018, same-sex couples across Australia have been legally able to adopt children. In fact, SOGI discrimination in the provision of all public services has been prohibited in every state and territory since 1 August 2013. Gender self-identification, including non-binary status, is sufficient for amending official ID documents such as passports and driving licences, though some states and territories require evidence of reassignment surgery for birth certificate amendment. The previously-mentioned overhaul of the practice of almost routinely referring children with intersex physiological characteristics for corrective surgery is also very relevant.

Trans persons and prisons

The 2018 profile of the Australian prison population compiled by the Australian Bureau of Statistics is detailed but for present purposes is mostly interesting for

126 [2007] VCAT 640.

its omissions: there is no information relating to LGBT inmates.[127] This probably indicates either a reluctance on the part of prison authorities to disaggregate inmates on that basis, as to do so would invite related service requests, or prisoner unwillingness to reveal SOGI status for fear of personal safety – or more simply, both. In any event, there would appear to be a distinct lack of caselaw on issues comparable with those generated in the UK and US penal systems. It can only be assumed that the Indigenous people who are overrepresented in the prison system are also underrepresented in having any SOGI issues met by appropriate services when incarcerated.

Private goods and service provision

The 2013 Act prohibits discrimination on the basis of sexual orientation, or gender identity or expression – subject to the religious exemption – throughout Australia.

The provision of accommodation has proven to be as problematic in Australia as elsewhere. Essentially, unless the accommodation is for six or fewer people, then access must be available on a non-discriminatory basis: same-sex couples or trans persons should be accommodated without reservation. The 2013 Act specifically directs religious organisations providing aged care services to refrain from excluding LGBT applicants or those in a same-sex relationship, although they are exempted from SOGI legislative provisions when considering applications to their schools and hospitals.

The difficulties that may arise in determining access to community facilities were demonstrated in the previously-mentioned *OV and OW*[128] and *Cobaw* cases.[129] The first concerned the right of Wesley Mission to withhold services by not accepting an application from a same-sex couple to become foster parents. It maintained that its religious beliefs would be breached if it treated such couples the same as it did those whose status complied with the core Wesleyan doctrine of "monogamous heterosexual partnership within marriage". Ultimately, eight years after refusal of the application and following several hearings by judicial and regulatory bodies, it was held that the Wesley Mission was able to avail of the statutory exemption as, at the relevant time, its doctrines were binding upon the Mission and could be construed as religious. In the second, Christian Youth Camps, established by the Christian Brethren Trust, had declined to make its resort facilities available to Cobaw Community Health Services because of the sexual orientation of the group it was sponsoring ("Way Out", a youth suicide

127 See further at: www.abs.gov.au/ausstats/abs@.nsf/Lookup/by%20Subject/4517.0~2018~Main%20Features~Prisoner%20characteristics,%20Australia~4.

128 *OV v. QZ (No 2)* [2008] NSWADT 115; *Member of the Board of the Wesley Mission Council v. OV and OW* (No 2) [2009] NSWADTAP 57; *OV & OW v. Members of the Board of the Wesley Mission Council* [2010] NSWCA 155.

129 *Cobaw Community Health Services Limited v. Christian Youth Camps Limited & Anor* [2010] VCAT 1613 (8 October 2010).

prevention project for same-sex attracted young people). It was found that the CYC refusal would constitute discrimination unless it could avail of the religious exemption. Justice Hampel's conclusion, endorsed by the Court of Appeal,[130] was that although CYC had genuine religious beliefs it was not necessary for them to refuse the booking in order to comply with them and in taking that step they had discriminated in breach of the Act.

Pensions, social security benefits etc.

Young v. Australia,[131] a landmark decision of the UN HR Committee on recognition for sexual orientation, concerned the denial of pension benefits to the same-sex partner of a deceased war veteran. The finding that this practice breached Article 26 of the ICCPR was of international significance because the Committee pointed out that Australia had failed to provide any justification for making a distinction on the basis of "sex or sexual orientation".

The Same-Sex Relationships (Equal Treatment in Commonwealth Laws–General Law Reform) Act 2008 and the Same-Sex Relationships (Equal Treatment in Commonwealth Laws–Superannuation) Act 2008 sought to establish – on a federal basis – equal treatment for same-sex couples, and any children raised by them, in a range of areas including taxation, superannuation, health, social security, aged care and child support, immigration, citizenship and veterans' affairs. Consequently, same-sex couples now receive the same rate of social security and family assistance payments as heterosexual couples. In addition, the Family Law Amendment (De Facto Financial Matters and Other Measures) Act 2008 allows same-sex and de facto couples access to the federal Family Court on property and maintenance matters.

Conscientious objection of service providers

The range of areas in which the conscientious objection of a service provider or recipient presents a legally valid justification for refusal to engage is steadily increasing. However, the traditionally accepted right of an individual to opt out from a mass vaccination programme is now attracting considerable controversy.

SOGI, public service and conscientious objection

In some states and territories, such as Victoria, medical practitioners can refuse to undertake or participate in abortion procedures – such a refusal may also become an issue in relation to contraception, IVF-assisted dying – if to do so would be against their religious beliefs. Similar carve-outs exist in relation to SOGI issues

130 *Christian Youth Camps Limited & Ors v. Cobaw Community Health Services Limited & Ors* [2014] VSCA 75.
131 CCPR/C/78/D/941/2000; 11 IHRR 146 (2004).

such as officiating at same-sex marriages. In 2018, the AMA's Ethics and Medico-Legal Committee launched a routine, five-year review of its *Position Statement on Conscientious Objection 2013*.

Conclusion

Australia is unusual in that it is the only "western" democratic country without a national Bill of Rights. This leaves judiciary and regulators relying upon the provisions of those international treaties and conventions to which Australia is a signatory, particularly the ICCPR. Nonetheless, in some respects – legal recognition for gender self-identification, intersex status and other non-binary gender identities – it could now be said to be at the forefront of the many nations currently adjusting to SOGI challenges. In other respects it is not: most states and territories still require trans people to produce evidence of surgery when applying for an amended birth certificate; a considerable swathe of public service provision is owned by religious organisations and as such are exempt from SOGI-related equality legislation; and the federally funded school chaplains programme, providing an exclusively Christian counselling service, reinforces the religion-based constraints on SOGI matters in schools. Moreover, civil registrars are statutorily entitled to avail of the conscientious objection privilege and refuse to officiate at LGBTI marriages, and, as noted earlier, medical practitioners may also withdraw their services in SOGI-related circumstances.

9 New Zealand

Introduction

In 2016, Statistics New Zealand established a global first by providing an official statistical standard for gender identity that offers guidance for the collection, analysis and reporting of official statistics on gender identity.[1] By way of context, the Attitudes and Values Study for that year, conducted under the auspices of the University of Auckland, found that 94.2% of New Zealanders identified as straight or heterosexual, 2.6% as gay or lesbian, 1.8% bisexual, 0.6% bicurious, 0.5% pansexual and 0.3% self-identified as asexual.[2]

This, the last of the jurisdiction-specific chapters, unfolds like the others. Beginning with an outline of the relevant domestic and international legal framework, it then considers the bearing of the more fundamental human rights – justice, expression, association and religion – on SOGI-related issues before examining the impact of human rights on the more intimate aspects of personal and family life for the LGBT community. As before, the chapter devotes most of its attention to the themes of SOGI-related caselaw as established in Chapter 3: the broad effects of equality and non-discrimination legislation and its more particular application in the fields of health, education, employment and service provision. Again, in keeping with its predecessors, this chapter concludes with an assessment of the significance of conscientious objection as a legally mandated opt-out for those professionals who decline to provide services – for example, officiating at same-sex marriages or teaching SOGI awareness to school children – on grounds of religion or other personal beliefs.

Legal framework: international and domestic

New Zealand acquired a measure of independence in 1840 with the Treaty of Waitangi – *te Tiriti o Waitangi*. The broad umbrella of the Treaty now functions alongside common law, statute law, international treaties and conventions.

1 Pega, F., Reisner, S., Sell, R. and Veale, J., Transgender Health: New Zealand's Innovative Statistical Standard for Gender Identity, *American Journal of Public Health*, 107(2), pp. 217–221 (2017).

2 See further at: www.psych.auckland.ac.nz/en/about/our-research/research-groups/new-zealand-attitudes-and-values-study.html.

International legislation

New Zealand has ratified a number of international conventions relating to non-discrimination and fundamental rights for all citizens, including minority groups[3] (see further Chapter 3). It is, for example, a signatory nation to the Universal Declaration of Human Rights, but not until 2010 did New Zealand decide to endorse the UN Declaration of Rights of Indigenous Peoples.[4]

The International Covenant on Civil and Political Rights (ICCPR)

New Zealand judiciary and regulators place considerable reliance upon the ICCPR and the accompanying Human Rights Committee decisions and the guidance offered in its *Comments* (see Chapter 3).

Domestic legislation

This country has in place a not untypical domestic platform of equality legislation, including the Human Rights Act 1993, the New Zealand Bill of Rights Act 1990, the Privacy Act 1993 and the Equal Pay Act 1972 and has introduced other legislative and policy frameworks to promote equality.[5]

The Constitution

New Zealand does not have a written Constitution,[6] though together with constitutional conventions, the following comprise a body of law with an overarching constitutional effect:[7] the Treaty of Waitangi; the Constitution Act 1986; the Imperial Laws Application Act 1988; the New Zealand Bill of Rights Act 1990; and the Human Rights Act 1993.

The Treaty of Waitangi

This founding document provided a broad statement of principles for establishing and guiding the relationship between the Crown and Māori. It offers

3 International Convention on the Elimination of All Forms of Racial Discrimination; International Covenant on Civil and Political Rights; International Covenant on Economic Social and Cultural Rights.

4 On 13 September 2007, the General Assembly adopted this landmark declaration outlining the rights of the world's estimated 370 million Indigenous people and outlawing discrimination against them: 143, ember States voted in favour; 11 abstained and four – Australia, Canada, New Zealand and the United States – voted against.

5 Citizenship Act 1977; Immigration Act 1987; State Sector Act 1988; Ethnic Perspectives in Policy 2003.

6 See further at: www.justice.govt.nz/policy/constitutional-law-and-human-rights/consideration-of-constitutional-issues-1/members-of-the-constitutional-advisory-panel.

7 See further Ekins, R. and Tomkins, D., *Constitutional Theory for the Constitutional Review*, Maxim Institute, Auckland, 2013.

a "constitutional" basis for recognising legal rights and for testing government policy in respect of all citizens, but it "has to be seen as an embryo rather than a fully developed and integrated set of ideas".[8] Articles 2 and 3 provide protection for Māori culture: the first does so by reference, in the Māori version, to *taonga*, that is, "everything that is held precious", and the second by providing for Māori to have "the same rights as those of the people of England".

The Marriage (Definition of Marriage) Amendment Act 2013

Amending the Marriage Act, this statute clarified that a marriage is between two people regardless of their sex, sexual orientation or gender identity.

The Human Rights Amendment Act 2001

This restructured the Human Rights Commission and introduced additional safeguards against discrimination on grounds such as age, disability or sexual orientation in the policies and practices of government agencies.

The Employment Relations Act 2000 (ERA)

In conjunction with the Employment Contracts Act 1991 (now repealed), this legislation provides employees with the right to take allegations of discrimination to the Employment Court.

The Births, Deaths and Marriages Registration Act 1995

As amended by the Births, Deaths, Marriages, and Relationships Registration Amendment Act 2009, the 1995 Act provides for the registration of information about births, adoptions, changes of name, sexual assignment and reassignment, marriages, civil unions and deaths.

The Human Rights Act 1993 (HRA)

This statute amalgamated the Race Relations Act 1971 and the Human Rights Commission Act 1977. It prohibits discrimination on the basis of specified grounds, which include sex or sexual orientation – though not specifically gender – in employment, in partnerships, in access to places, vehicles and facilities, in the provision of goods and services and in the provision of land, housing and other accommodation.

The New Zealand Bill of Rights Act 1990 (BORA)

This crucial statute declares the right to freedom from discrimination, s.19, and states that for everyone this right is available on the grounds provided in the

8 *New Zealand Māori Council v. Attorney-General*, op. cit., per Cooke, P.

Human Rights Act 1993, while s.20 asserts the "rights of minorities". Unlike equivalent legislation elsewhere, the 1990 Act is concerned with securing the freedom of the individual from arbitrary State intervention;[9] it does not specifically include free-standing rights in relation to principles of dignity, personal autonomy or the liberty and security of the person. It applies only to the actions of government and to persons exercising public functions; where such actions are found to infringe the 1990 Act, the courts may issue "indications of inconsistency" requiring the attention of Parliament.

The Constitution Act 1986

This is a major part of New Zealand's primary constitutional legal infrastructure. It consolidated the institutional and statutory powers necessary to clarify its relationship with the UK government and monarchy and provided for more coherent domestic governance.

The Race Relations Act 1971 (RRA)

This made incitement to racial disharmony a criminal offence and presaged the setting up of the Office of the Race Relations Conciliator in 1972, which was merged with the Human Rights Commission in 2002.

Other legislation

There is a considerable range of sector-specific legislation with a bearing on equality and non-discrimination, including the Crimes Act 1961; the Private Schools Conditional Integration Act 1975; and the Employment Relations Act 2000 (which repealed the Employment Contracts Act 1991) and the Employment Relations Amendment Bill 2013. The Sentencing Act 2002, s.9(1)(h), specifically includes SOGI criteria in its definition of hate crime.

Framework of courts and regulatory bodies

The court and regulatory system of New Zealand operates as an independent, unified and self-contained juridical entity, free of external judicial scrutiny.

International courts and regulatory bodies

New Zealand is subject to the monitoring processes of the treaties and conventions – in particular those established under CERD and the ICCPR – to which it is a signatory nation. Since 2003, it has not been amenable to Privy Council appeal procedures.

9 *Mendelssohn v. Attorney-General* (1999) 2 NZLR 268 (CA) at p. 273.

Domestic courts and regulatory bodies

The New Zealand legal system is a three-tiered model closely resembling its British counterpart.

The domestic judicial and regulatory systems

The Supreme Court is the highest court in the land and ultimate court of appeal. It determines issues where leave has been granted in the interests of justice or because the matter is one of general or public importance.[10] The Court of Appeal hears appeals from civil and criminal cases heard in the courts below, including appeals on questions of law from the Employment Court, which determines cases relating to employment disputes or challenges to decisions of the Employment Relations Authority. Also relevant are the Māori Land Court and the Māori Appellate Court – *Te Kooti Whenua Māori* – which deal with Māori land matters, and the Environment Court with its remit for resource management, planning and development.

The Human Rights Commission (HRC)

Established by the Human Rights Act 1993, the Commission was subsequently restructured by the Human Rights Amendment Act 2001. Its main functions are: to provide advocacy and support for human rights, cultural diversity and equal employment opportunities; to advise on the law and practice relating to the statutory grounds for unlawful discrimination; and to resolve or adjudicate upon any issues arising in the latter context. The HRC has issued a number of significant SOGI-related reports.[11]

The Human Rights Review Tribunal (HRRT)

The Tribunal is an independent judicial body, separate from the Employment Relations Authority and Employment Court. A complaint regarding alleged discrimination begins with a dispute resolution attempt; if that fails, then it is referred to the Office of Human Rights Proceedings, after which it goes to the HRRT, which must rule on the complaint and may issue restraining orders, award monetary damages or declare a breach of the Human Rights Act (which is reported to Parliament).

10 The Supreme Court Act 2003, s.13.

11 See, for example: "To Be Who I Am: Report of the Inquiry Into Discrimination Experienced by Transgender People, He Purongo mo te Uiuitanga mo Au- katitanga e Pangia ana e nga Tangata Whakawhitiira" (2009); and SOGI and Sex Characteristics Manual for NHRIs (2016). See further at: www.hrc.co.nz/news/new-sogi-and-sex-characeristics-manual-released/.

The Office of Human Rights Proceedings

Located within the Human Rights Commission, this agency provides free legal representation to complainants, enabling selected discrimination cases to proceed to the Human Rights Review Tribunal.

The Employment Relations Authority

The task of interpreting and applying the Employment Relations Act 2000 falls to the Employment Relations Authority, the Employment Court and the New Zealand Court of Appeal.

International reports on human rights in New Zealand

The practice of surgical intervention to "normalise" children born with atypical sex characteristics attracted comment from the UN Committee on the Rights of the Child, which in 2016 declared that "New Zealand is failing its obligations towards intersex people under the Convention on the Rights of the Child".[12] The second ICCPR Universal Periodic Review in 2014 recorded concerns that included: the delay in signing or ratifying certain Conventions; the lack of any overarching protection for human rights; and the disparities experienced by Māori as demonstrated by key social and economic indicators. The 2013 CERD report in its concluding observations noted with regret that the Treaty of Waitangi is still not a formal part of domestic law[13] and urged a raising of awareness to combat existing stereotypes and prejudices against certain ethnic and religious groups.

SOGI and related core human rights

While the absence of an overarching written Constitution is perhaps a weakness, the Human Rights Act 1993 (HRA) and the New Zealand Bill of Rights Act 1990 (BORA) together provide a baseline of recognition and protection for fundamental human rights which focuses the capacity of the law to address SOGI-related issues in New Zealand.

Right of access to justice

There are obstacles to accessing justice on SOGI-related issues. There is for example no explicit reference to gender identity in the Human Rights Act 1993 – a

12 United Nations; Committee on the Rights of Child, *The Fifth Periodic Report of New Zealand* (2016), at p. 15. See further at: http://intersex.shadowreport.org/public/2016-CRC-NZ-NGO-Zwischengeschlecht-Intersex-IGM.pdf.

13 Sue Barker (note to author, 15 June 2019) comments: "It is formally recognised in a number of Acts of Parliament". See: https://trc.org.nz/treaty_legal.

significant lacuna in such a statute – nor does it provide any recognition for non-binary people.

Access to relevant information

The Privacy Act 1993 includes many principles that govern the collection, use, retention and availability of personal information, such as sexual orientation. The Statistics New Zealand decision not to include questions on SOGI status in its 2018 national population survey has attracted criticism, not least because without relevant information on numbers, differentiation and geographic spread, the health authorities will be unable to accurately plan, and direct resources towards, SOGI-related health issues.

The Births, Deaths, Marriages, and Relationships Registration Bill 2018 (deferred in 2019) proposes to introduce measures that will allow gender diverse people to more easily change the sex on their birth certificates.

An effective remedy

The Crimes Act 1961, ss.169 and 170, provides an example of law being realigned to take into account SOGI-related issues. These provisions allowed a defence of provocation (a panic response when faced by an unwanted homosexual advance) to an alleged homophobic homicide and had the effect of reducing a murder conviction to one of homicide. This was amended by the Crimes (Provocation Repeal) Amendment Act 2009, which repealed the discriminatory provisions.

Asylum seekers/illegal immigrants

New Zealand is a signatory State to the Convention Relating to the Status of Refugees 1951 (see Chapter 3). The related refugee caselaw, in common with that of other such States, is clustered around the Convention's key definitional terms. In addition, the Immigration Act 2009, s.207, states that "exceptional circumstances of a humanitarian nature" provide valid grounds of appeal against deportation.

A central Convention term is "a particular social group", the meaning of which was examined in *Re GJ*,[14] when the Refugee Status Appeals Authority found that because sexual orientation is a characteristic which is either innate or unchangeable, or so fundamental to identity or to human dignity that an individual should not be forced to forsake or change the characteristic, it can therefore form the basis for the existence of a particular social group. This case concerned a gay man who claimed to fear SOGI-related persecution if he were returned to his native Iran. The Authority judged it crucial to establish whether homosexuals in Iran constituted a particular social group for Convention purposes. It therefore

14 Refugee Appeal No. 1312/93 (1995).

received and reviewed at length considerable expert evidence which demonstrated that because homosexuals were reviled by the Iranian authorities, discriminated against[15] and singled out for the most severe punishments, including execution, such persons could be held to come within the intended meaning of that Convention term.[16] By way of copper-fastening its reasoning, the Authority warned that it would be unreasonable to expect a gay person to avoid being classed as a member of such a group by concealing his homosexuality because "to expect of him the total denial of an essential part of his identity would be both inappropriate and unacceptable".[17] This rationale was subsequently applied, achieving the same effect, by the Immigration and Protection Tribunal in the similar case of *AO (Pakistan)*.[18]

The Convention requires that a refugee's "fear of persecution" on being returned to their country of origin must be "well-founded". The importance of establishing this, by objective standards, was demonstrated in *AM (Egypt)*,[19] when the Tribunal held the gay claimant had a well-founded fear of being persecuted in Egypt because his sexual orientation constituted membership of "a particular social group", the members of which were exposed to harm, as men suspected of being gay in Egypt were at risk of being subjected to imprisonment and serious physical abuse. A "well-founded fear of persecution" also provided successful grounds for appeal against the deportation of a married female couple in *Re Devi, Sangeeta*.[20] They were able to convince the Tribunal that the difficulties they would experience if they were to be returned to Fiji – in living openly as a gay couple and caring for a teenage daughter – would make their deportation unjust and unduly harsh.

Right to freedom of expression

This right is given express recognition in BORA, s.14, which declares that "everyone has the right to freedom of expression, including the freedom to seek, receive, and impart information and opinions of any kind in any form". This broadly worded right – encompassing free speech, a free press, social media, the sharing of ideas and information – was examined in *Living Word Distributors Ltd v. Human Rights Action Group Inc (Wellington)*,[21] which considered whether certain videos were sufficiently objectionable to breach the prohibition on sexual orientation discrimination in the HRA, s.21(1). The Court of Appeal concluded that while some material may breach the right to non-discrimination of some

15 Ibid., citing Refugee Appeal No. 3/91 *Re ZWD* (20 October 1992), paras. 70–73.
16 Ibid., paras. 59–85.
17 Note that the ICCPR, Articles 2, 17 and 26 entitle an asylum appellant not to have to suppress their sexuality in order to avoid persecution.
18 [2013] NZIPT 800322.
19 [2014] NZIPT 800656.
20 [2015] NZIPT 501973.
21 [2000] 3 NZLR 570.

individuals, this was insufficient, in this case, to cross the threshold of a State responsibility to protect the right of citizens to freedom of expression.

The moral majority

The 2002 decision of the UN HR Committee, in *Joslin v. New Zealand*[22] (see further below), to uphold the domestic court's refusal of a marriage licence to a lesbian couple was one which – in the absence of same-sex marriage legislation – favoured the moral majority as it then was in New Zealand. Coming 20 years after the ECtHR decision in *Dudgeon*,[23] it seemed to refute the rationale asserted in the latter case that to defend traditional cultural norms rather than allow an expression of human rights in relation to sexual orientation was to condone discrimination. Arguably, it marked a low point in the Committee's jurisprudence.

Missing from the caselaw is a Māori perspective – at any point in time and in relation to any SOGI issue.

Harm to others

Any exercise of free speech is conditional upon it not violating the HRA, s.61, which gives effect to Article 19 of the ICCPR by prohibiting expression that is "threatening, abusive, or insulting" and is considered "likely to excite hostility against or bring into contempt a person or group of persons on the ground of their colour, race or ethnic or national origins". Nor should any such expression be blasphemous as defined under the Crimes Act, s.123;[24] New Zealand is one of the few common law countries that have yet to repeal their blasphemy laws. While neither statute makes any specific reference to gender identity (the HRA mentions sexual orientation in s.21(m)(1)), the Sentencing Act 2002, s.9(1)(h), does make SOGI-related harmful conduct a hate crime.

Right to freedom of association and assembly

The right to peaceful assembly and to freedom of association is protected by the ICCPR, Articles 21 and 22 respectively, to which New Zealand is a signatory nation, while BORA, s.17, guarantees everyone "the right to freedom of association".

Constraints

Restrictions on the exercise of this right have been most usually on the grounds of prohibition where the purpose is deemed criminal or likely to present a threat

22 Communication No 902/1999 (2002).

23 *Dudgeon v. United Kingdom*, Application No. 7525/76 (1981).

24 Sue Barker points out that that s.123 was repealed by s/5 of the Crimes Amendment Act 2019.

to public order or safety. There have been few issues and an absence of caselaw in relation to LGBT associations and marches in New Zealand. However, the build-up of tensions associated with "identity politics" – exacerbated by the 2019 atrocity – is likely to trigger constraints in SOGI and other contexts as government searches for ways of ensuring protection for those who choose to assemble and associate for peaceful purposes.

Right to freedom of religion

BORA, s.15, provides for the right of any person to manifest their religion or belief in worship, observance, practice or teaching, either individually or in community, in public or in private. As with other BORA rights, this is one that under s.5 "may be subject only to such reasonable limits prescribed by law as can be demonstrably justified in a free and democratic society". Its exercise should be accommodated where feasible[25] but may be "modified in the public interest to take account of the rights of others and of the interests of the whole community".[26] The right to practice religion in general, and in particular the right of Muslims to do so, suffered its cruellest abuse on 15 March 2019 when 51 worshipers in two Christchurch mosques were massacred by a lone gunman.[27]

SOGI and religion

New Zealand has no legislative equivalent to the UK Racial and Religious Hatred Act 2006, which prohibits the inciting of hatred on the grounds of religion.

Religious organisations and the religious exemption

An exemption from equality and non-discrimination legislative provisions, on grounds of religion or belief, is available to religious organisations and is widely used to avoid SOGI-related legal requirements in many different contexts, including employment (see further below).

This exemption is established principally in BORA and the HRA but is also recognised in such legislation as the Education Act 1964; the Charities Act 2005; and the Marriage (Definition of Marriage) Amendment Act 2013. It privileges not just religious institutions but extends also to their offshoots, such as schools, hospitals and other health and social care facilities.

SOGI: personal relationships and human rights

New Zealand's reputation for demonstrating leadership by legally adjusting traditional familial roles, which began 130 years ago when it became the first country

25 *Feau v. Department of Social Welfare* (1995) 2 HRNZ 528.
26 *Noort v. MOT* [1992] 3 NZLR 260, at p. 283.
27 See further at: www.tvnz.co.nz/one-news/new-zealand/christchurch-terrorist-attack-death-toll-reaches-51-reports.

to grant women the right to vote, has continued with initiatives such as legalising abortion in 1977, de-criminalising homosexuality in 1985, enabling same-sex marriage in 2013 and in its recent introduction of non-binary registration.

Right to an identity

The capacity to self-identify – as a person and as one with a distinctive SOGI status – and to have that identity affirmed in law would seem to be gradually acquiring international recognition as a basic human right. ID documentation such as passports and birth certificates and changing names at schools and universities have often presented problems, but a proposed law[28] to permit self-identification in New Zealand was deferred by the government early in 2019 to allow for more comprehensive consideration of the legal implications of a self-declaration model and for formal public consultation.

Trans recognition in law

Until relatively recently, a trans person needed to provide evidence of medical intervention, sufficient to substantiate "physical confirmation" of their acquired gender, if they were to be issued with an appropriately changed birth certificate.[29] This was challenged in *Michael v. Registrar-General of Births*,[30] which concerned a person born female who self-identified as male from an early age, dressed in male clothing from the age of 9 and had been sexually attracted to females since puberty. In 2004 he was diagnosed by a psychiatrist as having gender dysphoria and underwent breast surgery (but not genital reconstruction surgery) and testosterone hormone treatment, after which he lived as a man for some years. Ultimately he sought official recognition for that gender status in an amended birth certificate and, on being refused, turned to the Family Court, requesting that it issue a declaration requiring the Registrar-General to make the amendment.[31] The issue for the court was whether the extent of Michael's treatment was sufficient to satisfy the requirement in the Births, Deaths, and Marriages Registration Act 1995, s.28, which declared that a birth certificate should contain the person's "nominated sex" if it was satisfied, on the basis of expert medical evidence, that the applicant "has assumed (or has always had) the gender identity of a person of the nominated sex, and has undergone such medical treatment as is usually regarded by medical experts as desirable". The court found that Parliament did not intend that all available procedures, including full genital surgery, should be necessary to satisfy the test, but that the "applicant's degree of comfort with, or physical conformity to their nominated gender identity is the proper focus of treatment decisions" and stated that what was intended was a case

28 The Births, Deaths, Marriages and Relationships Registration Bill.
29 Births, Deaths, Marriages and Relationships Registration Act 1995, s28(3)(c)(i)(B).
30 (2008) 27 FRNZ 58.
31 Births, Deaths and Marriages Registration Act 1995, s.30.

by case assessment of whether the steps taken satisfied the test.[32] It concluded that Michael could be given a new birth certificate reflecting his male sex but that under certain circumstances information about the change of sex would be disclosed by the Registrar-General, who could permit another person to inspect the records if the purpose was to investigate "whether or not the parties to a proposed marriage are a man and a woman". This significant decision determined that female-to-male transsexuals will not, in all cases, have to undergo full gender reassignment surgery in order to obtain an appropriately amended birth certificate.[33] Since 2013 it has been unnecessary to produce evidence of surgical intervention in order to change the declared gender identity on a passport.[34]

In 2018, a government select committee recommended changes to the process for amending gender on a person's birth certificate to allow people to change their gender identity on a birth certificate by signed declaration, rather than the current system involving a Family Court, in line with existing procedures for similarly amending other ID documentation such as passports and driving licenses. This recommendation, although welcomed by the HRC, was deferred by the government in 2019. Changes to gender on birth certificates currently still require Family Court authorisation with supporting medical evidence.

Non-binary gender identity

For some years, non-binary registration has been available on a variety of official documentation: the Department of Internal Affairs has been prepared to issue a birth certificate identifying the subject as being of "indeterminate" sex if there is evidence that neither "male" nor "female" is appropriate; while a similar designation on passports has been possible since 2012. In 2015, Statistics New Zealand introduced a new gender identity classification which included a gender diverse grouping comprising four different sub-categories.

Right to respect for private and family life

Due perhaps to its indigenous Māori community, its proximity to Pacific Rim cultures and the assimilation of successive waves of European and Asian immigrants, New Zealand has a well-established, flexible approach towards, and respect for, the different configurations that may constitute family life.

Sexual orientation, identity and private life

Sexual conduct between consenting same-sex adults was de-criminalised in 1986 under the Homosexual Law Reform Act. The Civil Union Act 2004 gave

32 Ibid., at paras. 68 and 71.

33 See further Seuffert, N., Case Comment: *"Michael" v. Registrar-General of Births, Deaths and Marriages*, at: www.nzlii.org/nz/journals/WkoLawRw/2009/7.pdf.

34 The Department of Internal Affairs, Information for Transgender Applicants, at: www.dia.govt.nz.

same-sex couples the same legal status as marriage and in 2013 the Marriage (Definition of Marriage) Amendment Act defined marriage in inclusive terms regardless of gender.

Family life

Some of the family support strategies pioneered in New Zealand – such as kinship adoption for children and family conferences – have contributed greatly to informing modern professional practice in the developed countries. Arguably, the early focus on "openness" has allowed evolving domestic practice to be particularly receptive and accepting of SOGI-related issues.

Private life, gender reassignment and divorce

The Births, Deaths and Marriages Registration Act 1995, s.30(2), required a trans person – married to a person of the same sex – to be divorced before they could be issued with documentation – such as a birth certificate – which officially registered them in their acquired gender identity. This was eventually repealed by the Marriage (Definition of Marriage) Amendment Act 2013.

SOGI, parenting and "the best interests of the child" principle

It is clear that in any parental dispute regarding the custody of a child, the best interests of that child will always be the main priority. From an early stage caselaw has established that a trans father can have access rights to his children under certain conditions – such as therapy for the children.[35] The HRC advise that:

> If, for any reason, living with a same sex couple would be detrimental to the child/children, then this should be taken into consideration when deciding on custody rights. In no case should the sexual orientation of either parent be the sole reason for making a final decision on which parent is awarded custody.[36]

Right to marriage and to found a family

Following a succession of cases in which the judiciary wrestled with new definitions of "family" and with the problems entailed in transposing familiar concepts into a reconfigured and more challenging social and legal landscape,[37] the Court

35 *C v. D* (1991) 8 FRNZ 338.

36 See further at: www.hrc.co.nz/our-work/sexual-orientation-and-gender-identity/faqs/.

37 See, for example: *VP v. PM* (1998) 16 FRNZ 61 (lesbian mother retains custody of two children); *Re An Application by T* [1998] NZFLR 769 (second parent adoption by lesbian mother of partner's child by donor insemination refused); *A v. R* [1999] NZFLR 249 (non-biological mother in *Re An Application by T*, ibid., held liable for child support payments as a step-parent); and *Re application of AMM and KJO to adopt a child* [2010] NZFLR 629 ("spouse" includes de facto heterosexual couples).

of Appeal in *Quilter*[38] considered same-sex marriage and held that the Marriage Act 1955 was incompatible with the anti-discrimination standards set out in s.19 of BORA and s.21 of the HRA.

Legal recognition for same-sex relationships and the right to marry

Quilter v. Attorney-General[39] concerned three lesbian couples who claimed that the reading of the Marriage Act 1955 as excluding same-sex couples – and therefore denying such couples the right to marry – was discriminatory. The court found that while BORA proclaimed the freedom from discrimination on grounds listed in the HRA – which include sex and sexual orientation – it did not define "discrimination" as such. Tipping J was of the view that even if there was discrimination inherent in the 1955 Act, the court could not intervene: it was bound by the traditional interpretation of marriage as construed in that Act, and it fell to the legislature and not the court to change that interpretation. Two of the couples subsequently took their case to the United Nations Human Rights Committee, claiming that the ban on same-sex marriage violated the ICCPR, but their claim was rejected.[40]

Not until the Civil Union Act 2004 was equality of rights for same-sex and heterosexual couples established. This was followed almost immediately by the Relationships (Statutory References) Act 2005, which extended that principle to most other legislation. Despite several legislative initiatives in the aftermath of the 1998 ruling in *Quilter*, statutory enactment of same-sex marriage was delayed until 17 April 2013, when Parliament passed the Marriage (Definition of Marriage) Amendment Act 2013.[41] In that same year the HRRT, in *Gay and Lesbian Clergy Anti-Discrimination Society Inc v. Bishop of Auckland*,[42] ruled that the religious exemption in s.39 of the HRA remained unaffected by the 2013 Act (see further below) and noted that

> while the State is free to determine what according to the secular law of the land is to be defined as marriage, the Anglican Church is free to decide how it will define marriage for the purposes of its own doctrine and teachings.

It therefore followed that the Act "did not amend the doctrine of any church, including in particular that of the Anglican Church, regarding the sacrament of marriage as conceived by that church"[43] and consequently the refusal to permit

38 *Quilter v. Attorney-General* [1998] 1 NZLR 523 1.
39 [1998] 1 NZLR 523.
40 *Joslin et al. v. New Zealand*, Communication No 902/1999 (2002).
41 Note also the Human Rights Commission, *To Be Who I Am: Report of the Inquiry Into Discrimination Experienced by Transgender People* (January 2008).
42 [2013] NZHRRT 36.
43 Ibid., at paras. 31 and 39.

the ordination of a person in a homosexual relationship as priest or deacon in the Anglican Church did not constitute discrimination on the grounds of sexual orientation.

Trans persons and marriage

M v. M[44] concerned the validity of a marriage of a trans person (mtf) who, following sex-reassignment surgery, had then married as a woman.[45] The marriage was upheld as valid on the grounds that the surgery had been sufficiently extensive to achieve physiological gender transformation. The need to have the characteristics of the acquired gender identity was reinforced by the Births, Deaths and Marriages Registration Act 1995. However, in *Attorney-General v. Otahuhu Family Court*,[46] the court took a broader view of what constituted a sexual relationship and was therefore prepared to reconsider the legal significance of being able to consummate a marriage. It suggested that neither sexual capacity nor procreation were legally essential for marriage and consequently transformative surgery need not be required as there was "no social advantage in the law not recognizing the validity of the marriage of a transsexual in the sex of reassignment". The court determined that an individual had the right to change their legal gender status without undergoing gender reassignment surgery.

Adoption, surrogacy and child care

The Marriage (Definition of Marriage) Amendment Act 2013 was enacted with a provision enabling eligible married same-sex parents to adopt children; however, existing adoption legislation presented obstacles. This had been evident in *Re AMM*,[47] when the court demonstrated a willingness to extend the meaning of "two spouses" in the Adoption Act 1955 to include opposite-sex couples in a stable committed relationship, but doubted whether this interpretation could stretch to include same-sex couples. Such doubts were confirmed by the HR Review Tribunal ruling in *Adoption Action Incorporated v. Attorney-General*[48] that the Adoption Act 1955 and the Adult Adoption Information Act 1985 contradicted the Human Rights Act and the Bill of Rights Act by discriminating against people based on sex, age, marital status and disability. Among other consequences, this outdated adoption legislation prevented same-sex unmarried couples from adopting. Not until the McHardy J decision, in *Application by SJD & TYW*,[49] did judicial interpretation of eligibility change. His ruling, that the phrase

44 [1991] NZFLR 337 (FC).
45 See further MacKenzie, R., Transsexuals' Legal Sexual Status and Same Sex Marriage in New Zealand: *M v. M*, *Otago Law Review*, 7, pp. 556, 557–558 (1992).
46 [1995] 1 NZLR 603.
47 [2010] NZFLR 629.
48 [2016] NZHRRT 9.
49 [2015] NZFC 9404.

"two spouses" should include same-sex de facto couples, not just those who are legally married, so as not to discriminate on the grounds of sexual orientation and thereby breach the HRA, was a landmark decision for New Zealand adoption law.

The fact that same-sex couples, married or unmarried, are now eligible to adopt presents traditional faith-based adoption agencies with the same forced choice as faced by their counterparts in the US and UK. Catholic Social Services in Christchurch and the Latter Day Saints Social Services, for example, are restricted by their religious beliefs in the range of services they can offer. Specifically, although both engage in ancillary adoption work, their discriminatory beliefs exclude the possibility of contracting with same-sex prospective adopters, and they are therefore excluded from registration and regulation by government as adoption agencies.

Adoption, surrogacy and IVF are often linked in practice and increasingly so in legal proceedings. This has resulted in many lesbian couples raising children and being facilitated by the Care of Children Act 2004.

Right to cultural life

The deeply rooted Māori community, with its distinctive culture and spiritual beliefs recognised and protected by the Treaty of Waitangi, has long offered a resolute counterpoint to the values, practices and laws of their westernised immigrant neighbours. The Māori term *takatāpui* (or *takataapui*), meaning a devoted partner of the same sex, preceded the European colonisation of New Zealand and perhaps prepared the ground for an acceptance of contemporary SOGI-related issues.

Cultural context

Adhar refers to "a steady pattern of dismantling . . . historic Christian remnants from the public square" accompanied by "a privileging of Maori spirituality".[50] The recognition given to Māori culture and beliefs, evident for many years in the *haka* rugby ritual, has also been affirmed more recently by the State in practices such as inclusive references in national ceremonies, in environmental and planning legislation, in the performance of *hikitapu* or spiritual cleansing rituals in overseas embassies, and in the increasing use of *karakia* (prayers) to commence court proceedings or public meetings. The healthier tension now growing between a Māori cultural imperative and western social mores, laws and institutions would seem conducive to a broad acceptance of SOGI differences, as is perhaps confirmed by the absence of much related caselaw.

50 See further Adhar, R. T., *The Religious Demography of New Zealand*, p. 547, at: www.iclrs.org/content/blurb/files/New%20Zealand.pdf.

SOGI: non-discrimination, affirmative action and equality

In the *Quilter* case,[51] the Court of Appeal noted that equality is one of the core principles underlying New Zealand's law on discrimination, even though that law contains no express reference to it. As Tipping J then observed, discrimination is discerned in "the difference of treatment in comparable circumstances. For discrimination to occur one person or groups of persons must be treated differently from another person or group of persons".

Equality before the law: sexuality and gender discrimination

A Crown Law opinion issued in 2006 confirmed that sex discrimination may also include discrimination on the basis of gender identity,[52] while the HRC has stated that intersex people are covered by the anti-discrimination provisions of the HRA.[53]

Sex discrimination and sexual orientation discrimination

The prohibition of discrimination on the grounds of sex and sexual orientation in the HRA, s.21, and in BORA, s.19, was examined in some detail in the previously-mentioned *Quilter* case. The proportion of annual complaints to the EEO Commission concerning sexual orientation is very small (approx. 2%),[54] and there is a dearth of related caselaw.

Gender identity and trans discrimination

There is no explicit reference to trans persons or to gender identity in the HRA. However, a prohibition on discrimination on the basis of gender is believed to be implied in the reference to sex and sexual orientation under s.21(1)(m) of the HRA, and it is mentioned in the Sentencing Act 2002, s. 30 of the Electronic Identity Verification Act 2012 and in an amendment to the Marriage Act 1955.

51 *Quilter v. Attorney-General*, op. cit.

52 "You have asked whether prohibition of discrimination on grounds of gender identity is already provided for in the Human Rights Act. In my view, it is". Crown Law Office "Opinion on Human Rights (Gender Identity) Amendment Bill" (Crown Law Office, Wellington, 2006), para 2.

53 Human Rights Commission, at: www.hrc.co.nz/our-work/sexual-orientation-and-gender-identity/faqs/.

54 See further at: www.neon.org.nz/trackingequalityatwork/sexualorientation/.

Affirmative action

BORA, s.19(2), states that:

> Measures taken in good faith for the purpose of assisting or advancing persons or groups of persons disadvantaged because of discrimination that is unlawful by virtue of Part II of the Human Rights Act 1993 do not constitute discrimination.

This and similar provisions in the HRA require, as a pre-condition, that any such measures are actually needed: the intended recipients must be disadvantaged relative to others; and they must need, or be reasonably supposed to need, assistance in order to achieve equality.[55]

LGBT issues and affirmative State action

The "affirmative action" mandated by s.73 of HRA and the above s.19(2) of BORA is most often deployed to facilitate access to tertiary education for Māori or those from other Polynesian ethnic groups. There is little evidence of State-sponsored programmes being similarly targeted towards the LGBT community. That said, the 2018 government investment of resources intended to reduce costs and waiting times for gender reassignment surgery could be seen in terms of affirmative action.[56]

Right to equality and non-discrimination: health

Reports indicate deficiencies in the provision of health services to the LGBT community in New Zealand:[57] insufficient research has been undertaken on best practice to improve health outcomes.[58] Studies have found significant gaps in health service provision,[59] while discrimination and stigma remain a problem resulting in poorer general health status for that community, a lower utilisation of health care facilities and a decreased quality of health services.[60] In particular,

55 See *Amaltal Fishing Co Ltd. v. Nelson Polytechnic (No.2)* (1996) 2 HRNZ 225 and *Avis Rent A Car Ltd v. Proceedings Commissioner* (1998) 5 HRNZ 501.

56 See further at: www.theguardian.com/society/2018/oct/19/new-zealand-reduces-30-year-wait-for-gender-reassignment-surgery.

57 See Women's Health Action Trust, UPR Submission on the Right to Health, *Improving the Health of Women in Aotearoa, New Zealand*, at: https://studylib.net/doc/6758210/improving-the-health-of-women-in-aotearoa-new-zealand.

58 Garcia, T. C., Primary Care of the Lesbian/Gay/Bisexual/Transgendered Woman Patient. *International Journal Fertility Women's Medicine*, 48(6), pp. 246–251 (2003).

59 Adams, J., Dickinson, P. and Asiasiga, L., *Mental Health Promotion and Prevention Services to Gay, Lesbian, Bisexual, Transgender and Intersex Populations in New Zealand: Needs Assessment Report*, Te Pou o Te Whakaaro Nui, Wellington, 2012.

60 Coker, T. R., Austin, S. B. and Schuster, M. A., The Health and Health Care of Lesbian, Gay, and Bisexual Adolescents. *Annual Review of Public Health*, 31, pp. 457–477 (2010).

"transgender people are often over represented in poor health outcomes. Few of these poor outcomes are caused by a transgender identity itself, but rather by discrimination from *whānau*, health services and those in wider society".[61]

Gender reassignment treatment

A diagnosis of gender identity disorder is most often a gateway requirement for entry into the gender reassignment process. The cost of health care can be a significant barrier: mental health professional input may be required for further treatment but is not government funded, limiting the service to those who can afford it. The costs of reassignment surgery together with lengthy waiting lists have forced many to complete the trans process overseas.[62]

In order to change their name and gender on official documents, including birth certificates, a trans person must provide medical evidence that they have "acquired a physical conformation that accords with their gender identity". This used to be legally interpreted as requiring evidence of surgery, but since the 2008 ruling in *Michael v. Registrar-General of Births*,[63] this is no longer essential.

Trans children

The Human Rights Commission's 2007 inquiry into trans discrimination[64] highlighted issues for children and young people, including barriers within schools, at work, playing sport, accessing health services and actively participating in their community. The recommended amendments to the Births, Deaths and Marriages Registration Act 1995, suggested by the Government Administration Select Committee in 2018 – permitting trans self-identification without evidence of medical intervention and extending this right to 16- and 17-year-old minors acting with the consent of parents and doctors – was deferred by government.

The long history of recourse to conversion therapy will end should the Prohibition of Conversion Therapy Bill 2018 ever become law. This Bill proposes to create an offence for any person who advertises, offers or performs conversion therapy on another person, or who removes another person from New Zealand for the purposes of conversion therapy.[65]

61 Ministry of Health, *Delivering Health Services to Transgender People: Advice to Health Professionals* (January 2019), at: www.health.govt.nz/our-work/preventative-health-wellness/delivering-health-services-transgender-people.

62 In the 1990s, New Zealand was a world leader in reassignment surgery, but by 2014 it had a 30-year-long waiting list.

63 (2008) 27 FRNZ 58.

64 Human Rights Commission, *To Be Who I Am: Report of the Inquiry Into Discrimination Experienced by Transgender People*, Wellington (2007).

65 Sue Barker comments: "there is no guarantee this will happen" (note to author, 15 June 2019).

Sports and recreational activities

The generally open and accepting social attitudes towards SOGI matters is increasingly evident across the range of New Zealand sports, with the All Blacks rugby demonstrating leadership in this field.[66] The absence of any related caselaw does not mean that the contention surrounding testosterone levels and hormone treatment for trans athletes is any less in New Zealand than elsewhere.[67]

Blood donors

The deferment period of 12 months of chastity, required before donations will be accepted from gay blood donors, is viewed by many in the LGBT community as discriminatory.

Right to equality and non-discrimination: education

The national education system was established by the Education Act 1877.

Schools

There are three main types of schools in New Zealand, providing education at primary and secondary levels, including immersion in Māori language and culture: State (public) schools (catering for approx. 85% of all students); State-integrated, mainly Catholic (12%); and private or independent schools.[68] There is no caselaw evidence of SOGI-related discrimination in any of these settings. However, in 2010 the HRC received a complaint from a gay netball coach who was fired from a Christchurch Christian school. The 28-year-old man was employed as a girls' netball coach but was dismissed by the board of trustees after members discovered his sexual orientation. The school principal said that the board had decided the coach's homosexuality was a problem. The sacked coach complained to the Commission and the matter was resolved through mediation.[69]

A report on bullying in schools found that lesbian, gay, bisexual, transgender, intersex and questioning (LGBTIQ) young people are overrepresented in bullying statistics.[70] Also, there has been some media attention about the installation of gender-neutral bathrooms in schools.[71]

66 See, for example, www.pinknews.co.uk/2018/04/27/new-zealand-rugby-rainbow-jerseys-lgbt-video-campaign-diversity/.

67 See the controversy regarding weightlifter Laurel Hubbard at: www.newshub.co.nz/home/new-zealand/2018/04/transgender-weightlifter-laurel-hubbard-might-have-unfair-advantage-expert.html.

68 See New Zealand Ministry of Education, *Roll by Education Regional & Authority*, 2015.

69 See further at: www.neon.org.nz/trackingequalityatwork/sexualorientation/.

70 New Zealand Ministry of Education, *Bullying Prevention and Response: A Guide for Schools*, 2015, p. 22. See further at: www.hrc.co.nz/files/5714/3226/0531/MOEBullyingGuide2015Web.pdf.

71 See further at: www.stuff.co.nz/dominion-post/news/wellington/77457959/wellington-high-onslow-college-get-genderneutral-bathrooms.

Curricula

Government has declared sexuality education to be one of seven key areas of learning in the health and physical education learning area of "The New Zealand Curriculum" and has mandated it for inclusion in teaching programmes at both primary and secondary school levels.[72] While the content is not explicitly SOGI oriented, it does require an affirming of diversity and the questioning of gender stereotypes.

Colleges/universities

Tertiary education is mainly available through eight universities, 16 polytechnics and institutes of technology. There would appear to be no SOGI-related caselaw emanating from this context.

Right to equality and non-discrimination: employment

The HRA, s.21 and s.22, prohibits discrimination in employment on grounds that include sex and sexual orientation, while the Employment Relations Act 2000 declares that employers may not discriminate when hiring, dismissing or retiring employees on a direct or indirect basis of the prohibited grounds of s.21.[73]

Religious exemption

The HRA, s.22(1)(c), stipulates that it is unlawful for an employer to terminate the employment of an employee by reason of the employee's religious beliefs (in circumstances in which the employment of other employees employed on work of that description would not be terminated). S.28 provides specific "exceptions for purposes of religion" to the anti-discrimination provisions, but their scope is uncertain due to both the broad legal interpretation now given to "religion" and to Mallon J's generous interpretation in *Liberty Trust* of activities that may be seen as "outworkings" of religious faith. Exemption is also available under the Marriage Act 1955, s.29, as amended by the New Zealand Marriage (Definition of Marriage) Amendment Act 2013, through the addition of s.2, to excuse churches and clergy from the obligation to solemnise marriages contrary to their religious beliefs. A similar exemption exists in relation to religion and conscience in the Contraception, Sterilization and Abortion Act 1977, s.46.

The general exemption, extended to religious organisations under s.28(2) of the HRA, from the prohibition against discrimination in relation to employment,

72 See New Zealand Ministry of Education, *Sexuality Education in the New Zealand Curriculum*, at: http://health.tki.org.nz/Teaching-in-HPE/Policy-guidelines/Sexuality-education-a-guide-for-principals-boards-of-trustees-and-teachers/Sexuality-education-in-The-New-Zealand-Curriculum.

73 No SOGI-related cases have been recorded in recent years by the Employment Court of New Zealand in its annual list of Judgements of Note at: www.employmentcourt.govt.nz/judgments/judgments-of-note/judgments-of-note-2/.

is specifically focused on grounds of sex (including sexual orientation) with respect to the appointment of clergy in s.39:

> (1) Nothing in section 38 shall apply where the authorisation or qualification is needed for, or facilitates engagement in, a profession or calling for the purposes of an organised religion and is limited to one sex or to persons of that religious belief so as to comply with the doctrines or rules or established customs of that religion.

In 2003, the Human Rights Commission sought the opinion of four experts on this exemption and its effect on the employment of gay and lesbian clergy and concluded that the HRA allows churches to discriminate on grounds of sex (including sexual orientation) with respect to the appointment of clergy to parish positions, though not to lay people e.g. doing pastoral work. Hospital chaplains are employees but are usually employed by hospitals or district health boards.[74] Ten years later the matter was revisited in the HR Review Tribunal hearing of the *Gay and Lesbian Clergy Anti-Discrimination Society Inc v. Bishop of Auckland*,[75] which concerned a gay man who alleged he had been barred from training to become an Anglican priest because he was in an "active" homosexual relationship. To become a priest in the Anglican Church an applicant must be single and celibate, or in a heterosexual marriage, which the court found to be a valid requirement notwithstanding the introduction of the Marriage (Definition of Marriage) Amendment Act 2013. It further found that s.39(1) provided an exemption for the Church (and all organised religions) in their ordaining of ministers but did not allow sexual orientation to be a ground of discrimination for a qualifying body (i.e. the Anglican Church) and was unaffected by the 2013 Act. The plaintiff's claim of indirect discrimination on the grounds of sexual orientation was dismissed.

Sexual orientation in the workplace

Discrimination on the grounds of sexual orientation is prohibited under the HRA, s.21, in any context, including the workplace. Where discrimination is alleged, the onus rests on the employer to show justification on grounds of "exception"[76] or "good reason";[77] under s.97, a "genuine occupational qualification (GOQ)" would constitute justification but only if the employer can show a functional link between the GOQ and the job requirements.[78] An

74 Author acknowledges advice from Bill Atkins on this matter (email comment, 31 January 2017).
75 [2013] NZHRRT 36. See further at: www.justice.govt.nz/tribunals/human-rights-review-tribunal.
76 Human Rights Act 1993, s.92F(2). See *Claymore Management Ltd v. Anderson* [2003] 2 NZLR 537.
77 Human Rights Act 1993, s.65.
78 *Claymore Management Ltd v. Anderson*, op. cit.

exemption from the prohibition on discrimination, including on the ground of sexual orientation, is available in respect of domestic employment in a private household.[79] The caselaw, such as it is, in this field is focused more on sex discrimination than on SOGI issues,[80] though the Employment Relations Authority does record a 2007 case of discrimination on grounds of sexual orientation. This concerned an Auckland publishing company employee who was found to have been hurt and humiliated due to infantile teasing in the workplace about his being gay.[81]

Trans persons and the workplace

The Human Rights Commission Inquiry Into Discrimination Experienced by Transgender People in 2008 confirmed that trans people face significant discrimination in day to day life. Consequently, the government has issued guidance to aid good practice for employers and employees in relation to gender transitioning.[82] The fact that some bad practice continues was illustrated in *Hemmingston v. Swan t/a Barker's Groom Room*,[83] which concerned the alleged unfair dismissal of a trans woman who worked as a hairdresser. The Employment Relations Tribunal (ERA) found that the employer had approached the situation with a pre-determined view that the employee's decision to transition did not suit the business.

Employment New Zealand has advised that

> an employee should be able to use facilities that match their gender identity, for example: trans women should be able to use a women's toilet, and trans men should be able to use a men's toilet. While a unisex toilet is a positive way to ensure facilities are inclusive (and may be more comfortable for a trans person early in their transition), a trans employee should not be stopped from using the appropriate single sex toilet.[84]

As yet there has been no judicial testing of the protection provided by the HRA against unlawful discrimination on the grounds of gender identity in the workplace.

79 Human Rights Act 1993, s.27(2).

80 See, for example: *Trilford v. Car Haulaways Ltd* [1996] 2 ERNZ 351 (female applicant rejected for job described to her by employer as being "more male orientated"; and *Parore v. Sheldon Hammond (Pty) Ltd* (2001) Employment Relations Authority Auckland AA 196/01 (older woman denied employment because employer wanted a younger, prettier woman).

81 See further at: www.nzherald.co.nz/business/news/article.cfm?c_id=3&objectid=10531484.

82 See further Employment New Zealand, at: www.employment.govt.nz/starting-employment/hiring/discrimination-when-hiring/transgender-employees/.

83 [2016] NZERA Auckland.

84 See further Employment New Zealand, op. cit.

Employment in the military

Since 1993, gays, lesbians and bisexuals have been legally entitled to serve in the military.

Right to equality and non-discrimination: services

The Human Rights Act 1993, s.44, prohibits discrimination in the provision of goods and services, but there seems to be little if any caselaw on associated legal issues.

Trans persons and gender-specific services

Gender Minorities Aotearoa argues that women-only places do not currently require birth certificates to enter, and there is "no credible evidence suggesting elevated levels of sexual violence as a result of similar legislation (permitting self-identification on birth certificates) passing in other countries".[85]

Provision of public services

Government activities, and any activities carried out on behalf of government, are required to be compliant with anti-discrimination standards, including discrimination on grounds of sexual orientation, as set out in s.19 of BORA and s.21 of the HRA.[86]

The Marriage (Definition of Marriage) Amendment Act 2013 is problematic in terms of guaranteeing gay couples access to a marriage service. While it is clear that a religious organisation is now enabled to conduct such a marriage ceremony, it remains somewhat uncertain as to what happens if clergy refuse to officiate and/or the couple are denied the use of their chosen church. Greater certainty, however, exists in relation to a Registrar: such a public official would be legally obliged to officiate at the civil wedding of a same-sex couple.

Trans persons and prisons

Service provision deficiencies in relation to SOGI issues arising in the penal system were revealed, to an extent, in *R. v. Glen Laurance Cooper DC*[87] when it was found to be a cruel and unusual punishment for inmates to be deprived of medication such as subsidised mainstream-allocated testosterone blockers and oestrogen. In 2015, the prison authorities responded to a trans woman's allegation of sexual assault in an Auckland prison by placing her in solitary confinement: such

85 See further at: www.newshub.co.nz/home/politics/2019/02/changing-sex-on-birth-certificates-both-sides-of-the-debate.html.
86 See the Human Rights Amendment Act 2001.
87 Whangarei CRI-2012–088–000223.

an increased level of punishment could be viewed as a questionable way of servicing a SOGI need[88] and contrary to the benchmark for cases concerning the rights of prisoners as established in *Taunoa v. Attorney-General*.[89] Otherwise, the dearth of caselaw prevents any insight into how the New Zealand prison service meets the SOGI-related needs of its inmates.

Private goods and service provision

While anecdotal evidence would suggest that some degree of antipathy towards the LGBT community persists, this is not supported by any recent services-related caselaw.

Pensions, social security benefits etc.

The ruling in *Hester v. Commissioner of Inland Revenue*[90] established that religious exemption privileges are subject to constraints. This case, concerning a superannuation scheme designed to provide for retired clergy and their families, concluded with a ruling which confirmed in principle that the scheme could be entitled to protection under BORA, if restricted to benefit only those beneficiaries (as such a scheme had been accepted as charitable in the case of *Presbyterian Church Fund of New Zealand v. The Commissioner of Inland Revenue*),[91] but as it in fact extended beyond clergy to include a wide range of Church employees, it was not accepted as charitable. An argument that this finding discriminated against a church which did not operate through paid clergy and was therefore prohibited under ss.15 and 19 of BORA and s.21 of HRA was rejected: "it is not possible to avoid discrimination on religious grounds when implementing those aspects of the law of charities which relate to the advancement of religion".[92]

Conscientious objection of service providers

While arising most acutely in times of war, conscientious objection has also become an issue in the context of medical treatment – accessing contraception, abortion, sterilisation – when public health care staff may wish to be excused from such service provision on religious grounds. In that context, specific statutory protection is available for such staff.

88 See further at: www.radionz.co.nz/news/national/286022/alleged-prison-assault-victim-trans-woman.

89 (2004) 7 HRNZ 379 (HC).

90 [2005] 2 NZLR 172 (CA).

91 [1994] 3 NZLR 363 (HC).

92 Ibid., at para. 101. Author acknowledges advice from Sue Barker on this matter (note to author, 15 June 2019).

SOGI, public service and conscientious objection

The right of public health care professionals to refuse to be engaged in service provision on grounds of conscientious objection is clearly stated in s.174 of the Health Practitioners Competence Assurance Act 2003 and in s.46(1) of the Contraception, Sterilisation and Abortion Act 1977.[93] However, the Supreme Court decision in *Right to Life New Zealand Inc v. Abortion Supervisory Committee*[94] confirmed that the Abortion Advisory Committee had the power to enquire into how the consultants involved in abortion procedures approached their decision-making in general (not in respect of any particular case). Should the Committee discover that a consultant's beliefs, or lack of such, influenced their approach to the circumstances in which abortion should be made available, this could have direct implications for their career prospects. As with registrars officiating at gay marriages, there is a probability that some consultants will have religious beliefs which, being SOGI adverse, may well be incompatible with continuing their public service functions.

Conclusion

Aside from some key rulings on issues associated with relationships – marriage, child care and custody, adoption etc. – there is a conspicuous lack of SOGI-related caselaw in New Zealand. Compared with other jurisdictions there would seem to be neither the volume, nor the landmark rulings by superior courts, on SOGI-related issues arising under equality and non-discrimination legislation. This is perhaps due to effective early intervention and mediation by the Human Rights Commission and the Ministry of Business, Innovation and Employment (MBIE) obviating the need for legal proceedings.

A comparison with other jurisdictions does, however, reveal areas of difference, some of which could be seen as weaknesses. These include: the lack of an explicit reference to gender identity in the human rights legislation; the fact that conversion therapy, and indeed corrective surgery to "normalise" genital ambiguity, both remain possible and legal; the deferment period of 12 months for gay blood donors; and an absence of legislation permitting trans self-declaration of gender identity without evidence of medical intervention. On the other hand, New Zealand has served as a model for other jurisdictions by providing non-binary registration on a variety of official documentation.

93 Author acknowledges advice from Sue Barker on this matter (note to author, 23 June 2019).
94 [2012] NZSC 68.

Part III

Evaluation

10 Themes of commonality and difference

Introduction

In 2017 an English judge confidently asserted that

> the law . . . recognises the reality that one's true sexuality and gender are no more matters of choice than the colour of one's eyes or skin.[1]

Only two years later, as society had grown more accepting of a non-binary spectrum, so too had awareness grown of the possible permutations of sexual orientation and gender identity, together with a greater understanding of the accompanying uncertainty. For some on that spectrum, choices do indeed need to be made.

In a few short decades, the penetration of equality laws has proven to be a powerful force for engineering social change – at least in all Part II jurisdictions. The moral imperative driving the requirements of equality and non-discrimination into all aspects of everyday life has become the cutting edge of contemporary human rights law. In challenging traditional practices and stereotypical attitudes across the range of arenas that constitute "the world of the individual person", this phenomenon would seem to be finally giving effect to the 60-year-old aspirations of Eleanor Roosevelt.[2]

This concluding chapter restricts itself to reflecting on the nature of jurisdictional characteristics that emerged from profiling the SOGI/human rights intersect in each of the Part II common law countries. It does so by focusing on the themes emerging from the four main sections: the legal framework; SOGI and related core human rights; SOGI, personal relationships and human rights; and SOGI, non-discrimination, affirmative action and equality. As a means of gauging relative jurisdictional progress, it employs the Yogyakarta Principles (YP+10) as a yardstick to identify and measure areas of significant jurisdictional commonality and difference. Justification for this approach can be found in the preamble to

1 *J v. B (Ultra-Orthodox Judaism: Transgender)* [2017] EWFC 4, per Jackson, J., at para. 179.
2 Speech to the UN at the Church Peace Union (New York, 1958), op. cit.

the Principles which, seemingly picking up on the Roosevelt outlook, recognises "that there is significant value in articulating in a systematic manner international human rights law as applicable to the lives and experiences of persons of diverse sexual orientations and gender identities".[3]

The legal framework for SOGI/human rights

The national and international legal frameworks of all Part II jurisdictions provide fully and similarly for recognising and giving effect to human rights, including those that relate to matters of sexual orientation and gender identity. As has been seen, however, this does not mean that they function with jurisdictional uniformity. Even though rooted in a shared common law heritage, differences in their subsequent political and socio-economic development have led to differences in culture, reflected in the pace and emphasis if not in the outcome of their respective responses to the sequence of SOGI challenges.

Legislation

> YP 30 – Everyone, regardless of sexual orientation, gender identity, gender expression or sex characteristics, has the right to State protection from violence, discrimination and other harm, whether by government officials or by any individual or group.

The principle that the State has a duty to protect the vulnerable is probably as old as the concept of a "State" and is central to contemporary international human rights law as first articulated in the UDHR and subsequently enlarged by the ICCPR. There are now some ten international treaties and innumerable additional international, regional and local legal instruments, all variously giving expression to that principle but not uniformly acceded to by all jurisdictions: there are various abstentions, reservations and failures to ratify. The relevance of the principle is most apparent in relation to the ECHR,[4] which is confined (for present purposes) to the UK and Ireland, where it has had a profound and lasting effect on the development of national legislation, and in general has often proven to be an effective resource for challenging outdated laws at the SOGI/human rights intersect.[5] The ICCPR, similarly viewed as an effective resource by the UN HR Committee,[6] provides a common platform

3 See further at: http://yogyakartaprinciples.org/preambule/.

4 The diverse constituency of the ECHR's 47 member States includes Russia, Turkey, Iceland and Azerbaijan.

5 See, for example: *Dudgeon v. United Kingdom*, Application No. 7525/76 [1981] 4 EHRR 149 [1981] ECHR 5.

6 The terminology in both instances is loosely derived from the rules of interpretation in Article 31 of the Vienna Convention on the Law of Treaties, 1969.

for all contracting States, most of which have fully incorporated its provisions into national law, but its ability to hold State parties to account for violations of the principle is constrained by the fact that neither the UK nor the US have adopted Optional Protocol 1.

National law governing the SOGI/human rights intersect is generally to be found in much the same raft of legislation comprising statutes on human rights, equality and non-discrimination, employment equality and racial hatred. Some countries have chosen to constitutionally embed core human rights principles or to assimilate convention provisions into statute law. In recent years, this has been added to by not dissimilar national provisions for gay marriage and other SOGI-related matters. The US is singular in that the principle of equality is firmly established as a primary foundation stone of its Constitution. Arguably, this gives equality an overriding legal weighting when it comes into conflict with other human rights.

The areas of jurisdictional difference are interesting: Ireland, most noticeably, has only very recently initiated steps to legislatively address the human rights shortcomings repeatedly noted by the UNHRC, but has progressed swiftly with some key pieces of SOGI legislation, while Australia conspicuously lacks a human rights statute and is often forced to rely upon race hatred statutes and/or the provisions of international treaties, conventions and protocols. The US can to some extent be differentiated from other jurisdictions by the attention now being given by judiciary and legislature to developing "religious liberty" laws and conscientious objection jurisprudence.

The majority of the Part II jurisdictions (the CANZUS nations) have a socially disadvantaged Indigenous population for whom the United Nations Declaration on the Rights of Indigenous Peoples (UNDRIP) 2006 is particularly important. However, despite the bearing of that dedicated set of provisions on their circumstances, in addition to the protection available under all other human rights instruments, the Indigenous people in all relevant jurisdictions continue to suffer from a higher incidence of human rights violation relative to their fellow citizens. Paradoxically, due to their well-established cultural acceptance of LGBT persons, the Indigenous communities had little need for the SOGI-related legislation introduced in the Part II jurisdictions.

Supra-national bodies

The varied adherence to international instruments is matched by a similar jurisdictional disparity in acceptance of international courts. Most obviously, the US rejects the possibility of any international court having jurisdiction over its citizens. Both the UK and Ireland accept the jurisdiction of the ECtHR and respect its rulings on issues arising from the domestic litigation of 47 member states, even if the decisions have no binding effect on their domestic law. The resulting body of jurisprudence has included formative principles – such as "proportionality" and "necessary in a democratic society" – which have proven influential in all Part II jurisdictions.

The UN, the world's largest human rights organisation, works on behalf of its almost 200 member States and has been responsible for formulating many foundational human rights instruments. The withdrawal of the US in 2018, citing dissatisfaction with the number of member States with a poor human rights record such as Algeria and Saudi Arabia, and also for reasons to do with the constant passing of resolutions criticising Israel, can only weaken the Council.

The quasi-judicial function exercised by the UN HR Committee has resulted in many influential adjudications that have added weight and some controversy to the jurisprudence on the SOGI/human rights intersect.[7] In at least two areas that controversy is likely to prove significant for the future: as regards the "margin of appreciation" rule; and in relation to the advice that "the Covenant should be interpreted as a living instrument and the rights protected under it should be applied in context and in the light of present-day conditions" (see further below). The "General Comments" issued from time to time by the Committee in respect of ICCPR implementation have also proven to be influential in guiding national practice and facilitating international congruence.[8]

National courts and regulatory bodies

In all Part II jurisdictions, the flow of SOGI-related issues very largely runs through regulatory bodies, with a relatively small proportion passing to the courts. Of the latter, their volume and the rate at which they end up in the national Supreme Court would seem to be stronger in the US than elsewhere. In recent years, the force of that flow has been generally driven by equality legislation and within that by an increase in SOGI-related issues.

SOGI and related core human rights

The Yogyakarta Principles affirm the primary obligation of States to implement international human rights, observing in Principle 1 that: "All human beings are born free and equal in dignity and rights. Human beings of all sexual orientations and gender identities are entitled to the full enjoyment of all human rights".[9] The more fundamental of those rights are access to justice and the freedoms of expression, assembly and association and religion.

7 For example, in *X v. Colombia*, Communication No 1361/2005, UN Doc CCPR/C/89/D/1361/2005 (2007), the Committee found that the State had unfairly discriminated against same-sex partners by denying them pension rights which were available to unmarried heterosexual partners.

8 See, for example, CCPR General Comment No. 34, Freedoms of Opinion and Expression (2011); No. 22, Freedom of Thought, Conscience or Religion (1993); and No. 18, Non-discrimination (1989). See further at: http://ccprcentre.org/ccpr-general-comments.

9 See further at: http://yogyakartaprinciples.org/principle-1/.

Right of access to justice

YP 8 (a) requires a State to

> take all necessary legislative, administrative and other measures to prohibit and eliminate prejudicial treatment on the basis of sexual orientation or gender identity at every stage of the judicial process, in civil and criminal proceedings and all other judicial and administrative proceedings which determine rights and obligations.

YP 28 – *Access to relevant information and to an effective remedy*

This requires "(d) that all persons have access to all necessary information about the processes for seeking remedies and redress". It has proved problematic in England and Wales (unlike in Ireland, Canada and Australia where gender identity is a matter of self-declaration) due to the failure of government bodies to amend official information systems to reflect acquired gender identity status.[10] It is of particular importance in relation to birth certificates. The USSC in *Pavan*[11] recently established that right, but it has yet to gain similar recognition in many states and has not done so in jurisdictions such as New Zealand. In the latter instance, that should change if and when the Births, Deaths, Marriages, and Relationships Registration Bill 2019 becomes law.

Provision for an effective remedy is also a requirement of YP 28 (e), which directs States to ensure "that financial aid is provided to those who are unable to afford the cost of securing redress, and that any other obstacles to securing such redress, financial or otherwise, are removed". In practice, the costs of litigation and the limitations on available legal aid make access to justice a somewhat qualified right in the US and Ireland, while in Australia the constraints on access by asylum seekers and Indigenous people are of similar effect. Accessing the information necessary to validate gender identity, specifically in the form of an amended birth certificate, is easier in some jurisdictions than in others and most readily secured in countries such as Ireland, Australia and Canada. Effectiveness may also be an issue in relation to whether young persons can give their consent to gender reassignment. In England and Wales statute law restricts lawful consent to those aged 18 or older, unlike countries such as Ireland, which accepts the consent of "*Gillick* competent" children.

YP 23 – *Asylum seekers/illegal immigrants*

This principle establishes the right to be granted asylum from persecution, including persecution related to sexual orientation or gender identity. YP 23 requires, among others, that (i) a well-founded fear of persecution on the basis of sexual orientation, gender identity, gender expression or sex characteristics

10 *JK v. Registrar General for England and Wales* [2015] EWHC 990 (Admin) and *C v. Secretary of State for Work and Pensions* [2017] UKSC 72.

11 *Marisa N. Pavan et al. v. Nathaniel Smith*, 582 U.S. (2017).

is accepted as a ground for the recognition of refugee status; (ii) States accept the self-identification of a person seeking asylum on the basis of sexual orientation, gender identity, gender expression or sexual characteristics as the starting point for consideration of their asylum claim; and (iii) the detention of asylum seekers is avoided and only used as a measure of last resort and for the shortest possible time. A State may not remove, expel or extradite a person to any other State where that person may face a well-founded fear of torture, persecution or any other form of cruel, inhuman or degrading treatment or punishment, on the basis of sexual orientation or gender identity. The Principle is reinforced by YP 7, the right to freedom from arbitrary deprivation of liberty, and YP 8, the right to treatment with humanity while in detention.

One consequence of the ongoing migrant crisis has been a sharper focus on SOGI status as grounds for human rights protection under the 1951 UN Convention on Refugees, the key terms of which structure the caselaw in all jurisdictions being considered. As many migrants are Muslims, or are from other countries or cultures with severe penalties for persons expressing SOGI characteristics, all Part II jurisdictions have experienced contentious legal battles as migrants rely on SOGI status as grounds for admission or for resisting deportation. Clearly, the US and Australia have taken the most stringent political and legislative measures to deny asylum, including on grounds of SOGI status, with the US specifically restricting admissions from Islamic countries, which necessarily adversely burdens those with SOGI status: judicial sophistication as regards SOGI grounds for resisting deportation from the US is at variance with the peremptory political approach. Canada, on the other hand, has exercised most leniency in that respect, and Ireland has legislation in effect which states that such status warrants asylum.[12]

Varying degrees of political concern, or panic, to establish national immigration controls have now resulted in a situation where there is no guarantee that the international human right to asylum, including on SOGI grounds, will be respected.[13]

Right to freedom of expression

YP 19 states the right to freedom of opinion and expression. It declares that

> everyone has the right to freedom of opinion and expression, regardless of sexual orientation or gender identity. This includes the expression of identity or personhood through speech, deportment, dress, bodily characteristics,

12 The International Protection Act 2015, s.8, which bears a strong resemblance to the US Immigration and Nationality Act 1965, initially enacted in 1952.

13 See further International Commission of Jurists, *Refugee Status Claims Based on Sexual Orientation and Gender Identity: A Practitioner's Guide* (February 2016), at: www.ilga-europe.org/sites/default/files/practitioners-guide-series-2016-eng.pdf.

> choice of name, or any other means, as well as the freedom to seek, receive and impart information and ideas of all kinds, including with regard to human rights, sexual orientation and gender identity, through any medium and regardless of frontiers.

It is reinforced by YP 19–21 (the importance of the freedom to express oneself, one's identity and one's sexuality, without State interference based on sexual orientation or gender identity).

For the LGBT community, probably more so than for most other minority groups, this right is singularly important and extends over a wide range of sexual and gender expression. The contemporary range of expressive mediums is now extensive: traditional forms of speech, publications etc. have been augmented by multi-social media options, many in real time, and all offer opportunities for the exercise and abuse of this human right. Long viewed as the hallmark of democracy, it is probably the single most staunchly defended of all human rights and one that enjoys greatest salience in the US.

The moral majority

The timeline of sequential stages in the legal recognition given to different aspects of SOGI status (see Chapter 2) provides a record of the challenges overcome by the LGBT community as they struggled to be free of the constraints imposed by the moral majority in all Part II jurisdictions. As the birthplace of the civil rights movement, it was natural that the US should lead the way in terms of articulating, addressing and adjudicating upon SOGI-related issues,[14] despite being nearly derailed by the AIDs epidemic.

The right to freedom of expression is often relied upon by both sets of protagonists engaged in conflicts between religious belief and sexual orientation, as illustrated in Canada by the *Trinity Western* cases.[15] For England and Wales, and indeed for the ECtHR, it was the *Dudgeon* case[16] some 40 years ago that exemplified the difficulties in balancing the merits of such rival claims. More recently, in Ireland the traditional religious ethos – for generations representing the moral majority – was overturned by constitutional referendum favouring LGBT rights, but only after the moral majority in the population had been reversed.[17] More broadly, this issue has been evident in the "gay baker" cases[18] and similar cases involving florists, photographers and other service providers.

14 Most notably the decision in *Obergefell v. Hodges*, 576 U.S. (2015).

15 *Trinity Western University v. British Columbia College of Teachers* (2001), 39 C.H.R.R. D/357. 2001 SCC 31; *Law Society of BC v. Trinity Western University*, 2018 SCC 32; and *Trinity Western University (TWU) v. Law Society of Upper Canada*, 2018 SCC 33.

16 *Dudgeon v. United Kingdom*, Application No. 7525/76 (1981).

17 The same-sex marriage national referendum (25 May 2015).

18 *Masterpiece Cakeshop v. Colorado Civil Rights Commission*, 584 U.S. (2018) and *Lee v. and Ashers Baking Co Ltd and Others* [2018] UKSC 49.

Harm to others

Offensive speech directed against the LGBT community or a member of it, or intended to cause harm to those with SOGI-related vulnerabilities, is generally prohibited in the Part II jurisdictions: in most it will only do so if it meets the definition of "hate speech", though in New Zealand there is no prohibition on inciting hatred on the grounds of religion; and in the US it must actually cause harm if it is to overcome the presumption of free speech.

In a number of countries, freedom of expression has become a contentious issue in relation to protests against abortion. In some – such as the US and Australia – the proven capacity for it to lead to harm has resulted in the erection of "safe access zones" to protect abortion clinics, their staff and patients.

Right to freedom of association and assembly

YP 20 states the right to freedom of peaceful assembly and association. YP 20(f) requires States to "respect, protect and facilitate the formation of associations for the purpose of promoting the rights of all persons, including on the basis of sexual orientation, gender identity, gender expression or sex characteristics". The right to form associations and the right to leave them, together with the right of assembly and to organise and participate in protest marches, are of fundamental importance to the LGBT community. In the US, it has traditionally been regarded as indicative of the independence of citizens in their relationship to the State but has been upheld as an important indicator of a democratic society in all Part II jurisdictions.

Constraints

The history of the LGBT community – particularly in the US, Canada and Australia – is one which records many instances of constraints being placed on LGBT marches and protest rallies on the grounds of anticipated breaches of public order. Similar reasons were given for police raids on bath houses in the same countries. Currently the issue of constraints is more likely to arise in respect of organisations seeking to prevent LGBT membership, most often instigated by Christian groups.[19] In every Part II jurisdiction, there are legal disputes regarding exclusionary practices to protect the beliefs and ethos of religious organisations; prevent trans persons from accessing gender-specific facilities, organisations and competitive sports; and in relation to gender neutral facilities and services. There is a strong probability of an escalation in such disputes as equality and non-discrimination legislation is brought to bear upon those who would constrain the rights of members of the LGBT community on grounds of health, safety or exemption privilege.

19 *Boy Scouts of America v. Dale* 530 U.S. 640, 648.

Right to freedom of religion

YP 21 states that everyone has the right to freedom of thought, conscience and religion, regardless of sexual orientation or gender identity. This right may not be invoked by the State to justify laws, policies or practices which deny equal protection of the law, or discriminate, on the basis of sexual orientation or gender identity.

SOGI and religion

The State duty to maintain neutrality and impartiality when engaged in religious matters is a common characteristic of all Part II jurisdictions. What they also have in common is the tendency for that duty to come into conflict with the provisions of equality and non-discrimination legislation requiring protection for those exercising their SOGI rights. As the legal interpretation of what constitutes "religion" continues to broaden, so too does the range and frequency of such conflicts.

Although obviously very strongly linked to both the "moral majority" (see earlier mention) and to "cultural life" (see next), the right to freedom of religion has its own distinct and uneasy relationship with SOGI issues: essentially, the beliefs and doctrines of the traditional religions – Christianity, Judaism and Islam – are non-SOGI compliant, causing social tensions that vary across the Part II jurisdictions in accordance with the number and commitment of adherents of those religions. This has proven most problematic in the US and Ireland and less so in Canada and the antipodes. In England and Wales, a pragmatic approach is usually evident but, as in Canada, the courts have generally held firmly to the principle that where beliefs and equality are in conflict, the latter should prevail.

Religious organisations and the religious exemption

A statutory exemption from the requirements of equality and non-discrimination law is granted to religious organisations in all Part II jurisdictions and applies not just to institutions, churches and the like but also to their offshoots, such as hospitals, residential care facilities, schools and universities owned by a religious organisation. Its extension to include organisations with a religious ethos and to persons on the grounds of their beliefs or conscience varies between the jurisdictions.

Currently, the US is rapidly extending the ambit of the exemption privilege by way of state "religious liberty laws" to excuse, on the grounds of religion or belief, a widening range of organisations and public service professionals from engaging in SOGI-related service provision. There have been indications that this approach may also be adopted, if to a lesser degree, in England and Wales, but there is least likelihood of it being followed in Canada due both to equality rights being entrenched in the Charter, s.15, and to judicial precedents establishing the principle that there can be no hierarchy of Charter rights. In Ireland, the constitutional guarantee favouring religion has had the effect of impeding any developments in the law which might be incompatible with or constrain the exercise of that freedom. In Australia, as in Ireland, a large proportion of public service provision – hospitals, schools etc. – remain in the hands of religious organisations which avail of the exemption when staffing and determining service access. However, in both Australia and New Zealand the courts tend to interpret the exemption privilege narrowly and the equality and non-discrimination requirements broadly so as to restrict carve-outs on religious grounds.

SOGI: personal relationships and human rights

The Yogyakarta Principles recognise and affirm the central importance of personal relationships in a SOGI context and emphasise the State duty to ensure their protection through international human rights.

Right to recognition as a person before the law

YP 3 asserts that everyone has the right to recognition everywhere as a person before the law. Persons of diverse sexual orientations and gender identities shall enjoy legal capacity in all aspects of life. This is further developed in YP 31 by a declaration that the right is to be exercisable "without reference to, or requiring assignment or disclosure of, sex, gender, sexual orientation, gender identity, gender expression or sex characteristics". It states that everyone has the right to obtain identity documents, including birth certificates, regardless of sexual orientation, gender identity, gender expression or sex characteristics. In addition, "everyone has the right to change gendered information in such documents while gendered information is included in them". For members of the LGBT community, there is no more important right, but it is one which the Part II jurisdictions have been slow to acknowledge.

Trans recognition in law

Currently neither the law nor practice in England and Wales is compliant with YP 31. Instead, an initial medical diagnosis, with mental health implications, is required in order to obtain a Gender Recognition Certificate (restricted to those aged 18 or over), and no provision is made for self-declaration of gender identity. This is in sharp contrast to equivalent Irish, Australian and Canadian law, which allow for gender recognition and the issue of a GRC on the basis of self-declaration (including for "*Gillick* competent" applicants aged 16–18). The law varies across the US with some states requiring evidence of surgery before the issue of amended gender ID. In New Zealand, such evidence is no longer required, but official recognition of trans identity cannot be issued unless sanctioned by a Family Court.

Non-binary gender identity

England and Wales, together with Ireland, make no legal provision for official recognition of non-binary identity. However, non-binary birth certificates have been issued in Canada, on the basis of self-declaration, since 2018; in New Zealand with Family Court approval supported by medical evidence; and in a minority of States in the US, which provide similar official recognition at least on passports. Australia, unusually, has been to the forefront in human rights compliant practice, having introduced non-binary recognition to passports in 2003, extending it to birth certificates in 2014.

Right to respect for private and family life

YP 6 states that everyone, regardless of sexual orientation or gender identity, is entitled to the enjoyment of privacy without arbitrary or unlawful interference, including with regard to their family, home or correspondence as well as to protection from unlawful attacks on their honour and reputation. This was augmented by YP+10 additional clause (g), which requires States to ensure that requirements for individuals to provide information on their sex or gender are relevant, reasonable and necessary as required by the law for a legitimate purpose in the circumstances where it is sought, and that such requirements respect all persons' right to self-determination of gender. Embodied in Article 8 of the ECHR and given effect by the ECtHR, there is probably no right that has been as important in shaping the development of SOGI-related law in England and Wales, Ireland and further afield.

Sexual orientation, identity and private life

All Part II jurisdictions made the same transition from de-criminalising same-sex relationships, granting them legal recognition and protection, adjusting ages of consent and doing so over much the same time period from the early 1980s to the turn of the century, probably beginning with the ECtHR ruling in *Dudgeon*[20] and continuing through to decisions that included *Toonen*[21] and *Young*[22] in Australia and *Lawrence v. Texas* in the US.[23] This process, a consequence of the relative ease in construing sexual orientation as an inferred or extrapolated aspect of "sex", was not so readily emulated with regard to gender identity. Indeed, thereafter it became increasingly problematic – in general towards recognition of

20 *Dudgeon v. the United Kingdom*, Application No. 7525/76 [1981] 4 EHRR 149 [1981] ECHR 5.

21 *Toonen v. Australia*, Communication No. 488/1992, UN Doc CCPR/C/50/D/488 (1992).

22 *Young v. Australia*, CCPR/C/78/D/941/2000; 11 IHRR 146 (2004).

23 539 U.S. 558 (2003).

non-binary status and in particular in relation to recognising "intersex" – in terms of disaggregating, and acquiring legal recognition for, distinct SOGI identities.

Family life

Traditional boundaries for what in law can be construed as a "family", with gender-determined roles, have in general long since disappeared, though in Ireland this continues to enjoy constitutional protection. The UN HR Committee,[24] followed somewhat tardily by the ECtHR,[25] has extended recognition to families formed by same-sex married couples. The traditional legal definition has been replaced in effect by "household" as many permutations of "parent" and "child of the family" have gained acceptance for purposes such as assigning responsibilities for maintenance, child support and protection.

Private life, gender reassignment and divorce

Endless ramifications of the privacy right of the individual have been developed in all Part II jurisdictions for many purposes, including to prevent those with SOGI status from enjoying their right of equal access to all aspects of family life. It has, for example, been relied upon to remove the legal obstacle that required a spouse to divorce as a pre-condition recognition of gender identity.

YP 3 states that "no one shall be forced to undergo medical procedures, including sex reassignment surgery, sterilisation or hormonal therapy, as a requirement for legal recognition of their gender identity". Until very recently, this was a right mostly honoured in its breach, with many countries requiring evidence of irreversible surgery. Although England and Wales and many states in the US continue to be non-compliant, no other Part II jurisdictions insist on medical procedures, though some require medical affirmation, to establish gender identity. Increasingly, in line with the privacy principle as expanded in clause (g), the international trend is to accept self-declaration as sufficient for purposes of obtaining relevant official ID.

SOGI, parenting and "the best interests of the child" principle

YP 24 (c) requires the best interests of the child to be a primary consideration in all decisions taken concerning children, adding that "the sexual orientation or gender identity of the child or of any family member or other person may not be considered incompatible with such best interests".

All Part II jurisdictions are signatories to Article 3(1) of the Convention on the Rights of the Child, which requires the welfare interests of the child to be the

24 *Young v. Australia*, op. cit. *X v. Colombia*, Communication No. 1361/2005, U.N. Doc. A/62/40.

25 *Schalk and Kopf v. Austria*, Application No. 30141/04 (2010).

"primary consideration" in all actions concerning children. Consequently, there is now little if any disparity between them as regards addressing a SOGI dimension in parental care decisions, though the decisions of some US states may be at variance with this principle,[26] and overseas surrogacy arrangements can introduce complications

Right to marriage and to found a family

YP 24 declares that:

> Everyone has the right to found a family, regardless of sexual orientation or gender identity. Families exist in diverse forms. No family may be subjected to discrimination on the basis of the sexual orientation or gender identity of any of its members.

YP 24 (e) refers to a right of non-discriminatory treatment in relation to same-sex marriage in those States which already recognise it. Of considerable relevance to current developments in the US is YP 17 with its additional clause (p) requiring the removal of "any barriers that may hinder timely access to affordable and quality abortion services, without discrimination based on sexual orientation, gender identity, gender expression or sex characteristics". It also remains problematic in Ireland, if less so than it was, but in all other jurisdictions there is reasonable access.

Family life in all Part II jurisdictions takes many varied forms which now find recognition in law, though in some, such as Ireland, the traditional heterosexual marital family is accorded preferential treatment.

Legal recognition for same-sex relationships and the right to marry

Unlike the UN HR Committee and the ECtHR, the right to same-sex marriage is recognised in YP 4–26 and is now established in the statute law of all Part II jurisdictions. Again, though, a caveat must be entered in relation to the US: although a federally established right, some states have yet to enact legislation enabling same-sex marriage.

Trans persons and marriage

As marriage is now legally gender neutral in all Part II jurisdictions, trans people have the same right to marry as anyone else, regardless of whether their partners are legally considered to be of the same or opposite sex.

26 *In re Marriage of Magnuson*, 170 P. 3d 65, 66 (Wash. Ct. App. 2007).

Adoption, surrogacy and child care

YP 24 (a) requires the State to take "all necessary legislative, administrative and other measures to ensure the right to found a family, including through access to adoption or assisted procreation (including donor insemination), without discrimination on the basis of sexual orientation or gender identity". YP+10 added clause (k) requiring States to "ensure that surrogacy, where legal, is provided without discrimination based on sexual orientation, gender identity, gender expression or sex characteristics".

The laws specific to surrogacy and adoption are complicated, and as these two routes become more popular, particularly as a resource for same-sex couples to achieve family life, so their interaction with SOGI-related law can produce further complications. However, while in general adoption, surrogacy and child care arrangements no longer generate any SOGI-specific legal issues, it can be foreseen that in the US those states introducing "religious liberty laws" are very likely to do so.

Right to cultural life

YP 26 states that "everyone has the right to participate freely in cultural life, regardless of sexual orientation or gender identity, and to express, through cultural participation, the diversity of sexual orientation and gender identity". YP 26 (b) requires States to

> foster dialogue between, and mutual respect among, proponents of the various cultural groups present within the State, including among groups that hold different views on matters of sexual orientation and gender identity, consistently with respect for the human rights referred to in these Principles.

Further, YP 38 adds that "everyone has the right to practise, protect, preserve and revive cultures" and that States are required to "ensure the right to practice, protect, preserve and revive the diversity of cultural expressions of persons of all sexual orientations, gender identities, gender expressions and sex characteristics on the basis of the equal dignity of and respect for all".

In the multicultural context that characterises developed western nations, the issue of the circumstances in which one culture may or should "trump" another is politically fraught, but for the Indigenous people in the CANZUS nations, those circumstances have never worked to their advantage. Other religious and culturally defined minority groups have tended to function in parallel with their "host" mainstream western society: in it, but not of it; mutual ignorance serves to maintain cultural boundaries. This may perhaps be true of the Amish, Mennonites, Hutterites and Mormons in the US and of Muslims, Charedi Jews and others in the UK.

Cultural context

SOGI-related laws, principles and practices have tended to remain confined within culturally defined boundaries. However, as indicated by the first FGM prosecution in England and Wales, the TWU cases in Canada and the introduction of SOGI-compliant teaching materials to primary schools in a number of countries, there would now seem to be a more concerted policy to use equality and non-discrimination legislation to ensure that this iteration of international human rights transfers across cultural and religious barriers. A contrary policy may well be emerging in the US.

SOGI: non-discrimination, affirmative action and equality

The YP Preamble notes that:

> international human rights law imposes an absolute prohibition of discrimination in regard to the full enjoyment of all human rights, civil, cultural, economic, political and social, that respect for sexual rights, sexual orientation and gender identity is integral to the realisation of equality between men and women and that States must take measures to seek to eliminate prejudices and customs based on the idea of the inferiority or the superiority of one sex or on stereotyped roles for men and women, and noting further that the international community has recognised the right of persons to decide freely and responsibly on matters related to their sexuality, including sexual and reproductive health, free from coercion, discrimination, and violence.

Equality before the law: sexuality and gender discrimination

YP 2 declares that "everyone is entitled to enjoy all human rights without discrimination on the basis of sexual orientation or gender identity . . . whether or not the enjoyment of another human right is also affected" and warns that SOGI-based discrimination is often "compounded by discrimination on other grounds including gender, race, age, religion, disability, health and economic status".

The process of disaggregating sexual orientation from its binary (men/women) stereotyping and more broadly from medical, psychological and legal contexts has been problematic in all Part II jurisdictions, though all now recognise it as a distinct legal concept constituting separate grounds for discrimination proceedings. This was followed by further and not dissimilar contortions in acceding legal recognition to gender identity, and unlike Canada, some jurisdictions – such as England and Wales and the federal government in the US – have not legislated to prohibit discrimination based specifically on gender identity or transgender status. Problems continue to obstruct recognition in general of non-binary people and in particular of those who are intersex. Arguably, the reason why the YP 2 declaration has proven difficult to realise is to do with the issue being compounded by cultural context.

Affirmative action

In relation to YP 20: additional clause (j) requires States to "take positive measures, including affirmative action measures, to overcome specific challenges to the enjoyment of the freedom of association of groups that are marginalised and made vulnerable on grounds of sexual orientation, gender identity, gender expression or sex characteristics"; while clause (k) requires States to "take positive measures to protect the right to association of service providers working with those discriminated against on grounds of sexual orientation, gender identity, gender expression or sex characteristics".

Socially disadvantaged groups lack leverage and need the additional support of State institutions if they are to be enabled to play an equitable role alongside others in a democratic society, but offsetting this by way of affirmative action does have a downside. Such intervention by State bodies in support of those disadvantaged or discriminated against has often been crudely operationalised by introducing a quota system which, while guaranteeing the inclusion of a more representative number of those normally excluded, does so at the cost of stigmatising the group concerned, generating resentment from those who have to make way and can threaten overall efficiency. It is, however, specifically mandated in relation to SOGI-related issues by the equality and anti-discrimination legislation of the Part II jurisdictions. However, there is little evidence that the mandate has resulted in a significant State investment of targeted resources. Instead, affirmative action tends to be interpreted as discretionary rather than mandatory and achieves little more than subsidised access to education or preferential ranking in quotas for employment opportunities.

Right to equality and non-discrimination: health

YP 17 states that "everyone has the right to the highest attainable standard of physical and mental health, without discrimination on the basis of sexual orientation or gender identity. Sexual and reproductive health is a fundamental aspect of this right". YP 18 declares that

> no person may be forced to undergo any form of medical or psychological treatment, procedure, testing, or be confined to a medical facility, based on sexual orientation or gender identity. Notwithstanding any classifications to the contrary, a person's sexual orientation and gender identity are not, in and of themselves, medical conditions and are not to be treated, cured or suppressed.

Supplementary clauses require: (a) "all necessary legislative, administrative and other measures to ensure full protection against harmful medical practices based on sexual orientation or gender identity, including on the basis of stereotypes"; and (f) "that any medical or psychological treatment or counselling does not, explicitly or implicitly, treat sexual orientation and gender identity as medical conditions to be treated, cured or suppressed".

Gender reassignment treatment

YP 32 directs that "no one shall be subjected to invasive or irreversible medical procedures that modify sex characteristics without their free, prior and informed consent, unless necessary to avoid serious, urgent and irreparable harm to the concerned person". YP 17 (g) requires States to "facilitate access by those seeking body modifications related to gender reassignment to competent, non-discriminatory treatment, care and support". A supplementary clause (l) to YP 17 adds that States must "ensure that gender affirming health care is provided by the public health system or, if not so provided, that the costs are covered or reimbursable under private and public health insurance schemes". Also relevant is YP 13, which states that "everyone has the right to . . . health insurance or care or benefits (including for body modifications related to gender identity)".

The main factors governing access to such treatment are the need for a mental health diagnosis; consent; costs; and availability. A diagnosis of gender dysphoria is a prerequisite for referral for gender reassignment treatment – and, arguably, discriminatory – in England and Wales, Ireland, the US and usually in New Zealand. The consent of a minor (16- and 17-year-old teenagers) is not legally valid in some countries, including England and Wales. Costs can be a very real factor in determining treatment access. The lack of a guarantee that all costs will be met, particularly relating to necessary body modifications, and that procedures will be readily available remain a significant area of jurisdictional difference. In the UK, full costs are borne by the NHS after diagnosis, but lengthy waiting lists can push applicants to either defer treatment or pay privately. In the US, some insurance companies will cover hormone therapy and gender reassignment surgeries while others will not, though the Affordable Care Act 2014 requires stated health insurance providers not to exercise discrimination based on gender or health history. In Ireland, the costs are borne by the public health service under the Treatment Abroad scheme, which requires a diagnosis of gender identity disorder for referral to a clinic. In Canada, hormone replacement therapy (HRT) and gender confirmation surgery are not covered by public health services in all provinces and territories; however, the majority do offer some or even full coverage. In Australia, the cost of some, but not all, treatment is covered by the national Medicare public health scheme. In New Zealand, only a very small proportion of those on the waiting list are funded through the government's Special High Cost Treatment Pool funds, and until 2018 there was a cap on annual operations which led to a 30-year waiting list. The availability problem in New Zealand, now greatly eased, effectively negated eligibility for treatment. In Ireland, also, access is a problem as there is no Irish treatment facility and referrals are made to the waiting lists in other countries.

When ready access to treatment is compromised by such factors – or is treated as cosmetic surgery – this may well constitute a violation of the basic human right to health.

Trans children

YP 24(i) states that birth certificates for children should be issued upon birth that reflect the self-defined gender identity of the parents.

A distinction must be made between medical intervention undertaken to facilitate gender reassignment and to "correct" gender incongruity, though both are perhaps equally governed by gender stereotyping. The latter is distinctive in that the intervention is directed towards infants or very young children, at parental initiative, with medical support and most often on court authority. Consent of the child concerned is clearly not a factor. For some, this raises issues as to the "binary is best" presumption, the corollary that an "intersex" identity is to be avoided, that surgery on a healthy child is compatible with the "best interests" test and ultimately that the intervention serves the interests of the parents rather than the child. In Ireland, New Zealand and Australia, and some states in the US, such genital "normalising surgery" continues to be lawful but is clearly in breach of YP 32 and, arguably, also is in breach of a child's human rights.

In relation to reassignment surgery there is a cautionary tale from Sweden. Researchers, while noting that "detransition and rates of 'transition regret' are known to be very low, even after surgery – depending on the study cited", nonetheless conclude that the rate can reach a maximum of 4%.[27] This would seem to indicate that a number of trans people – while children – were facilitated to make what was for them a wrong decision with presumably deeply unsettling long-term consequences for their sense of identity, not to mention the accompanying family turmoil. It may be that while much attention is rightly given to the very real risks of bullying and stigma that can trouble trans children, there is also good reason to consider the risks that go with what might be a growing willingness to affirm gender identity choices and cause for concern regarding the "it's cool to be trans" approach that would seem to be evolving among some in this age group. Age limits for consenting to irreversible treatment is an issue and the law varies between the Part II jurisdictions.

Sports and recreational activities

Supplementary clauses to YP 2 require States to: (i) ensure that all individuals can participate in sport in line with the gender with which they identify, subject only to reasonable, proportionate and non-arbitrary requirements; and (j) ensure that

27 See further at: www.researchgate.net/publication/262734734_An_Analysis_of_All_Applications_for_Sex_Reassignment_Surgery_in_Sweden_1960-2010_Prevalence_Incidence_and_Regrets.

all individuals can participate in sport without discrimination on the grounds of sexual orientation, gender identity, gender expression or sex characteristics. Further, additional clause (r)[28] requires sporting organisations to (ii) ensure that all individuals who wish to participate in sport are supported to do so irrespective of sexual orientation, gender identity, gender expression and sex characteristics, and that all individuals are able to participate, without restriction, subject only to reasonable, proportionate and non-arbitrary requirements to participate in line with their self-declared gender; and (iii) remove, or refrain from introducing, policies that force, coerce or otherwise pressure women athletes into undergoing unnecessary, irreversible and harmful medical examinations, testing and/or procedures in order to participate as women in sport.

SOGI issues can be amplified in this context and have the potential to be more so in Ireland where gender identity in a competitive sport may rest solely on self-identification. In England and Wales, trans athletes (mtf) may be prohibited from competing in female events. The difficulties were apparent in the 2019 ruling by the Court of Arbitration for Sport against Caster Semenya, preventing her from competing in female track events because of her high levels of testosterone; this was subsequently overturned.[29] Acknowledging that its ruling was discriminatory, the court explained that "such discrimination is a necessary, reasonable and proportionate means of achieving the IAAF's aim of preserving the integrity of female athletics". While recognising that a high level of testosterone ("hyperandrogenism") in some elite female athletes is a differentiating feature that gives them a competitive edge, regulators remain deeply divided as to what to do about it. The status of intersex or other non-binary competitors is uncertain in all Part II jurisdictions.

Blood donors

YP 17 (h) requires States to "ensure that all health service providers treat clients and their partners without discrimination on the basis of sexual orientation or gender identity". Also significant is the additional recommendation (r) that "legal provisions, regulations or any other administrative measures on the donation of blood, gametes, embryos, organs, cells or other tissues do not discriminate on grounds of sexual orientation, gender identity, gender expression or sex characteristics".

The public stigma associated with homosexuality, once expressed through criminalisation, has more recently been replaced by the disgrace of being denied the opportunity to be a blood donor, due to a misconception that such a contribution to the public good would necessarily be tainted by a perceived proximity to HIV/AIDS. This anomaly has lingered on in some countries longer than in others: in Ireland, the US, Australia and New Zealand, donations are only

28 http://yogyakartaprinciples.org/additional-recommendations-yp10/.
29 See further at: www.bbc.co.uk/sport/athletics/48504205.

permitted from those who have abstained from sex for a year; in England and Wales and Canada, the deferral period is three months, though the fact that some are protesting by deliberately ignoring this legal requirement raises questions as to its effectiveness.[30] Given the sophisticated filtering systems now available, it's hard to avoid the suspicion that a mandatory deferral period applied only in respect of prospective donors with SOGI status is discriminatory.

Right to equality and non-discrimination: education

YP 16 declares that "everyone has the right to education, without discrimination on the basis of, and taking into account, their sexual orientation and gender identity". This lengthy statement of principle (eight clauses) strives, among other things, to balance the requirements that education methods and materials "enhance understanding of and respect for, inter alia, diverse sexual orientations and gender identities" with that education is directed to the development of "respect for each child's parents and family members, cultural identity, language and values". An additional clause (i) strengthens the requirement to provide SOGI teaching material in school curricula but, significantly, adds that this should "take into consideration the evolving capacity of the child".

Schools and curricula

In many Part II jurisdictions – notably in Canada, England and Wales and Australia – the public protests indicate that for significant numbers of parents there can be no satisfactory balancing of the above requirements. Particularly for Muslims, but also for those of other beliefs and for some of none, their cultural identity and values are wholly irreconcilable with SOGI teaching. The fact that inclusion of SOGI material in school curricula is often interpreted by education authorities as mandatory – in accordance with equality and non-discrimination legislation – for all primary schools has become highly contentious.

The exemption of faith schools from the requirements of equality and non-discrimination enables such schools in all jurisdictions to avoid integrating SOGI awareness into school curricula, though this exemption may be forfeited if, as in the US, such schools are in receipt of government funding. In Ireland, an entrenched religious ethos may militate against legislative reforms designed to ensure greater accommodation of diversity, including the use of SOGI teaching material. A concern regarding SOGI-related pupil bullying and harassment is evident in all jurisdictions.

Colleges/universities

The human right to freedom of expression is naturally highly valued in a tertiary educational context. Nonetheless, reports of tensions between university

30 See further at: www.bbc.co.uk/news/health-48598461.

authorities and student LGBT and religious groups are common in most Part II jurisdictions.

Right to equality and non-discrimination: employment

YP 12 proclaims the right of everyone "to decent and productive work, to just and favourable conditions of work and to protection against unemployment, without discrimination on the basis of sexual orientation or gender identity". SOGI-related discrimination in relation to employment is prohibited in all Part II jurisdictions by both domestic legislation and international measures.

Religious exemption

The religious exemption applies to permit the exclusion of persons from being employed, and to permit their firing, where there is conflict with the beliefs of an organisation. It is supplemented by the "genuine occupational requirement" rule. In operational terms, it functions as a significant caveat to the YP 12 principle in all Part II jurisdictions. Where the organisation is government funded to provide services, then they are bound by equality and non-discrimination legislation and are unable to rely on the religious exemption; though, as in Ireland and Australia, this may not entirely negate the exemption. In the US, the law is more complicated and uncertain, rendered increasingly more so by the ongoing introduction of "religious liberty laws" in many states.

SOGI in the workplace

SOGI-related discriminatory treatment in the workplace is not uncommon. It most often comes before national regulatory bodies in the form of allegations of homophobia involving direct discrimination, harassment or victimisation. Most jurisdictions now treat such issues as discrimination on the basis that the conduct amounts to violation of a protected characteristic. In the US, the caselaw has revolved around an approach which simply examines whether there has been discriminatory treatment based on sexual stereotyping, which is perhaps more to the point. However, the law there has now become more complicated and uncertain where these issues arise for consideration under Title VII.

In Canada, the role played by "the duty to accommodate" is of central importance, and this is in keeping with the requirement in YP 2 additional clause (g) that States

> take all appropriate steps to ensure that reasonable accommodation is provided, where needed, in order to promote equality and eliminate discrimination on the basis of sexual orientation, gender identity, gender expression or sex characteristics, including in education, employment, and access to services.

In Australia, the law offers specific recognition and protection for SOGI issues in the workplace.

Employment in the military

In all Part II jurisdictions, government policy relating to the enlistment, or employment in any capacity, of members of the LGBT community in the nation's armed forces, and their treatment while serving in that capacity, has developed to comply with equality and non-discrimination human rights requirements. In the US, however, that policy has recently become a good deal more equivocal. The current position – that trans persons are not permitted to enlist or serve in the US armed forces – presents a forthright challenge to their human rights.

Right to equality and non-discrimination: services

YP 2 (c) requires States to "adopt appropriate legislative and other measures to prohibit and eliminate discrimination in the public and private spheres on the basis of sexual orientation and gender identity". Domestic legislation in the Part II jurisdictions prohibits discriminatory practice in the public or private provision of and access to goods, services, facilities or accommodation. This prohibition is generally subject to an exemption in favour of religious organisations unless they are government funded.

Trans persons and gender-specific services

The availability of gender-specific and/or trans-specific services has recently emerged as a contentious social issue in relation to facilities such as bathrooms, swimming pools, women's refuges etc. but has yet to receive much attention from judicial and regulatory bodies. Generally domestic law permits a narrow degree of exclusion where a trans person is considered likely to present a risk of harm to others, while religious organisations are entitled to exclude in circumstances where inclusion would violate religious beliefs. The right to exclude would seem to be broadening in the US as the rights of trans persons are now being steadily constrained by state laws and by Trump administration initiatives.

Provision of public services

The existence of national equality and non-discrimination legislation, or the ratification of equivalent international measures, requires the government of the nation concerned to ensure that all services and other facilities provided by its various departments and by bodies contracted to provide on its behalf do so in a manner that is fully compliant with such legislation. The US, at state and federal levels, is once again developing laws at variance with that requirement: public health officials are to be excused from equality and non-discrimination provisions if compliance would compromise their religion or beliefs (see further below). The fact that government officials – and organisations acting on behalf of government departments – should be exempted from equality legislation is difficult to square with the above YP 2 (c) and with basic human rights.

Trans persons and prisons

YP 5 states that "everyone, regardless of sexual orientation or gender identity, has the right to security of the person and to protection by the State against violence or bodily harm, whether inflicted by government officials or by any individual or group". This is reinforced by the YP 6 requirement that States respect the right to privacy; the YP 9 (c) requirement "that all prisoners participate in decisions regarding the place of detention appropriate to their sexual orientation and gender identity"; and more specifically by YP 9 additional principle (i) requiring States to

> adopt and implement policies on placement and treatment of persons who are deprived of their liberty that reflect the needs and rights of persons of all sexual orientations, gender identities, gender expressions, and sex characteristics and ensure that persons are able to participate in decisions regarding the facilities in which they are placed.

Clearly, if multiculturalism, social diversity, equality and non-discrimination are to be more than empty slogans, then government public services must be as inclusive as possible and should model best practice. It would seem that only in Canada does that practice come close to meeting the above YP requirements, while in the US current federal penal policy is decidedly SOGI adverse.

Private goods and service provision

YP 2 (c) requires States to "adopt . . . measures to prohibit and eliminate discrimination in the . . . private spheres on the basis of sexual orientation and gender identity".

In all Part II jurisdictions, there are numerous cases of SOGI-based discrimination in relation to the provision of a range of goods or services, most usually involving refusal to provide accommodation or sell goods such as cakes or flowers on the grounds that a retailer's religious beliefs would be breached by service provision to a member of the LGBT community. These are pretty much uniformly treated as unlawful discrimination unless the service provider is a religious organisation and is entitled to claim exemption from the relevant legislation. In the latter case, it could be argued that the State in all Part II jurisdictions is remiss in not complying with the above YP 2 (c) requirement.

Pensions, social security benefits etc.

YP 13 states that

> everyone has the right to social security and other social protection measures, without discrimination on the basis of sexual orientation or gender identity including employment benefits, parental leave, unemployment benefits,

health insurance or care or benefits (including for body modifications related to gender identity), other social insurance, family benefits, funeral benefits, pensions and benefits with regard to the loss of support for spouses or partners as the result of illness or death.

For same-sex couples and trans persons, as for everyone else, rights to property, inheritance and entitlements to welfare benefits, pensions etc. are vital for personal security and independence. Marriage is an important legal means of acquiring many such rights. As is revealed in the caselaw, these benefits were hard fought for but have now been fairly evenly attained in all jurisdictions. As noted earlier, access to full gender reassignment procedures – from insurance companies, national welfare benefit schemes or national health service provision – constitutes a serious derogation from YP 13 obligations.

Conscientious objection of service providers

YP 2 (c) requires States to "adopt appropriate legislative and other measures to prohibit and eliminate discrimination in the public . . . sphere(s) on the basis of sexual orientation and gender identity". Additional clause (j) imposes an obligation to "protect all persons from discrimination . . . on the basis of sexual orientation, gender identity, gender expression and sex characteristics in healthcare settings".

SOGI, public service and conscientious objection

The European Committee of Social Rights, in *FAFCE v. Sweden*,[31] has taken up a position that wholly complies with the earlier YP requirements. Finding that the EU Charter of Fundamental Rights "does not impose on States a positive obligation to provide a right to conscientious objection for health care workers", the Committee made a clear statement of principle that runs counter to the US-led conscientious objection jurisprudence. Several states in the US and to a more limited extent in Australia, together with Ireland, now permit public health professionals to refuse to engage in the delivery of services they object to on grounds of conscience.

Conclusion

The same formative human rights principles – established internationally by the UDHR, the ICCPR and other instruments; supplemented by much the same domestic legislation; and applied by the same tiers of judicial and regulatory bodies (excepting the UK and Ireland, which are subject to the same supra-national tier) – have clearly not impacted uniformly on all six Part II common law jurisdictions.

31 Complaint No. 99/2013 (2015).

As regards the legal framework, not all jurisdictions have wholly acceded to the YP 30 standard, embodying the principle of State protection for the vulnerable, when dealing with issues arising at the SOGI/human rights intersect. This can be seen, for example, in the jurisdictional difference of approach towards asylum seekers, prisoners and in relation to "normalising" surgery for children with genital abnormalities. It is apparent also when jurisdictions fail to legislate for human rights or fail to ensure that such legislation specifically addresses SOGI issues.

In relation to the core international human rights – justice, free speech, association/assembly and religion – because they have been long recognised as crucial to democracy, they are all assured of protection. The freedoms of expression, association/assembly and religion are staunchly defended in the Part II jurisdictions in keeping with the requirements of YP 19, 20 and 21 respectively; the latter is particularly strongly supported by the State in some jurisdictions. Costs, however, unless defrayed by national legal aid schemes, can be a constraint on accessing justice in accordance with YP 28.

Human rights as they relate to personal relationships are of particular importance in a SOGI context. The relevant standards set by a clutch of YP+10 principles reveal considerable jurisdictional variation, particularly evident in respect of YP 3 and 31 relating to identity: specifically that of trans persons, intersex and others on the non-binary spectrum and the need for surgery to substantiate gender identity. In all jurisdictions, the right to privacy has had significant strategic leverage and a proven capacity for maximising the standard set by YP 6. The right to family life, as emphasised in YP 24, has been realised in all jurisdictions, but with considerable variation in timescales. Currently in the US, the interaction of this right with religious belief has led to a spiralling clash between YP 24 and the access to abortion requirement in YP 17 which shows every sign of spilling over into other SOGI-related issues and sending this jurisdiction down a route divergent from its common law companions and a great deal less YP compliant. Cultural integrity, as asserted by YP 26 and 38, would seem an unattainable aspiration in all Part II jurisdictions but particularly so in the CANZUS nations, where that of the Indigenous people is probably irretrievably compromised.

Finally, as regards the intersect between equality legislation and SOGI-related issues in "the world of an individual person", it is clear from the volume and range of caselaw in each jurisdiction that the standard set by YP 2, of global entitlement to all human rights without SOGI-based discrimination, will not be met by any Part II jurisdiction in the foreseeable future. Moreover, leaving aside political initiatives to reverse or constrain SOGI-compliant policies, it remains to be seen what the long-term impact will be of a steadily burgeoning body of conscientious objection jurisprudence.

Conclusion

In the introduction, this book referenced Eleanor Roosevelt's observation in 1958 that the ultimate test of human rights rests on how they play out in "the world of the individual person; the neighbourhood he lives in; the school or college he attends; the factory, farm, or office where he works".[1] The SOGI-related aspects of that world are unlikely to have featured much in her ruminations, but in the intervening 60 years they have come to form a distinct strand of human rights that touches on many aspects of the life of her notional individual person. Driven by the inexorable moral authority of laws that insist on equality, SOGI considerations now greatly influence such a person's participation in health and social care, in employment and education and in the ever-expanding arena of service provision. In this brief conclusion, it seems appropriate to reflect on how Eleanor Roosevelt might have viewed these developments: firstly, as regards sexuality and gender; then in relation to human rights in general.

The UN Special Rapporteur once suggested that

> fundamental human rights principles, as well as existing human rights norms, lead ineluctably to the recognition of sexual rights as human rights. Sexual rights include the right of all persons to express their sexual orientation, with due regard for the well-being and rights of others, without fear of persecution, denial of liberty or social interference.[2]

The truth of his observation has been apparent in the legislative steps taken by the Part II jurisdictions as each progressed resolutely through the same stages in their recognition of sexual orientation and gender identity as human rights, albeit at different speeds and with caveats in relation to the latter. However, it is also true that the caselaw reveals a considerable degree of jurisdictional disparity as regards the extent to which sexual orientation may be expressed: cultural context and political

1 See Eleanor Roosevelt's speech to the UN at the Church Peace Union, *In Your Hands: A Guide for Community Action on the 10th Anniversary of the UDHR*, New York, 1958.

2 Report of the Special Rapporteur on the right of everyone to the enjoyment of the highest attainable standard of physical and mental health, E/CN.4/2004/49/Add.1 (2004), at para. 54.

exigency have clearly played their part. Some jurisdictions, for example, continue to practice State-authorised "normalising" surgery on infants, have not prohibited "conversion therapy" and have not extended legal recognition to intersex status nor included gender identity as a prohibited characteristic in discrimination legislation. In others, a resurgence of conservative politics has resulted in a change in SOGI-compliant laws. Then there is the fact that the right to express sexual orientation often conflicts with the right to freedom of religion, and the resulting considerable "social interference" in all those jurisdictions may well be feeding cultural dissonance between the democratic and Islamic nations. So, while the destination may in the long term be ineluctable, the routes taken to get there can be many and varied and, at times, vigorously contested.

For Eleanor Roosevelt, many facets of this would have been intriguing. Foreseeing the extension of human rights to the LGBT community would not in itself have been problematic; even predicting the somewhat forced legal interpretation of "sex" as encompassing sexual orientation and gender identity could have logically followed. The next step, though, would have been a bit of a stretch. Requiring human rights not only to recognise and address SOGI status but to also accommodate post-binary and intersex concepts and then to configure the application of SOGI-related human rights to issues arising in the complicated contemporary "world of the individual person" would most probably have been outside her contemplation. Curiously, 60 years ago the world of such an Indigenous person was – and for centuries had been – post-binary. It is an irony that the struggle of adjusting to a SOGI-compliant world, which as this book records all Part II jurisdictions have undergone, had long been largely accomplished – the non-binary and intersex accommodated – in most of those jurisdictions in the parallel world of the individual person in their Indigenous community.

The body of human rights has also changed. Seventy years ago, in the aftermath of two world wars and ideological turmoil, the 30 articles of the UDHR established very fundamental red lines for balancing the rights/responsibilities of the individual with the interests of the State: restricting the grounds justifying the intervention of the latter into the life of the former and thereby offering the best bet for consolidating society and building a peaceful comity of nations. When Eleanor Roosevelt made her comments, international human rights consisted of those listed in the Declaration, but they have since greatly increased in volume and range from that basic UDHR iteration. This has correspondingly increased the legal complexities.

Like the common law, human rights jurisprudence is constructed on the basis of categories of people (children, disabled, asylum seekers, women etc.) and of grounds (health, employment, education etc.) judged to be particularly deserving of protection. Human rights proceedings are contingent upon an entity having a legal identity that fits within the specified characteristics of a protected category. This classification system functions on the basis of a correlation between a legally recognised entity and a "cause of action". In a human rights context, as defined by the UDHR, such a correlation was straightforward if selectively utilised: most issues were addressed through normal legislative proceedings, with human rights litigation reserved for the more unusual and significant issues with potentially wider implications. However, every subsequent human rights instrument has caused this correlation to become more complicated, with cross-referencing across several international instruments now often necessary. In recent years, first sexual orientation, then gender identity, then non-binary identity – the latter with some equivocation – have acquired recognition and legal status in human rights instruments. At the same time, the range of "causes of action" on SOGI-related issues have multiplied, mostly in the form of proceedings initiated under domestic equality and non-discrimination legislation.

The vast weight of contemporary human rights would have surprised and possibly alarmed Eleanor Roosevelt: it is unlikely that she could have envisaged the world of her notional individual person becoming filled with catalogues of internationally guaranteed protective measures; and she could well have been troubled by a suspicion that the increase in volume was accompanied by a dilution in effectiveness.[3] While she might well have been heartened by the current expansion of the equality right and impressed by its capacity to leverage improvements in the private life of the individual, she might have found its elevation to the status of a human rights grundnorm[4] and its impact upon other rights a bit unsettling. Then, as now, it was accepted that human rights, being anchored on the circumstances of the individual, cannot be selectively distributed: every member of a small, newly emerging, socially disadvantaged group is entitled to the same respect and protection as someone from a structurally disadvantaged sector of society with longer-established human rights credentials; there is an equivalence in the protection entitlements of, say, a refugee, an Indigenous person and a trans prisoner. However, responding in a legal and morally coherent manner to contemporary complex and entangled human rights issues, taking into account the cross-cutting equality and non-discrimination imperative, has become increasingly problematic. There is an argument for retreating to a classification system that clearly differentiates between fundamental human rights and all others. Balance, after all, was the essence of the UDHR and would have been at the forefront of Eleanor Roosevelt's mind when she reflected on "the world of the individual person".

3 Arguably the continuous stream of international instruments, each with their designated tranche of human rights customised to fit the needs of yet another group judged to be particularly disadvantaged, prompts a reflexive "not another Ten Commandments" response from lawyers and the general public and risks devaluing the currency of international human rights and desiccating civil society.

4 See Kelsen, H., *The General Theory of Law and State*, Harvard University Press, 1949.

Index

For Product Safety Concerns and Information please contact our EU representative GPSR@taylorandfrancis.com
Taylor & Francis Verlag GmbH, Kaufingerstraße 24, 80331 München, Germany

www.ingramcontent.com/pod-product-compliance
Ingram Content Group UK Ltd.
Pitfield, Milton Keynes, MK11 3LW, UK
UKHW020021200926
475702UK00014B/2001
9781032086750